train_man
densha otoko ™

Hidenori Hara
Based on Densha Otoko by Hitori Nakano

story thus far

He Just Happened to Sit Next to Her

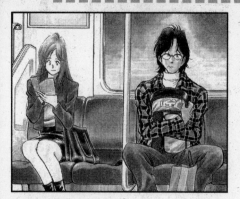

It all started on this young man's way home from Akihabara. When he took a seat on the train, he glanced over to see a beautiful woman seated to his right. This young man will come to be called "Train_Man." No one would expect a beautiful woman like her to be interested in an otaku like him, but an unexpected fate awaits this couple!

I'm So Uncool

KYA!
WHACK
WHOA!
WHOA
WHOA!

STOP IT!!

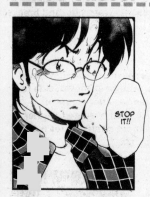

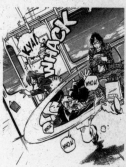

Train_Man musters up his courage and saves the woman from a bothersome drunk. She tries to show her gratitude, but he gets nervous and runs away. Later on, he feels disgusted with himself for his cowardly behavior and regrets not asking for her contact information.

Hermess

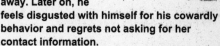

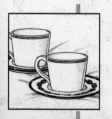

Two days later, a thank-you gift arrives via an express delivery service. Best of all, the waybill contains the woman's telephone number! The thank-you gift turns out to be a nice pair of teacups. Train_Man writes about his experience on an online forum and is inspired by the sincere support offered by the other forum members. The forum members get excited when they find out the cups were made by Hermes, a high-end designer brand. Train_Man's love for the woman nicknamed "Hermess" begins to grow.

w00t?? (´∀`)·ω·)ﾟДﾟ)ﾟ∀ﾟ)·∀·) ￣-￣)´_ゝ`)-_)ﾞ∋)´ Дﾟ)ﾞ-) ??!!!!

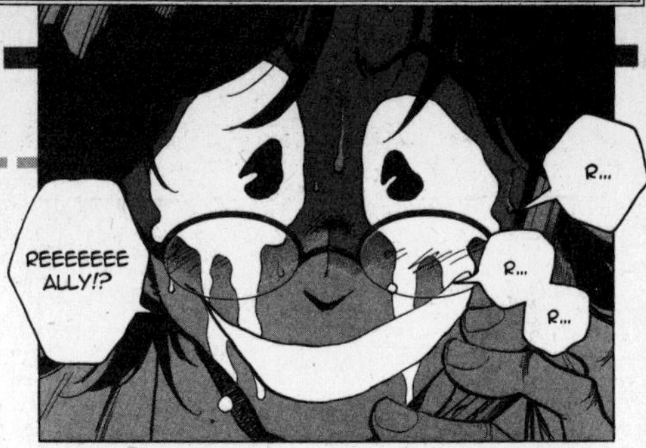
R...
R...
R...
REEEEEEE ALLY!?

Ask Her Out!

Advice from the forum members comes fast and furious. With their encouragement, he calls her, but gets a recording. Later, the two are able to have a phone conversation. The forum members urge him to "Ask her out to dinner!" Train_Man finally succeeds in asking Hermess out to dinner, but she insists that they split the bill.

The Transformation of Train_Man!!

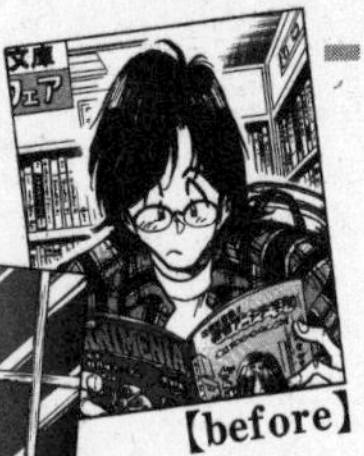
【before】

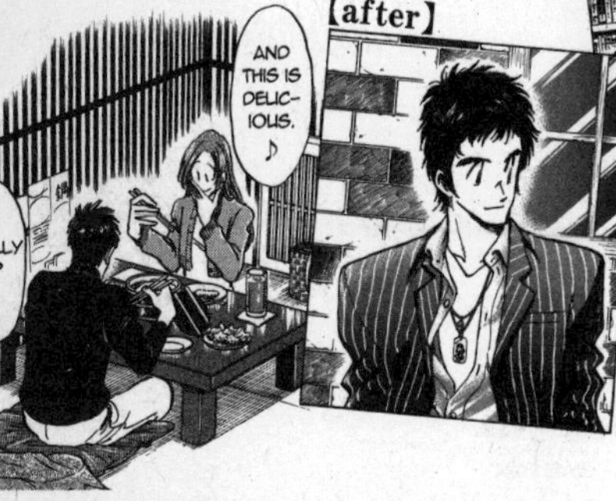
AND THIS IS DELICIOUS. ♪
REALLY ...?
I'M GLAD
【after】

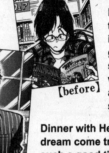

His next mission is to transform himself into a good-looking guy! He gets his hair styled, upgrades his wardrobe, and breaks away from his Akiba-style look.

Dinner with Hermess is like a dream come true. And they have such a good time, they decide to go for a drink after the meal! However, their evening together ends without arranging for a second date.

The Second Dinner

Train_Man thinks about Hermess night and day. It's definitely love. The forum members support Train_Man, and help him set up another dinner date. But this time, Hermess brings along a friend. The forum members grow impatient as they wait for his report...but he still hasn't returned home. Is Train_Man in trouble!?

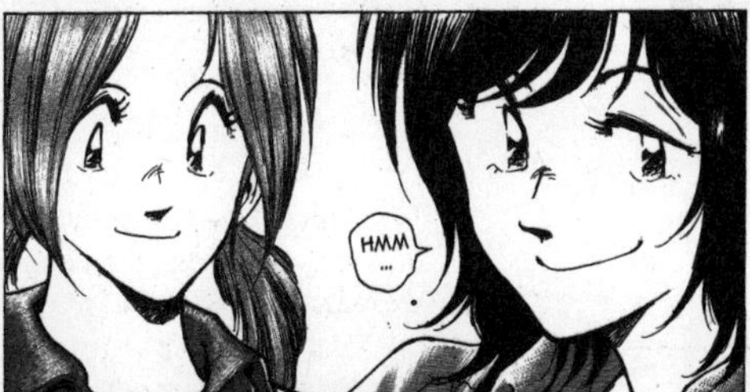
HMM ...

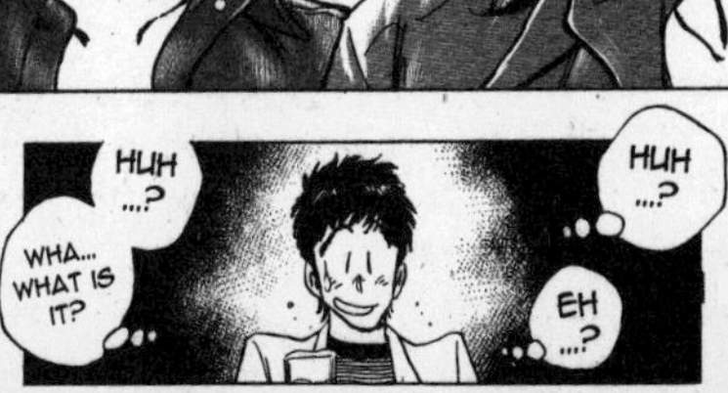
HUH ...?
EH ...?
HUH ...?
WHA... WHAT IS IT?

Table of Contents !!--(ﾟ∀ﾟ)--!!

episode 10:
Good Job, Train_Man

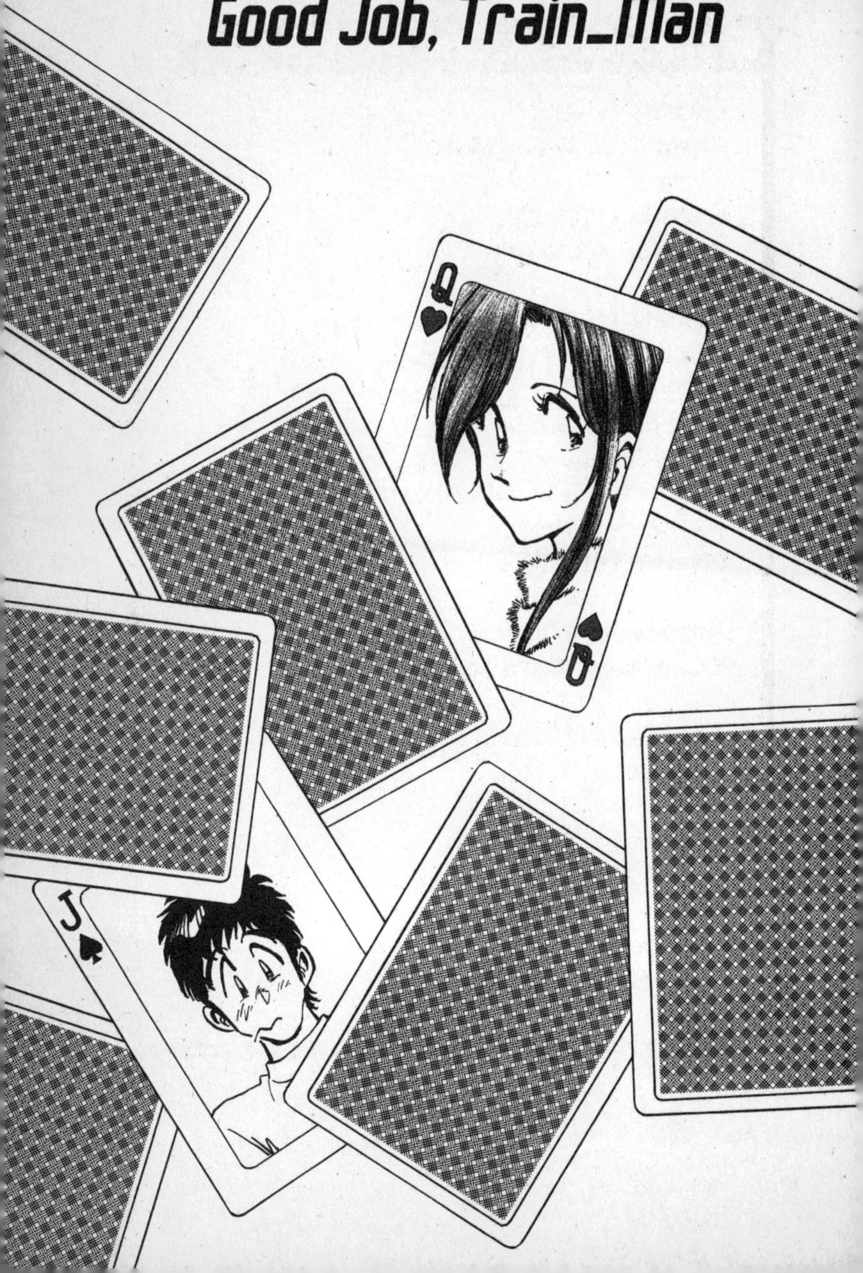

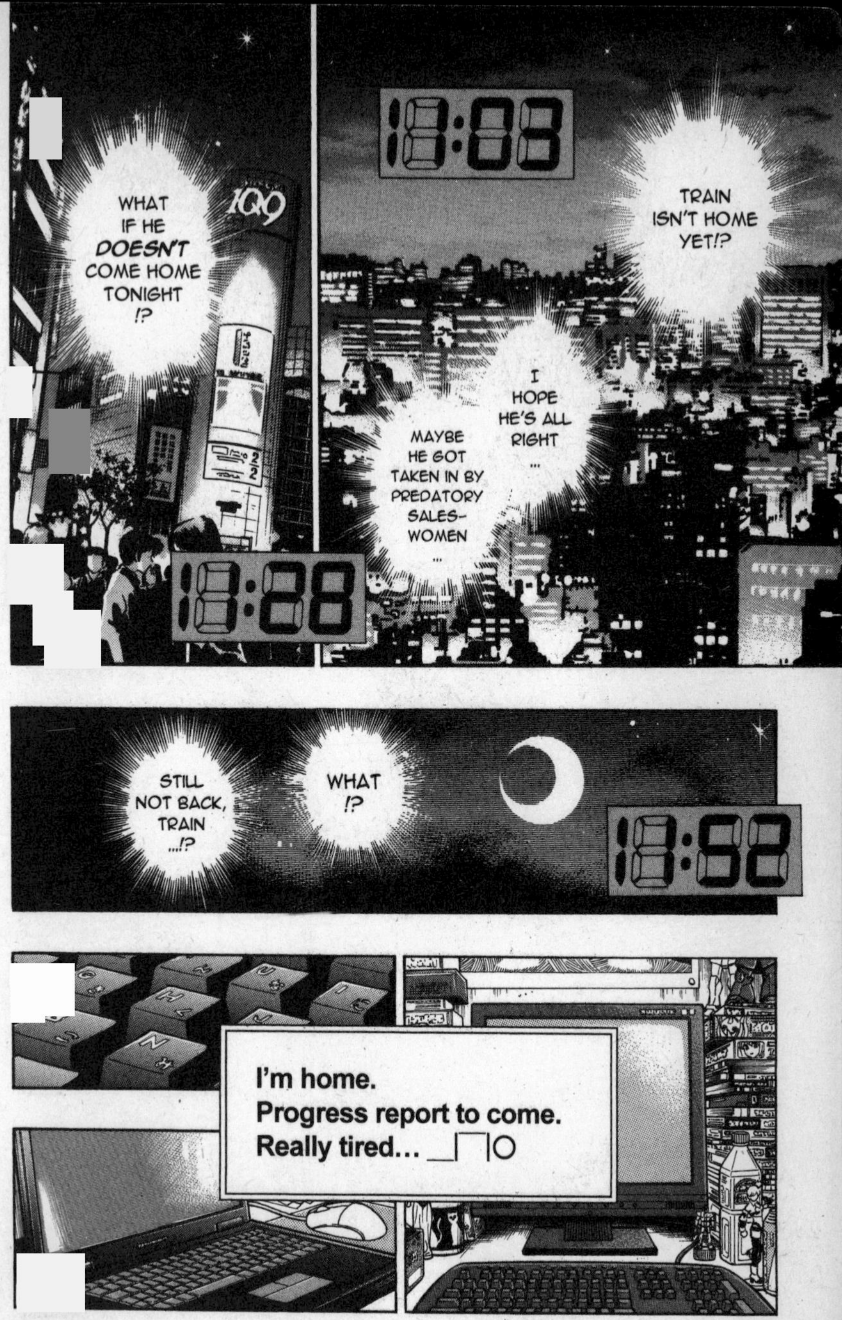
TRAIN ISN'T HOME YET!?
I HOPE HE'S ALL RIGHT ...
MAYBE HE GOT TAKEN IN BY PREDATORY SALES-WOMEN ...
WHAT IF HE *DOESN'T* COME HOME TONIGHT !?
WHAT !?
STILL NOT BACK, TRAIN ...!?
I'm home.
Progress report to come.
Really tired… _|¯|○

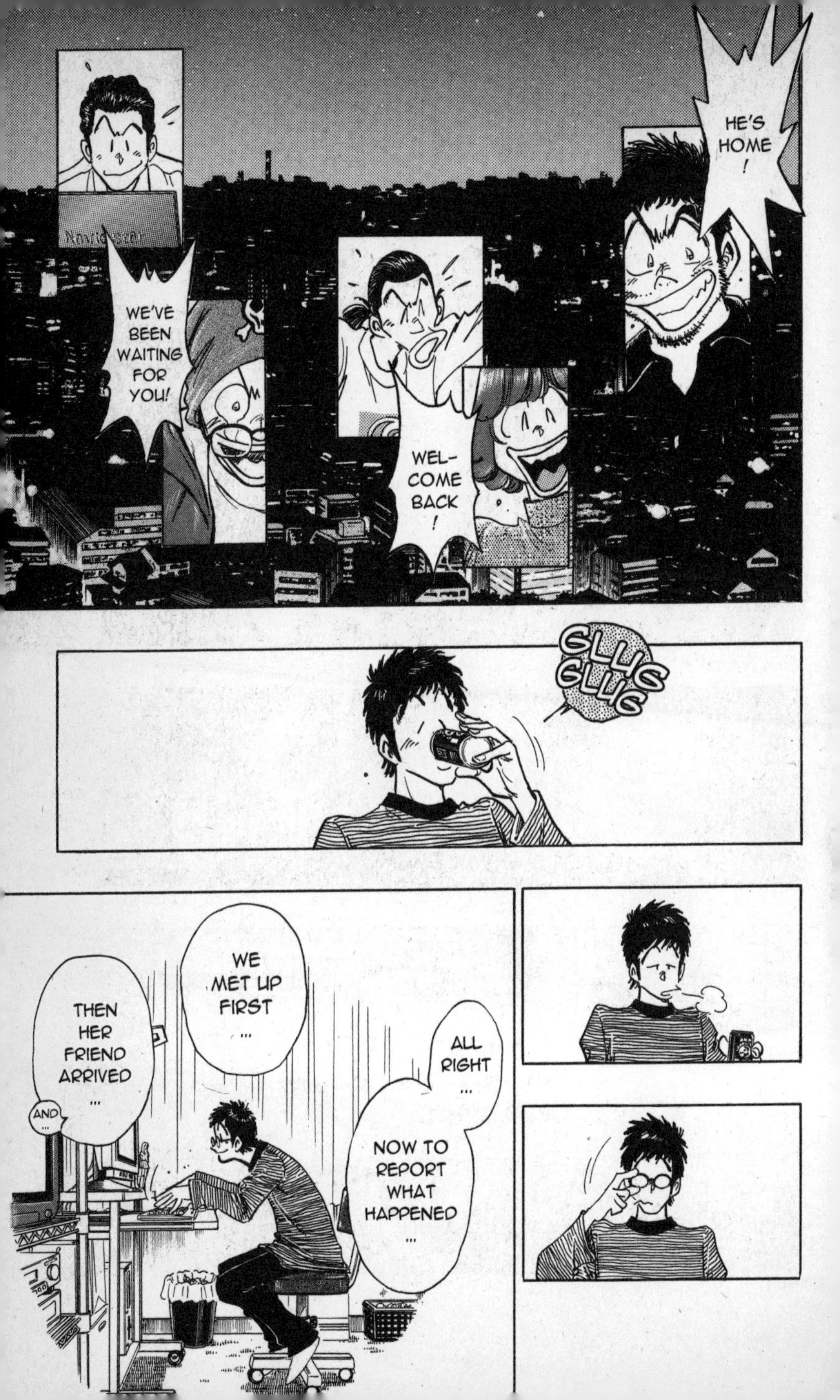
HE'S HOME!
WEL-COME BACK!
WE'VE BEEN WAITING FOR YOU!
GLUG GLUG
ALL RIGHT ...
NOW TO REPORT WHAT HAPPENED ...
WE MET UP FIRST ...
THEN HER FRIEND ARRIVED ...
AND ...

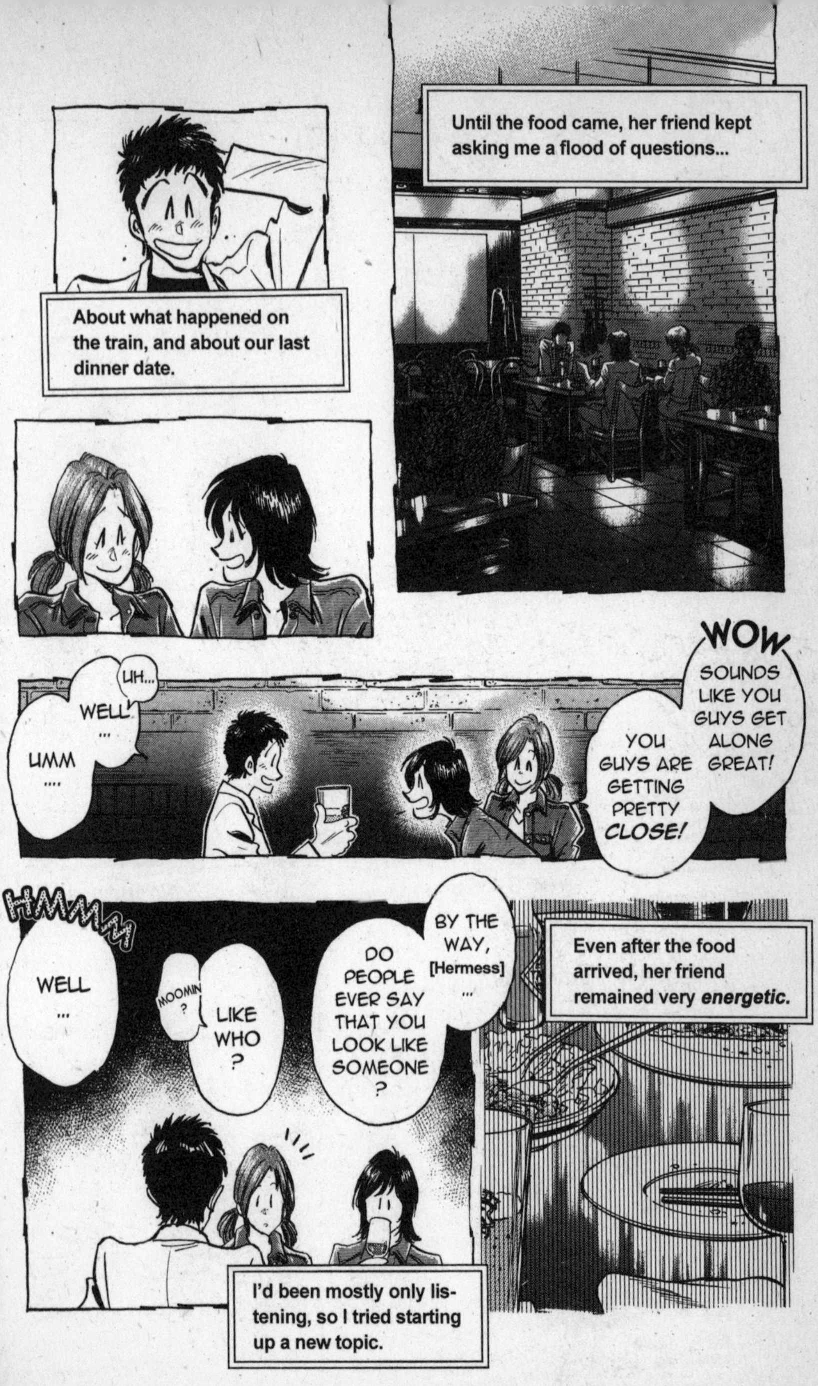
Until the food came, her friend kept asking me a flood of questions...
About what happened on the train, and about our last dinner date.
WOW
SOUNDS LIKE YOU GUYS GET ALONG GREAT!
YOU GUYS ARE GETTING PRETTY CLOSE!
UH...
WELL...
UMM....
Even after the food arrived, her friend remained very *energetic.*
BY THE WAY, [Hermess]...
DO PEOPLE EVER SAY THAT YOU LOOK LIKE SOMEONE?
LIKE WHO?
MOOMIN?
WELL...
HMMMM
I'd been mostly only listening, so I tried starting up a new topic.

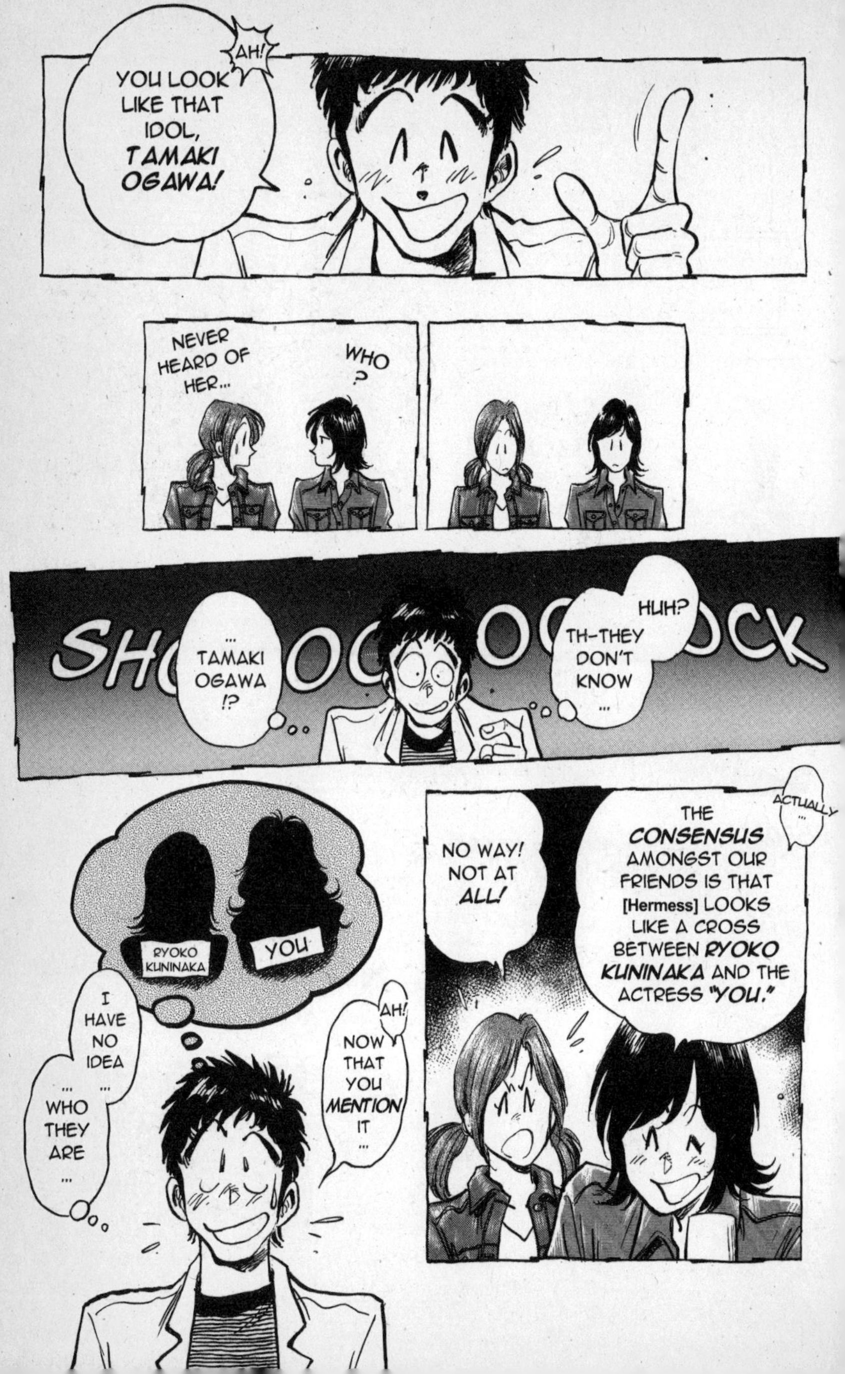
AH!
YOU LOOK LIKE THAT IDOL, TAMAKI OGAWA!
WHO ?
NEVER HEARD OF HER...
SH OO OC OCK
HUH?
TH-THEY DON'T KNOW ...
... TAMAKI OGAWA !?
ACTUALLY ...
THE CONSENSUS AMONGST OUR FRIENDS IS THAT [Hermess] LOOKS LIKE A CROSS BETWEEN RYOKO KUNINAKA AND THE ACTRESS "YOU."
NO WAY! NOT AT ALL!
RYOKO KUNINAKA
YOU
AH!
NOW THAT YOU MENTION IT ...
I HAVE NO IDEA ... ... WHO THEY ARE ...

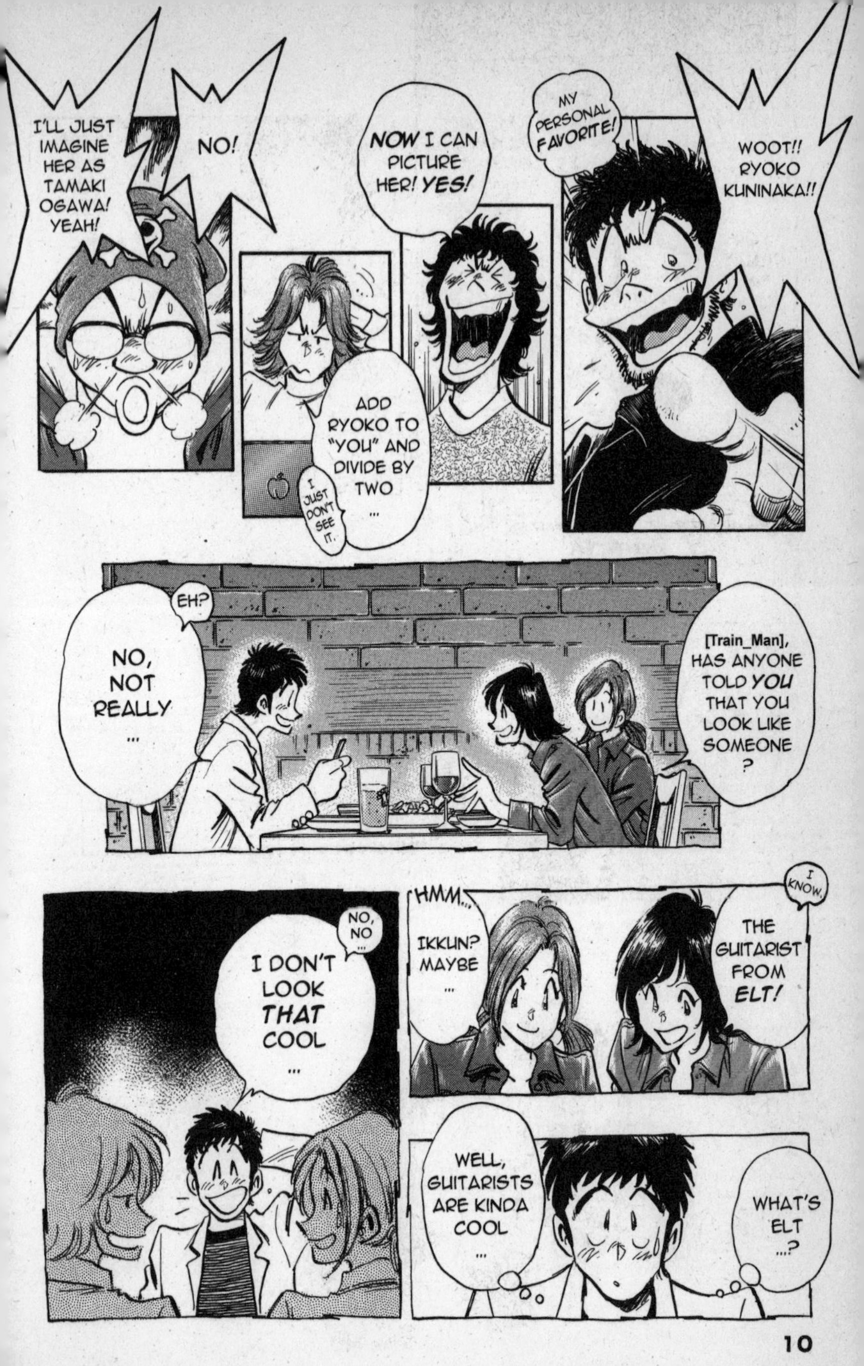
WOOT!! RYOKO KUNINAKA!!
MY PERSONAL FAVORITE!
NOW I CAN PICTURE HER! YES!
ADD RYOKO TO "YOU" AND DIVIDE BY TWO ...
I JUST DON'T SEE IT.
NO!
I'LL JUST IMAGINE HER AS TAMAKI OGAWA! YEAH!
[Train_Man], HAS ANYONE TOLD YOU THAT YOU LOOK LIKE SOMEONE ?
EH?
NO, NOT REALLY ...
I KNOW.
THE GUITARIST FROM ELT!
HMM...
IKKUN? MAYBE ...
WHAT'S ELT ...?
WELL, GUITARISTS ARE KINDA COOL ...
NO, NO ...
I DON'T LOOK THAT COOL ...

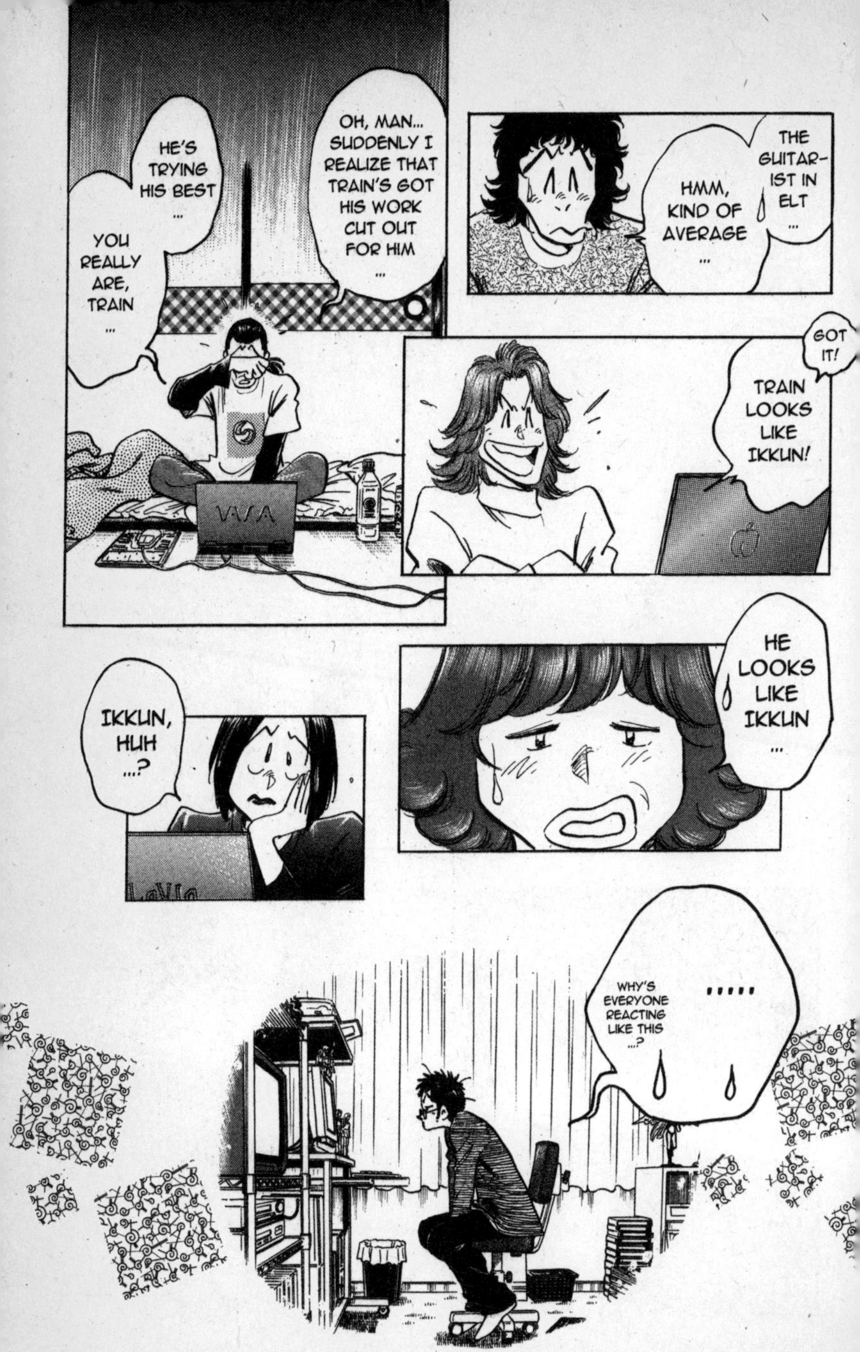
THE GUITARIST IN ELT ...
HMM, KIND OF AVERAGE ...
GOT IT!
TRAIN LOOKS LIKE IKKUN!
OH, MAN... SUDDENLY I REALIZE THAT TRAIN'S GOT HIS WORK CUT OUT FOR HIM ...
HE'S TRYING HIS BEST ... YOU REALLY ARE, TRAIN ...
HE LOOKS LIKE IKKUN ...
IKKUN, HUH ...?
.....
WHY'S EVERYONE REACTING LIKE THIS ...?

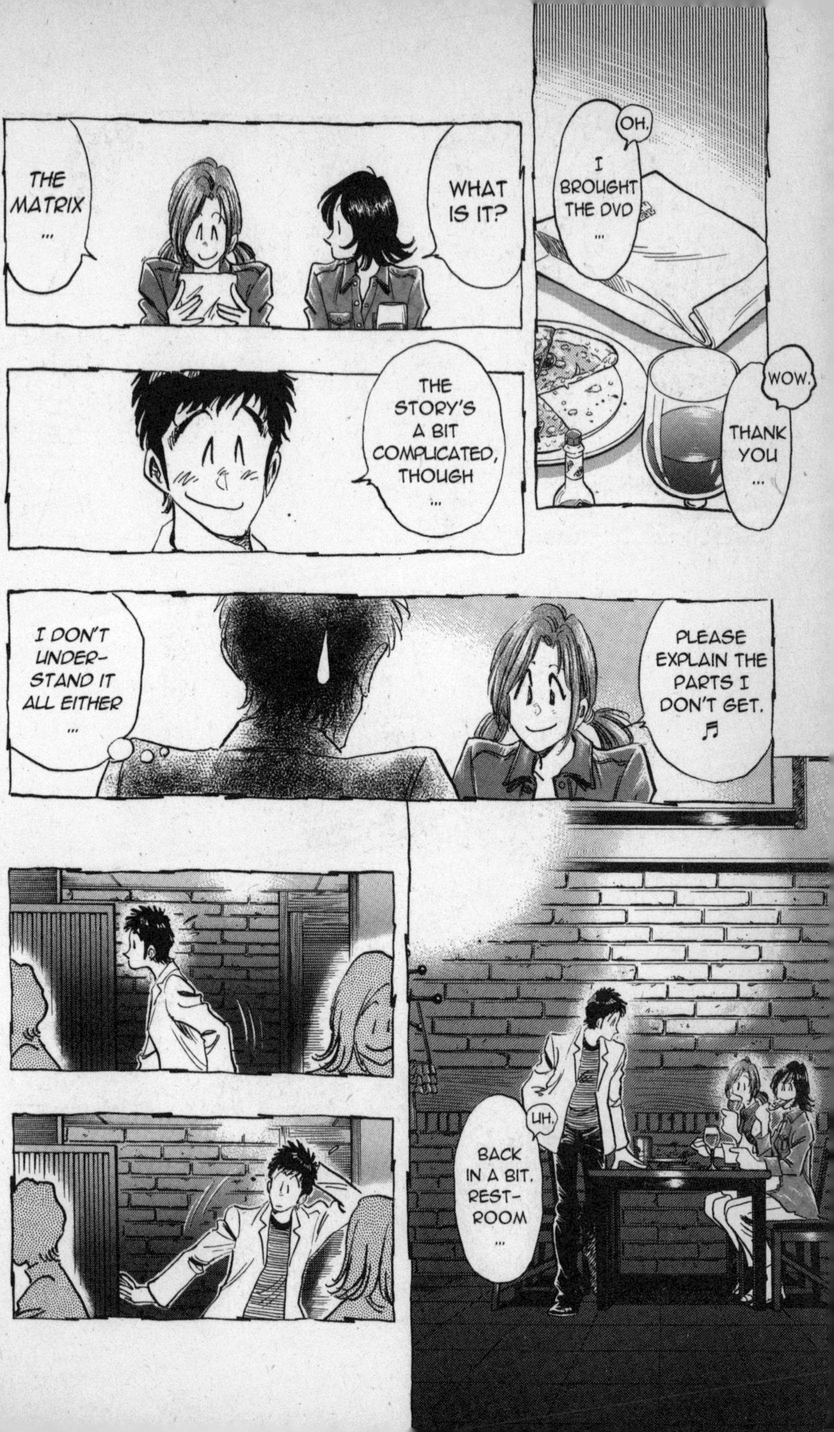

OH.
I BROUGHT THE DVD ...
WOW.
THANK YOU ...
WHAT IS IT?
THE MATRIX ...
THE STORY'S A BIT COMPLICATED, THOUGH ...
PLEASE EXPLAIN THE PARTS I DON'T GET. ♫
I DON'T UNDER-STAND IT ALL EITHER ...
UH.
BACK IN A BIT. REST-ROOM ...

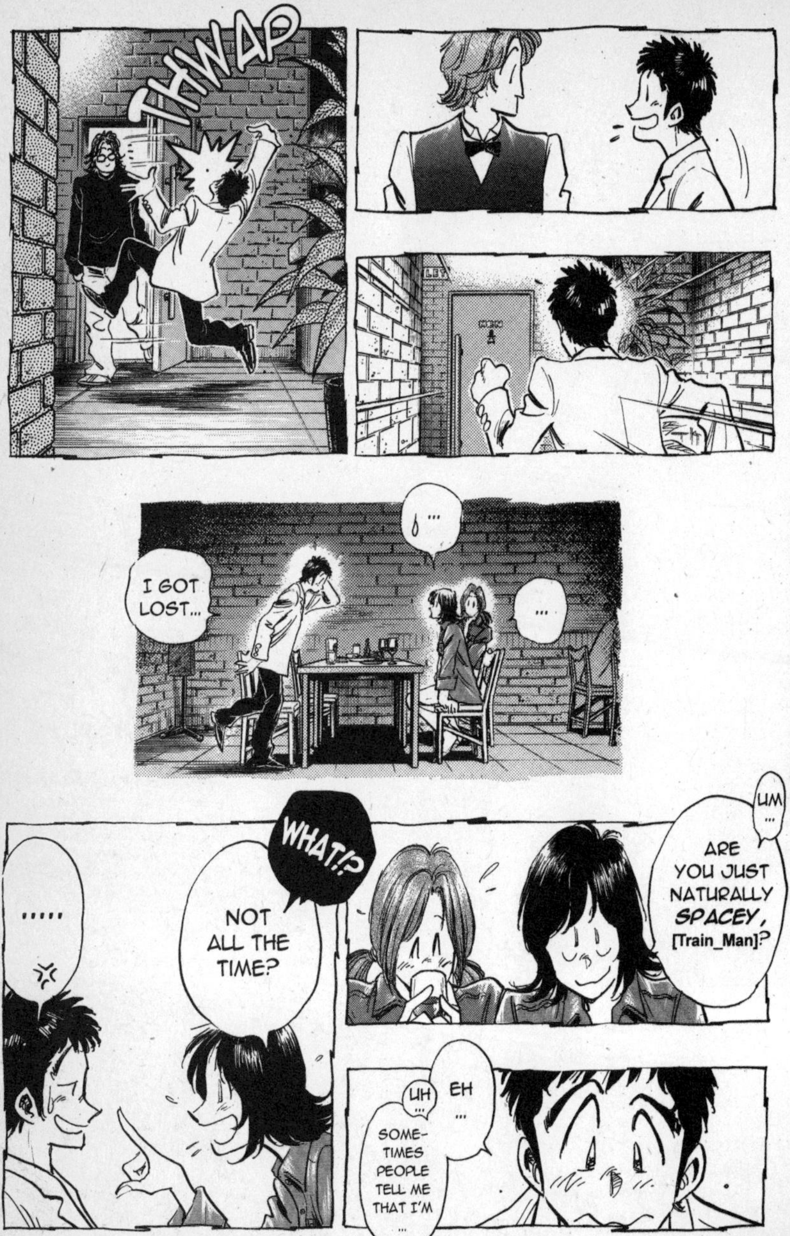
THWAP
...
...
I GOT LOST...
UM ...
ARE YOU JUST NATURALLY SPACEY, [Train_Man]?
EH ...
UH ...
SOME-TIMES PEOPLE TELL ME THAT I'M ...
WHAT!?
NOT ALL THE TIME?
......

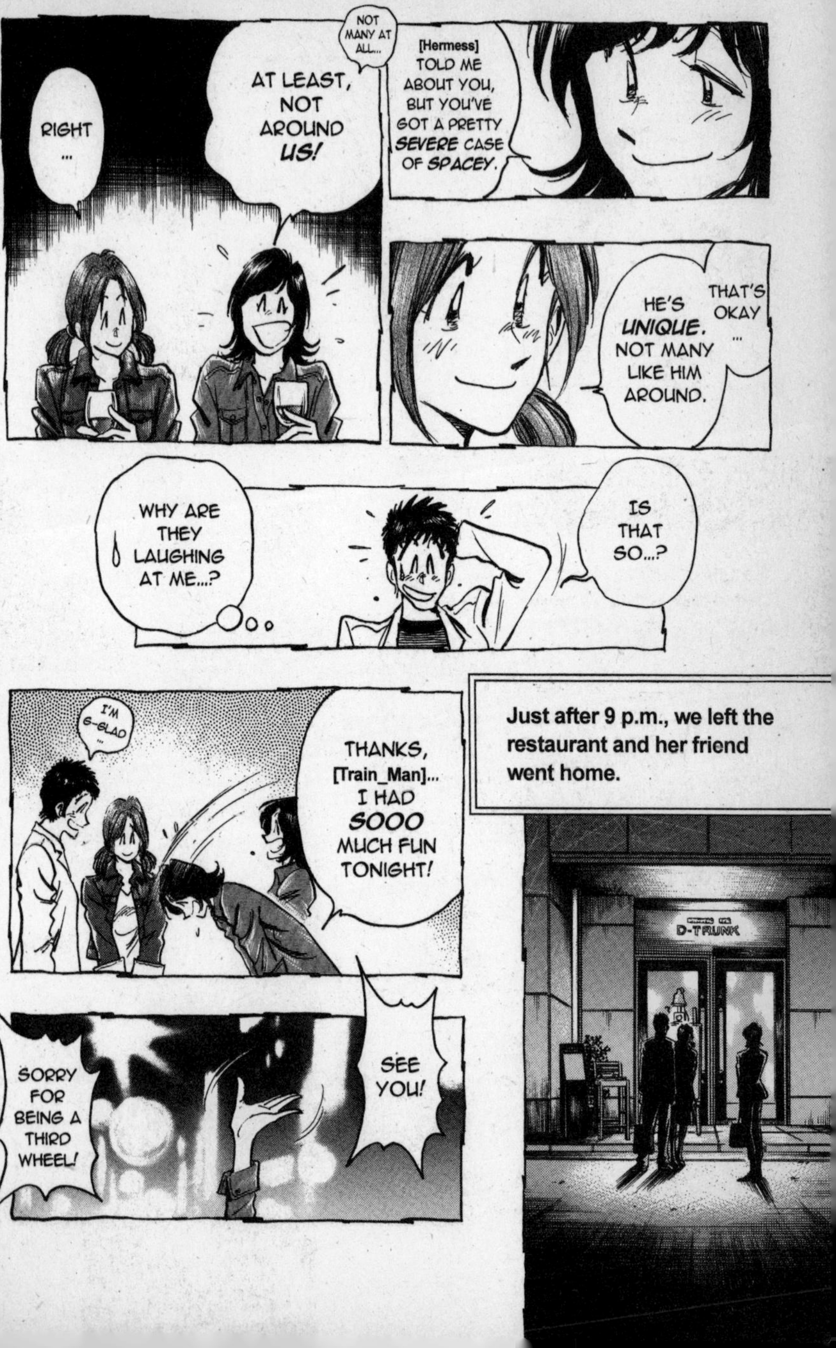
[Hermess] TOLD ME ABOUT YOU, BUT YOU'VE GOT A PRETTY SEVERE CASE OF SPACEY.
THAT'S OKAY ...
HE'S UNIQUE. NOT MANY LIKE HIM AROUND.
NOT MANY AT ALL...
AT LEAST, NOT AROUND US!
RIGHT ...
IS THAT SO...?
WHY ARE THEY LAUGHING AT ME...?
Just after 9 p.m., we left the restaurant and her friend went home.
D-TRUNK
THANKS, [Train_Man]... I HAD SOOO MUCH FUN TONIGHT!
I'M G-GLAD ...
SEE YOU!
SORRY FOR BEING A THIRD WHEEL!

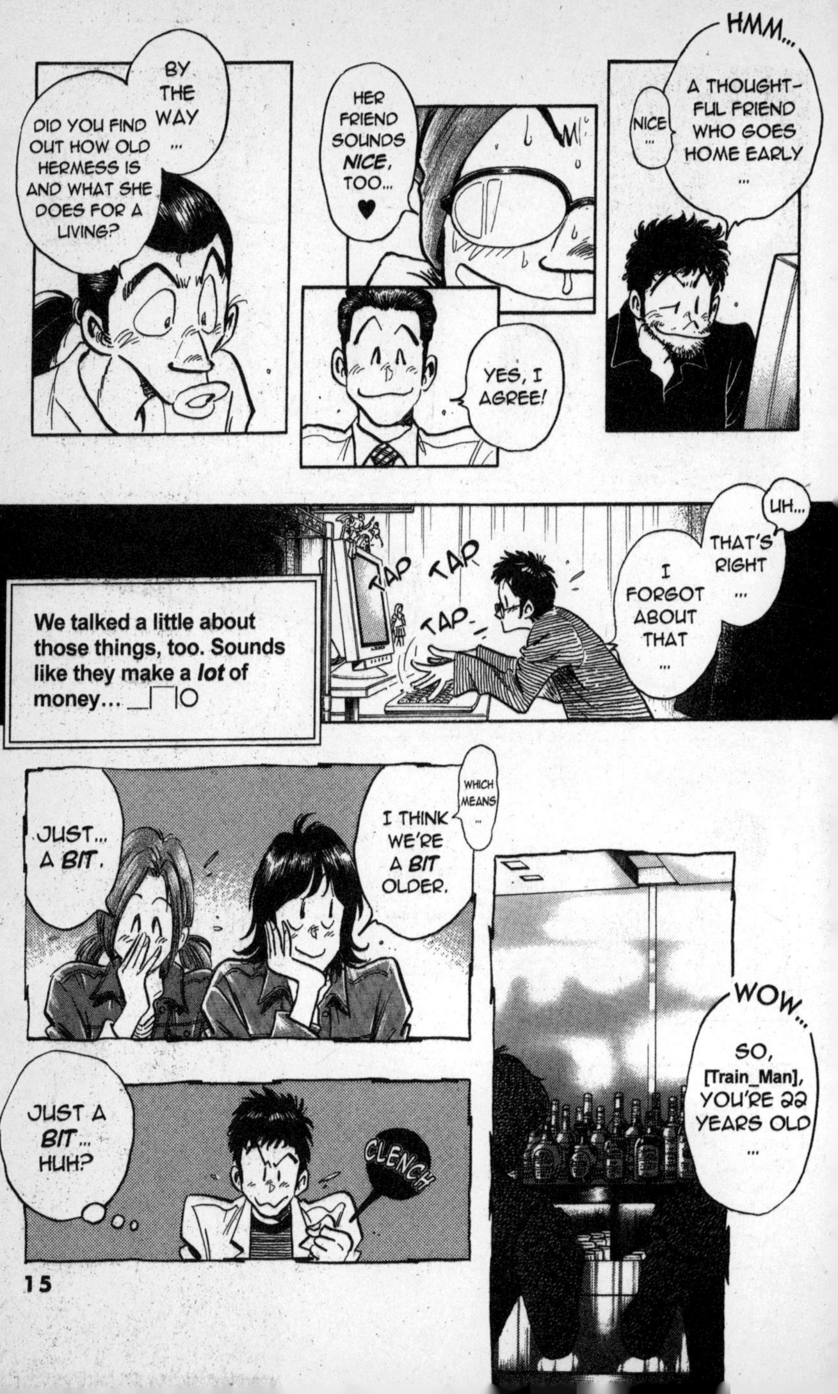
HMM...
A THOUGHT-FUL FRIEND WHO GOES HOME EARLY ...
NICE ...
HER FRIEND SOUNDS *NICE*, TOO... ♥
YES, I AGREE!
BY THE WAY ...
DID YOU FIND OUT HOW OLD HERMESS IS AND WHAT SHE DOES FOR A LIVING?
UH...
THAT'S RIGHT ...
I FORGOT ABOUT THAT ...
TAP TAP
TAP
We talked a little about those things, too. Sounds like they make a *lot* of money... _|¯|○
WOW...
SO, [Train_Man], YOU'RE 22 YEARS OLD ...
WHICH MEANS ...
I THINK WE'RE A *BIT* OLDER.
JUST... A *BIT*.
CLENCH
JUST A *BIT*... HUH?

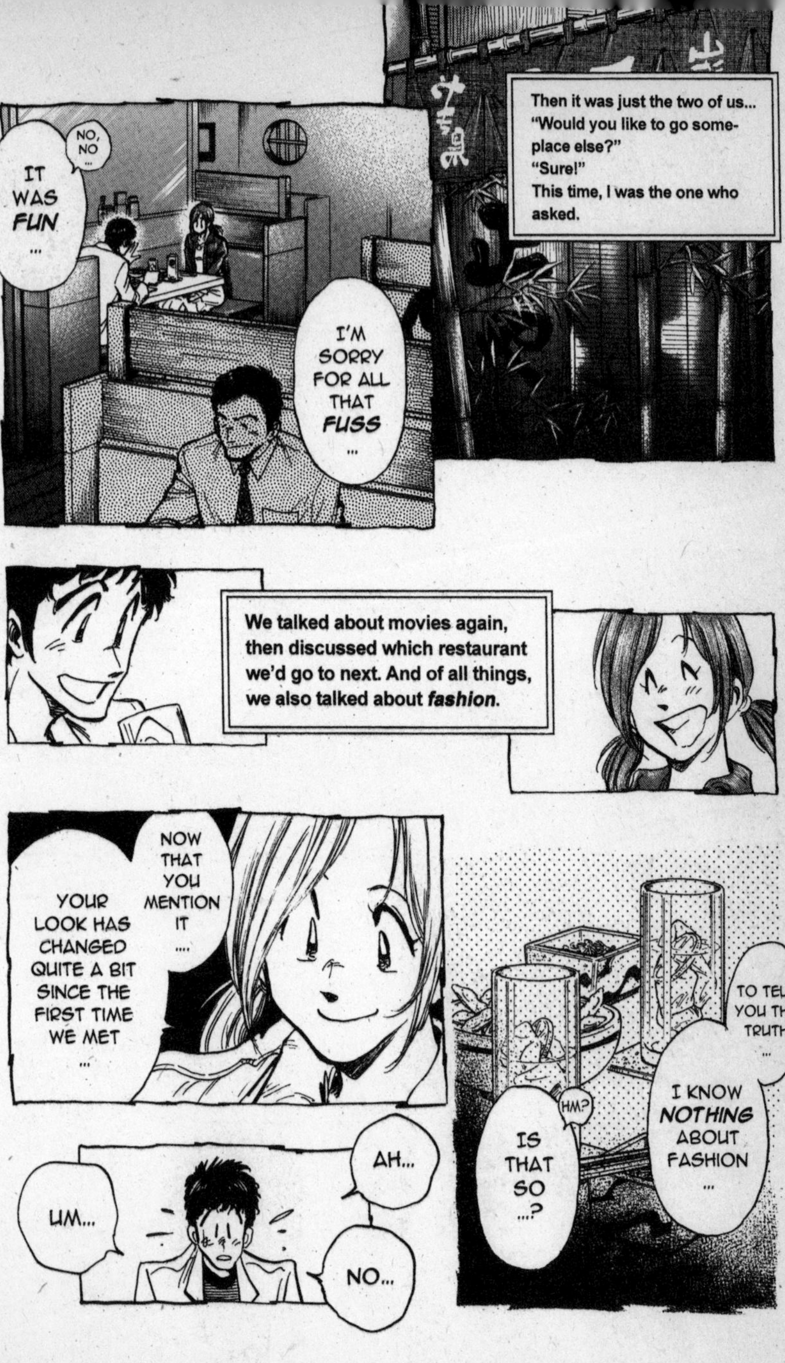
Then it was just the two of us...
"Would you like to go someplace else?"
"Sure!"
This time, I was the one who asked.
I'M SORRY FOR ALL THAT FUSS ...
NO, NO ...
IT WAS FUN ...
We talked about movies again, then discussed which restaurant we'd go to next. And of all things, we also talked about *fashion*.
TO TELL YOU THE TRUTH ...
I KNOW NOTHING ABOUT FASHION ...
HM?
IS THAT SO ...?
NOW THAT YOU MENTION IT ....
YOUR LOOK HAS CHANGED QUITE A BIT SINCE THE FIRST TIME WE MET ...
AH...
NO...
UM...

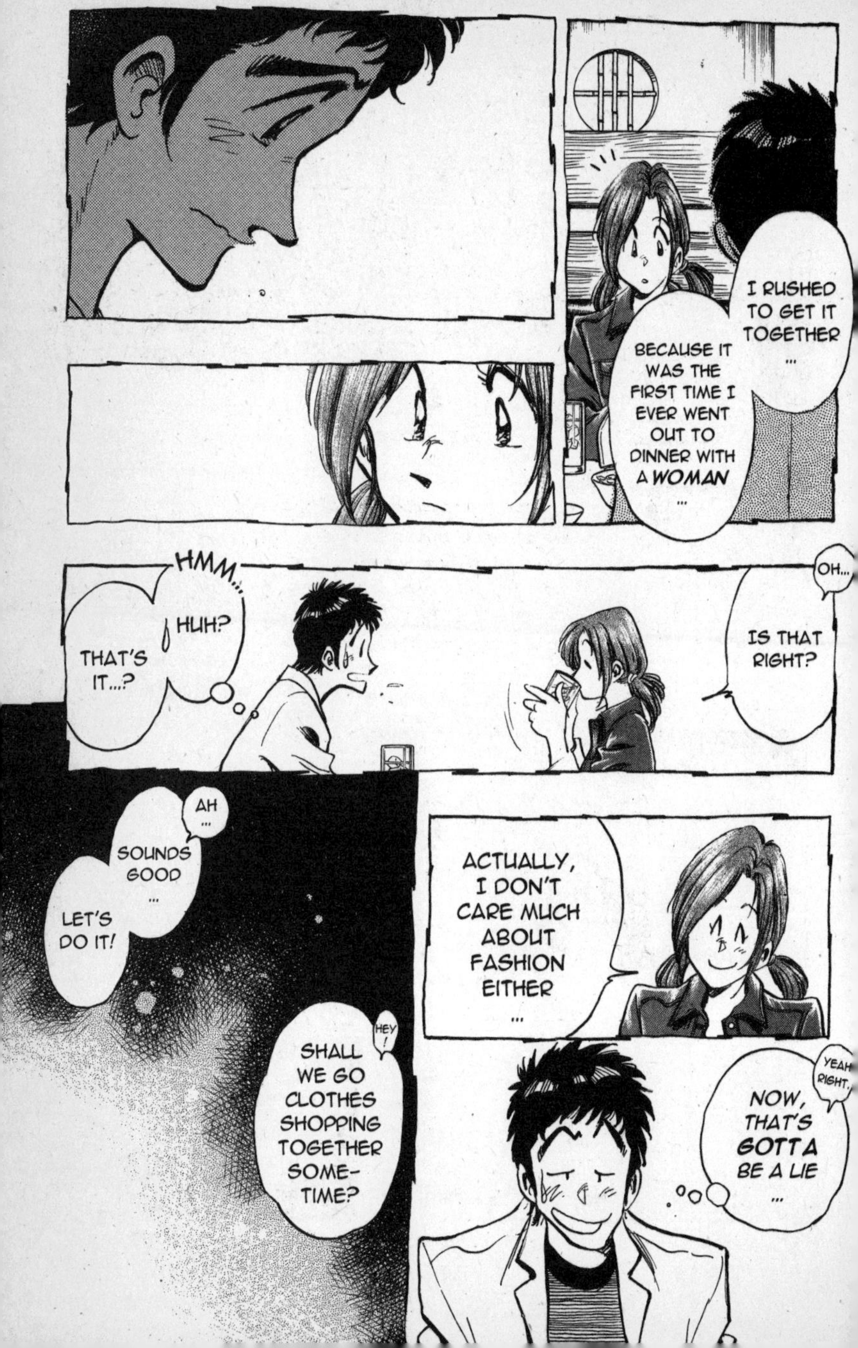
I RUSHED TO GET IT TOGETHER ...
BECAUSE IT WAS THE FIRST TIME I EVER WENT OUT TO DINNER WITH A *WOMAN* ...
OH...
IS THAT RIGHT?
HMM...
HUH?
THAT'S IT...?
ACTUALLY, I DON'T CARE MUCH ABOUT FASHION EITHER ...
YEAH RIGHT.
NOW, THAT'S **GOTTA** BE A LIE ...
HEY!
SHALL WE GO CLOTHES SHOPPING TOGETHER SOME-TIME?
AH ...
SOUNDS GOOD ...
LET'S DO IT!

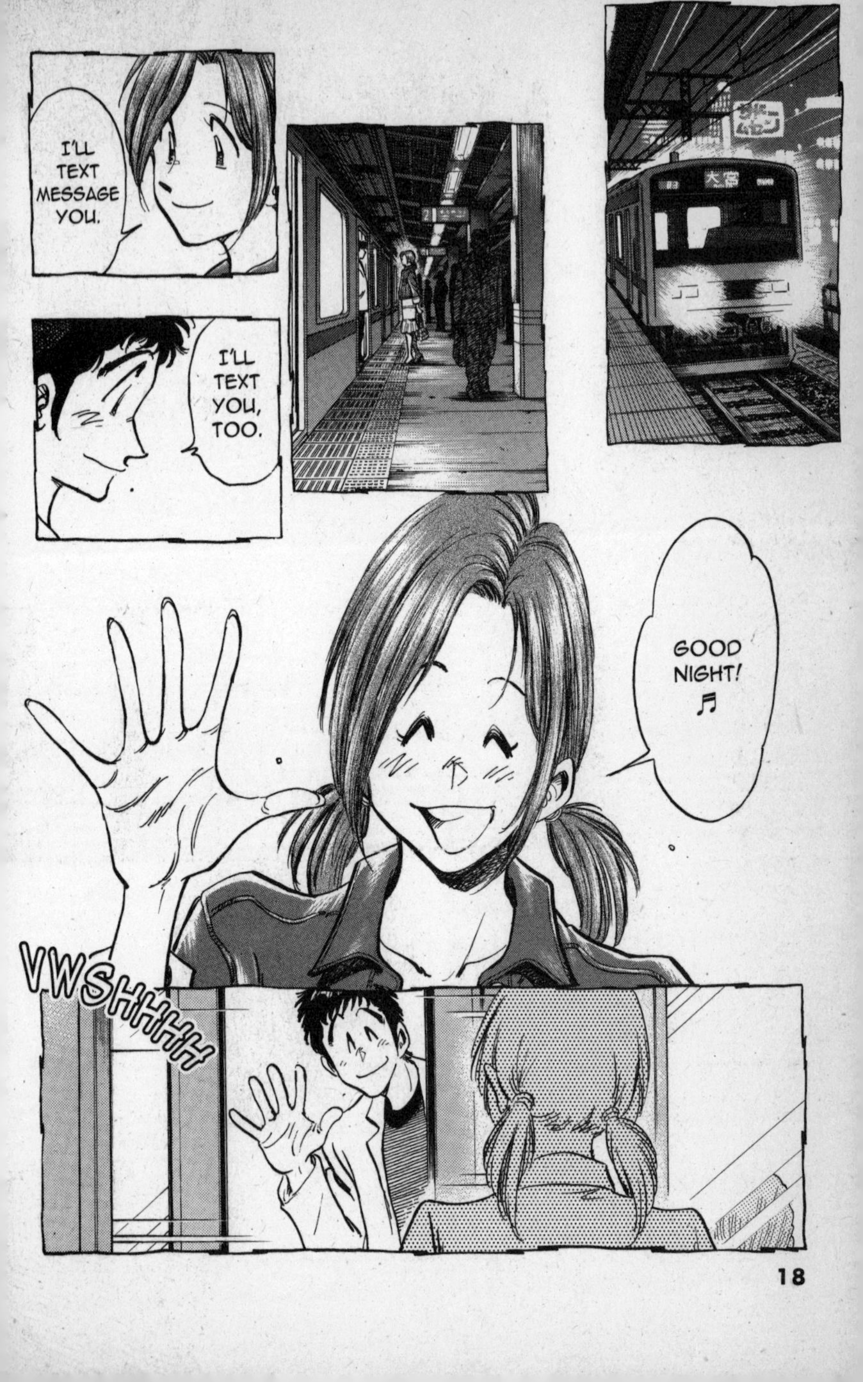
I'LL TEXT MESSAGE YOU.
I'LL TEXT YOU, TOO.
GOOD NIGHT! ♬
VWSHHHHH

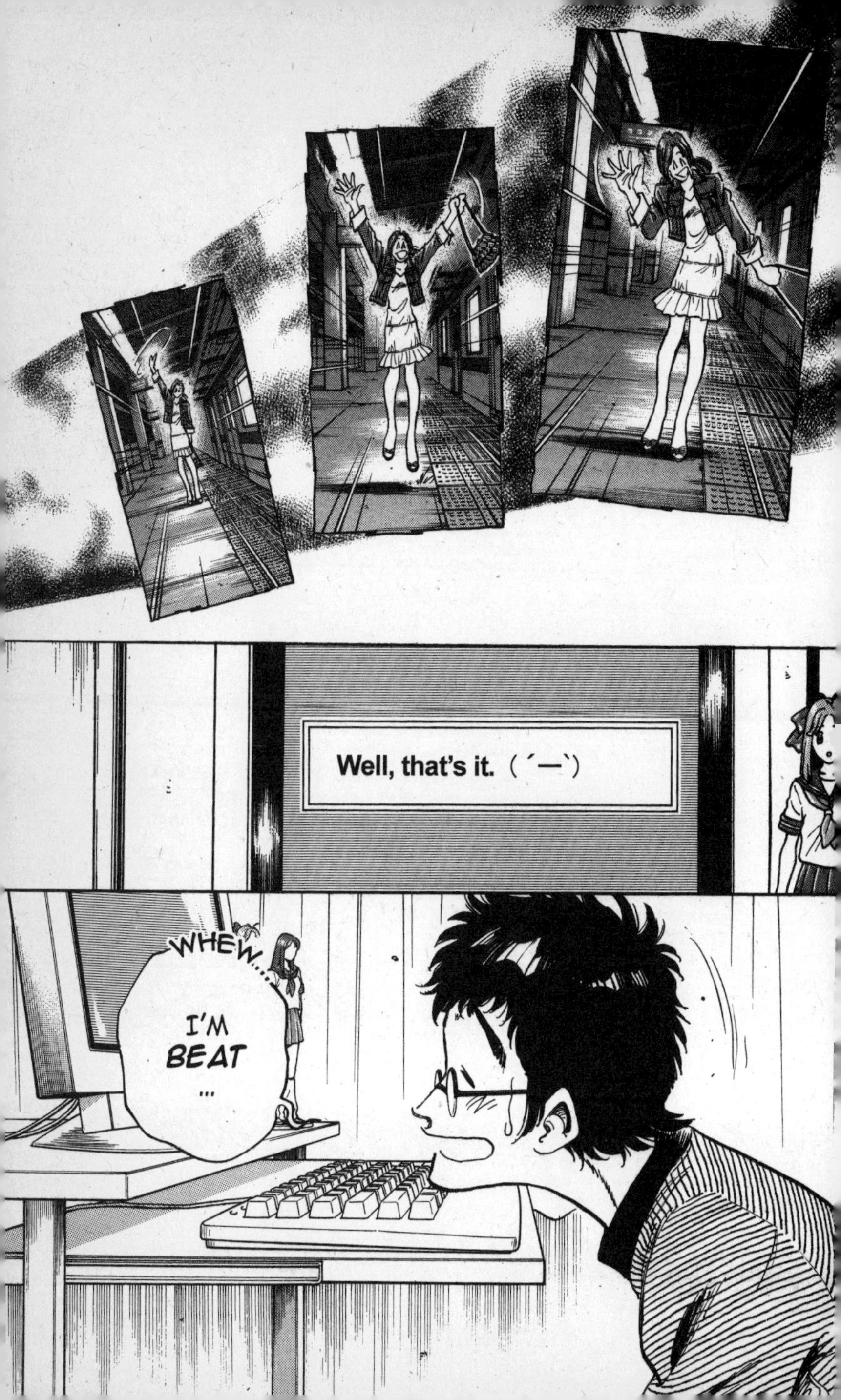
Well, that's it. (´—`)
WHEW...
I'M BEAT ...

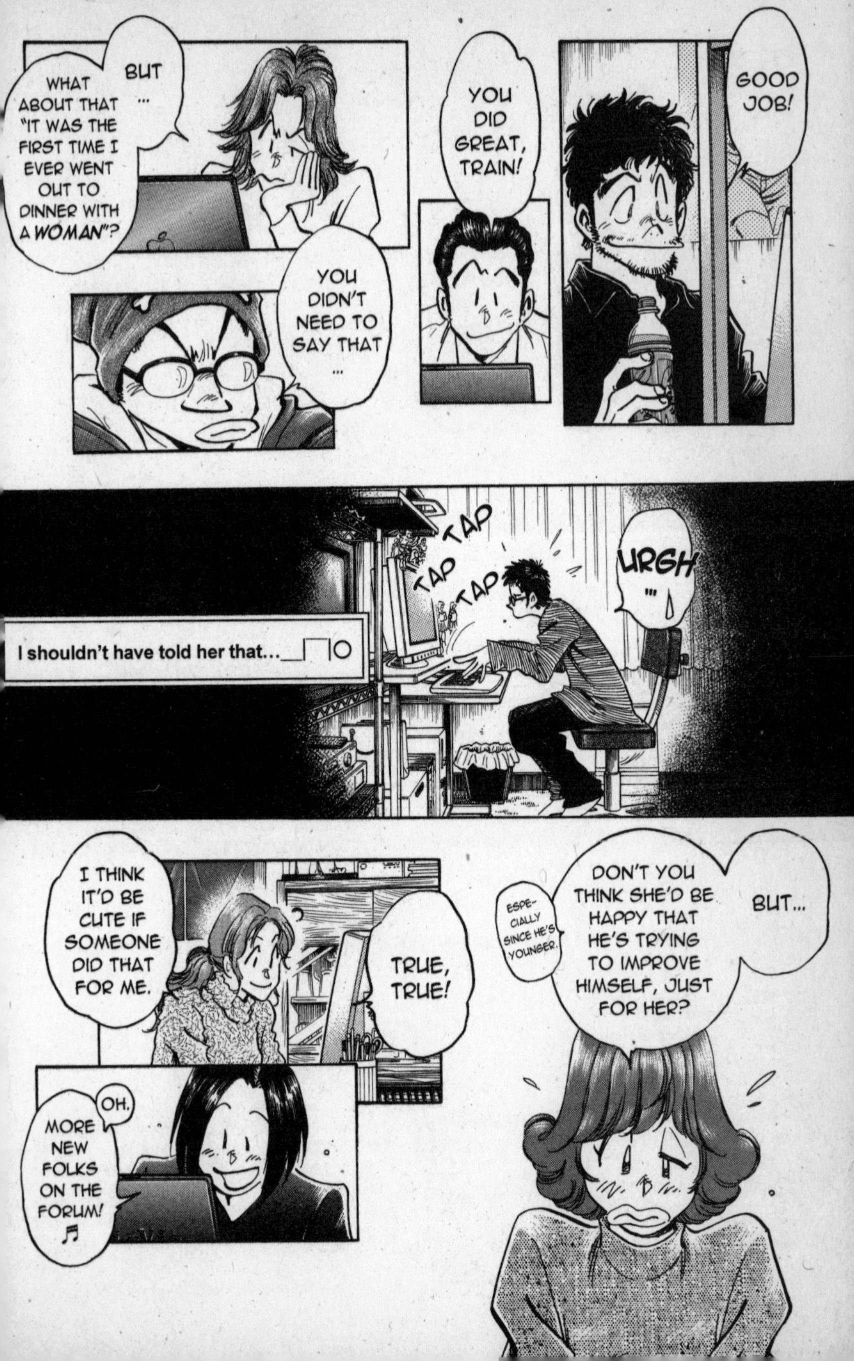
GOOD JOB!
YOU DID GREAT, TRAIN!
BUT ...
WHAT ABOUT THAT "IT WAS THE FIRST TIME I EVER WENT OUT TO DINNER WITH A *WOMAN*"?
YOU DIDN'T NEED TO SAY THAT ...
URGH ...
TAP TAP TAP TAP
I shouldn't have told her that... _|￣|○
BUT...
DON'T YOU THINK SHE'D BE HAPPY THAT HE'S TRYING TO IMPROVE HIMSELF, JUST FOR HER?
ESPECIALLY SINCE HE'S YOUNGER.
TRUE, TRUE!
I THINK IT'D BE CUTE IF SOMEONE DID THAT FOR ME.
OH,
MORE NEW FOLKS ON THE FORUM! ♫

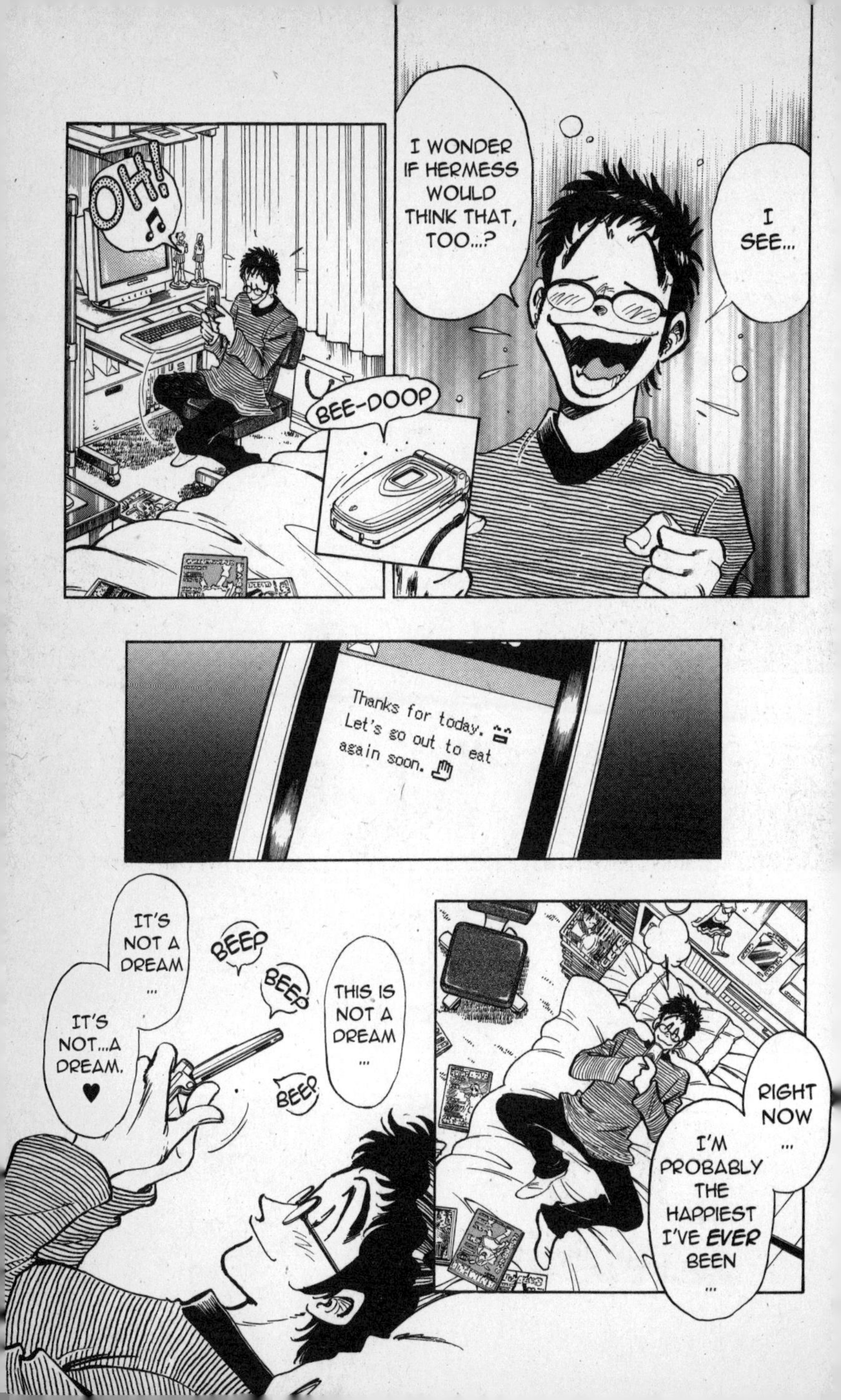
I SEE...
I WONDER IF HERMESS WOULD THINK THAT, TOO...?
BEE-DOOP
OH! ♪
Thanks for today.
Let's go out to eat again soon.
RIGHT NOW ...
I'M PROBABLY THE HAPPIEST I'VE *EVER* BEEN ...
THIS IS NOT A DREAM ...
BEEP
BEEP
BEEP
IT'S NOT A DREAM ...
IT'S NOT...A DREAM. ♥

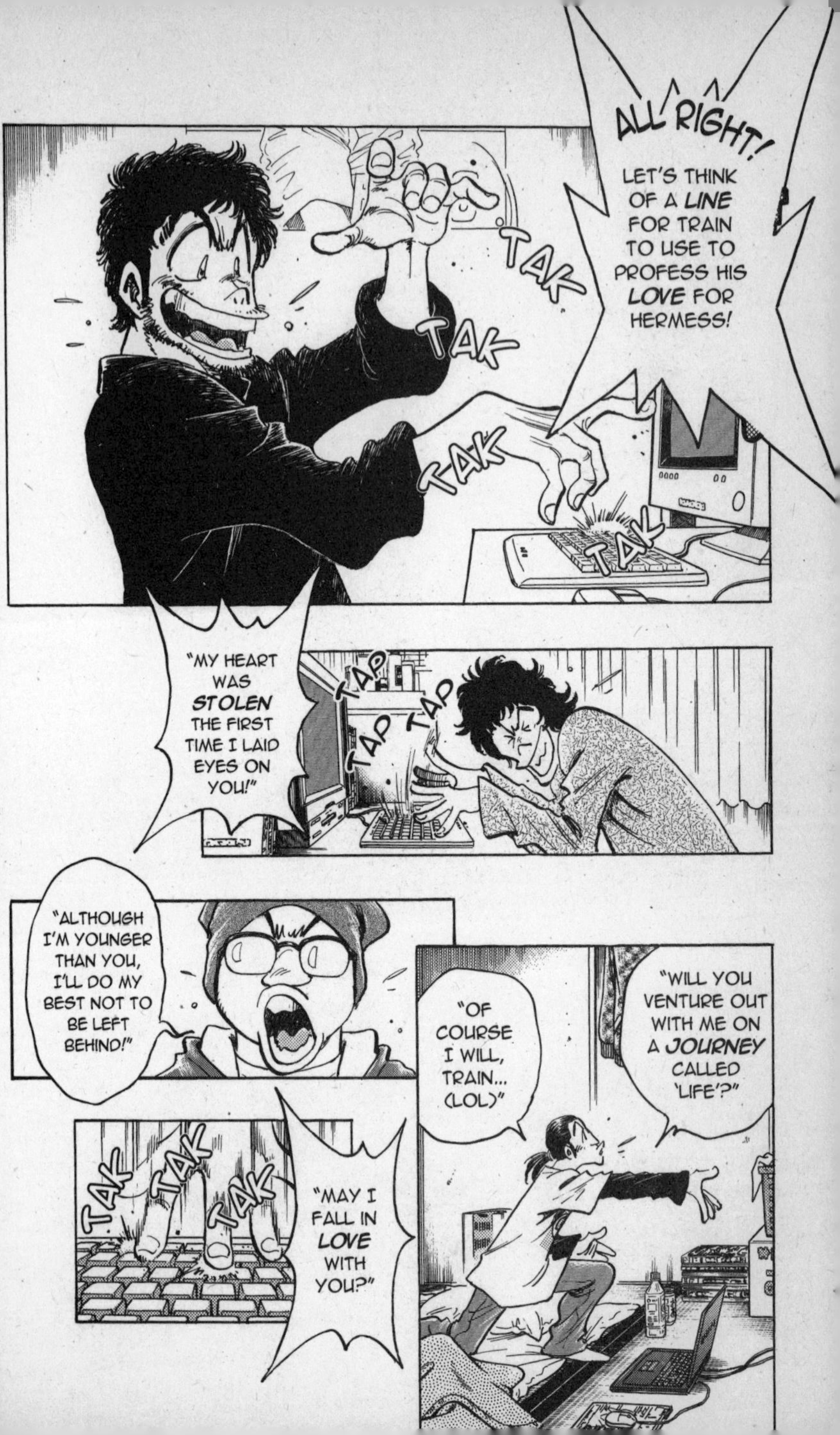
ALL RIGHT!
LET'S THINK OF A ***LINE*** FOR TRAIN TO USE TO PROFESS HIS ***LOVE*** FOR HERMESS!
TAK
TAK
TAK
TAK
"MY HEART WAS ***STOLEN*** THE FIRST TIME I LAID EYES ON YOU!"
TAP
TAP
TAP
"WILL YOU VENTURE OUT WITH ME ON A ***JOURNEY*** CALLED 'LIFE'?"
"OF COURSE I WILL, TRAIN... (LOL)"
"ALTHOUGH I'M YOUNGER THAN YOU, I'LL DO MY BEST NOT TO BE LEFT BEHIND!"
TAK
TAK
TAK
"MAY I FALL IN ***LOVE*** WITH YOU?"

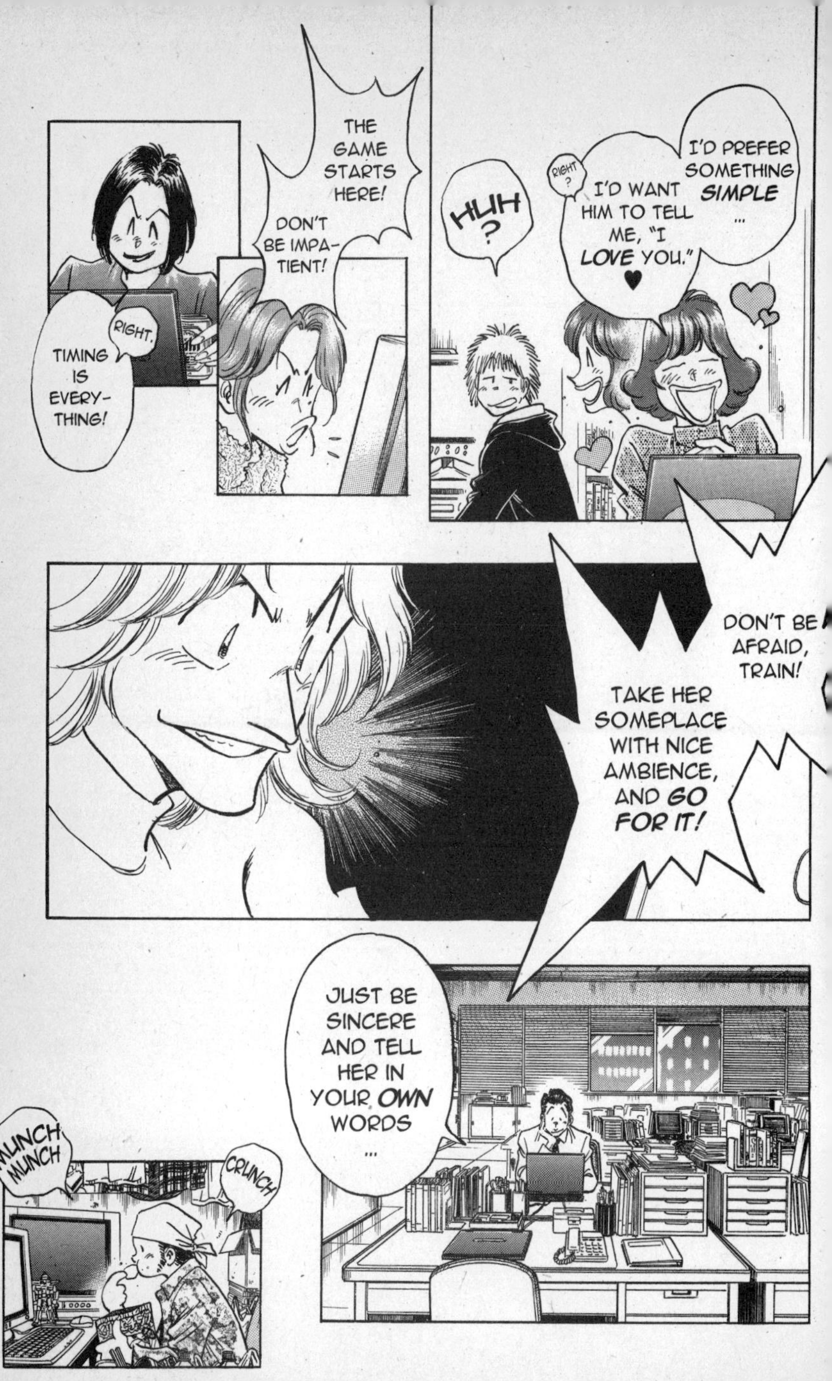
I'D PREFER SOMETHING SIMPLE ...
RIGHT ?
I'D WANT HIM TO TELL ME, "I LOVE YOU." ♥
HUH ?
THE GAME STARTS HERE!
DON'T BE IMPA-TIENT!
RIGHT.
TIMING IS EVERY-THING!
DON'T BE AFRAID, TRAIN!
TAKE HER SOMEPLACE WITH NICE AMBIENCE, AND GO FOR IT!
JUST BE SINCERE AND TELL HER IN YOUR OWN WORDS ...
CRUNCH
MUNCH MUNCH

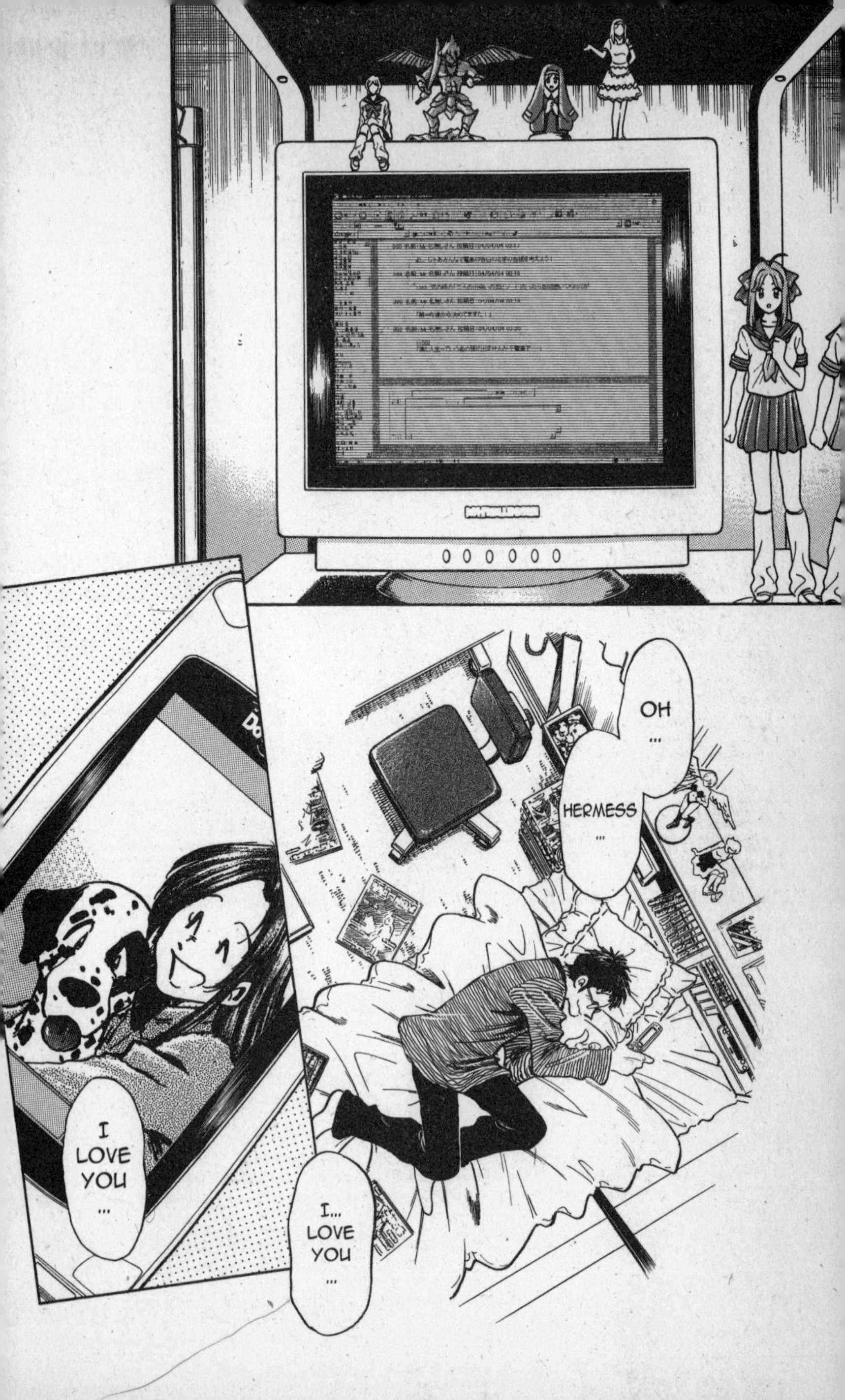
OH ...
HERMESS ...
I... LOVE YOU ...
I LOVE YOU ...

episode 11: Are You All Right?

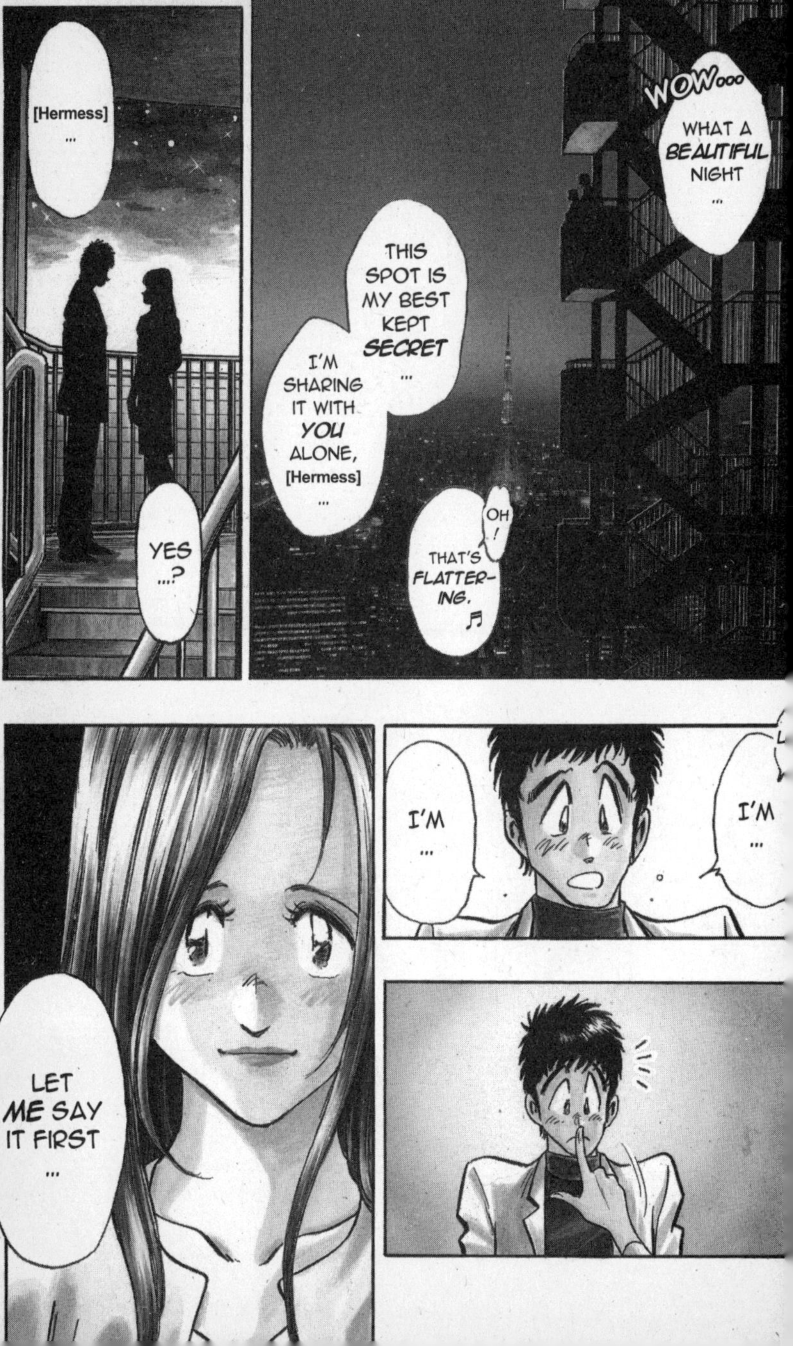
WOW...
WHAT A BEAUTIFUL NIGHT ...
THIS SPOT IS MY BEST KEPT SECRET ...
I'M SHARING IT WITH YOU ALONE, [Hermess] ...
OH! THAT'S FLATTERING. ♬
[Hermess] ...
YES ...?
I'M ...
I'M ...
LET ME SAY IT FIRST ...

episode 11:
Are You All Right?

FROM THE TIME YOU SAVED ME ON THE TRAIN ...

I'M OLDER THAN YOU, BUT ...

I'VE BEEN IN *LOVE* WITH YOU, [Train_Man] ...

I'LL TRY NOT TO BE LEFT BEHIND, SO PLEASE ... WON'T YOU BE MINE ?

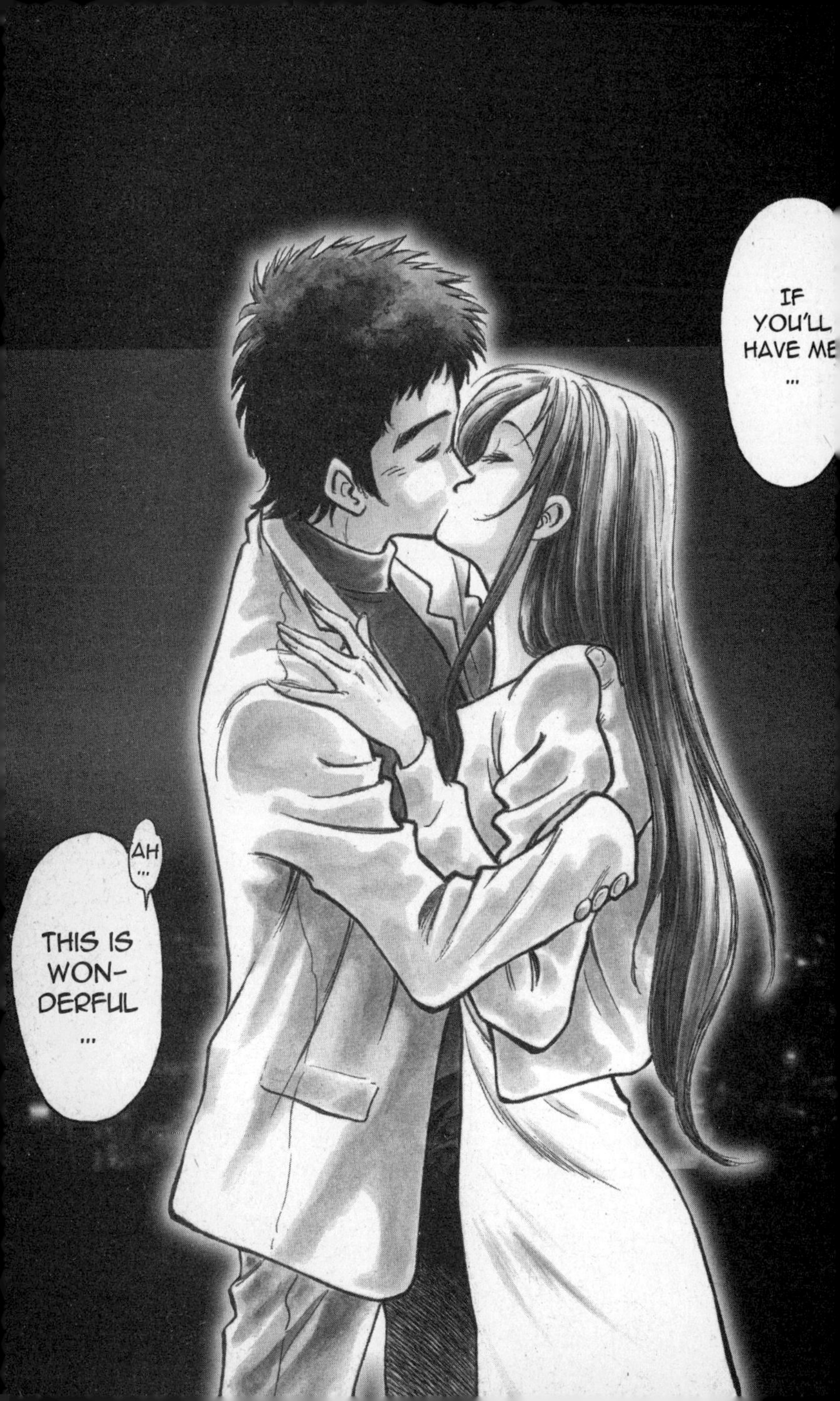
IF YOU'LL HAVE ME ...
AH ...
THIS IS WON-DERFUL ...

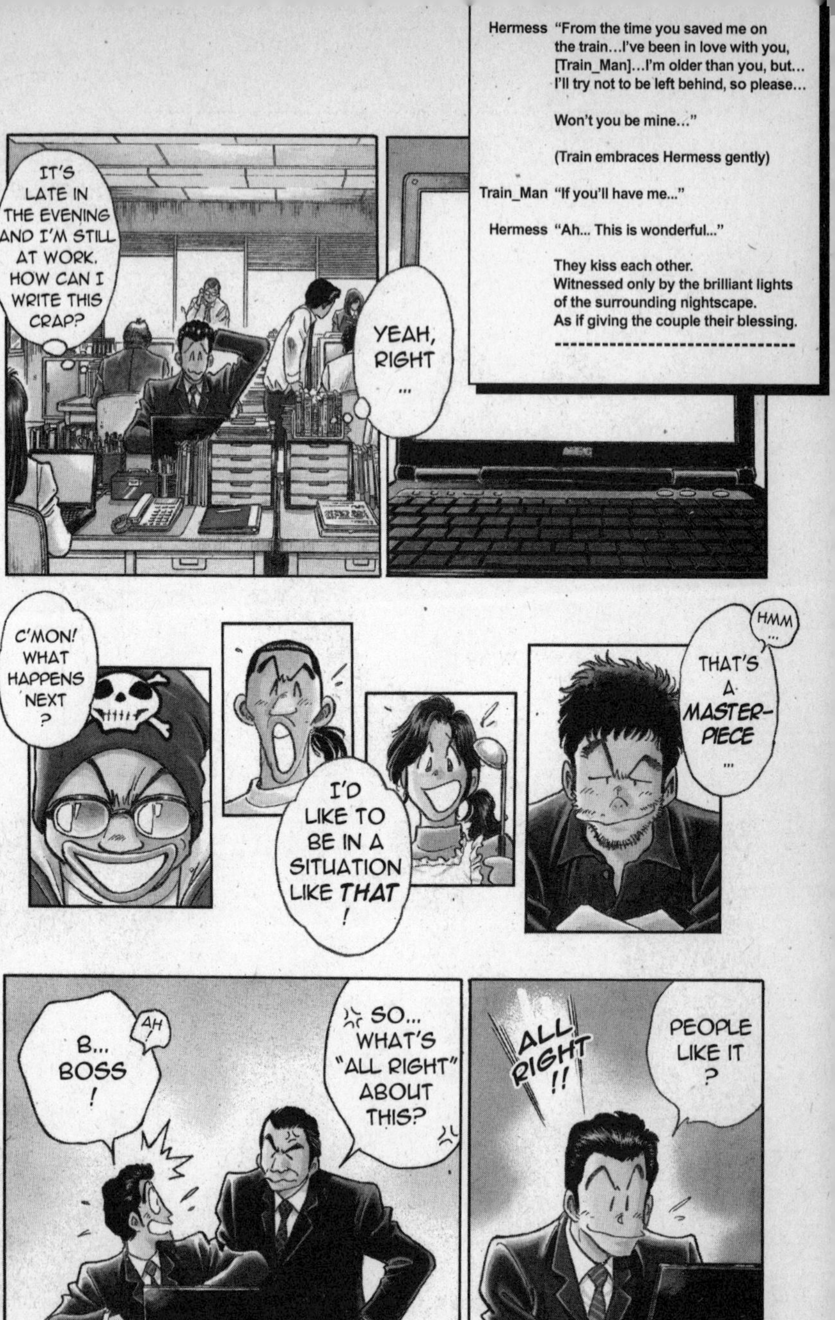

Hermess “From the time you saved me on the train…I’ve been in love with you, [Train_Man]…I’m older than you, but… I’ll try not to be left behind, so please…
Won’t you be mine…”
(Train embraces Hermess gently)
Train_Man “If you’ll have me...”
Hermess “Ah... This is wonderful...”
They kiss each other.
Witnessed only by the brilliant lights of the surrounding nightscape.
As if giving the couple their blessing.
IT'S LATE IN THE EVENING AND I'M STILL AT WORK. HOW CAN I WRITE THIS CRAP?
YEAH, RIGHT ...
HMM ...
THAT'S A MASTER-PIECE ...
I'D LIKE TO BE IN A SITUATION LIKE THAT !
C'MON! WHAT HAPPENS NEXT ?
PEOPLE LIKE IT ?
ALL RIGHT !!
SO... WHAT'S "ALL RIGHT" ABOUT THIS?
AH !
B... BOSS !

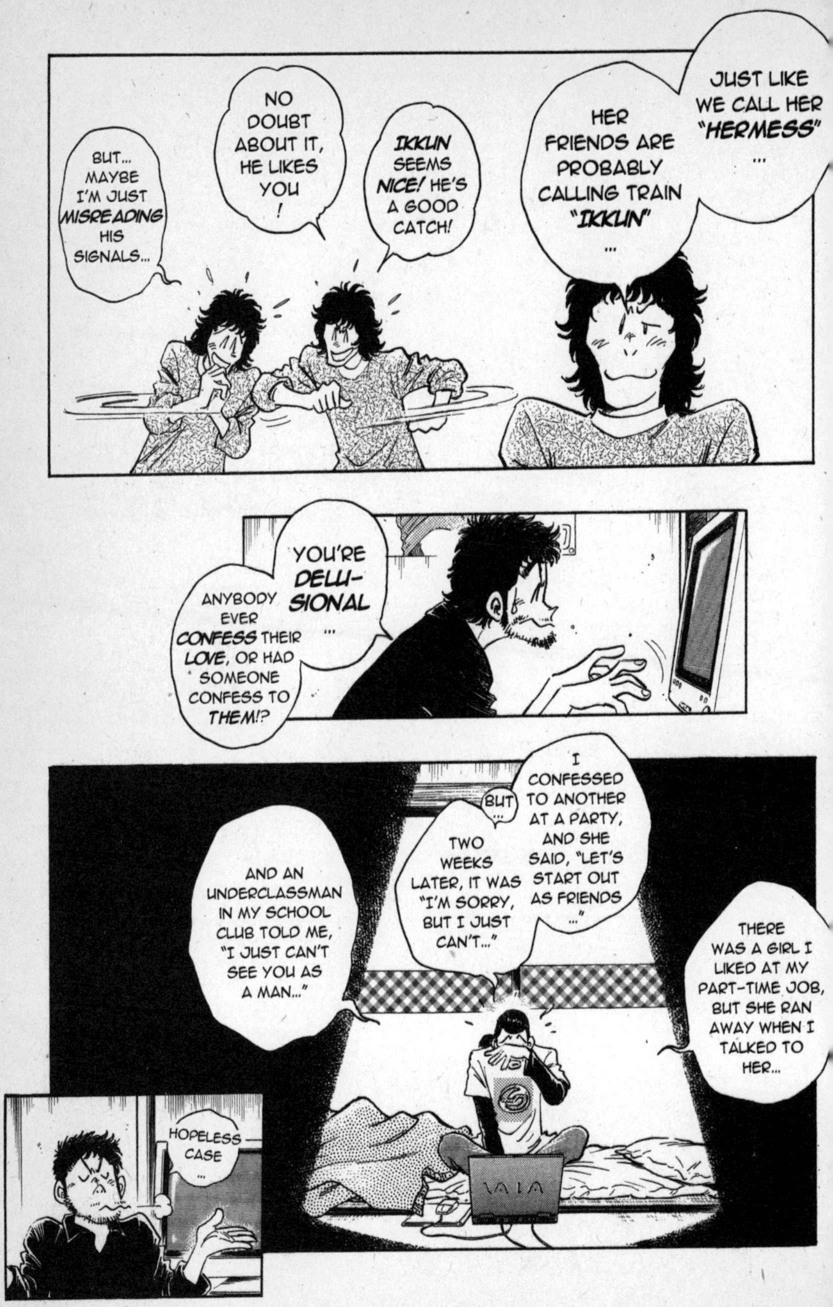
JUST LIKE WE CALL HER "HERMESS"...
HER FRIENDS ARE PROBABLY CALLING TRAIN "IKKUN"...
IKKUN SEEMS NICE! HE'S A GOOD CATCH!
NO DOUBT ABOUT IT, HE LIKES YOU!
BUT... MAYBE I'M JUST MISREADING HIS SIGNALS...
YOU'RE DELUSIONAL...
ANYBODY EVER CONFESS THEIR LOVE, OR HAD SOMEONE CONFESS TO THEM!?
THERE WAS A GIRL I LIKED AT MY PART-TIME JOB, BUT SHE RAN AWAY WHEN I TALKED TO HER...
I CONFESSED TO ANOTHER AT A PARTY, AND SHE SAID, "LET'S START OUT AS FRIENDS..."
BUT...
TWO WEEKS LATER, IT WAS "I'M SORRY, BUT I JUST CAN'T..."
AND AN UNDERCLASSMAN IN MY SCHOOL CLUB TOLD ME, "I JUST CAN'T SEE YOU AS A MAN..."
HOPELESS CASE...

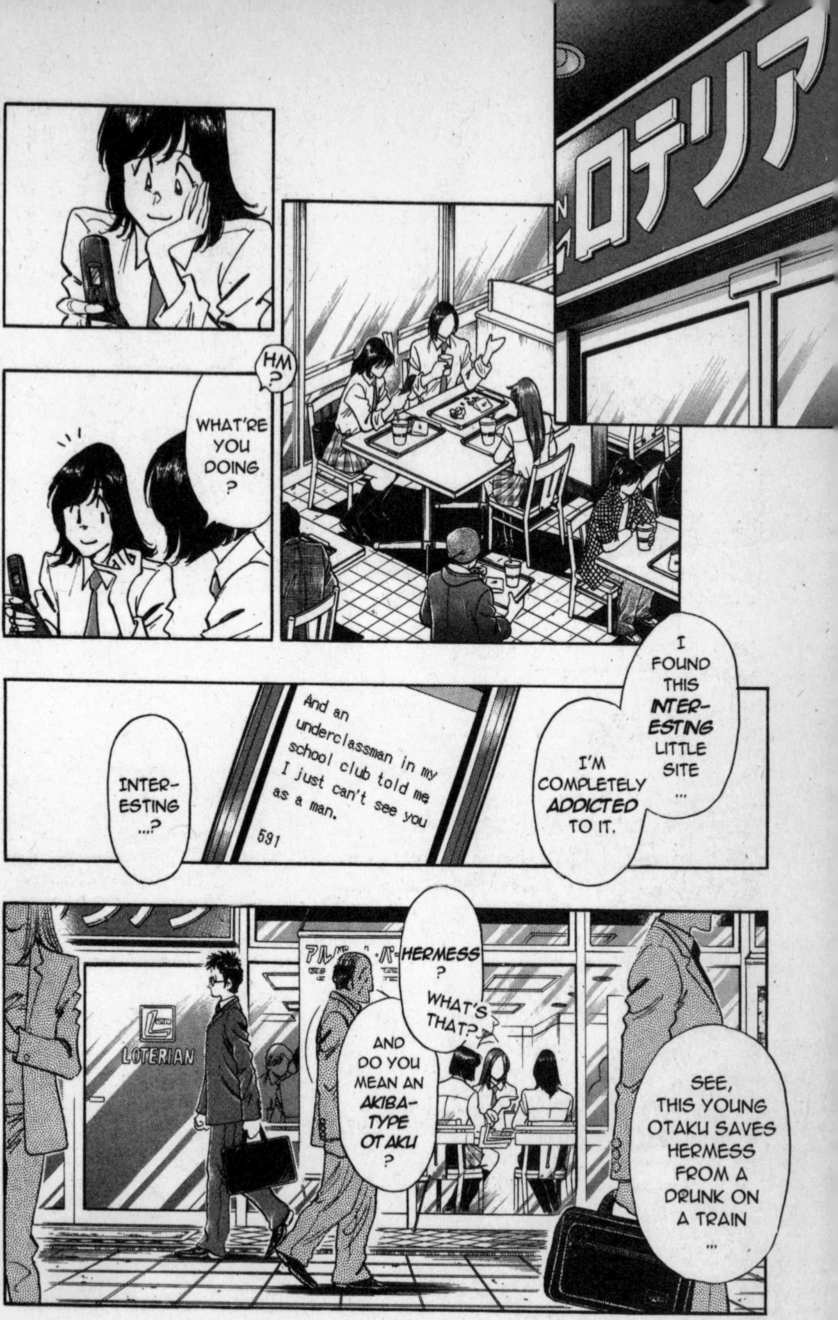
ロテリア
HM?
WHAT'RE YOU DOING?
I FOUND THIS INTERESTING LITTLE SITE ...
I'M COMPLETELY ADDICTED TO IT.
And an underclassman in my school club told me I just can't see you as a man.
591
INTERESTING ...?
SEE, THIS YOUNG OTAKU SAVES HERMESS FROM A DRUNK ON A TRAIN ...
HERMESS? WHAT'S THAT?
AND DO YOU MEAN AN AKIBA-TYPE OTAKU?
LOTERIAN

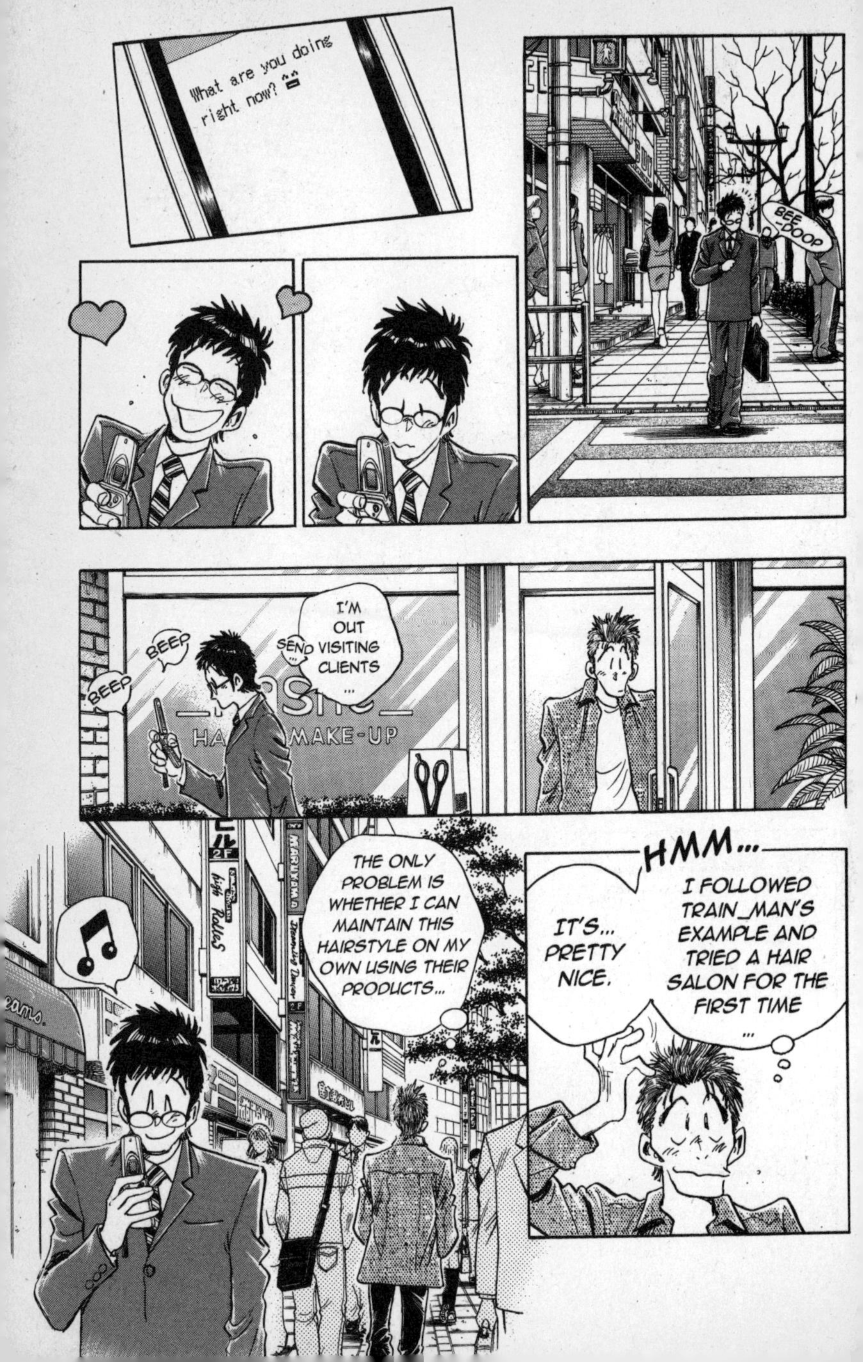
BEE-DOOP
What are you doing right now?
BEEP
BEEP
SEND...
I'M OUT VISITING CLIENTS...
HMM...
I FOLLOWED TRAIN_MAN'S EXAMPLE AND TRIED A HAIR SALON FOR THE FIRST TIME...
IT'S... PRETTY NICE.
THE ONLY PROBLEM IS WHETHER I CAN MAINTAIN THIS HAIRSTYLE ON MY OWN USING THEIR PRODUCTS...

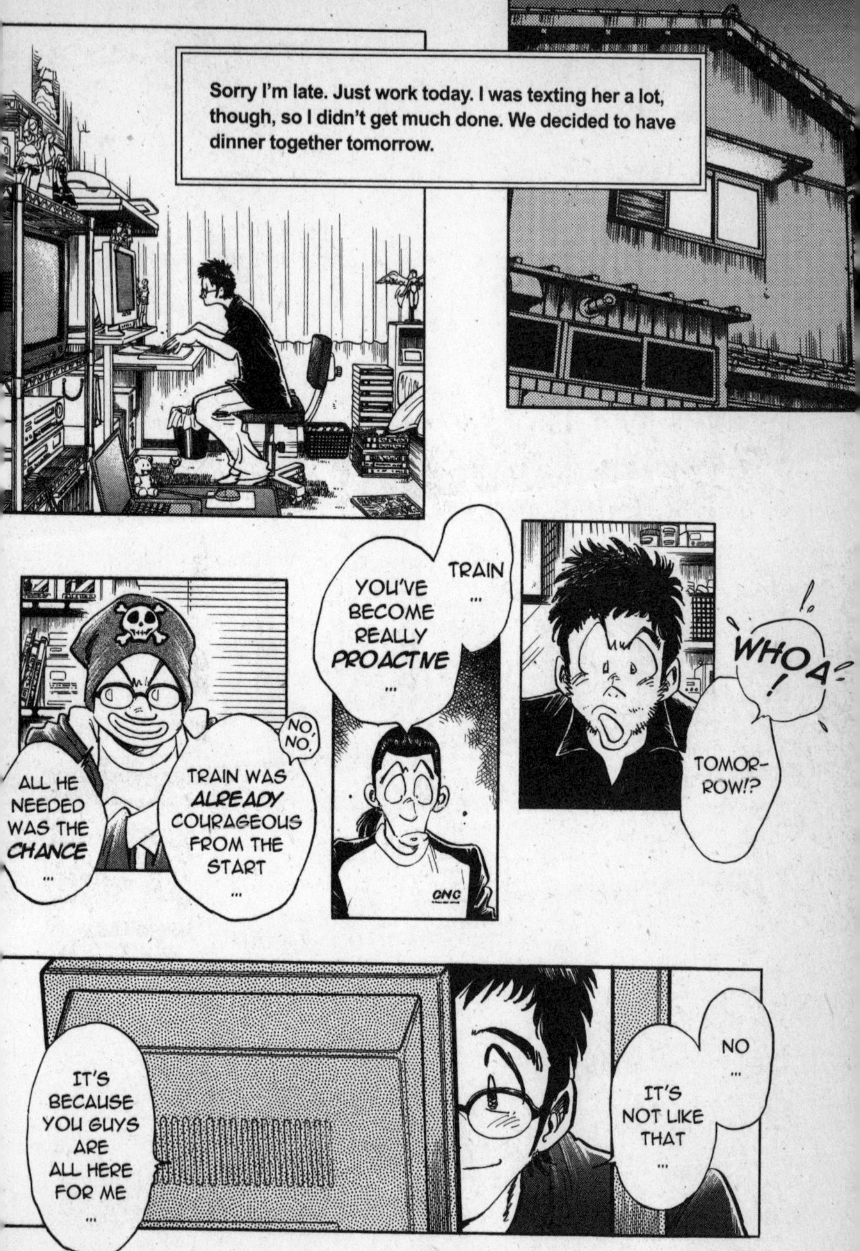

Sorry I'm late. Just work today. I was texting her a lot, though, so I didn't get much done. We decided to have dinner together tomorrow.
WHOA!
TOMORROW!?
TRAIN ...
YOU'VE BECOME REALLY PROACTIVE ...
NO, NO.
TRAIN WAS ALREADY COURAGEOUS FROM THE START ...
ALL HE NEEDED WAS THE CHANCE ...
NO ...
IT'S NOT LIKE THAT ...
IT'S BECAUSE YOU GUYS ARE ALL HERE FOR ME ...

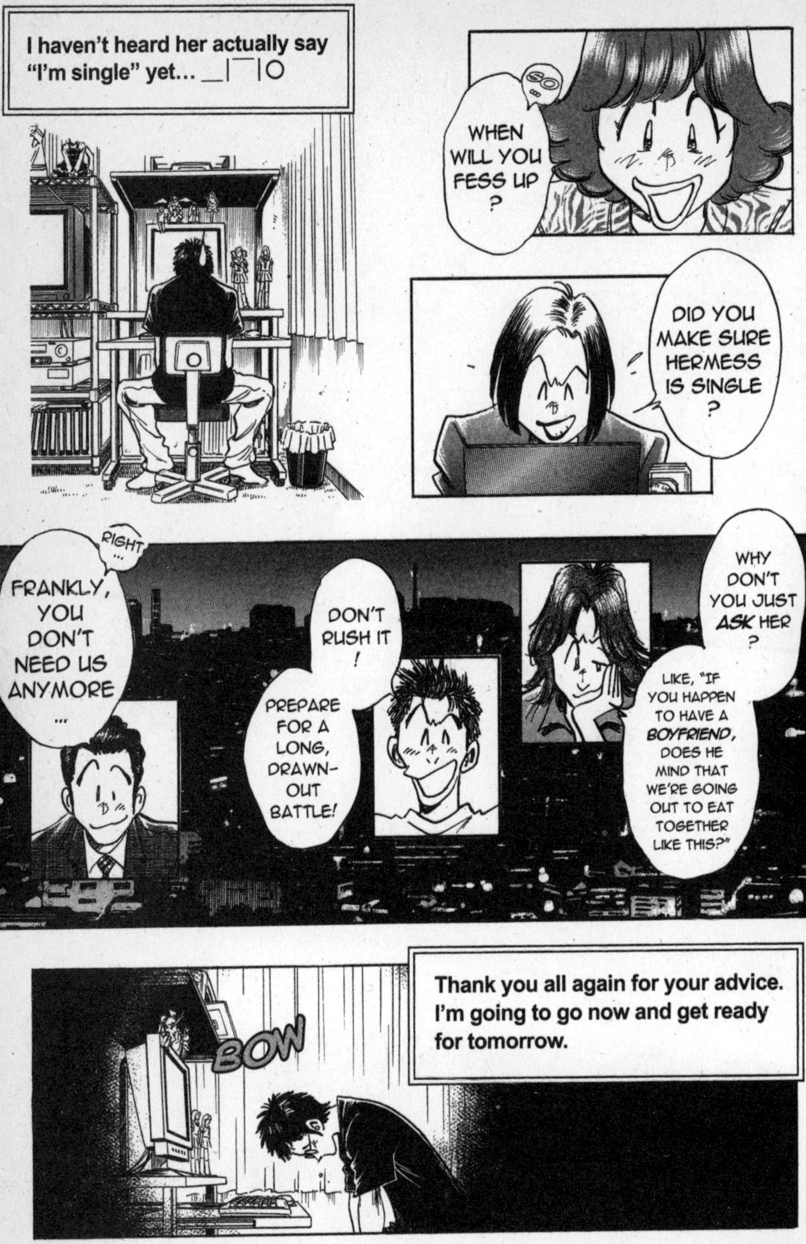
SO
WHEN WILL YOU FESS UP?
DID YOU MAKE SURE HERMESS IS SINGLE?
I haven't heard her actually say "I'm single" yet... _|￣|○
WHY DON'T YOU JUST ASK HER?
LIKE, "IF YOU HAPPEN TO HAVE A BOYFRIEND, DOES HE MIND THAT WE'RE GOING OUT TO EAT TOGETHER LIKE THIS?"
DON'T RUSH IT!
PREPARE FOR A LONG, DRAWN-OUT BATTLE!
RIGHT...
FRANKLY, YOU DON'T NEED US ANYMORE...
Thank you all again for your advice. I'm going to go now and get ready for tomorrow.
BOW

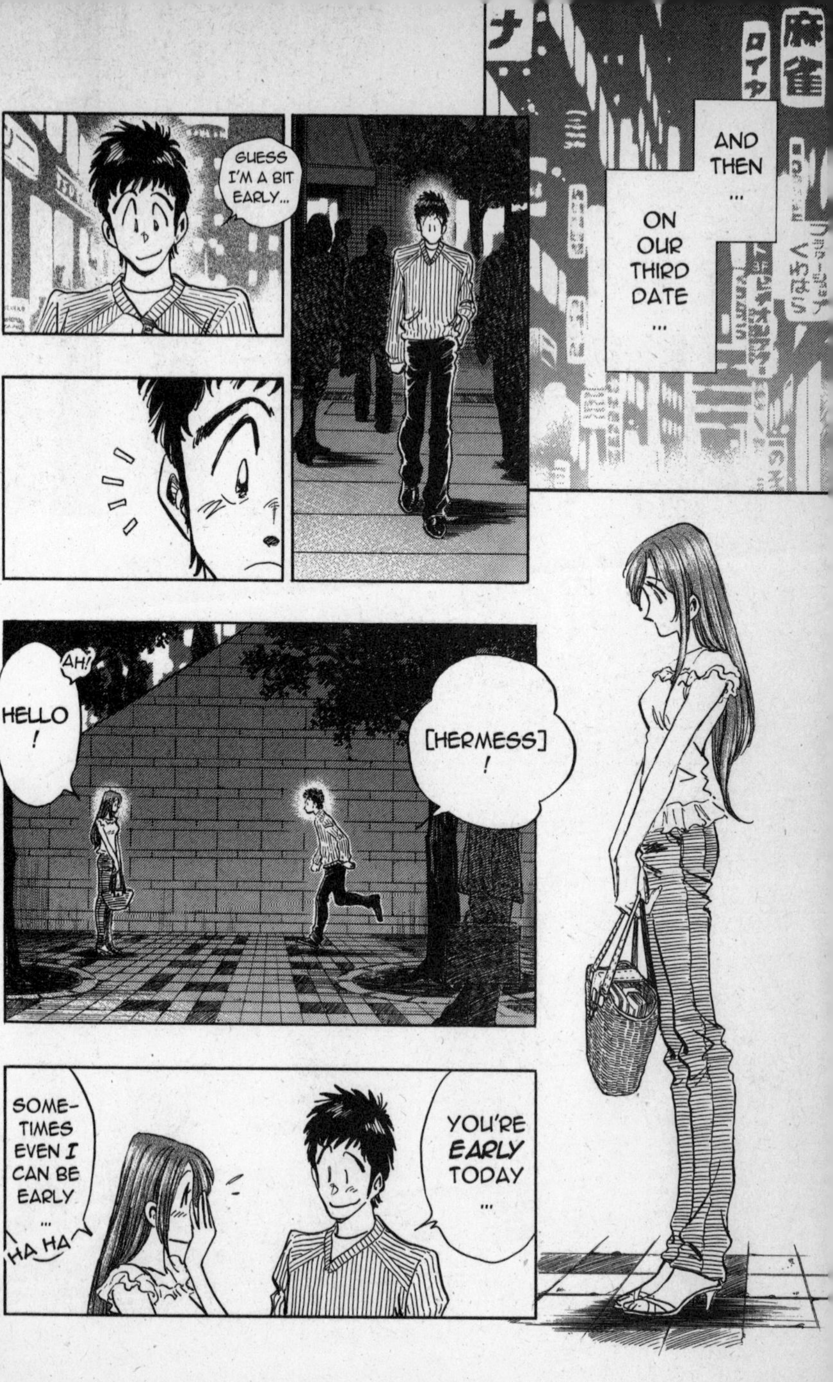

麻雀
AND THEN ...
ON OUR THIRD DATE ...
GUESS I'M A BIT EARLY...
[HERMESS] !
AH!
HELLO !
YOU'RE *EARLY* TODAY ...
SOME-TIMES EVEN *I* CAN BE EARLY ...
HA HA

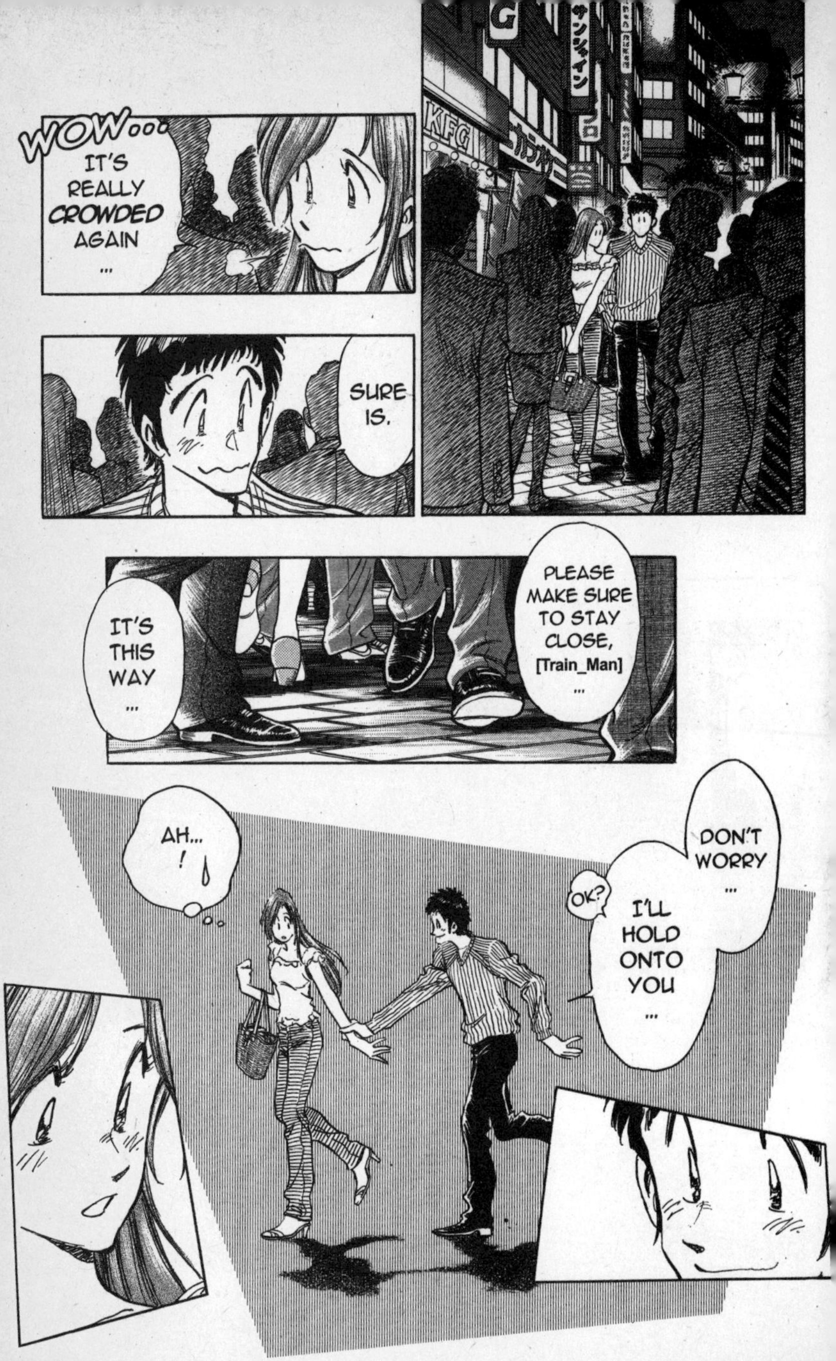
KFG
サンシャイン
WOW...
IT'S REALLY CROWDED AGAIN ...
SURE IS.
PLEASE MAKE SURE TO STAY CLOSE, [Train_Man] ...
IT'S THIS WAY ...
DON'T WORRY ...
OK?
I'LL HOLD ONTO YOU ...
AH... !

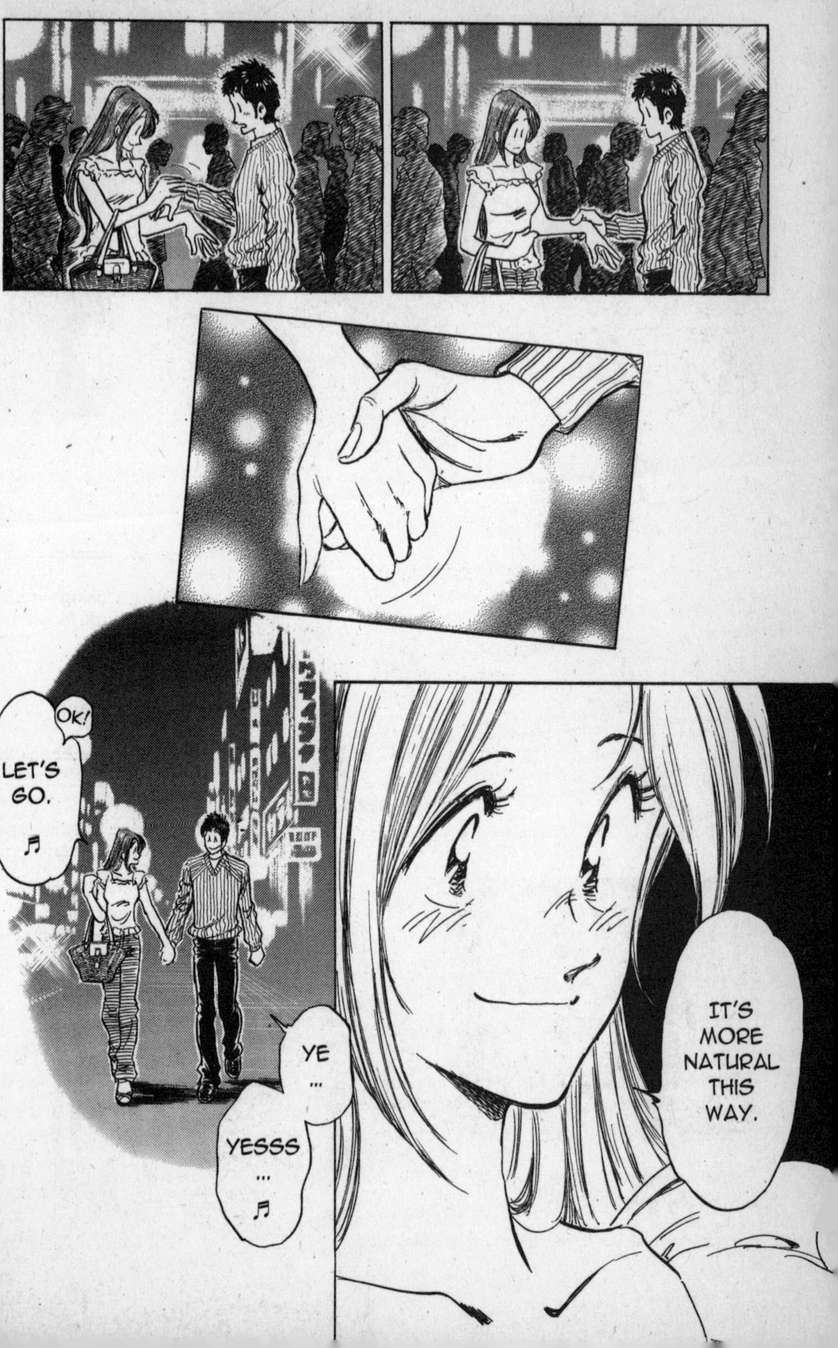
IT'S MORE NATURAL THIS WAY.
LET'S GO. ♪
OK!
YE... YESSS... ♪

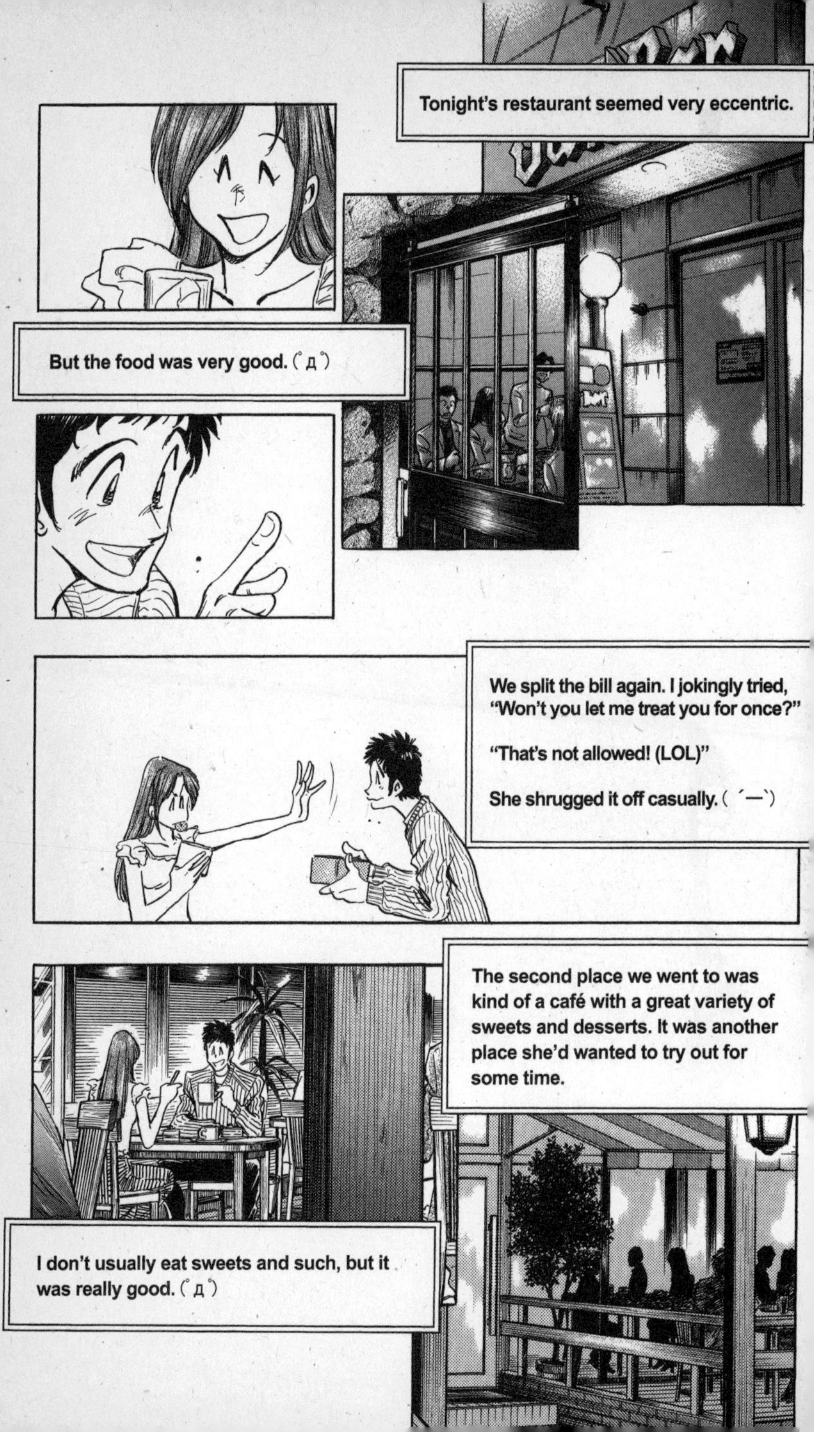

Tonight's restaurant seemed very eccentric.
But the food was very good. (゜д゜)
We split the bill again. I jokingly tried, "Won't you let me treat you for once?"
"That's not allowed! (LOL)"
She shrugged it off casually. (´ー`)
The second place we went to was kind of a café with a great variety of sweets and desserts. It was another place she'd wanted to try out for some time.
I don't usually eat sweets and such, but it was really good. (゜д゜)

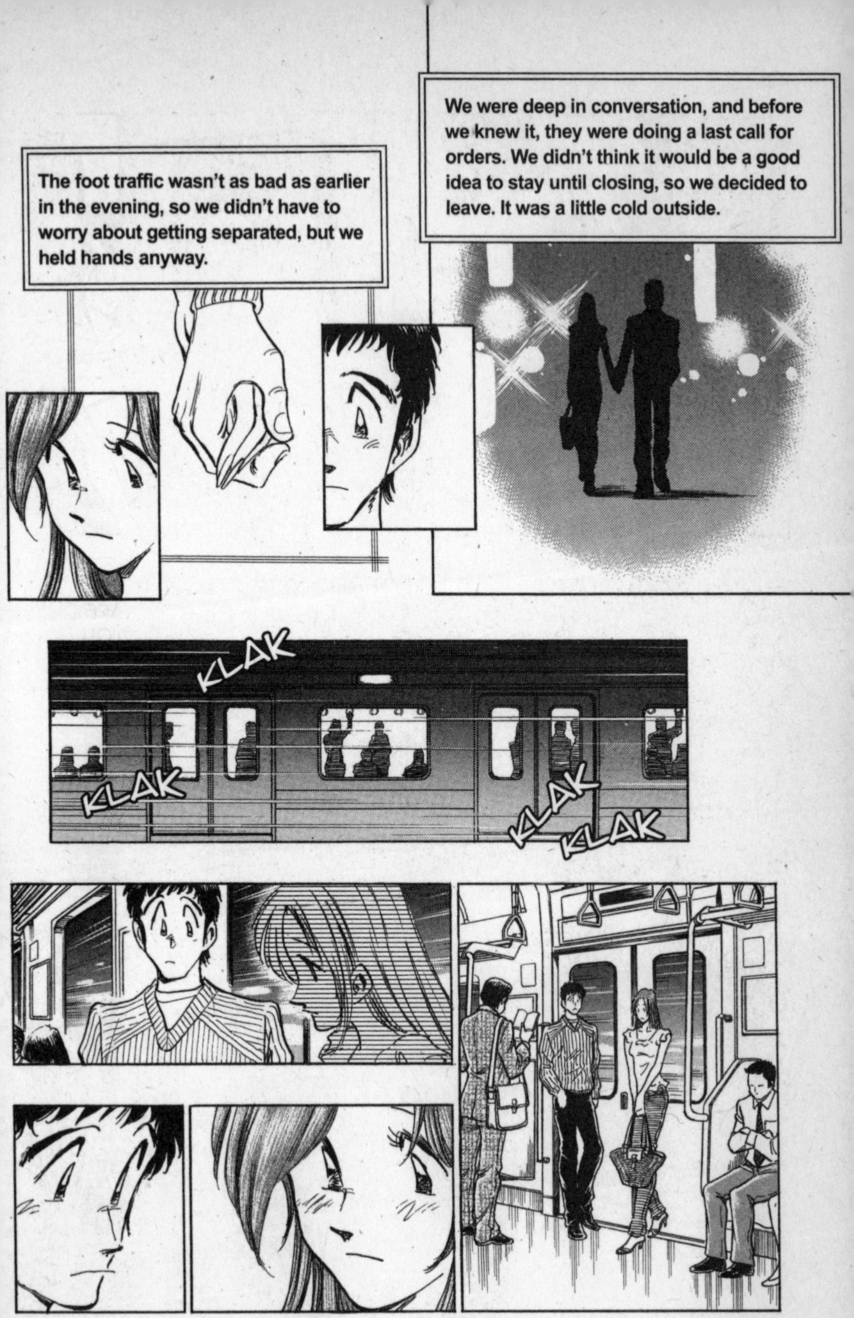
We were deep in conversation, and before we knew it, they were doing a last call for orders. We didn't think it would be a good idea to stay until closing, so we decided to leave. It was a little cold outside.
The foot traffic wasn't as bad as earlier in the evening, so we didn't have to worry about getting separated, but we held hands anyway.
KLAK
KLAK
KLAK
KLAK
KLAK

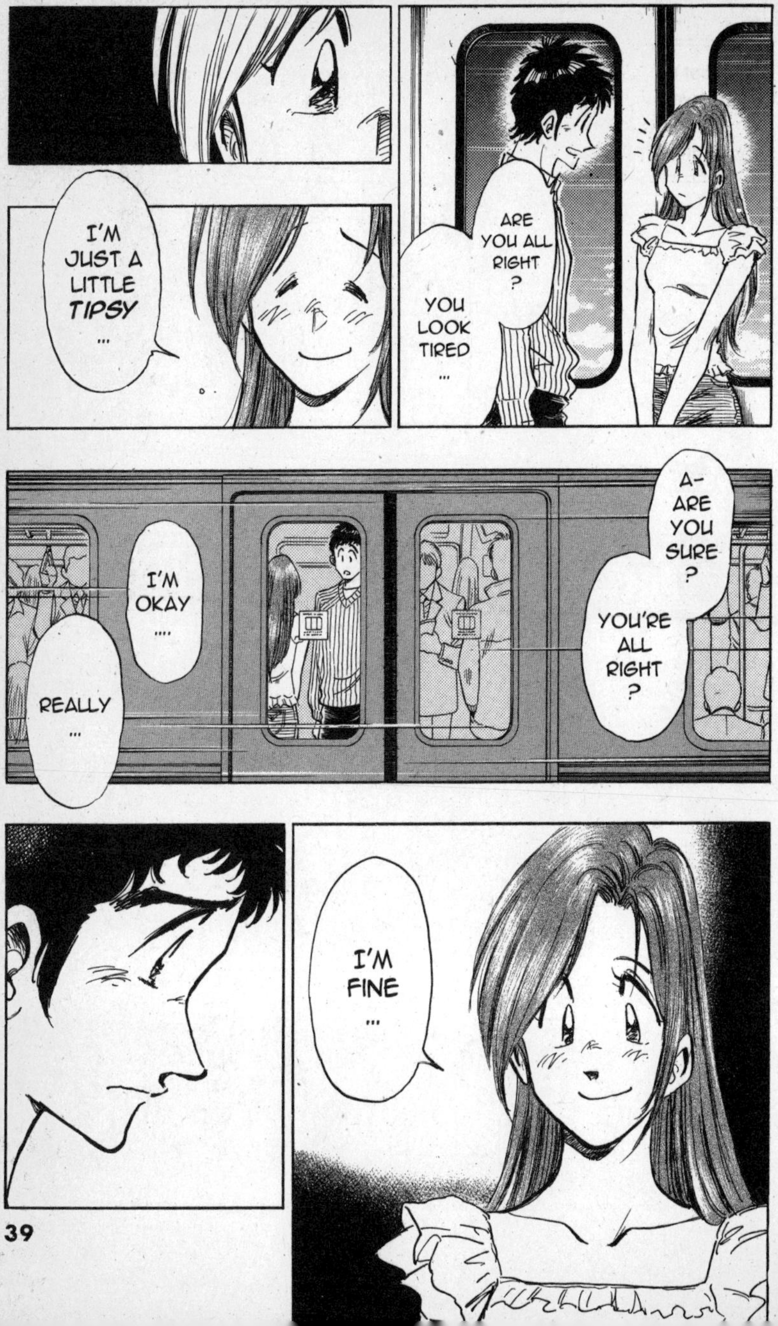

ARE YOU ALL RIGHT?
YOU LOOK TIRED ...
I'M JUST A LITTLE *TIPSY* ...
A-ARE YOU SURE?
YOU'RE ALL RIGHT?
I'M OKAY ....
REALLY ...
I'M FINE ...

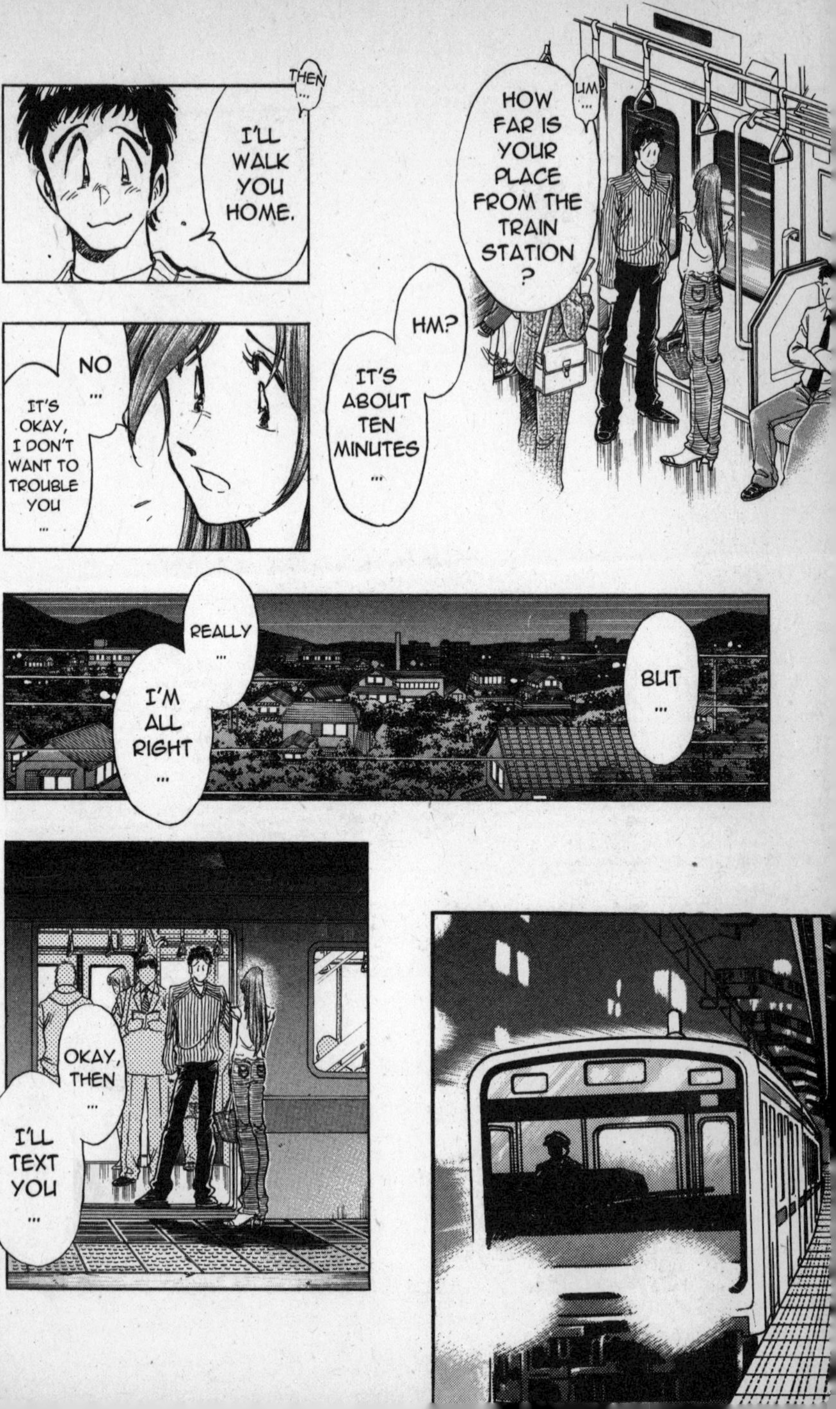

UM ...
HOW FAR IS YOUR PLACE FROM THE TRAIN STATION?
HM?
IT'S ABOUT TEN MINUTES ...
THEN ...
I'LL WALK YOU HOME.
NO ...
IT'S OKAY, I DON'T WANT TO TROUBLE YOU ...
BUT ...
REALLY ...
I'M ALL RIGHT ...
OKAY, THEN ...
I'LL TEXT YOU ...

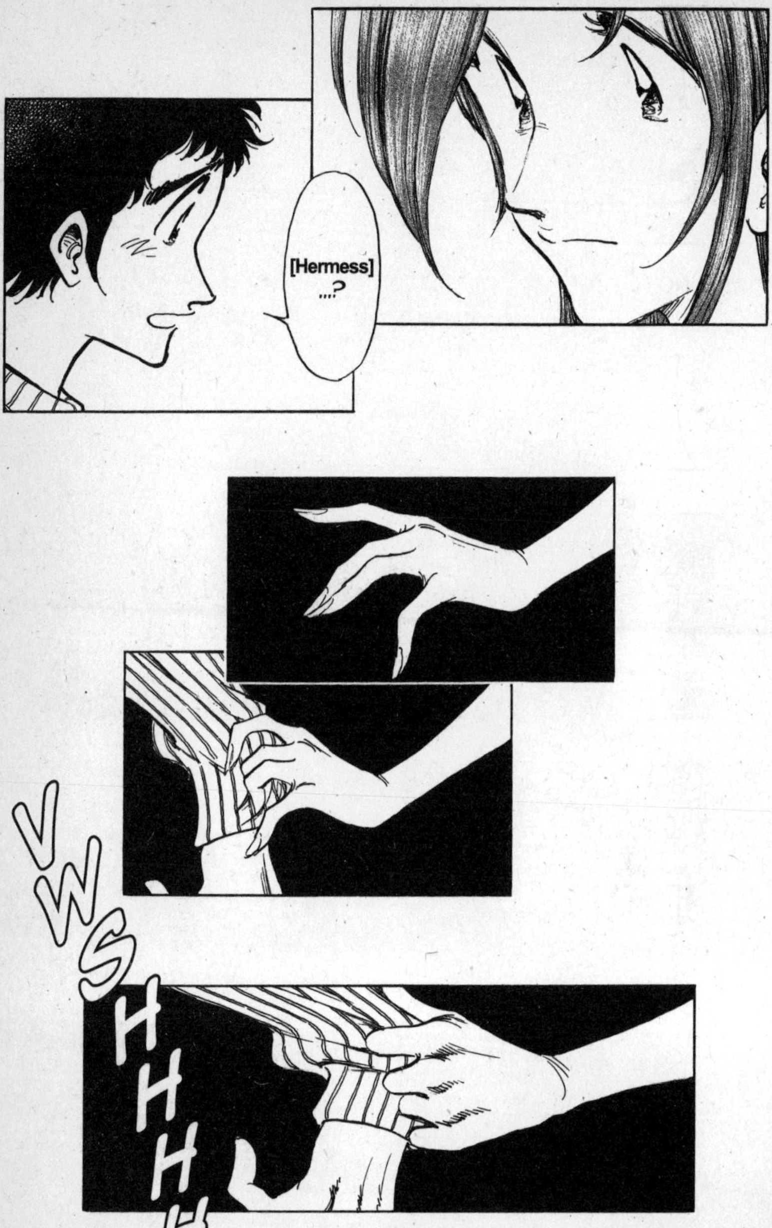
[Hermess]
...?
VWSHHHH

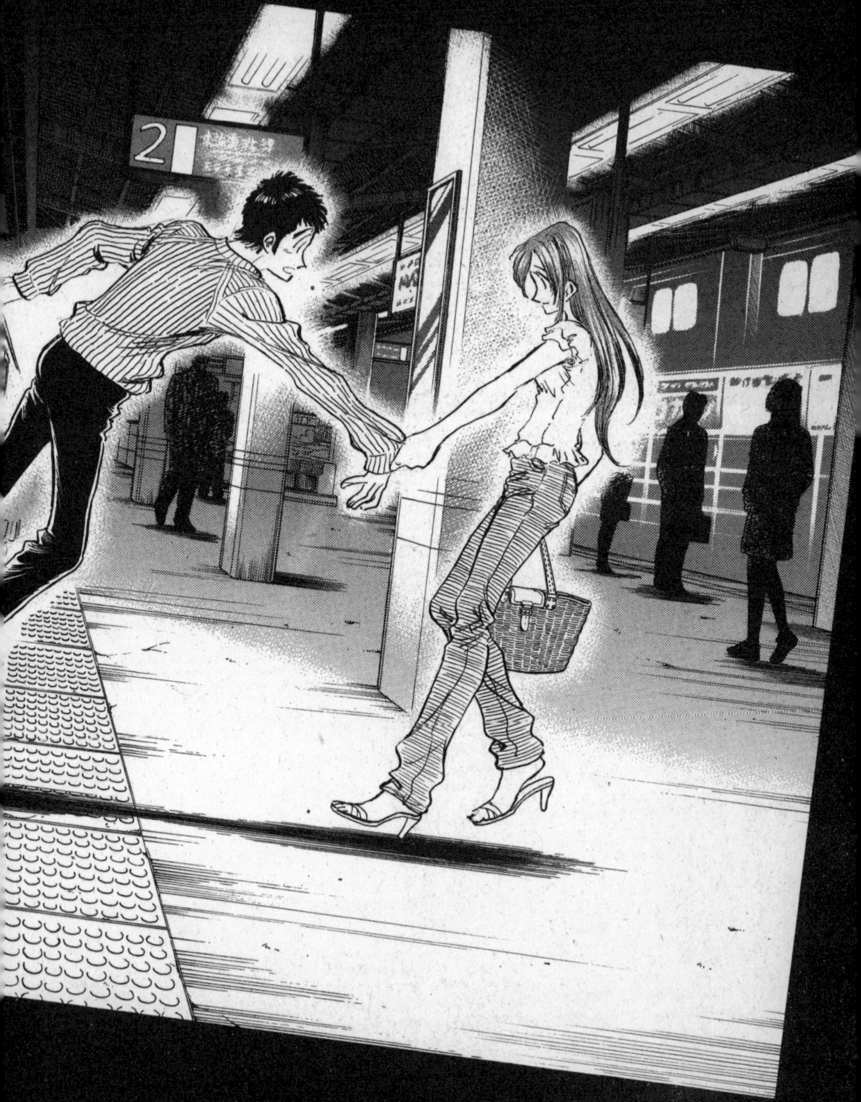
2

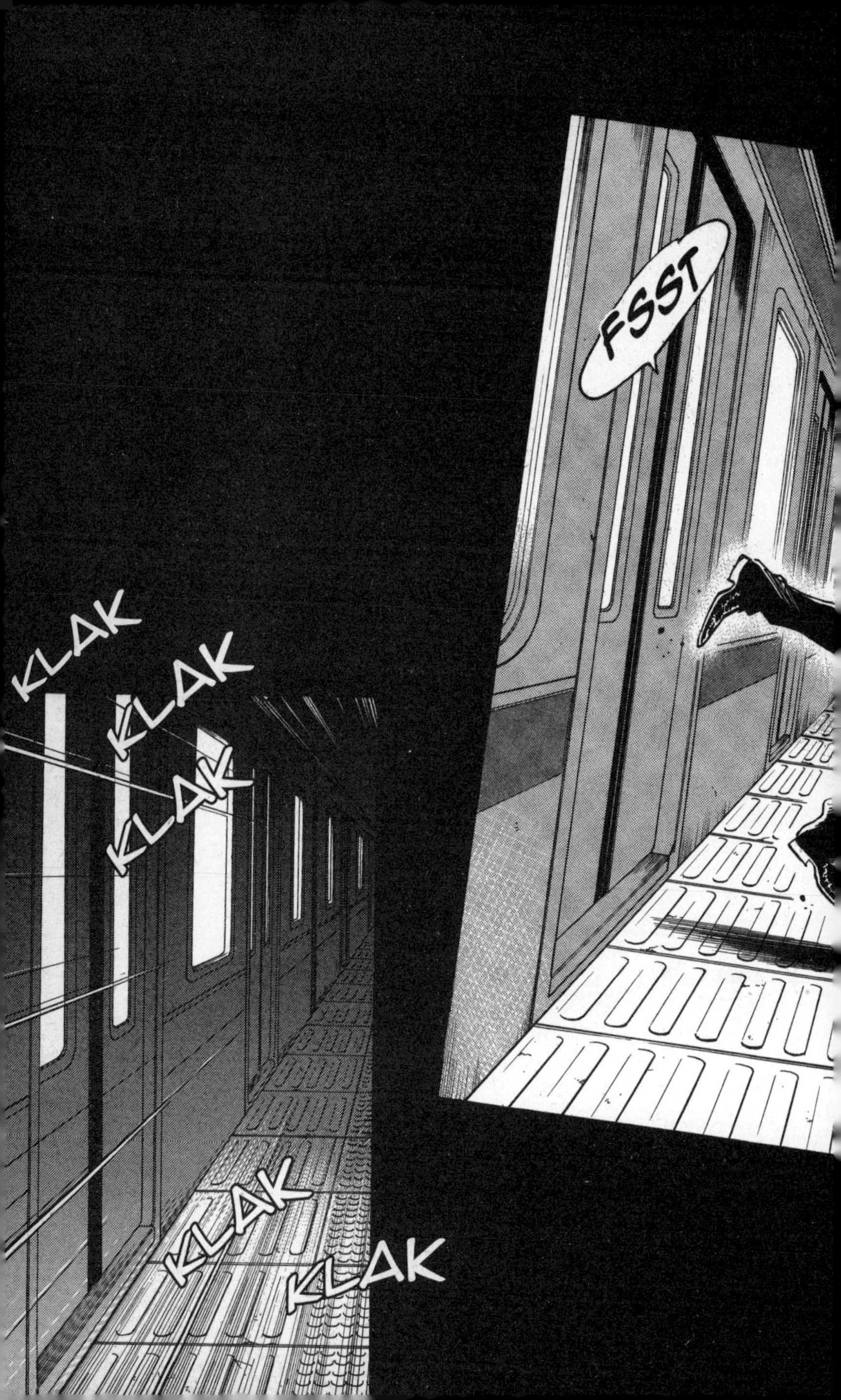
FSST
KLAK
KLAK
KLAK
KLAK
KLAK

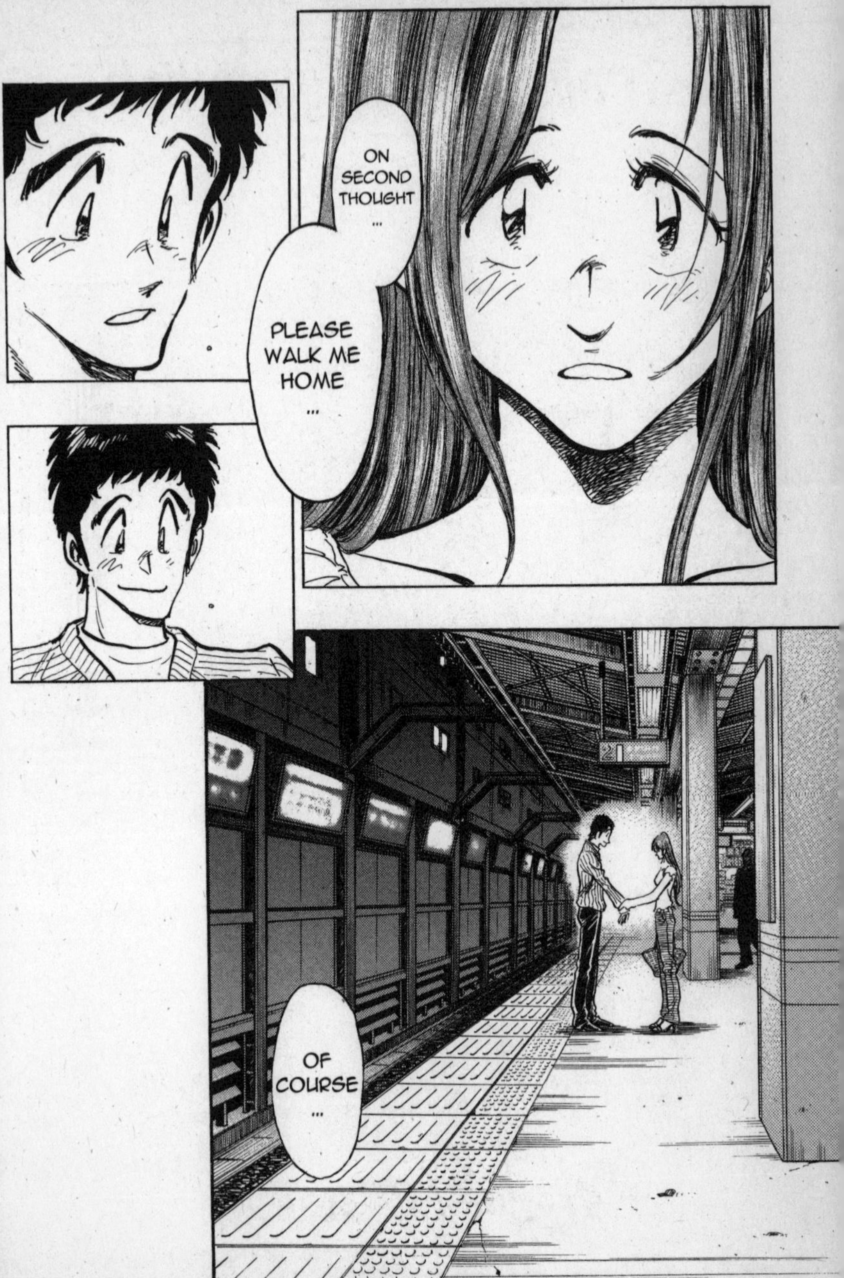
ON SECOND THOUGHT ...
PLEASE WALK ME HOME ...
OF COURSE ...

episode 12:
Train_Man, Flying High

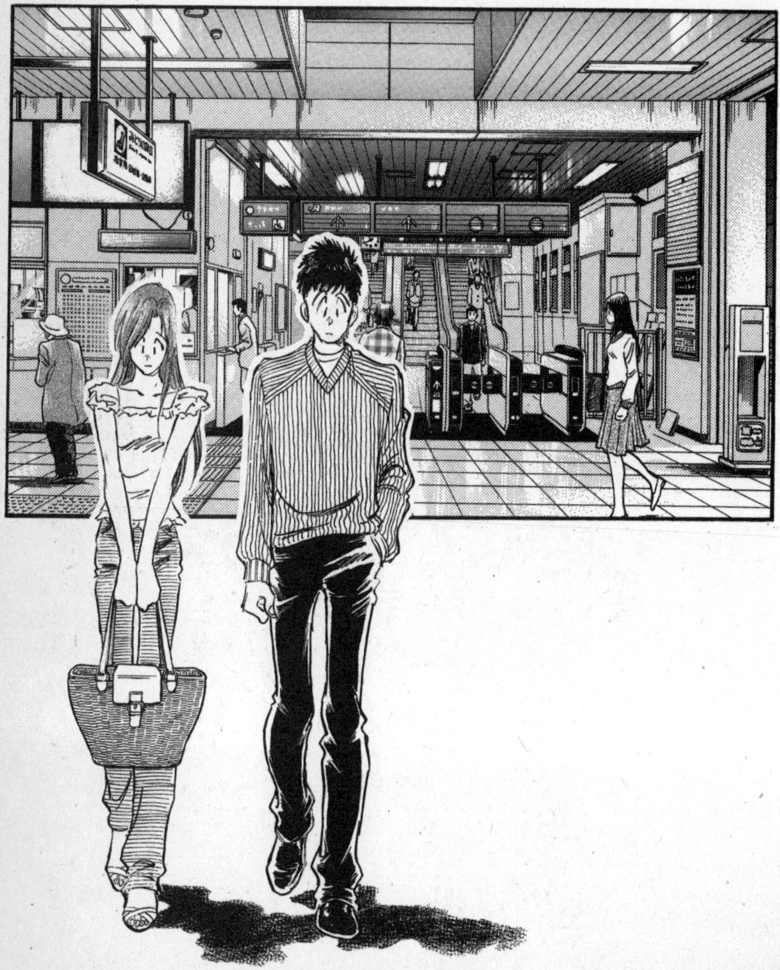

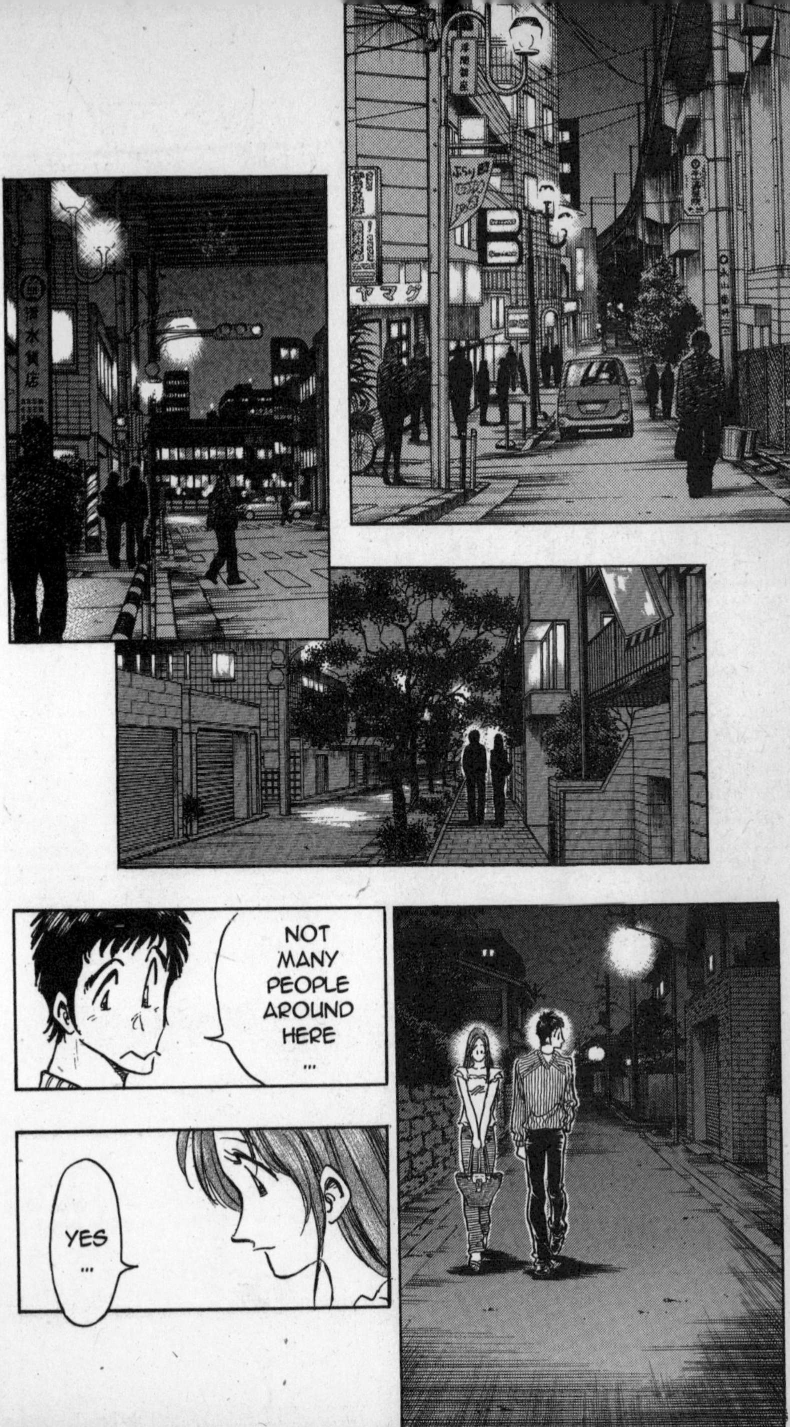
NOT MANY PEOPLE AROUND HERE ...
YES ...

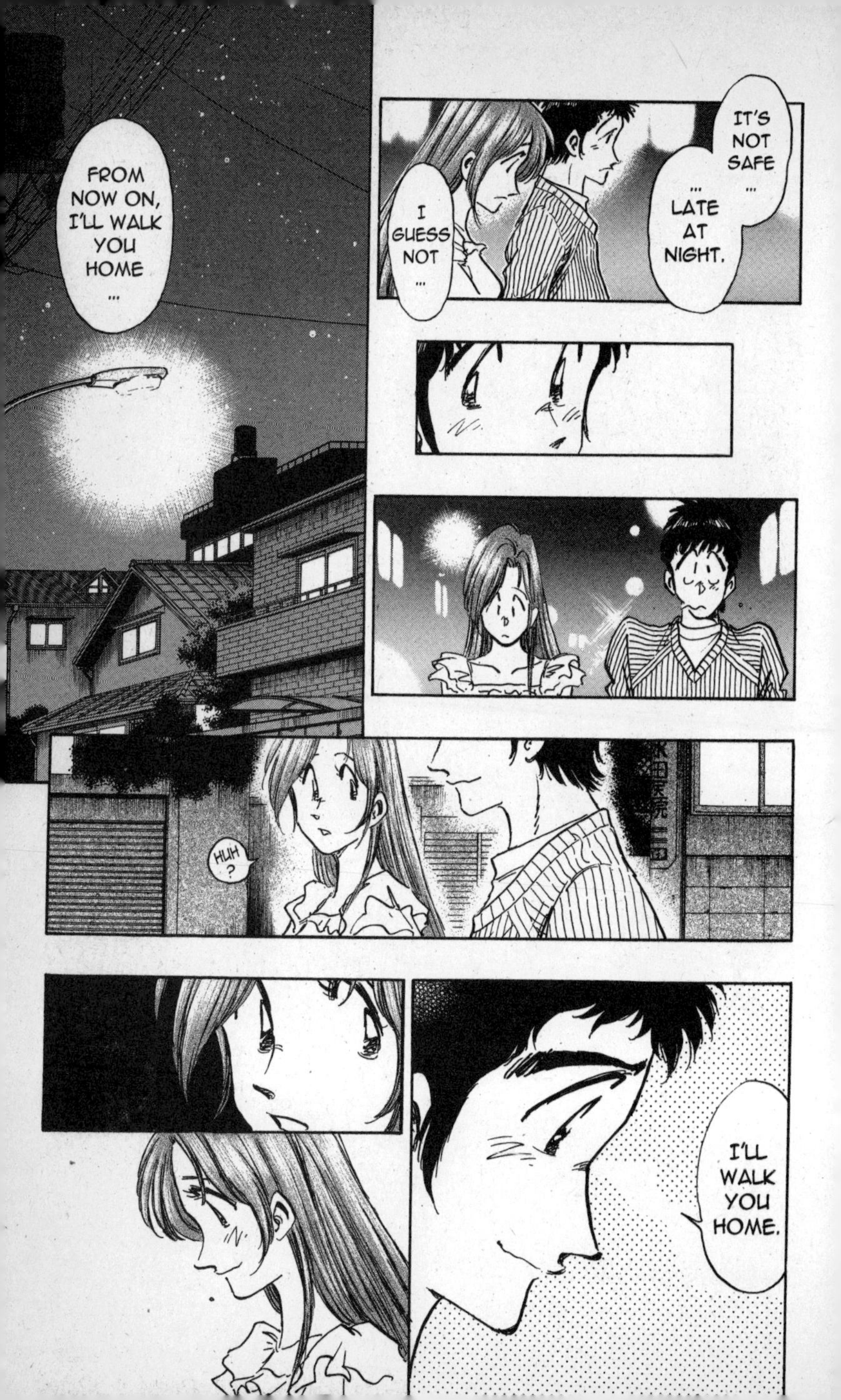

IT'S NOT SAFE ...
... LATE AT NIGHT.
I GUESS NOT ...
FROM NOW ON, I'LL WALK YOU HOME ...
HUH ?
I'LL WALK YOU HOME.

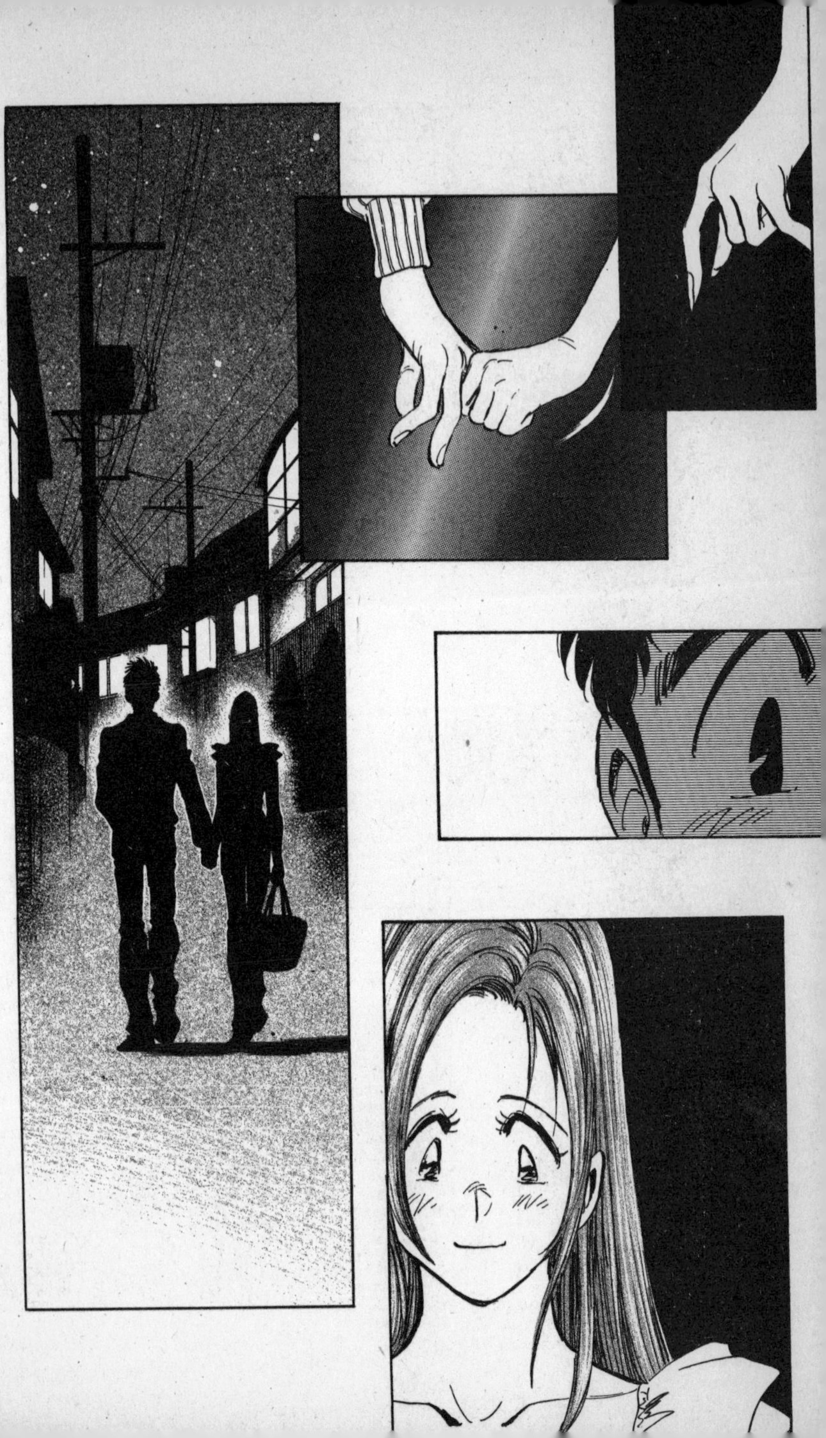

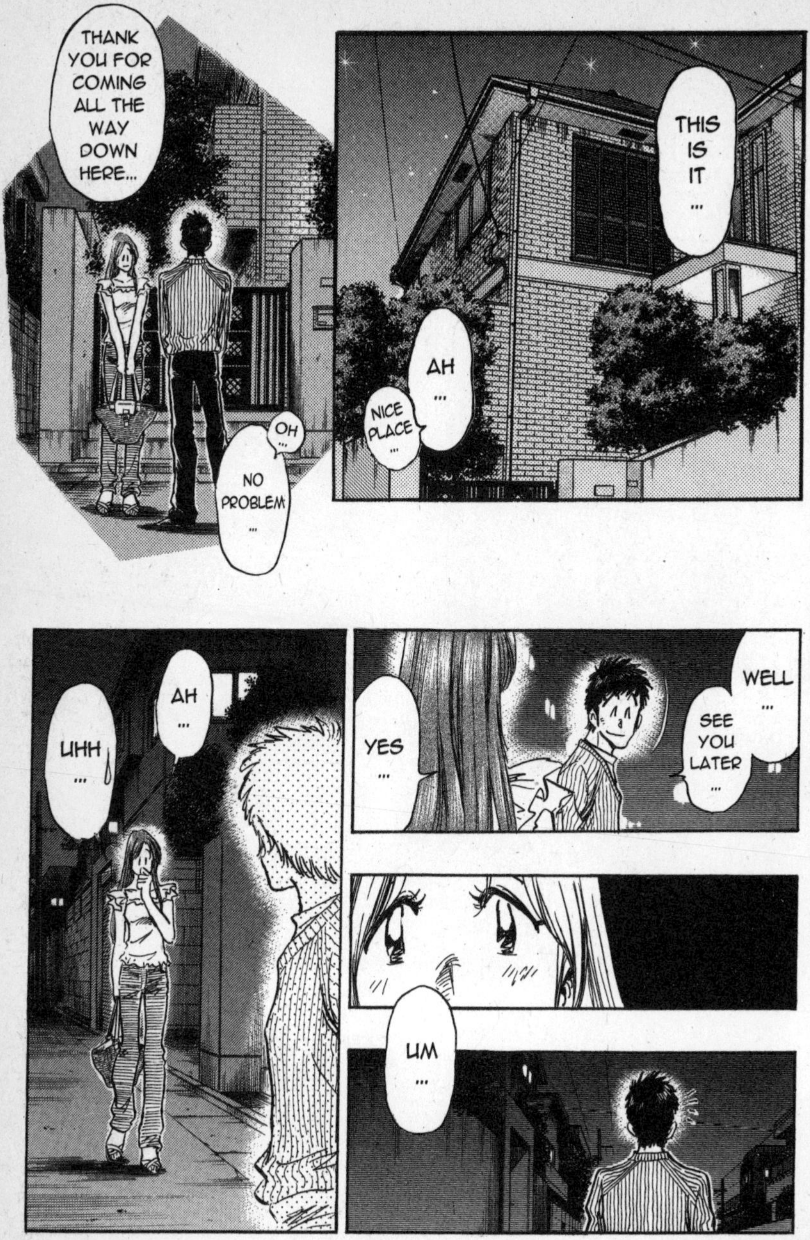
THIS IS IT ...
AH ...
NICE PLACE ...
THANK YOU FOR COMING ALL THE WAY DOWN HERE...
OH ...
NO PROBLEM ...
WELL ...
SEE YOU LATER ...
YES ...
UM ...
AH ...
UHH ...

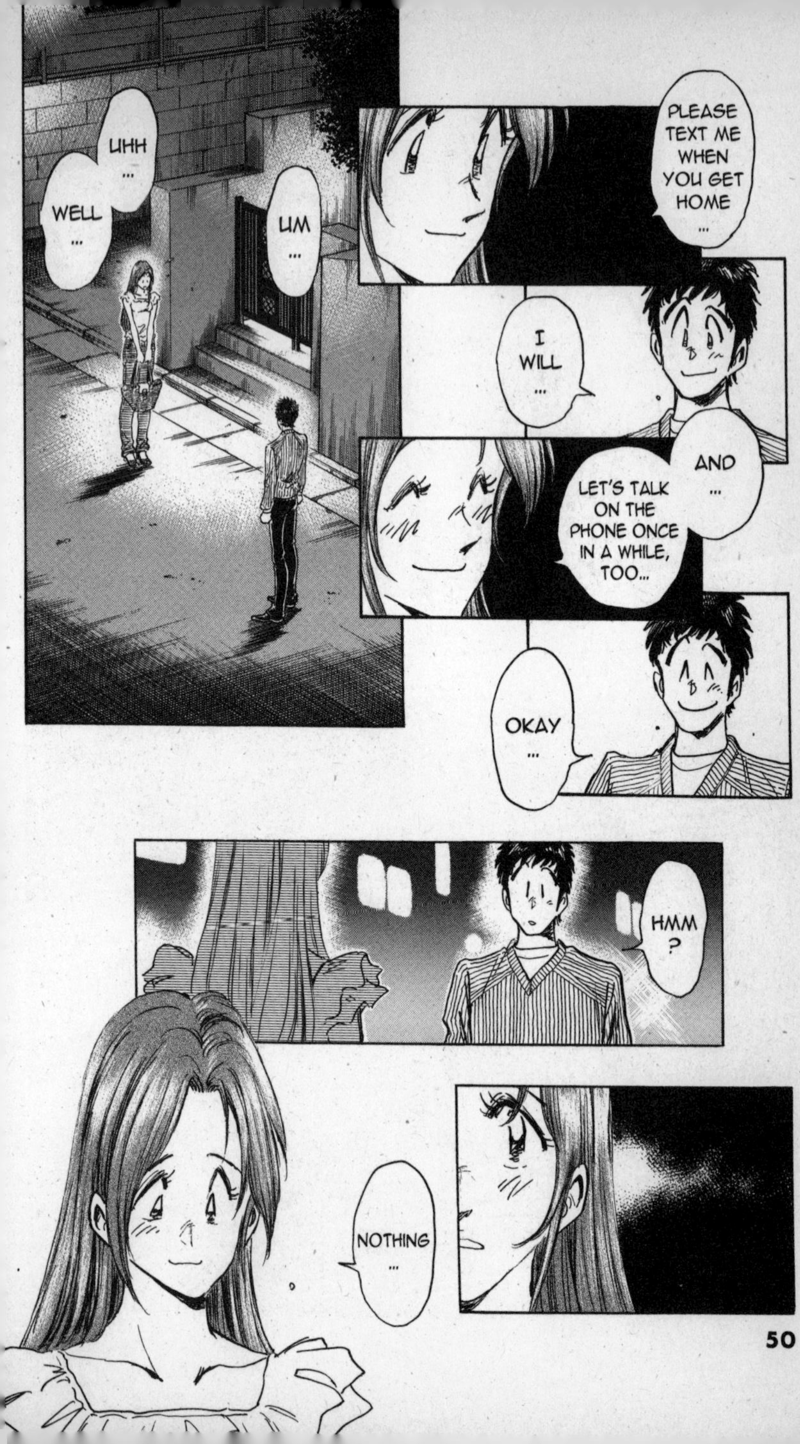
PLEASE TEXT ME WHEN YOU GET HOME ...
I WILL ...
AND ...
LET'S TALK ON THE PHONE ONCE IN A WHILE, TOO...
OKAY ...
UM ...
UHH ...
WELL ...
HMM ?
NOTHING ...

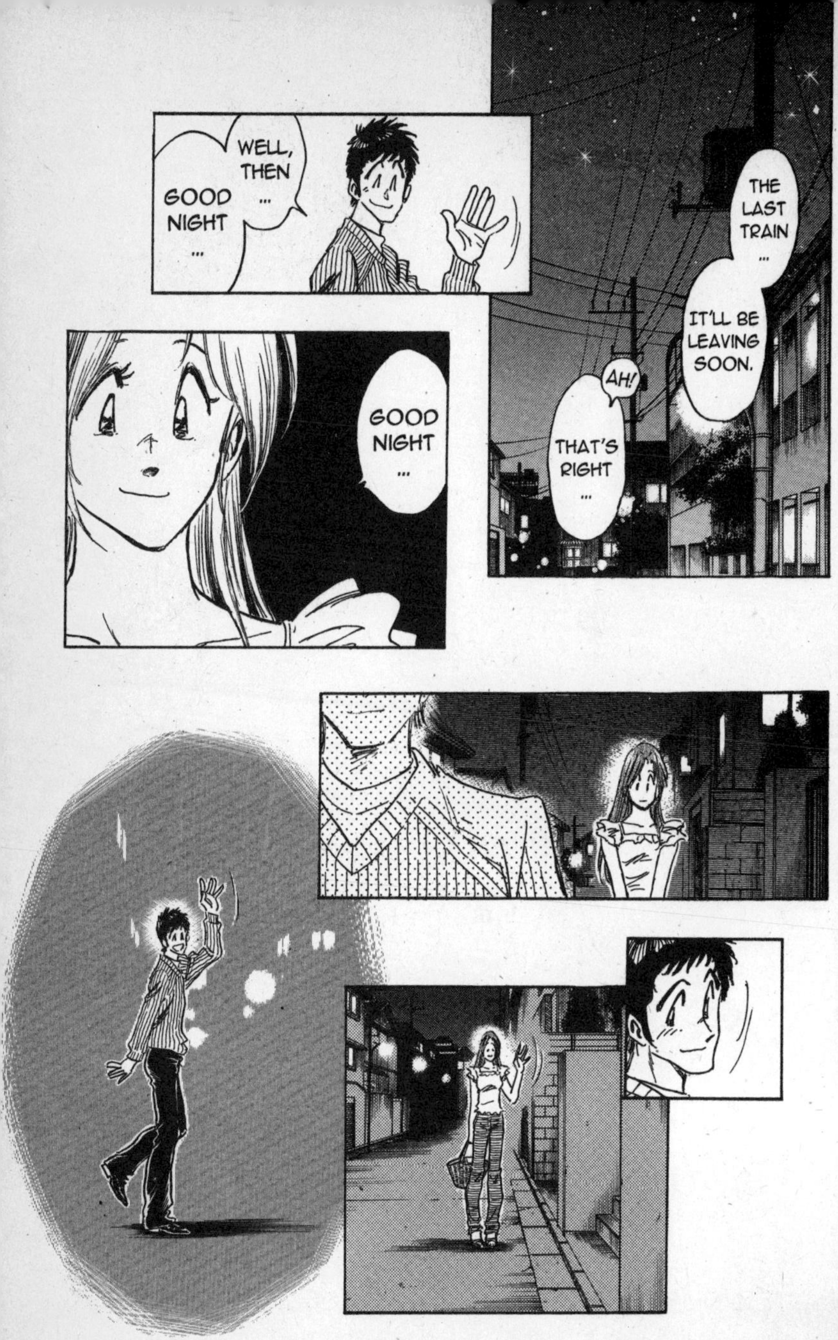
THE LAST TRAIN ...
IT'LL BE LEAVING SOON.
AH!
THAT'S RIGHT ...
WELL, THEN ...
GOOD NIGHT ...
GOOD NIGHT ...

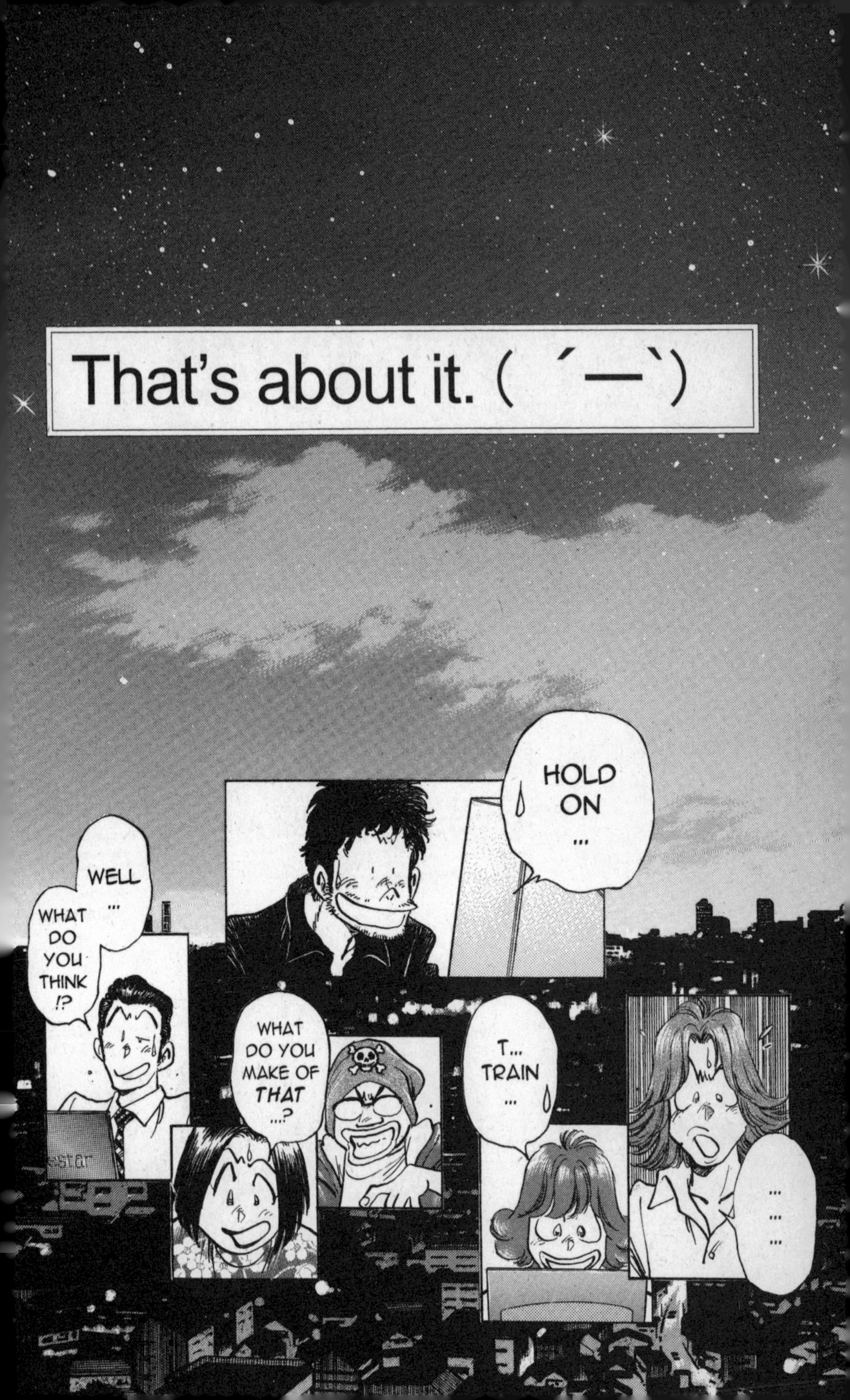
That's about it. (´—`)
HOLD ON ...
WELL ...
WHAT DO YOU THINK !?
... ...
T... TRAIN ...
WHAT DO YOU MAKE OF THAT ...?

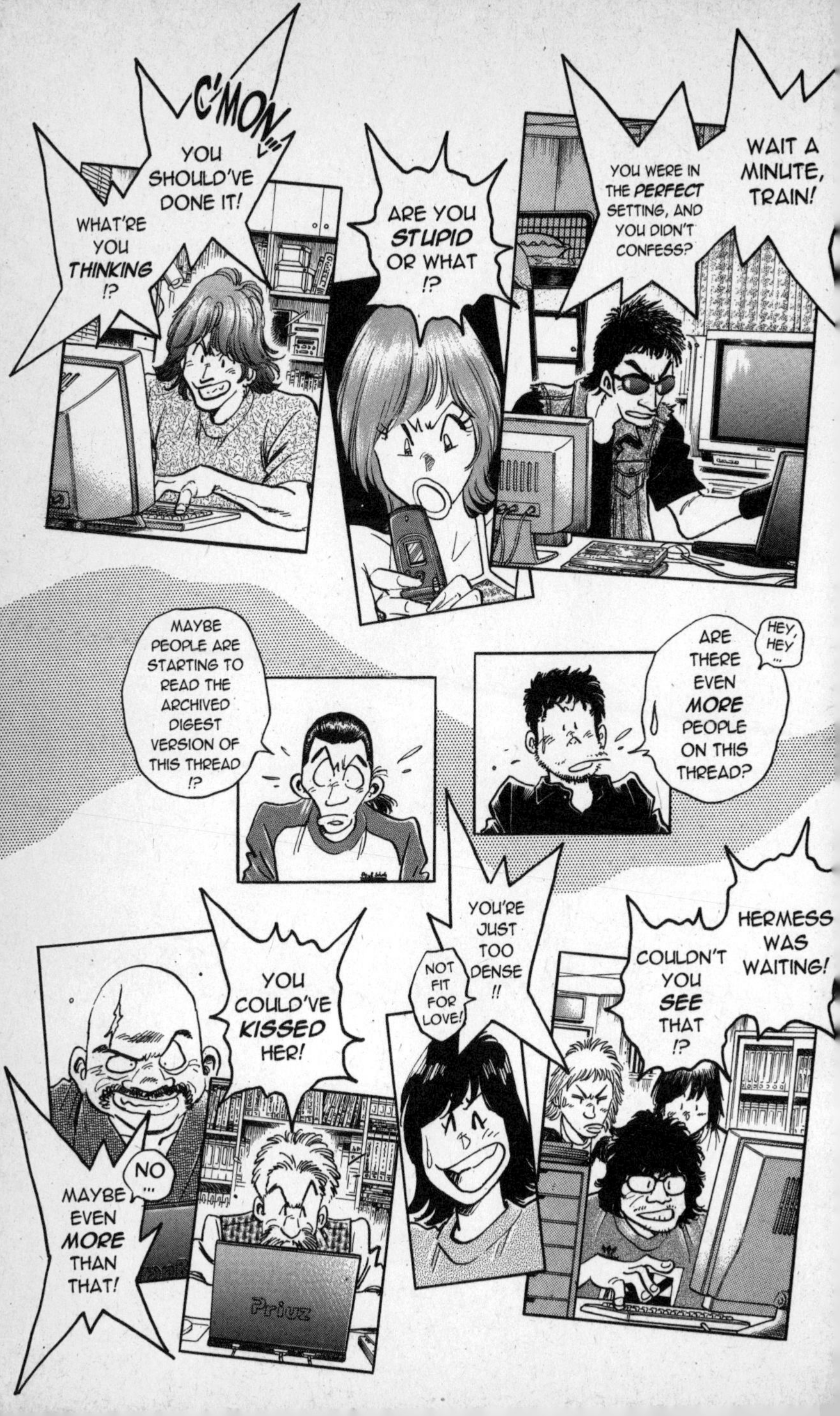
WAIT A MINUTE, TRAIN!
YOU WERE IN THE PERFECT SETTING, AND YOU DIDN'T CONFESS?
ARE YOU STUPID OR WHAT!?
C'MON...!!
YOU SHOULD'VE DONE IT!
WHAT'RE YOU THINKING!?
HEY, HEY...
ARE THERE EVEN MORE PEOPLE ON THIS THREAD?
MAYBE PEOPLE ARE STARTING TO READ THE ARCHIVED DIGEST VERSION OF THIS THREAD!?
HERMESS WAS WAITING!
COULDN'T YOU SEE THAT!?
YOU'RE JUST TOO DENSE!!
NOT FIT FOR LOVE!
YOU COULD'VE KISSED HER!
NO...
MAYBE EVEN MORE THAN THAT!
Prius

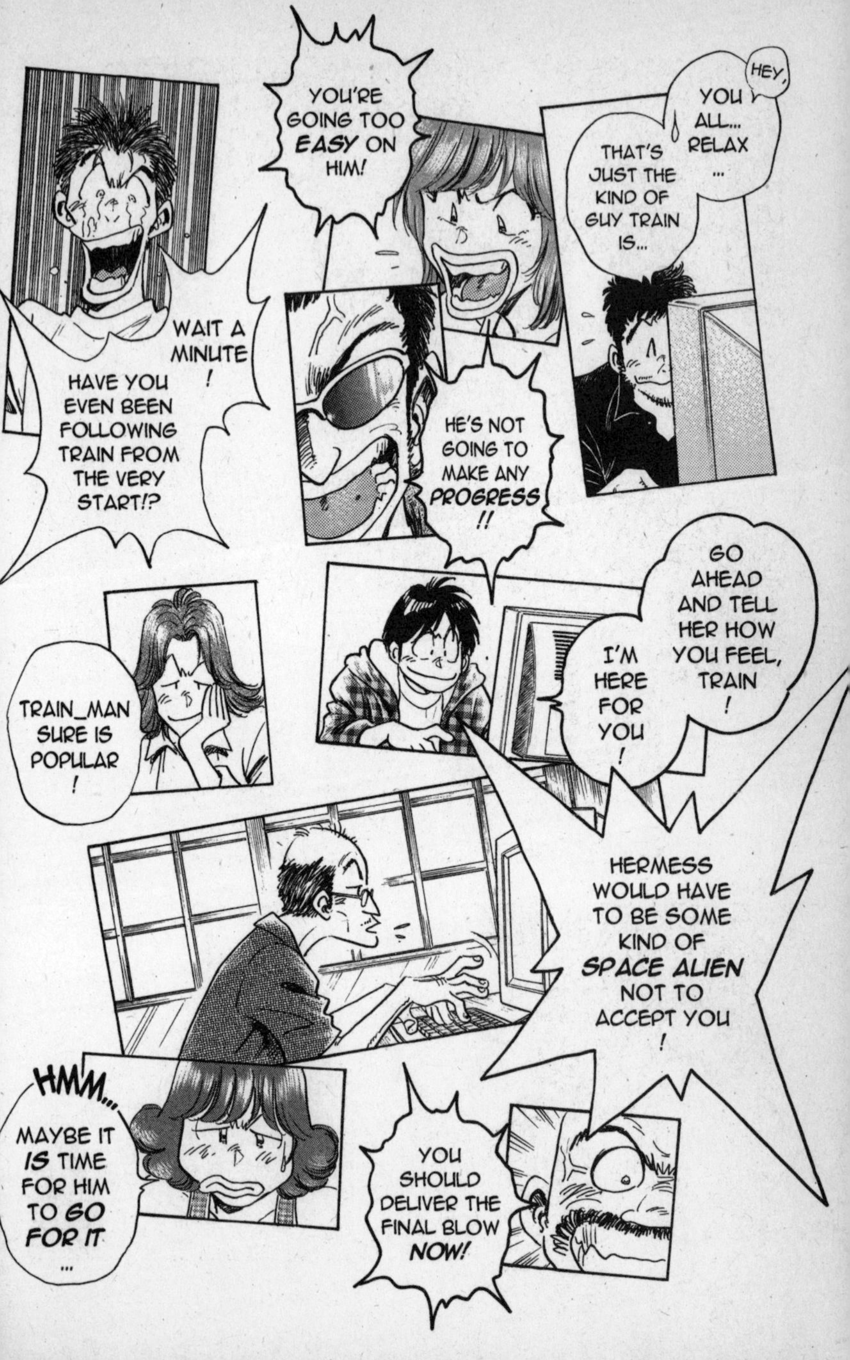
HEY,
YOU ALL... RELAX ...
THAT'S JUST THE KIND OF GUY TRAIN IS...
YOU'RE GOING TOO *EASY* ON HIM!
HE'S NOT GOING TO MAKE ANY *PROGRESS* !!
WAIT A MINUTE !
HAVE YOU EVEN BEEN FOLLOWING TRAIN FROM THE VERY START!?
GO AHEAD AND TELL HER HOW YOU FEEL, TRAIN !
I'M HERE FOR YOU !
TRAIN_MAN SURE IS POPULAR !
HERMESS WOULD HAVE TO BE SOME KIND OF *SPACE ALIEN* NOT TO ACCEPT YOU !
YOU SHOULD DELIVER THE FINAL BLOW *NOW!*
HMM...
MAYBE IT *IS* TIME FOR HIM TO *GO FOR IT* ...

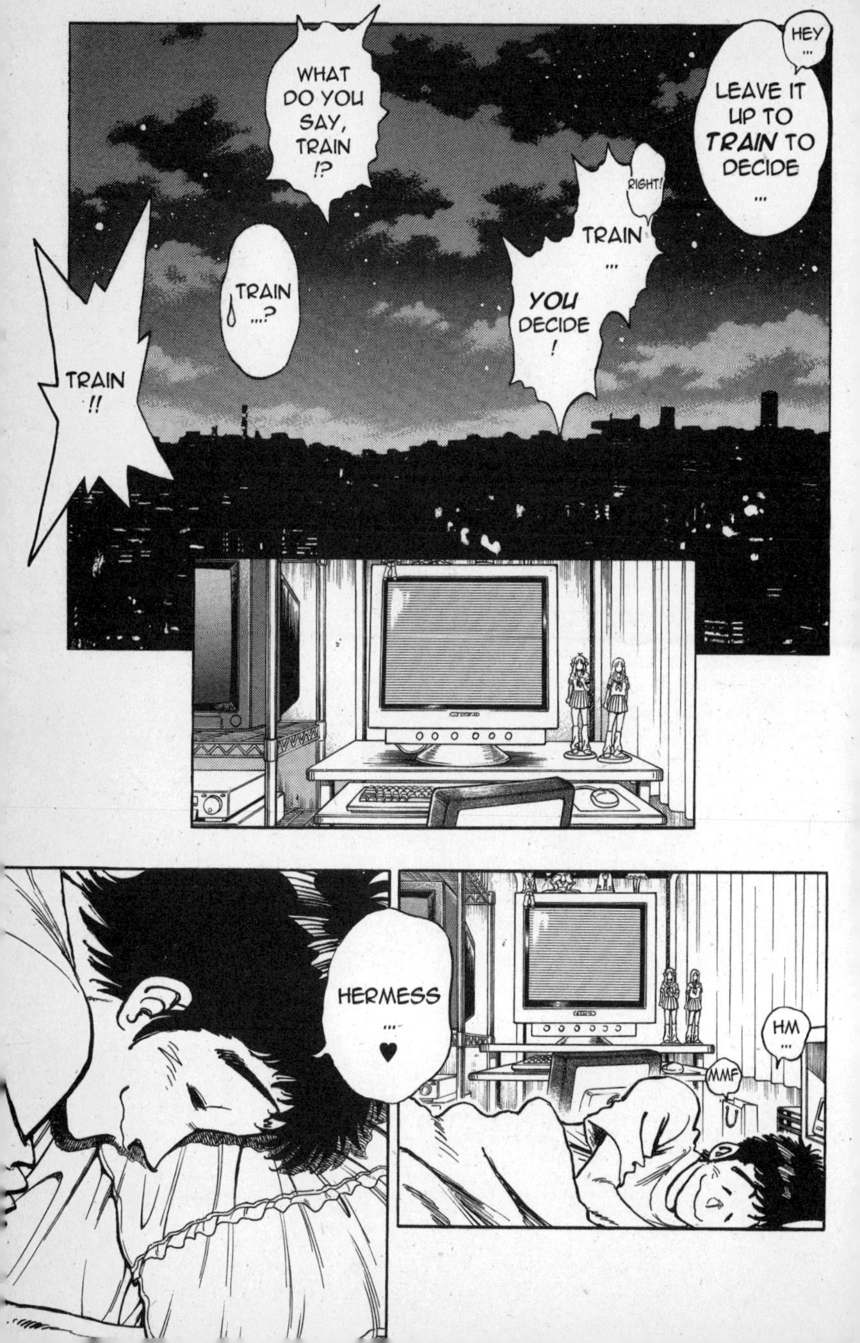
HEY ...
LEAVE IT UP TO TRAIN TO DECIDE ...
RIGHT!
TRAIN ... YOU DECIDE !
WHAT DO YOU SAY, TRAIN !?
TRAIN ...?
TRAIN !!
HM ...
MMF
HERMESS ... ♥

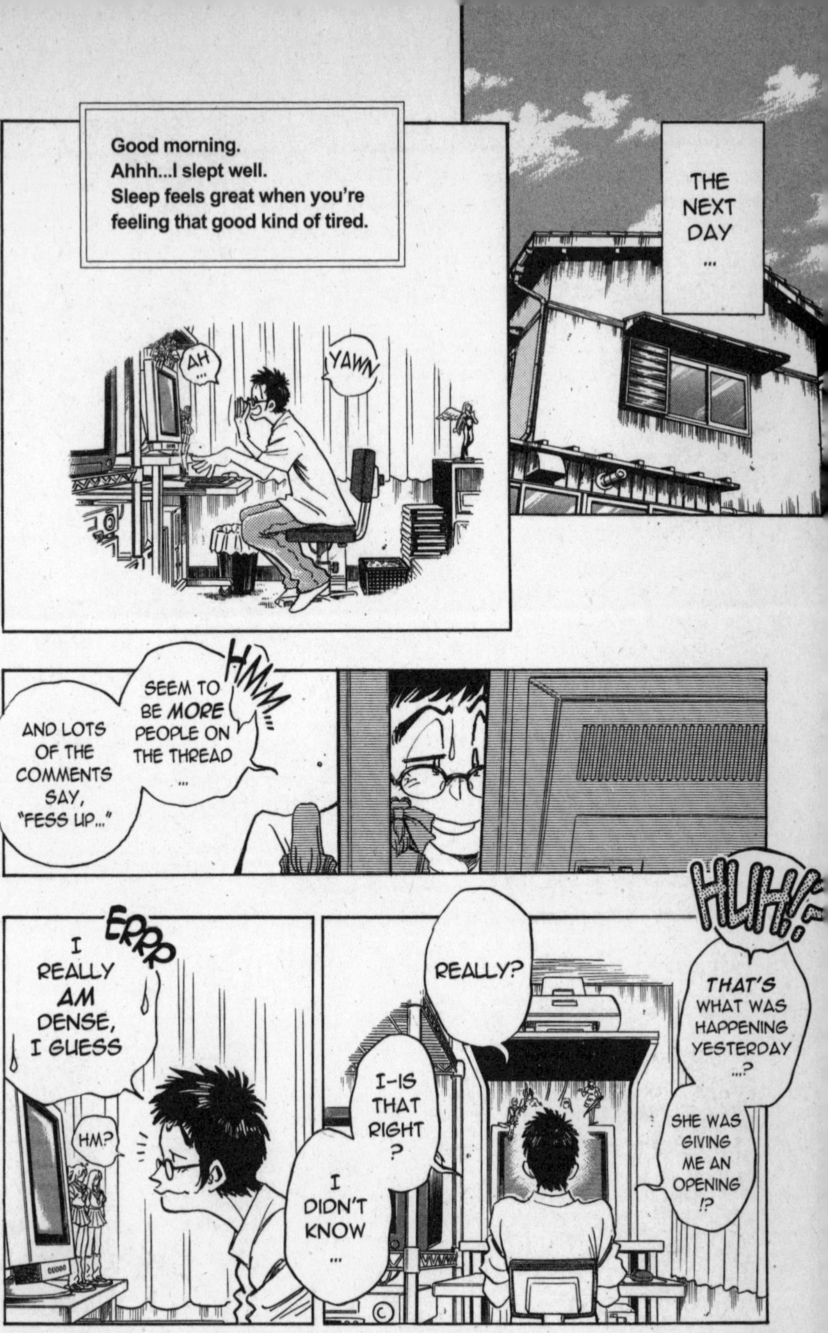

THE NEXT DAY ...
Good morning.
Ahhh...I slept well.
Sleep feels great when you're feeling that good kind of tired.
YAWN
AH ...
HMM
SEEM TO BE MORE PEOPLE ON THE THREAD ...
AND LOTS OF THE COMMENTS SAY, "FESS UP..."
HUH!?
THAT'S WHAT WAS HAPPENING YESTERDAY ...?
SHE WAS GIVING ME AN OPENING !?
REALLY?
I-IS THAT RIGHT ?
I DIDN'T KNOW ...
ERRR
I REALLY AM DENSE, I GUESS
HM?

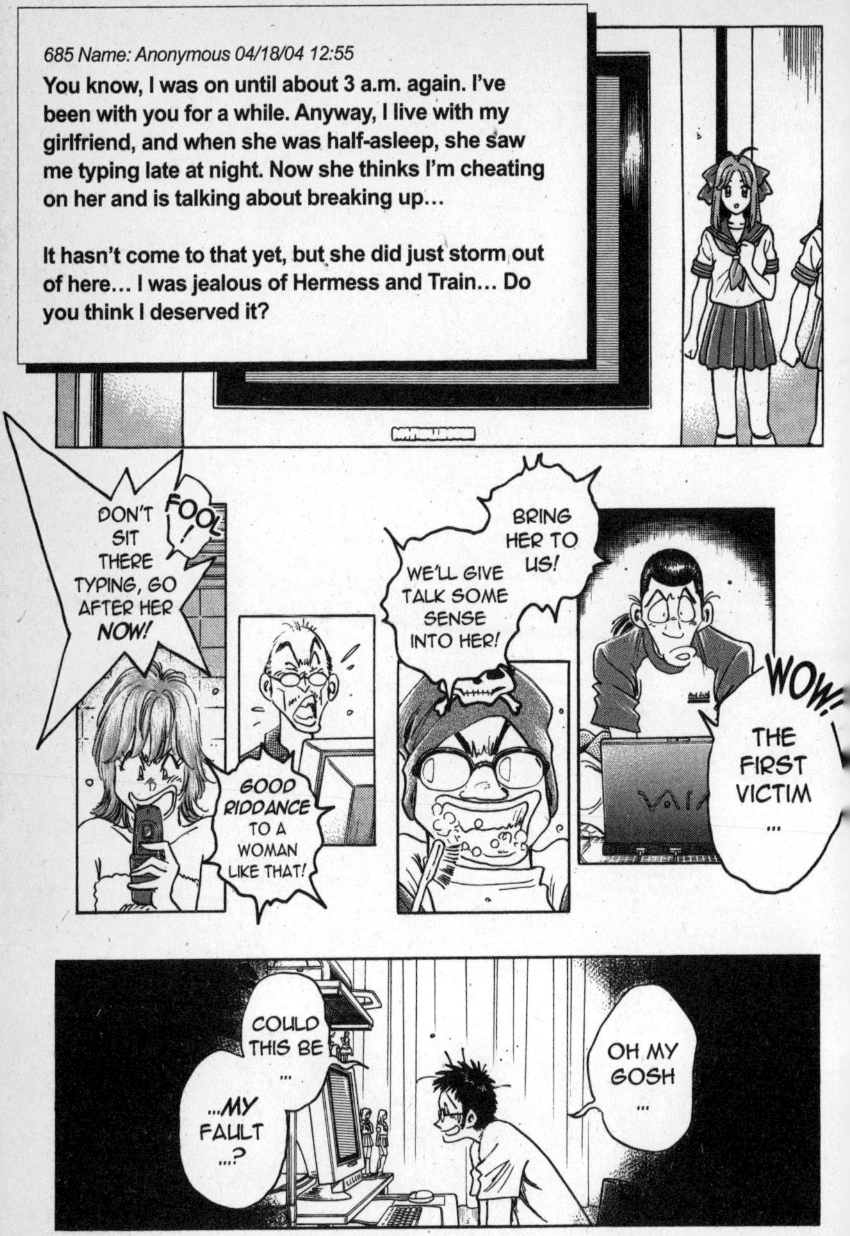
685 Name: Anonymous 04/18/04 12:55
You know, I was on until about 3 a.m. again. I've been with you for a while. Anyway, I live with my girlfriend, and when she was half-asleep, she saw me typing late at night. Now she thinks I'm cheating on her and is talking about breaking up…
It hasn't come to that yet, but she did just storm out of here… I was jealous of Hermess and Train… Do you think I deserved it?
WOW!
THE FIRST VICTIM ...
BRING HER TO US!
WE'LL GIVE TALK SOME SENSE INTO HER!
GOOD RIDDANCE TO A WOMAN LIKE THAT!
FOOL!
DON'T SIT THERE TYPING, GO AFTER HER NOW!
OH MY GOSH ...
COULD THIS BE ...
...MY FAULT ...?

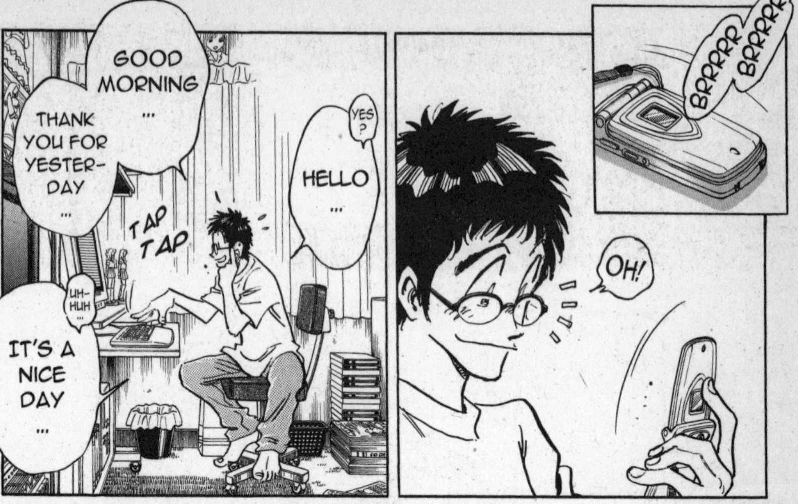
BRRRRR BRRRRR
OH!
YES ?
HELLO ...
GOOD MORNING ...
THANK YOU FOR YESTER-DAY ...
TAP TAP
UH-HUH ...
IT'S A NICE DAY ...

fone caL!

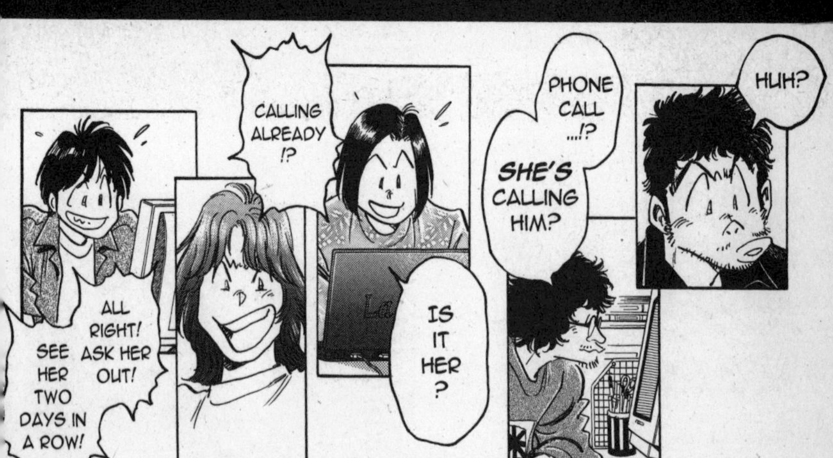
HUH?
PHONE CALL ...!?
SHE'S CALLING HIM?
CALLING ALREADY !?
IS IT HER ?
ALL RIGHT! ASK HER OUT!
SEE HER TWO DAYS IN A ROW!

goin 2
c hr

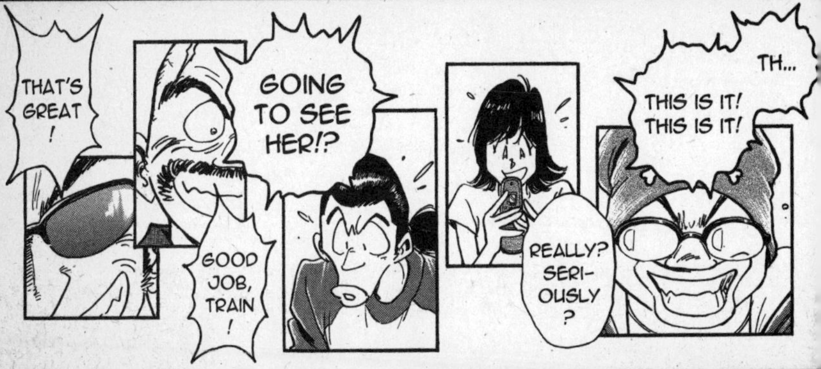
TH...
THIS IS IT! THIS IS IT!
REALLY? SERIOUSLY?
GOING TO SEE HER!?
GOOD JOB, TRAIN!
THAT'S GREAT!

5in 2 hr hows

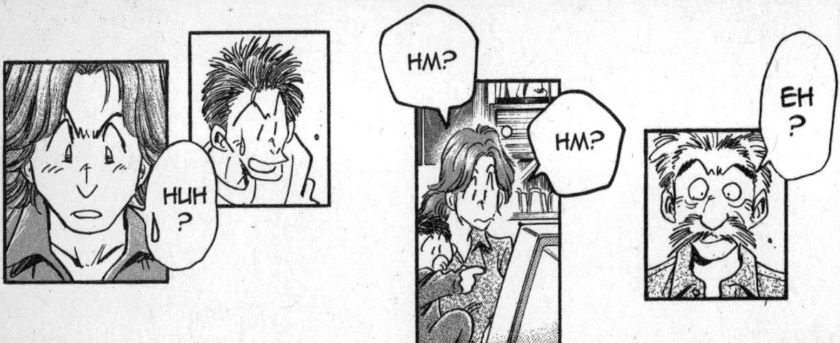
EH?
HM?
HM?
HUH?

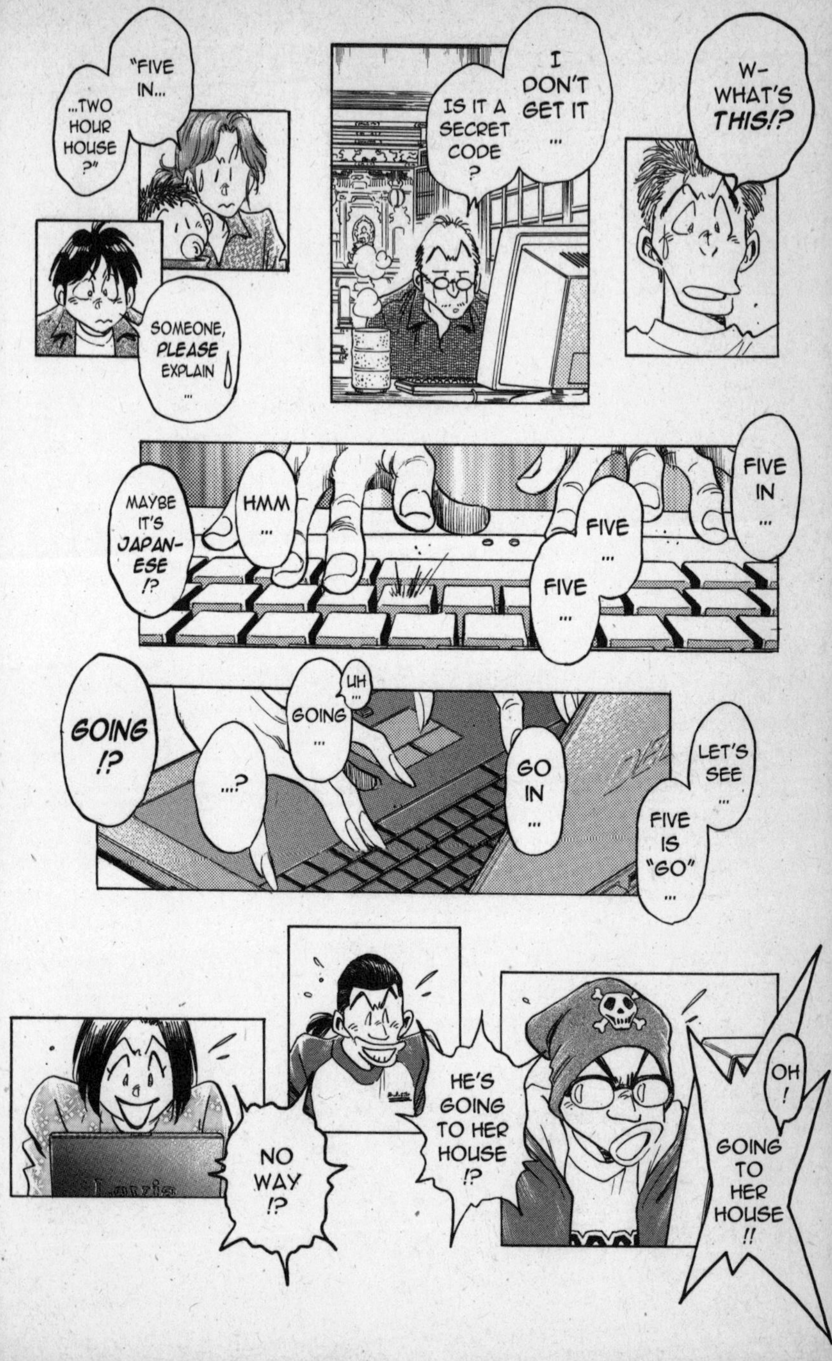
W-WHAT'S *THIS!?*
I DON'T GET IT ...
IS IT A SECRET CODE ?
"FIVE IN...
...TWO HOUR HOUSE ?"
SOMEONE, *PLEASE* EXPLAIN ...
FIVE IN ...
FIVE ...
FIVE ...
HMM ...
MAYBE IT'S JAPAN-ESE !?
LET'S SEE ...
FIVE IS "GO" ...
GO IN ...
UH ...
GOING ...
...?
GOING !?
OH !
GOING TO HER HOUSE !!
HE'S GOING TO HER HOUSE !?
NO WAY !?

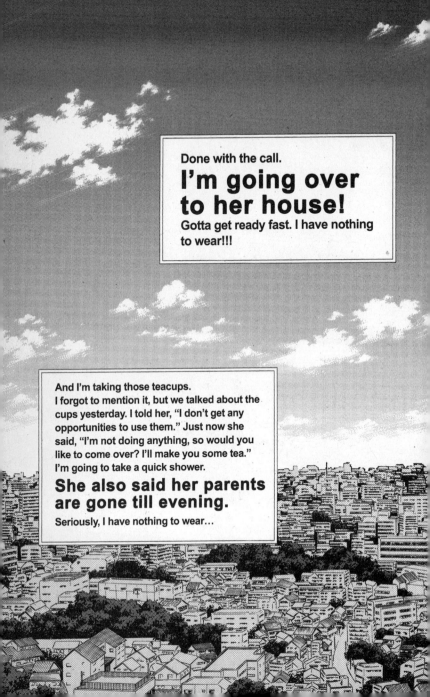

Done with the call.

I'm going over to her house!

Gotta get ready fast. I have nothing to wear!!!

And I'm taking those teacups.
I forgot to mention it, but we talked about the cups yesterday. I told her, "I don't get any opportunities to use them." Just now she said, "I'm not doing anything, so would you like to come over? I'll make you some tea." I'm going to take a quick shower.

She also said her parents are gone till evening.

Seriously, I have nothing to wear…

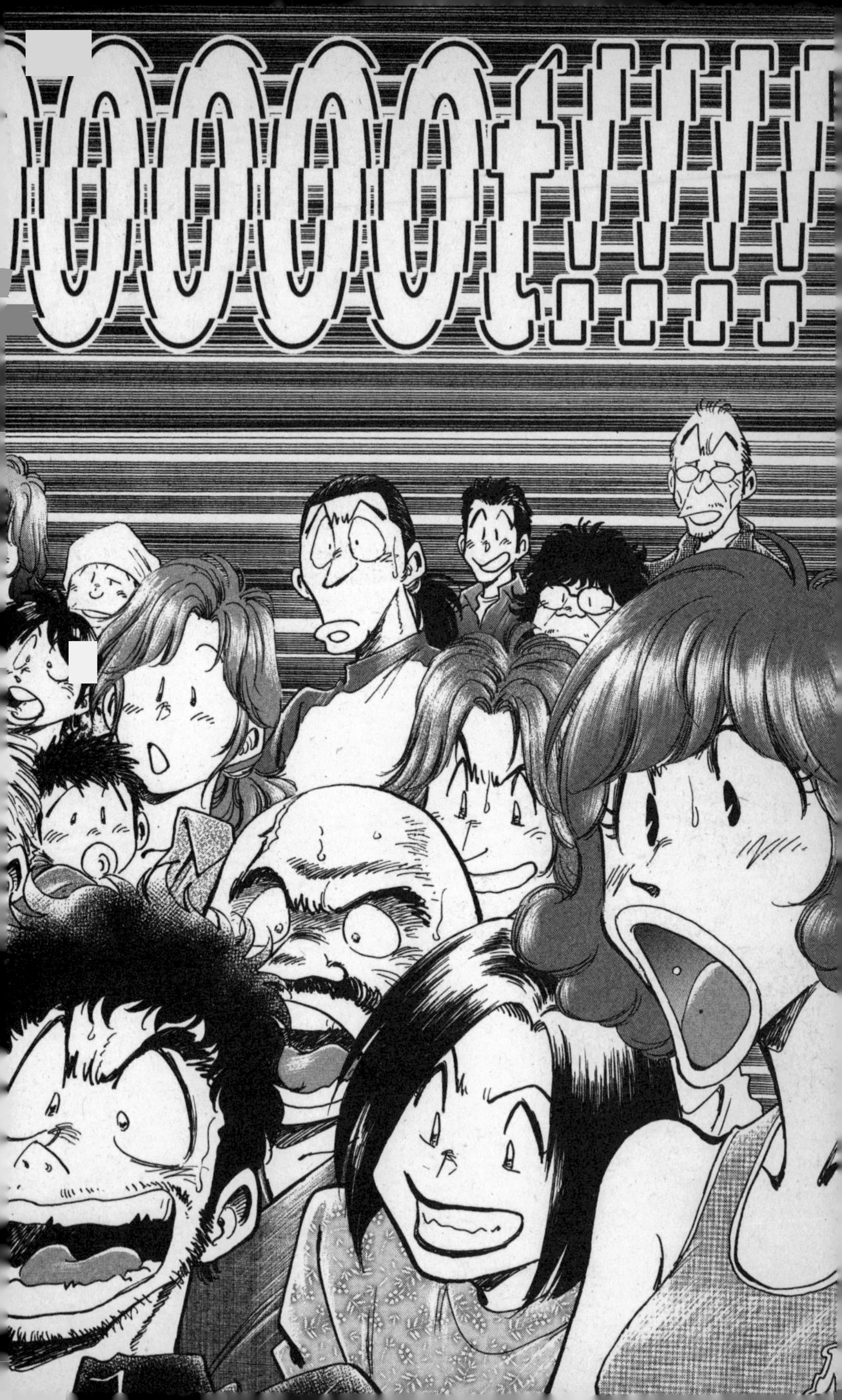
OOOOO!!!!

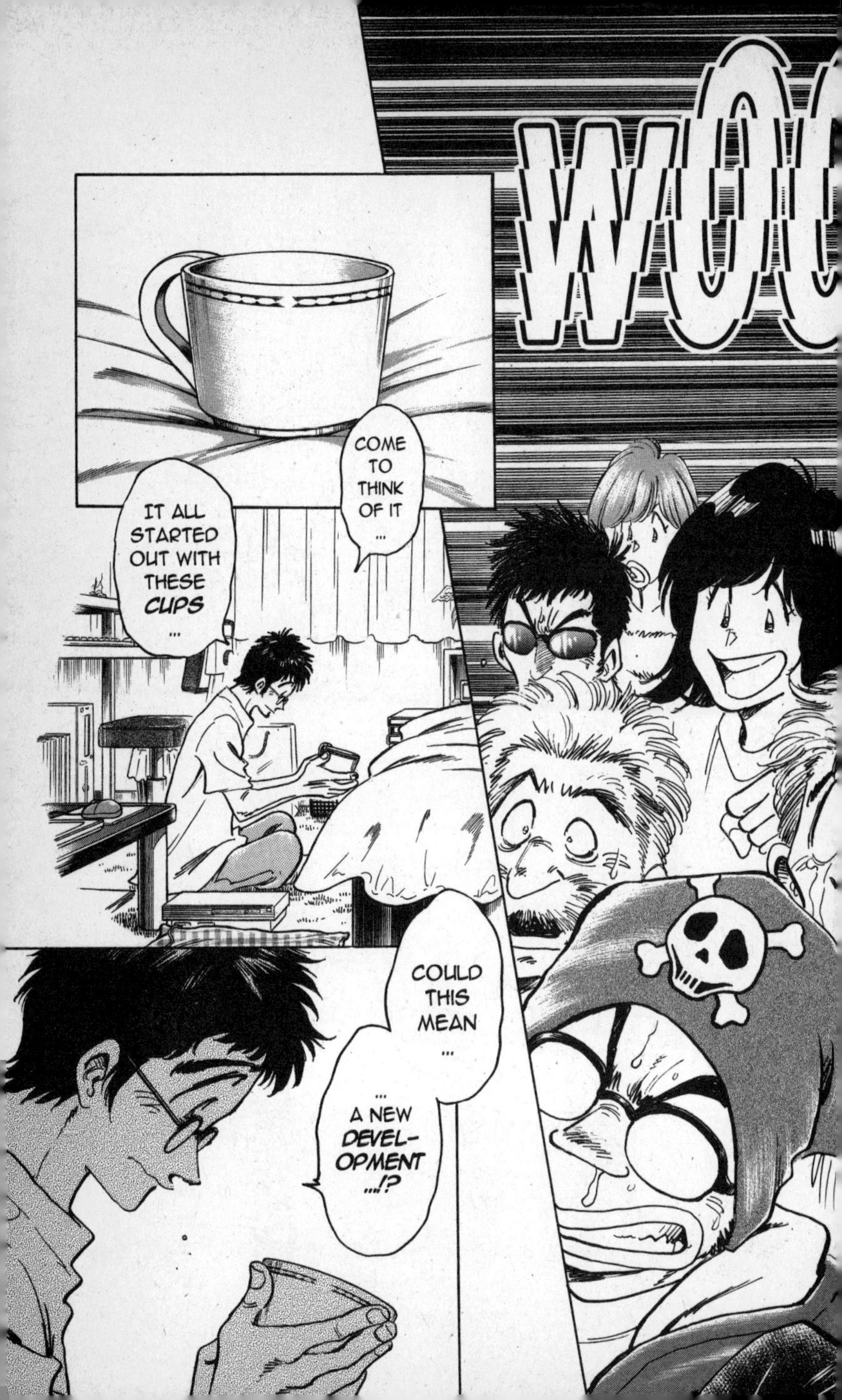
WOO
COME TO THINK OF IT ...
IT ALL STARTED OUT WITH THESE *CUPS* ...
COULD THIS MEAN ...
... A NEW *DEVELOPMENT* ...!?

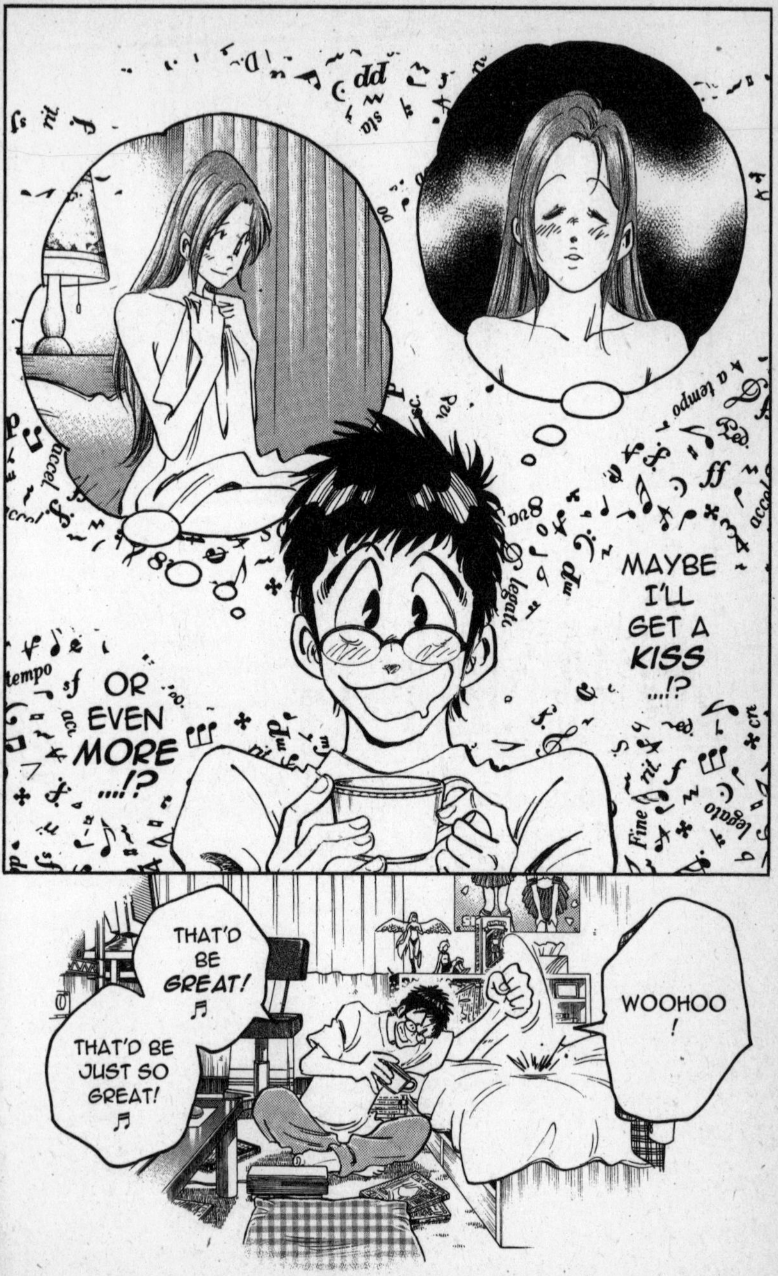
MAYBE I'LL GET A KISS ...!?
OR EVEN MORE ...!?
WOOHOO!
THAT'D BE GREAT! ♬
THAT'D BE JUST SO GREAT! ♬

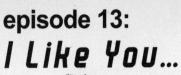

episode 13:

I Like You...

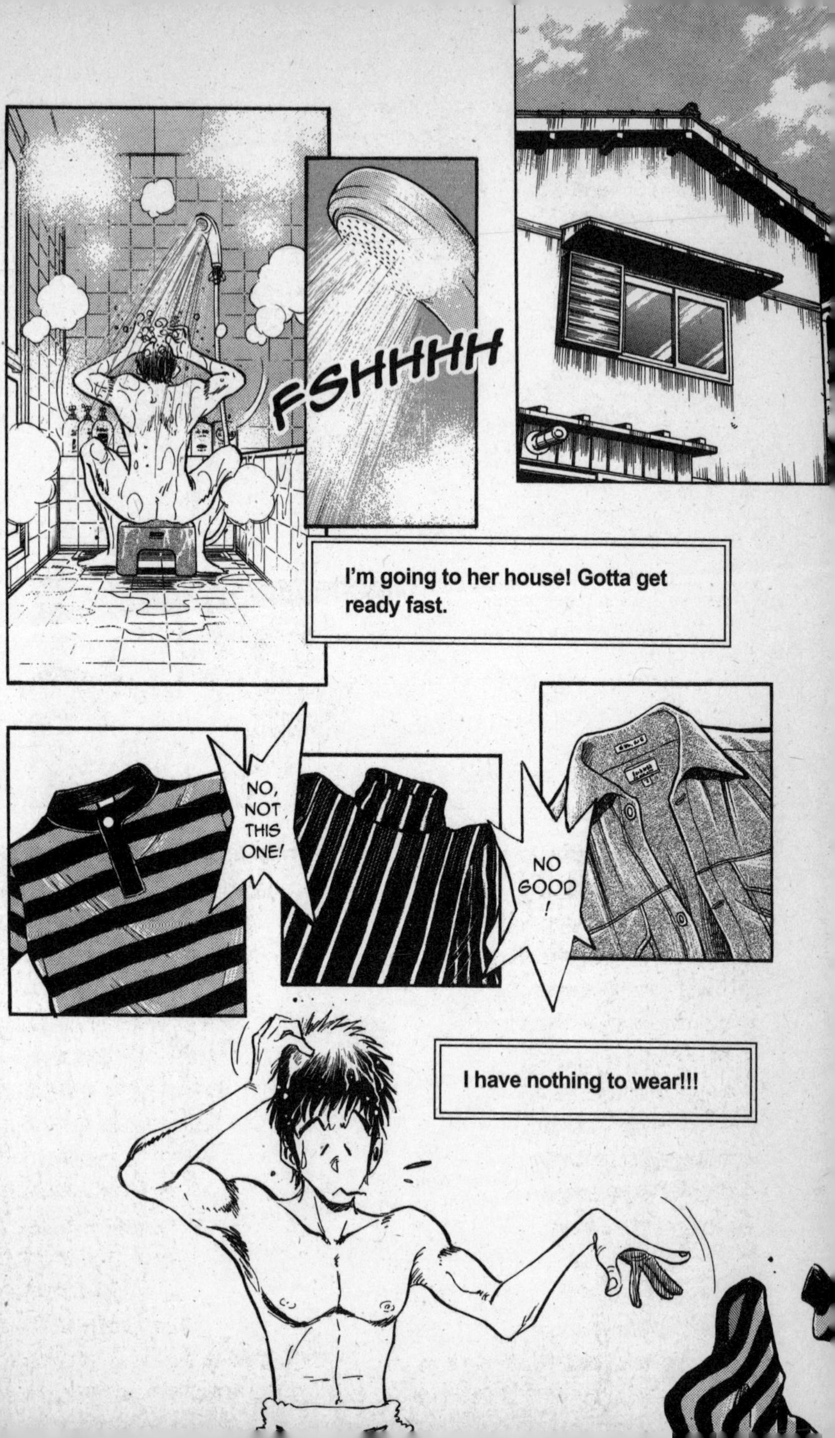
FSHHHH
I'm going to her house! Gotta get ready fast.
NO GOOD!
NO, NOT THIS ONE!
I have nothing to wear!!!

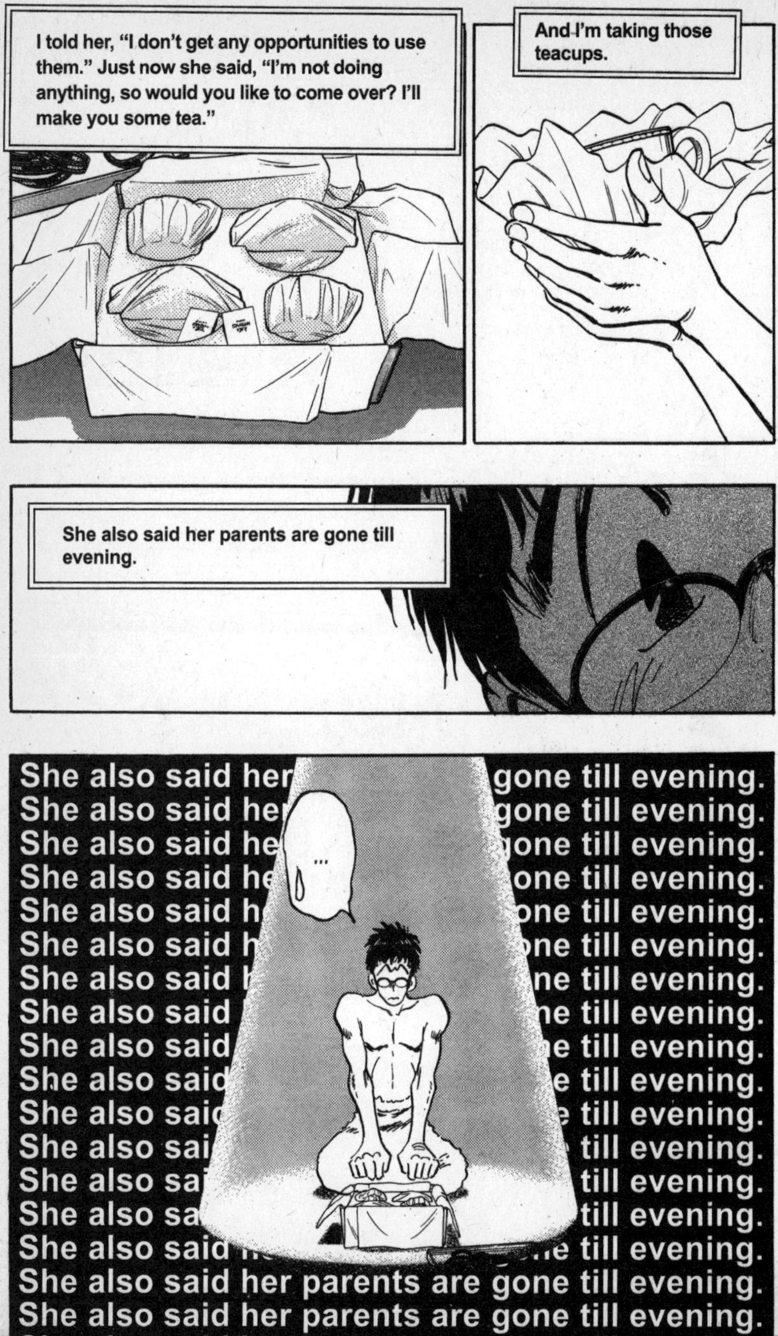
And I'm taking those teacups.
I told her, "I don't get any opportunities to use them." Just now she said, "I'm not doing anything, so would you like to come over? I'll make you some tea."
She also said her parents are gone till evening.
...
She also said her gone till evening.
She also said her gone till evening.
She also said he one till evening.
She also said he one till evening.
She also said h one till evening.
She also said h ne till evening.
She also said ne till evening.
She also said ne till evening.
She also said e till evening.
She also said e till evening.
She also sai e till evening.
She also sai till evening.
She also sai till evening.
She also sa till evening.
She also said e till evening.
She also said her parents are gone till evening.
She also said her parents are gone till evening.

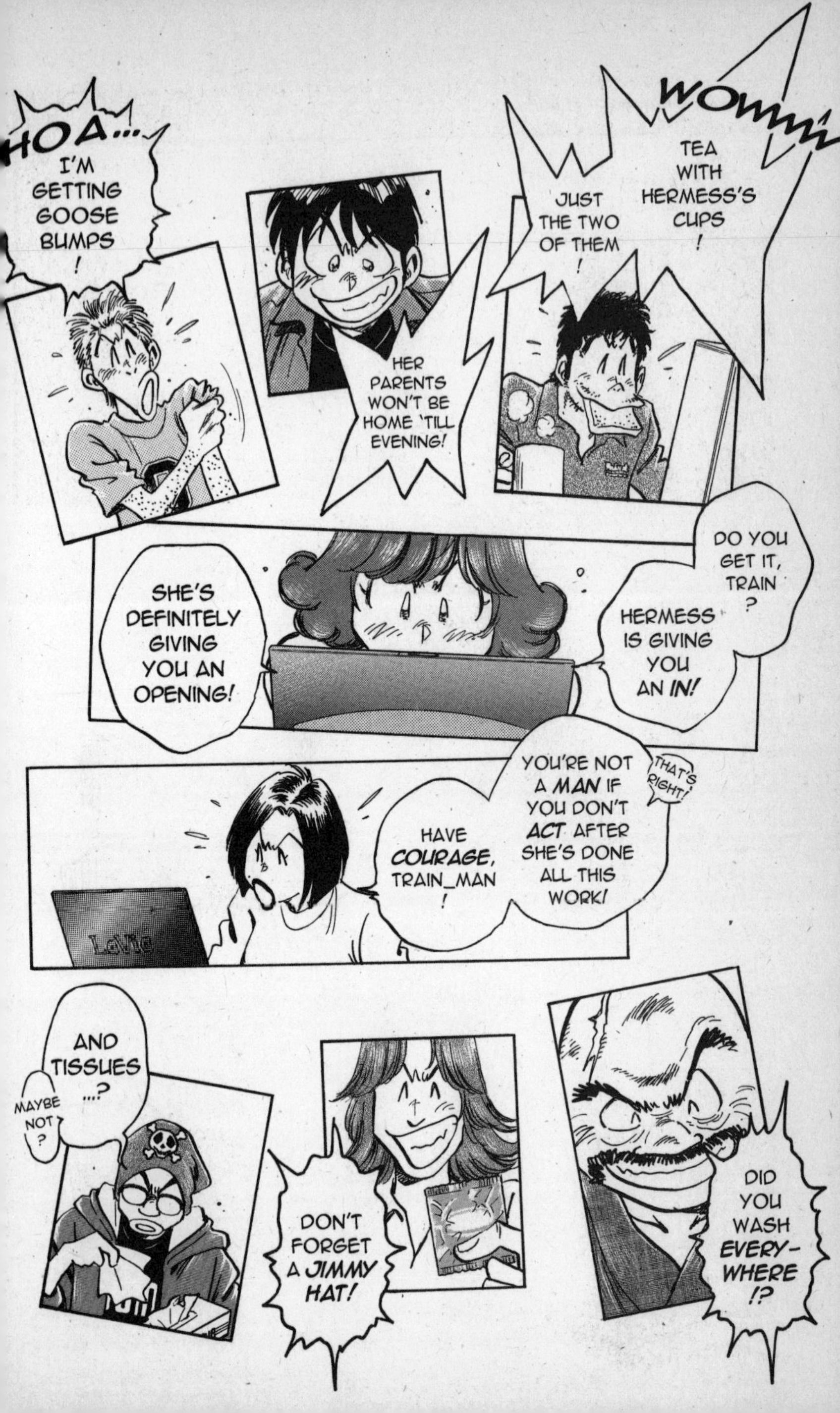
WOWWW
TEA WITH HERMESS'S CUPS!
JUST THE TWO OF THEM!
HER PARENTS WON'T BE HOME 'TILL EVENING!
HOA... I'M GETTING GOOSE BUMPS!
DO YOU GET IT, TRAIN?
HERMESS IS GIVING YOU AN IN!
SHE'S DEFINITELY GIVING YOU AN OPENING!
YOU'RE NOT A MAN IF YOU DON'T ACT AFTER SHE'S DONE ALL THIS WORK!
THAT'S RIGHT!
HAVE COURAGE, TRAIN_MAN!
DID YOU WASH EVERY-WHERE!?
DON'T FORGET A JIMMY HAT!
AND TISSUES ...?
MAYBE NOT?

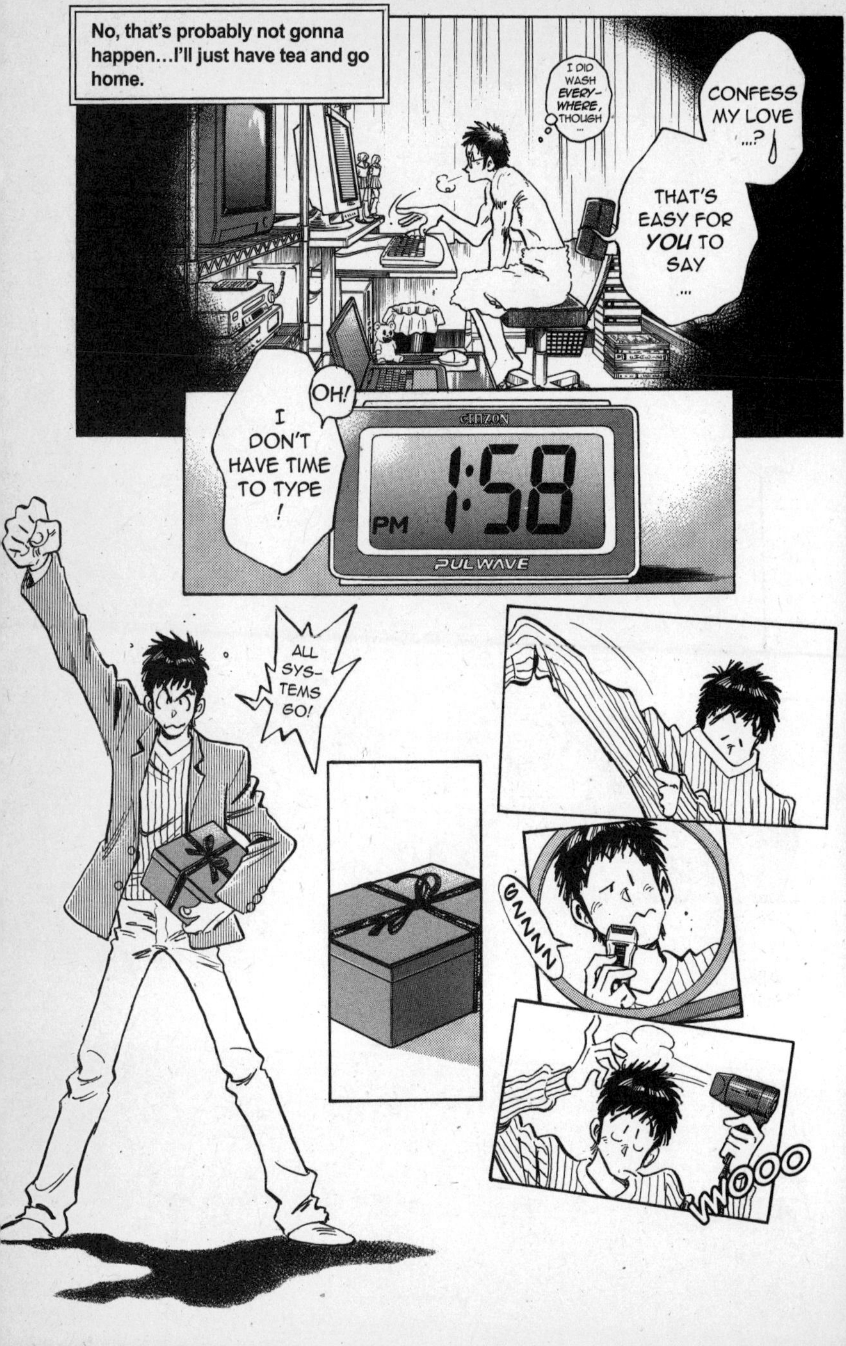

CONFESS MY LOVE ...?
THAT'S EASY FOR YOU TO SAY ...
I DID WASH EVERY-WHERE, THOUGH ...
No, that's probably not gonna happen…I'll just have tea and go home.
OH!
I DON'T HAVE TIME TO TYPE!
CITIZON
PM 1:58
PULWAVE
GNNNN
WOOO
ALL SYS-TEMS GO!

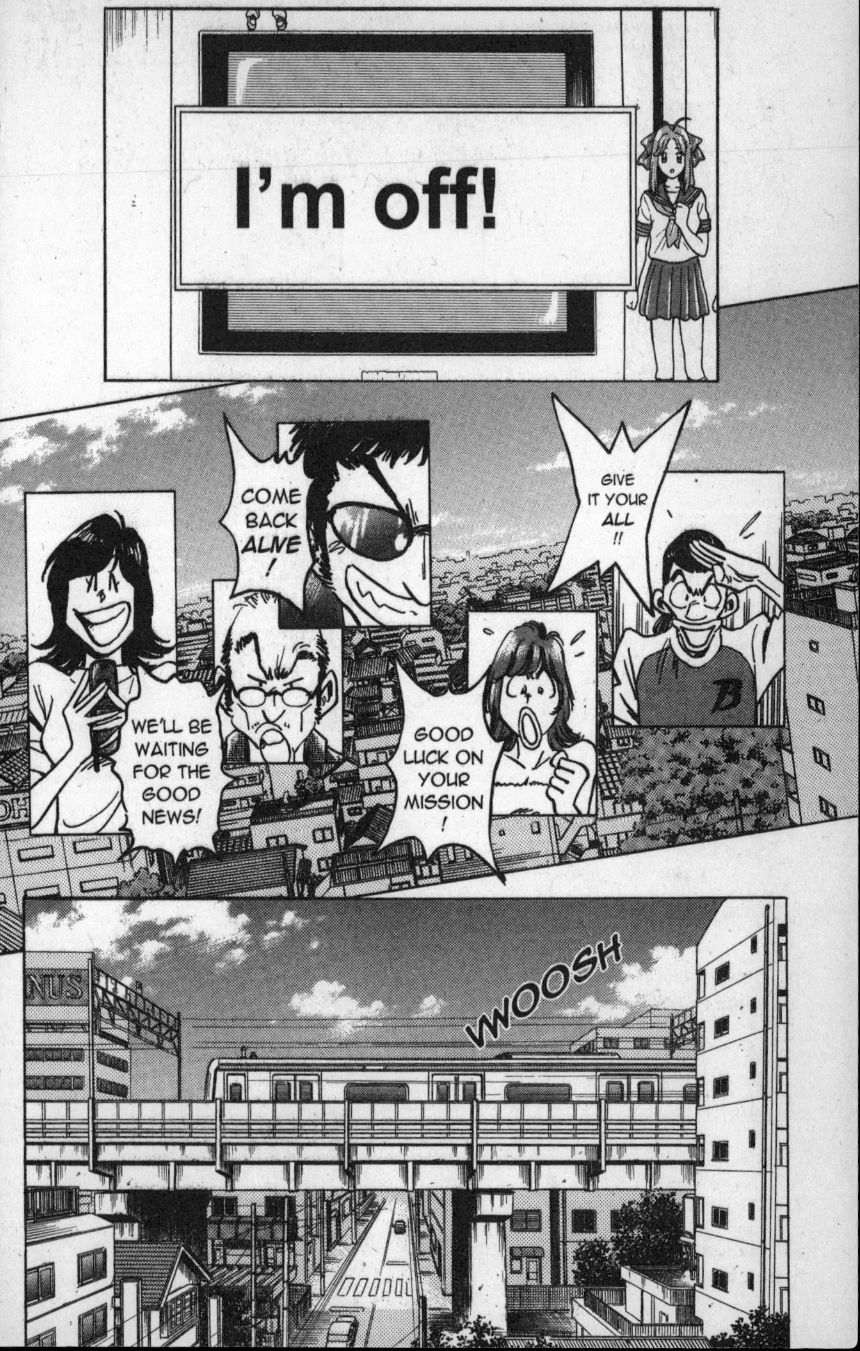
I'm off!
GIVE IT YOUR ALL!!
COME BACK ALIVE!
GOOD LUCK ON YOUR MISSION!
WE'LL BE WAITING FOR THE GOOD NEWS!
WOOSH

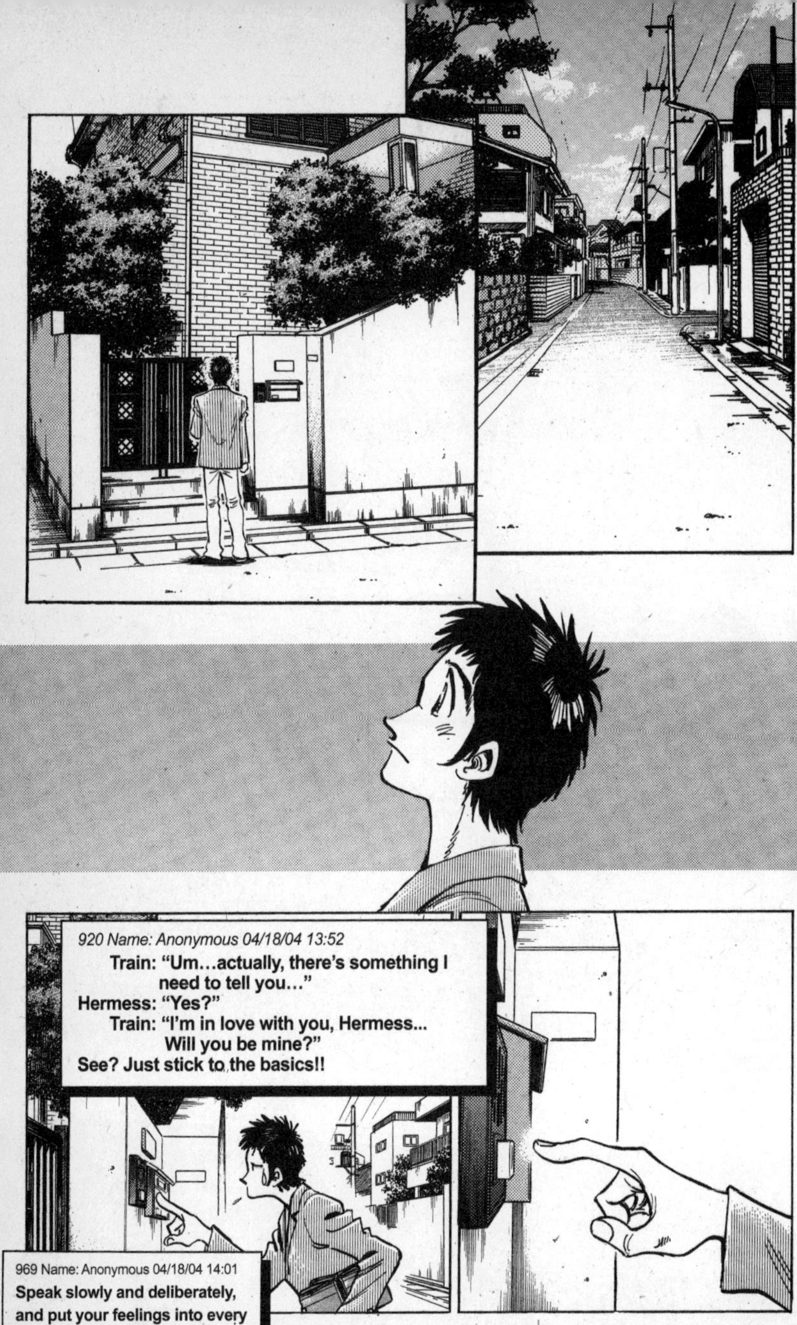
920 Name: Anonymous 04/18/04 13:52
Train: "Um…actually, there's something I need to tell you…"
Hermess: "Yes?"
Train: "I'm in love with you, Hermess... Will you be mine?"
See? Just stick to the basics!!
969 Name: Anonymous 04/18/04 14:01
Speak slowly and deliberately, and put your feelings into every word. She'll fall for you for sure.

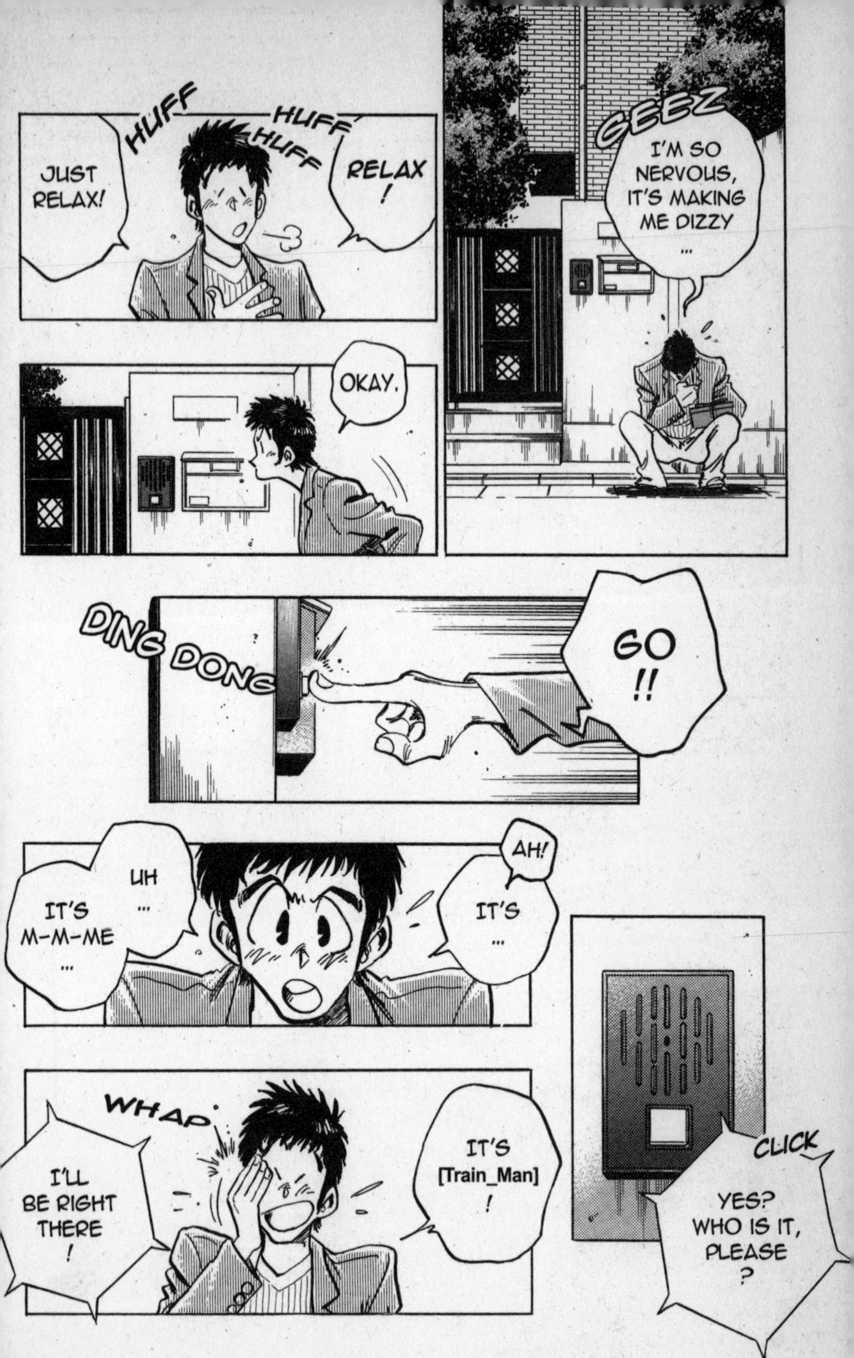
GEEZ
I'M SO NERVOUS, IT'S MAKING ME DIZZY ...
HUFF HUFF HUFF
RELAX!
JUST RELAX!
OKAY.
GO!!
DING DONG
CLICK
YES? WHO IS IT, PLEASE?
AH!
IT'S ...
UH ...
IT'S M-M-ME ...
IT'S [Train_Man]!
WHAP
I'LL BE RIGHT THERE!

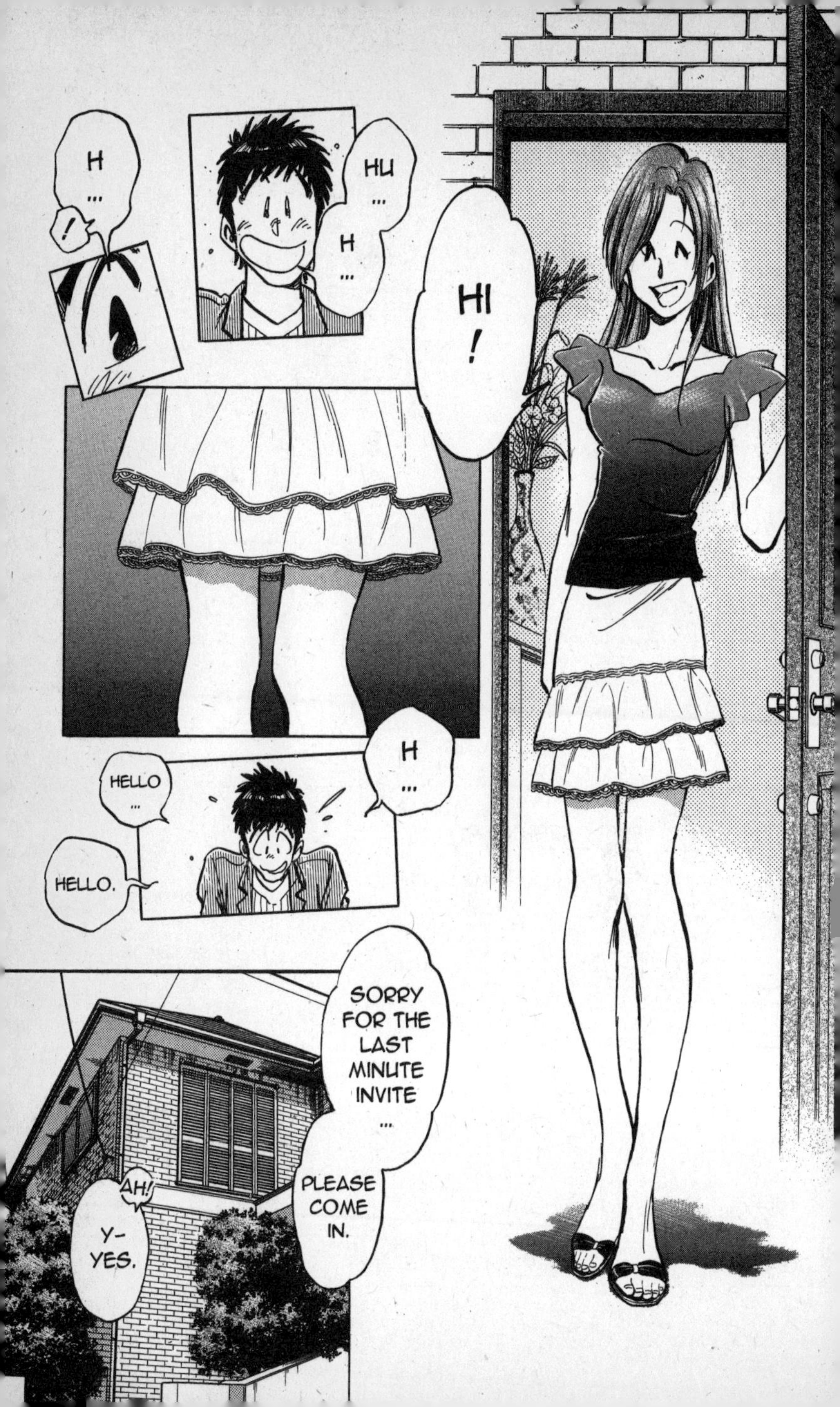
HI!
HU... H...
H... !
H...
HELLO...
HELLO.
SORRY FOR THE LAST MINUTE INVITE...
PLEASE COME IN.
AH!
Y-YES.

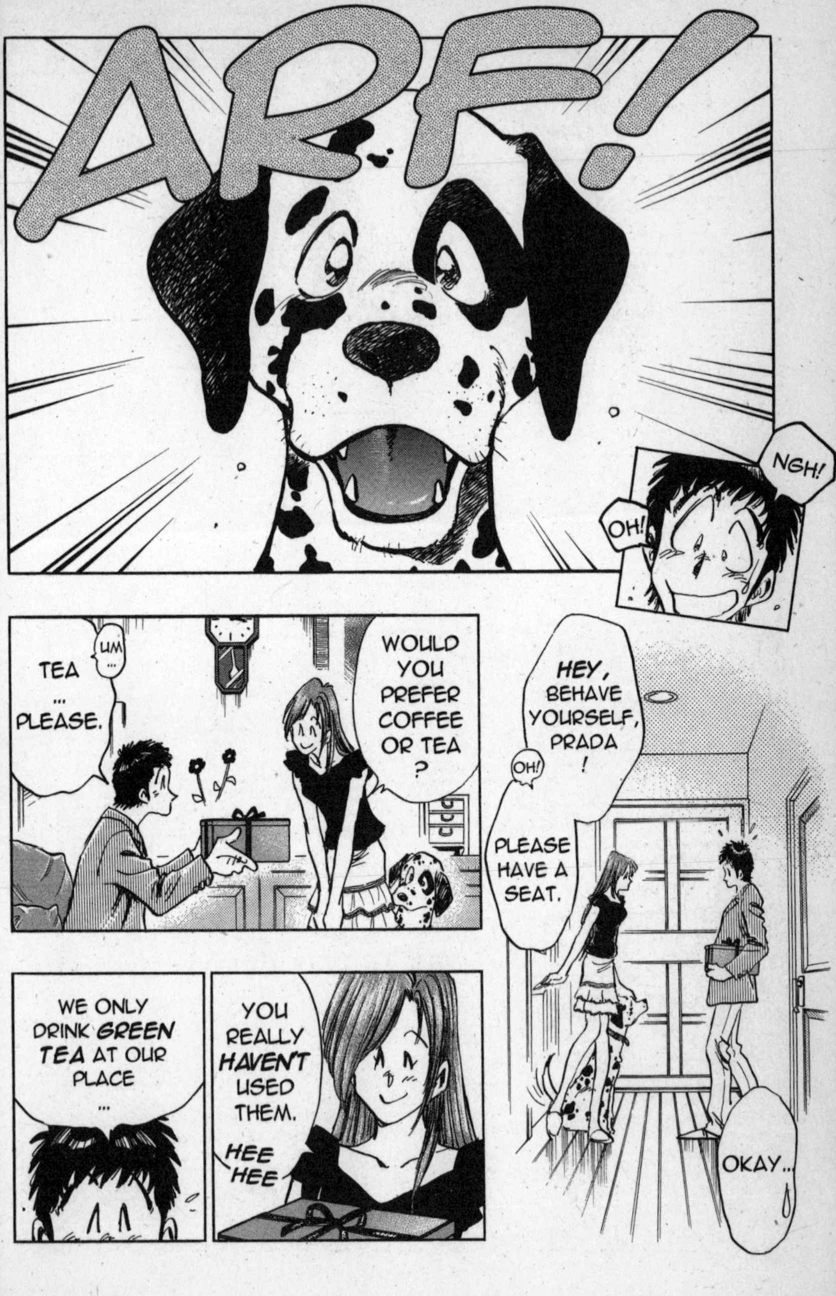
ARF!
NGH!
OH!
HEY, BEHAVE YOURSELF, PRADA!
OH!
PLEASE HAVE A SEAT.
OKAY...
WOULD YOU PREFER COFFEE OR TEA?
UM...
TEA... PLEASE.
YOU REALLY HAVEN'T USED THEM.
HEE HEE
WE ONLY DRINK GREEN TEA AT OUR PLACE...

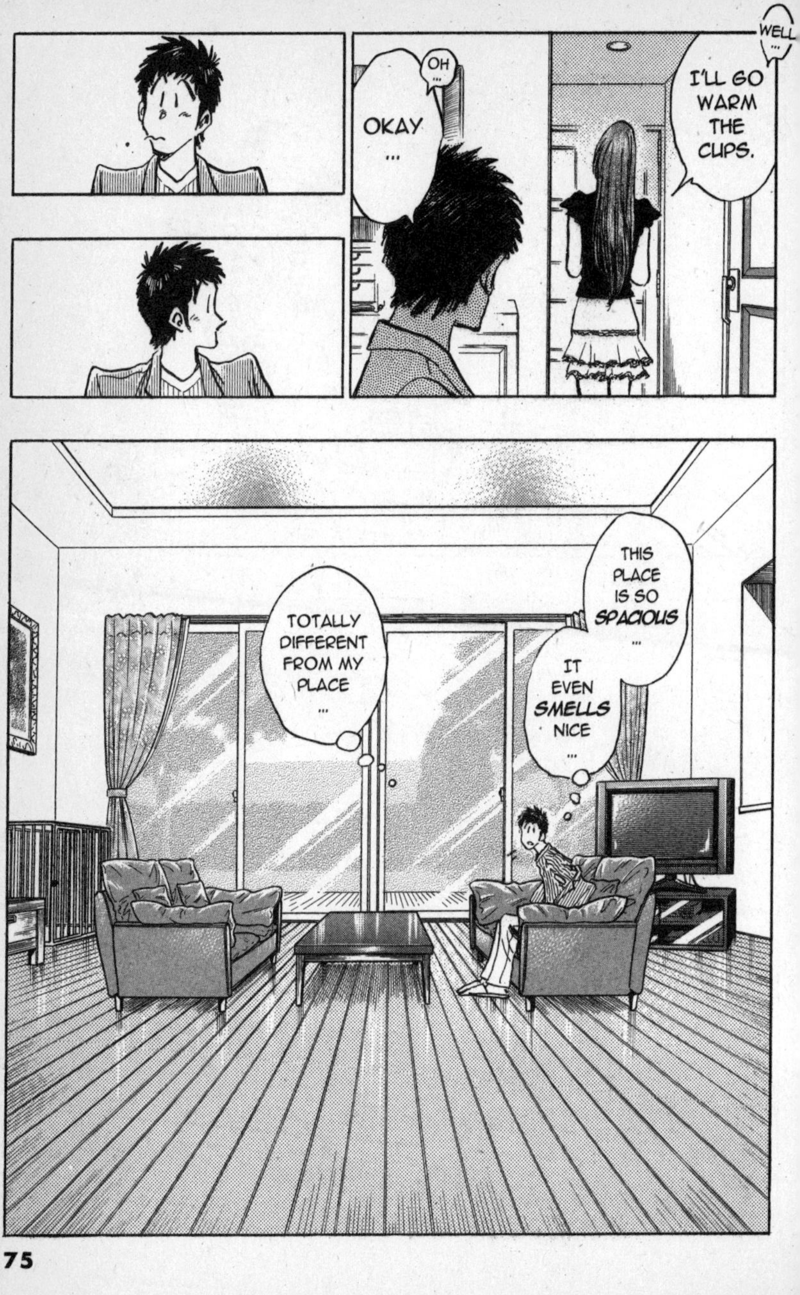
WELL ...
I'LL GO WARM THE CUPS.
OH ...
OKAY ...
THIS PLACE IS SO SPACIOUS ...
IT EVEN SMELLS NICE ...
TOTALLY DIFFERENT FROM MY PLACE ...

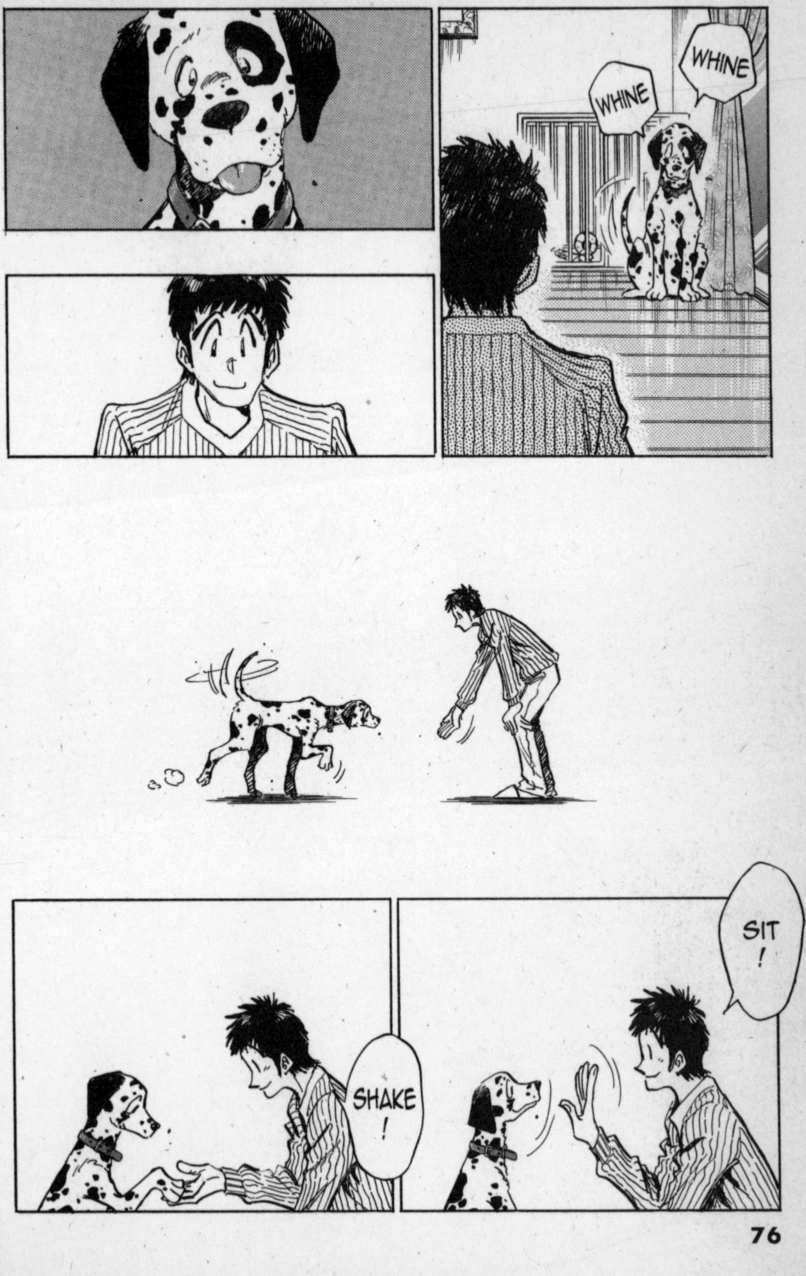

WHINE
WHINE
SIT!
SHAKE!

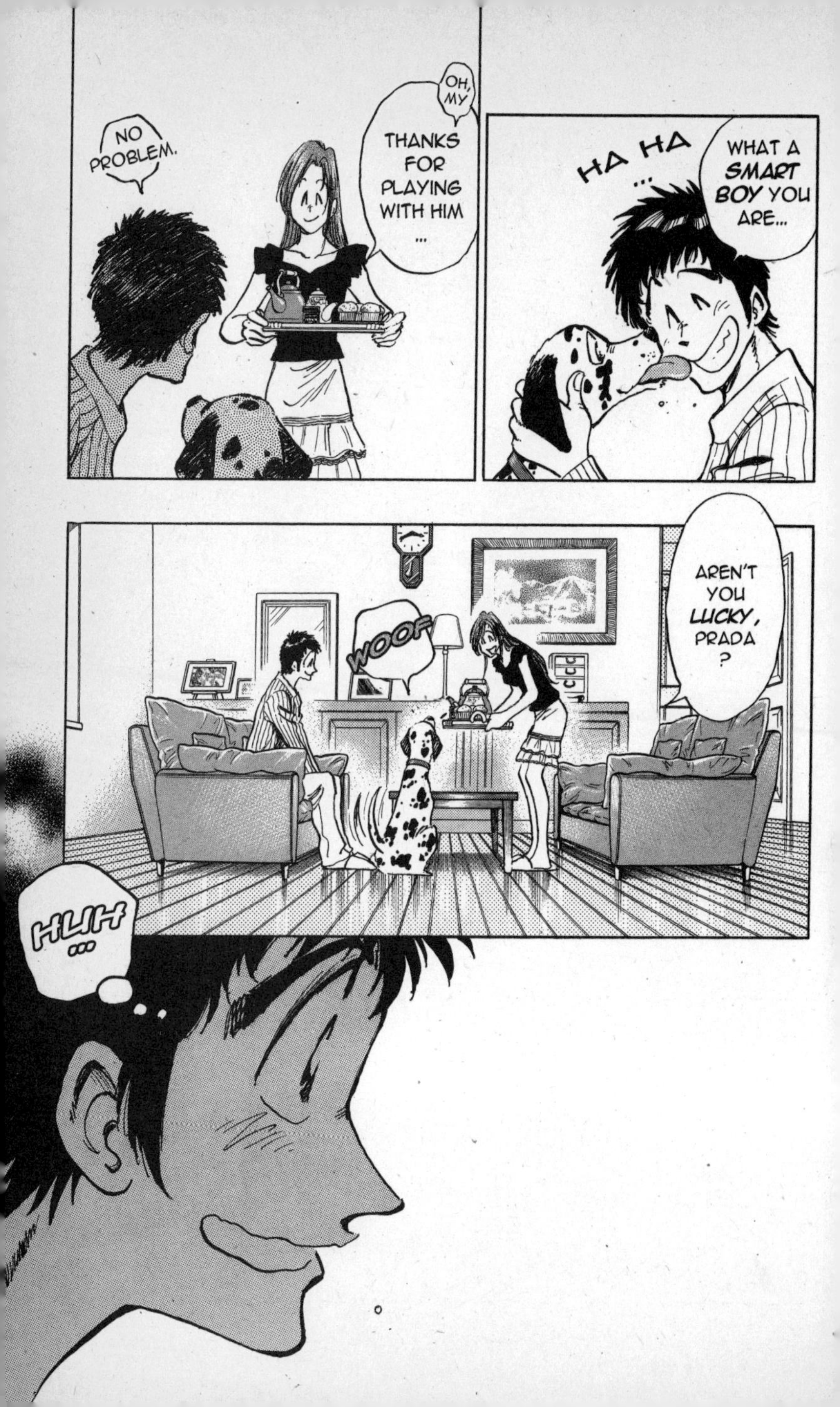
WHAT A SMART BOY YOU ARE...
HA HA ...
OH, MY
THANKS FOR PLAYING WITH HIM ...
NO PROBLEM.
AREN'T YOU LUCKY, PRADA?
WOOF
HUH ...

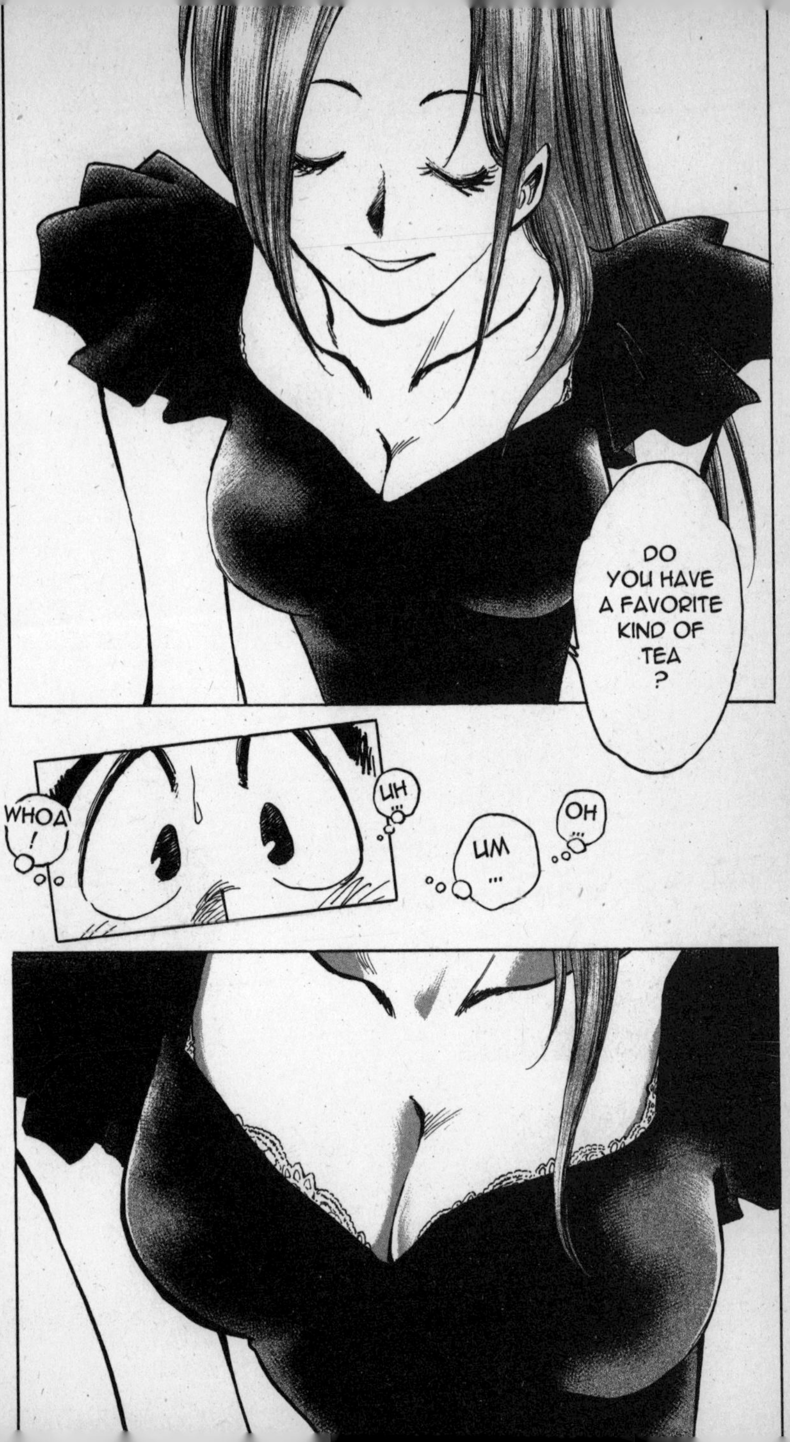
DO YOU HAVE A FAVORITE KIND OF TEA?
OH...
UM...
UH...
WHOA!

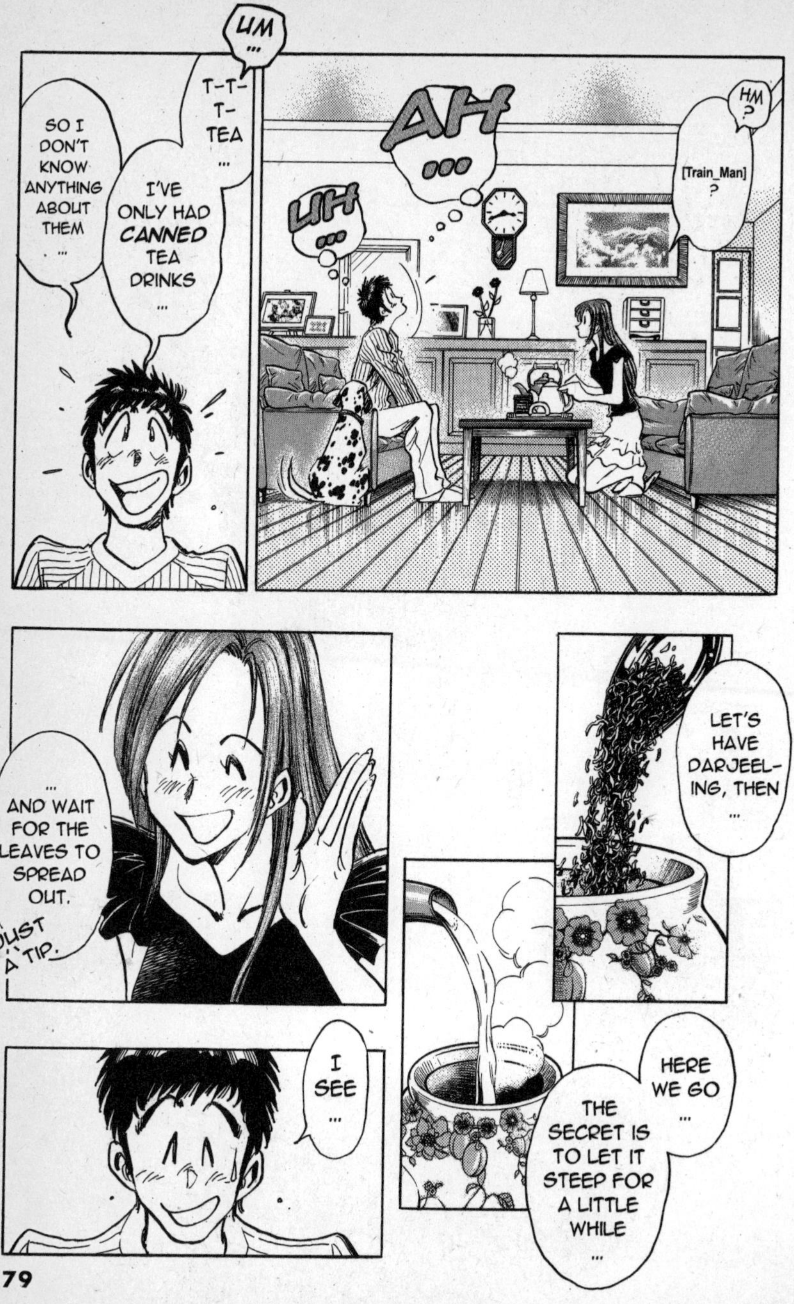

HM?
[Train_Man]?
AH...
UH...
UM...
T-T-T-TEA...
I'VE ONLY HAD CANNED TEA DRINKS...
SO I DON'T KNOW ANYTHING ABOUT THEM. ...
LET'S HAVE DARJEELING, THEN...
HERE WE GO...
THE SECRET IS TO LET IT STEEP FOR A LITTLE WHILE...
...AND WAIT FOR THE LEAVES TO SPREAD OUT.
JUST A TIP.
I SEE...

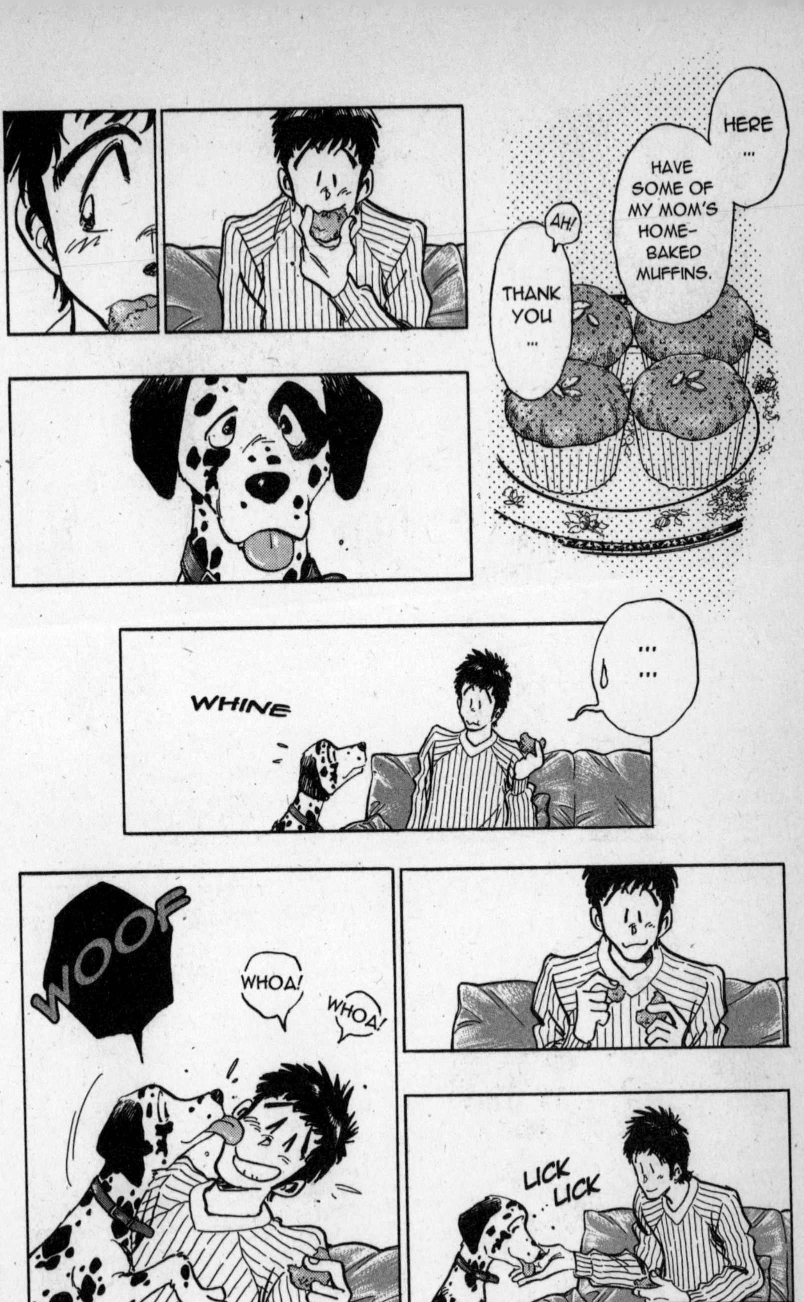
HERE ...
HAVE SOME OF MY MOM'S HOME-BAKED MUFFINS.
AH!
THANK YOU ...
... ...
WHINE
LICK LICK
WOOF
WHOA!
WHOA!

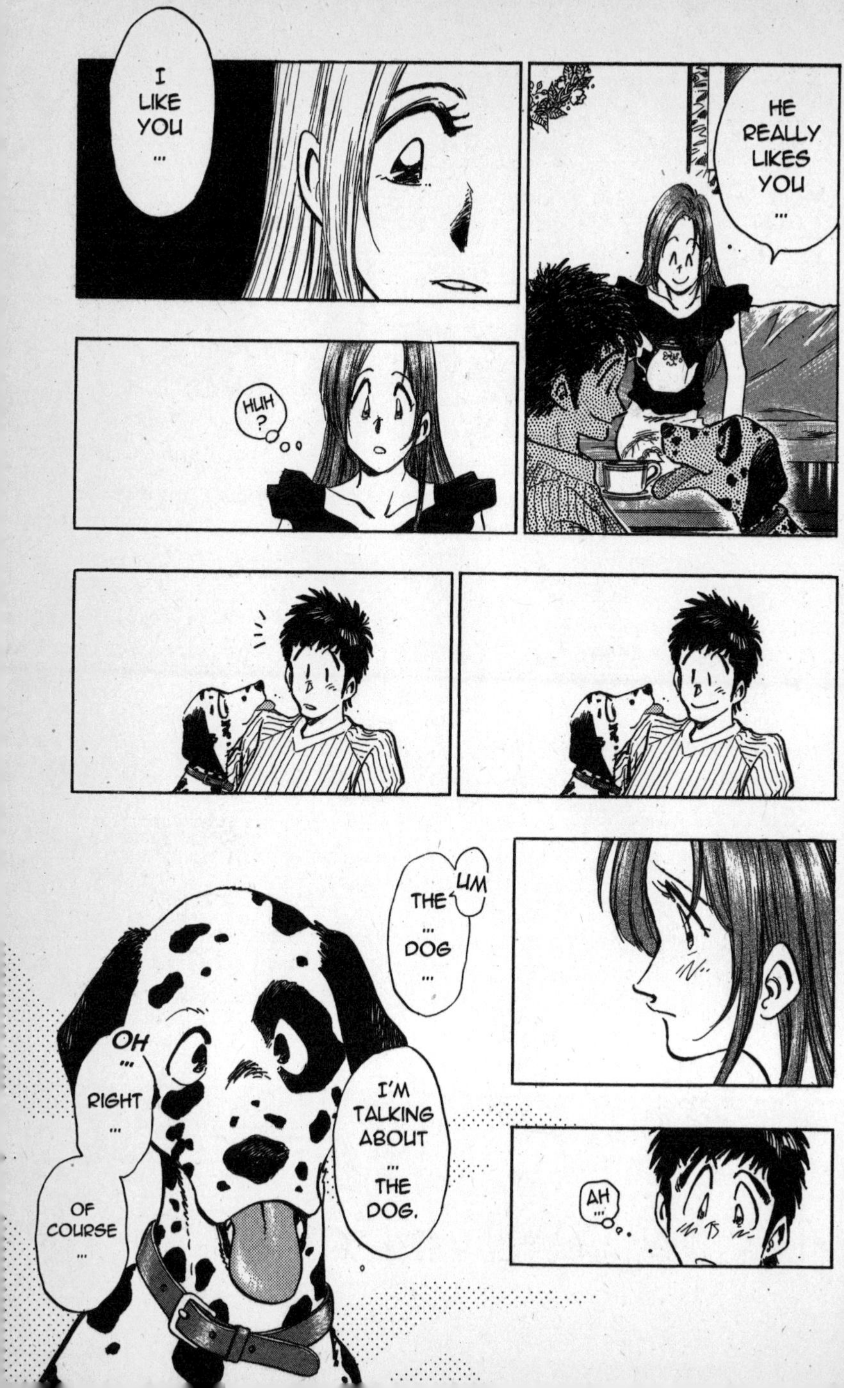
HE REALLY LIKES YOU ...
I LIKE YOU ...
HUH ?
AH ...
UM
THE ... DOG ...
I'M TALKING ABOUT ... THE DOG.
OH ... RIGHT ...
OF COURSE ...

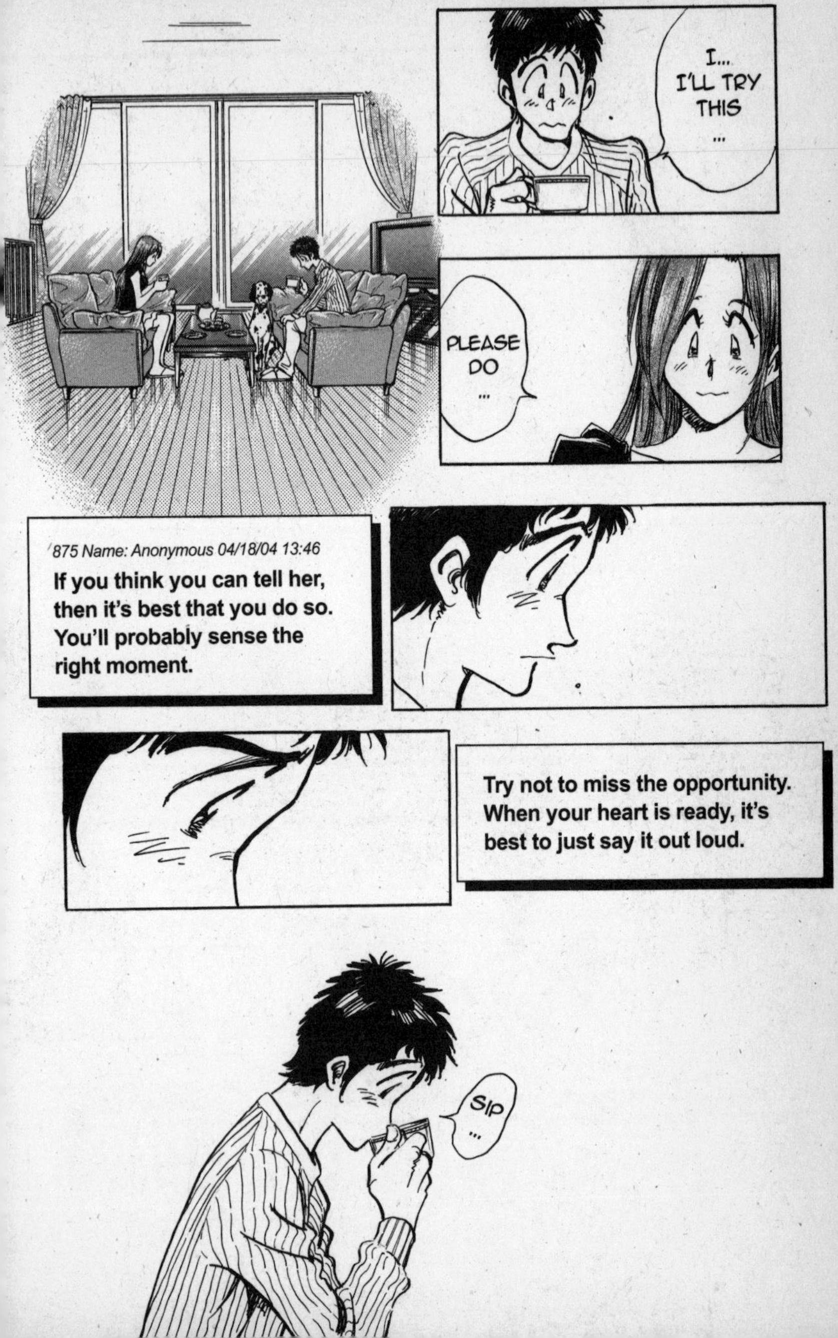
I... I'LL TRY THIS ...
PLEASE DO ...
875 Name: Anonymous 04/18/04 13:46
If you think you can tell her, then it's best that you do so. You'll probably sense the right moment.
Try not to miss the opportunity. When your heart is ready, it's best to just say it out loud.
Sip ...

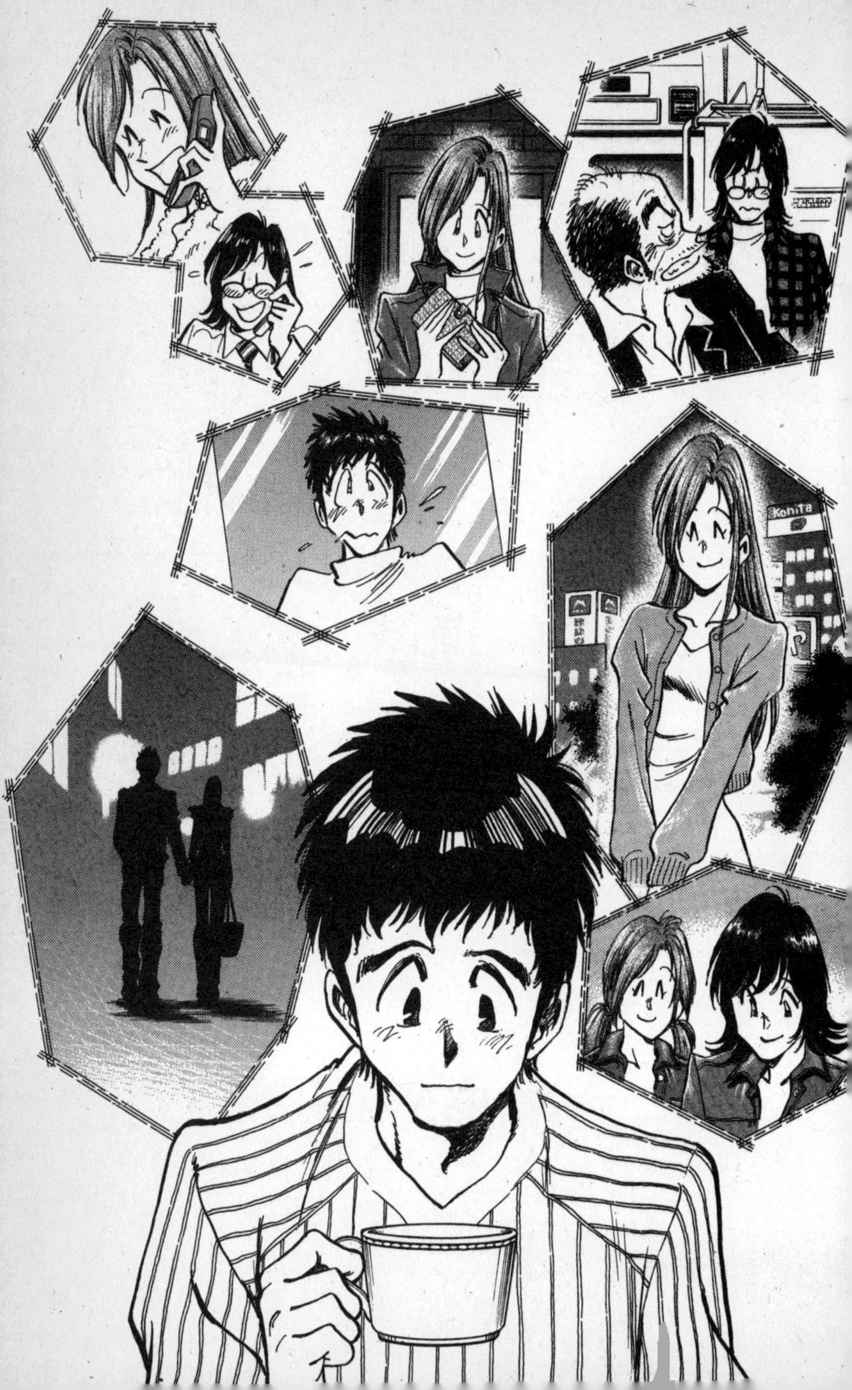
KohiTa

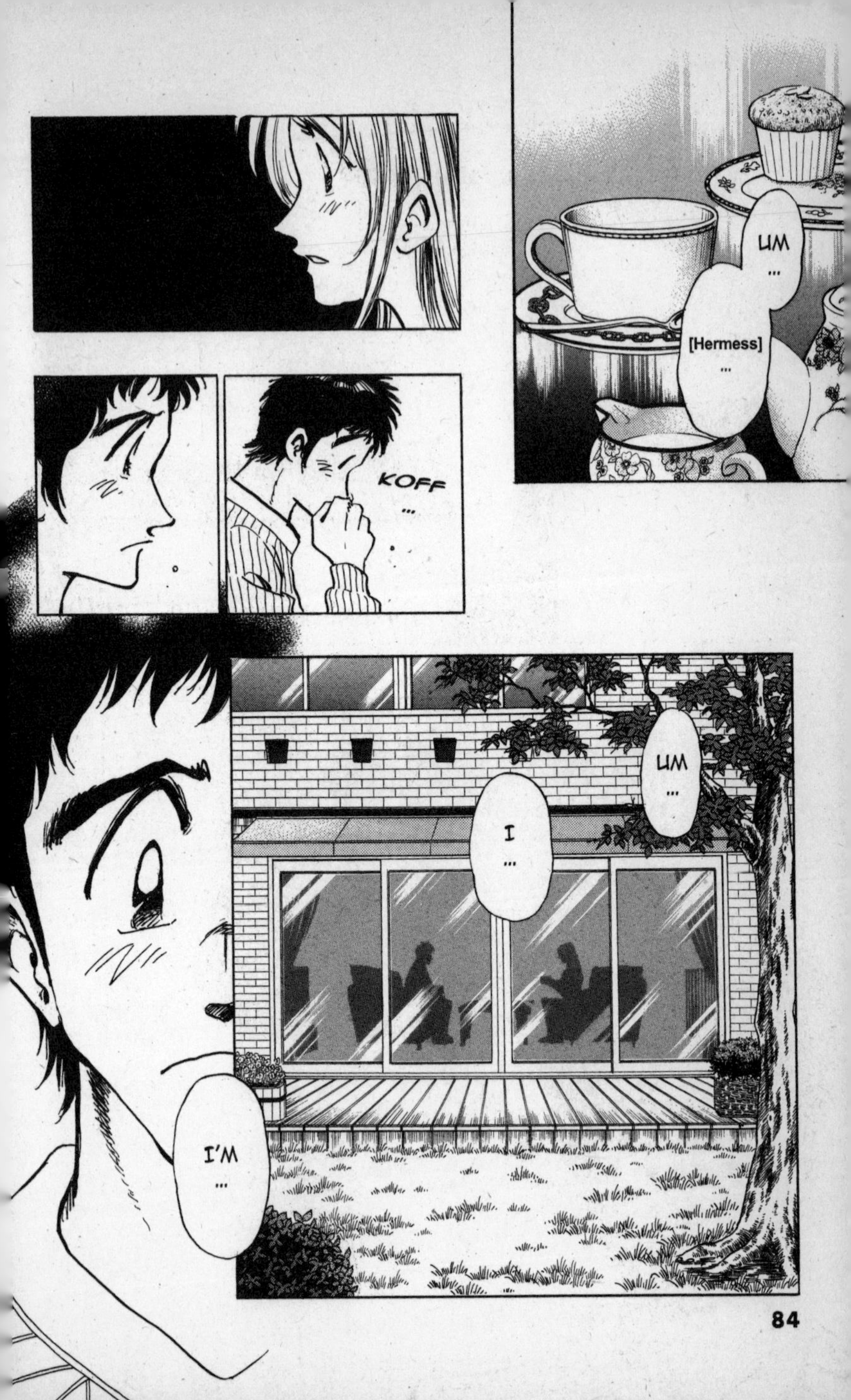
UM ...
[Hermess] ...
KOFF ...
UM ...
I ...
I'M ...

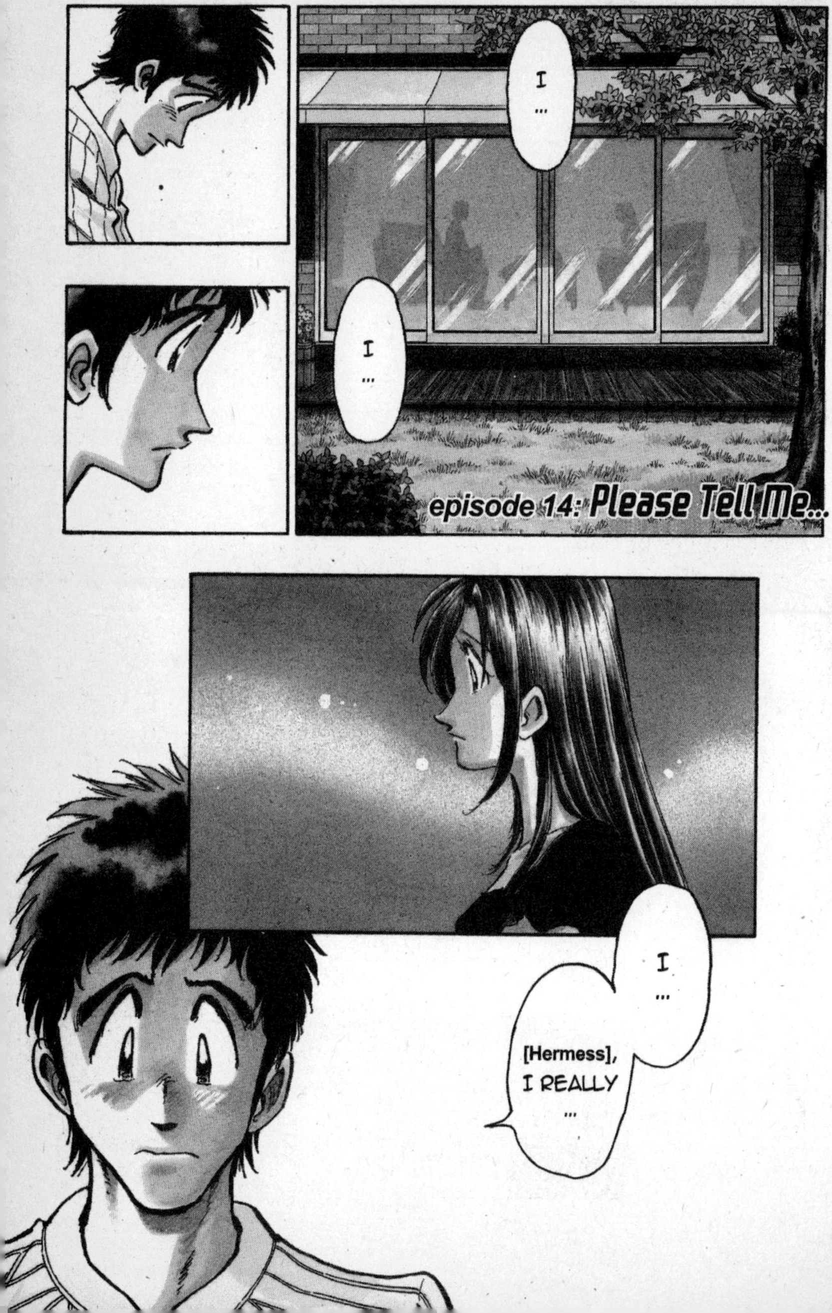
I ...
I ...
episode 14: Please Tell Me...
I ...
[Hermess], I REALLY ...

episode 14:
Please Tell Me...

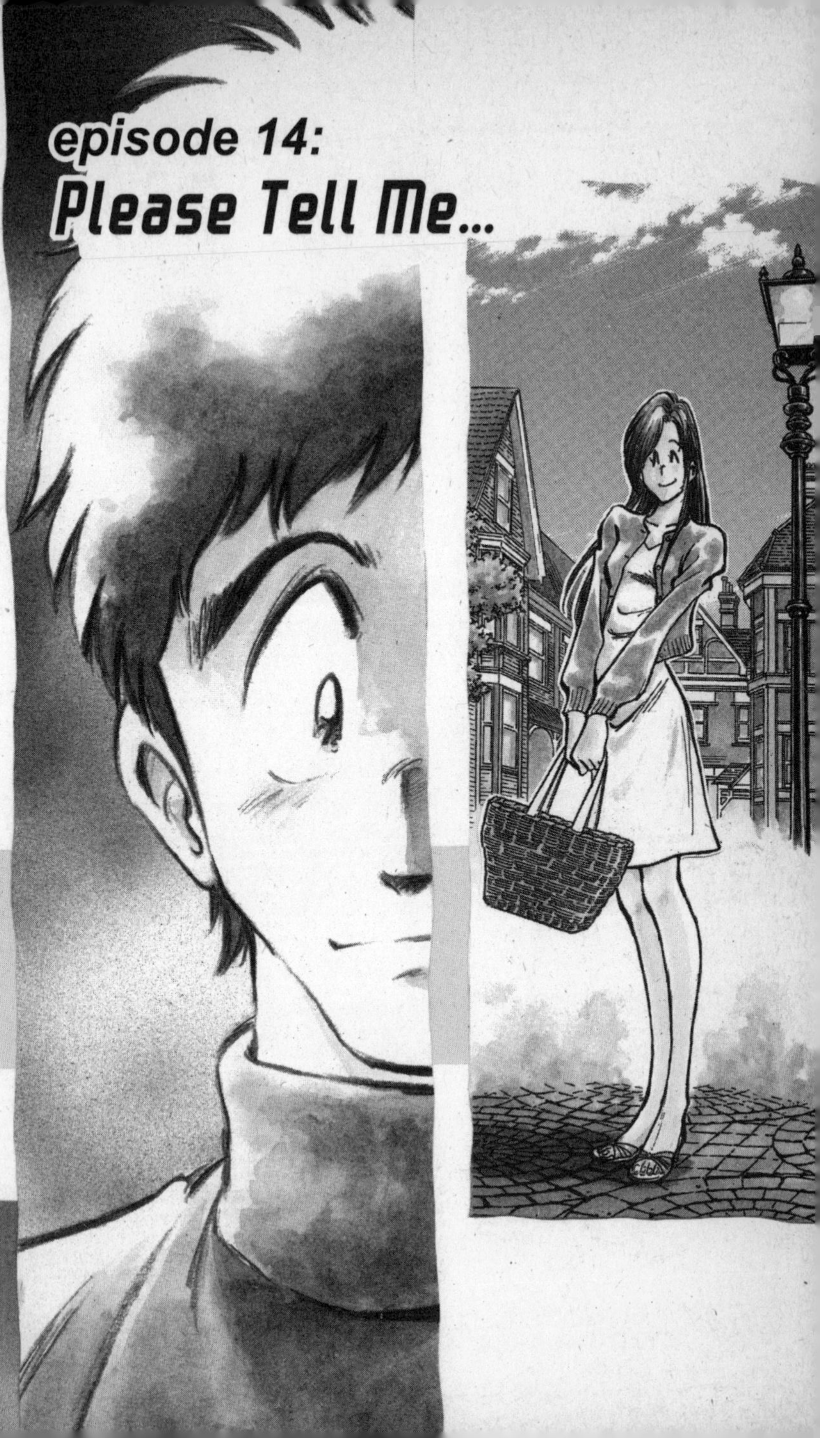

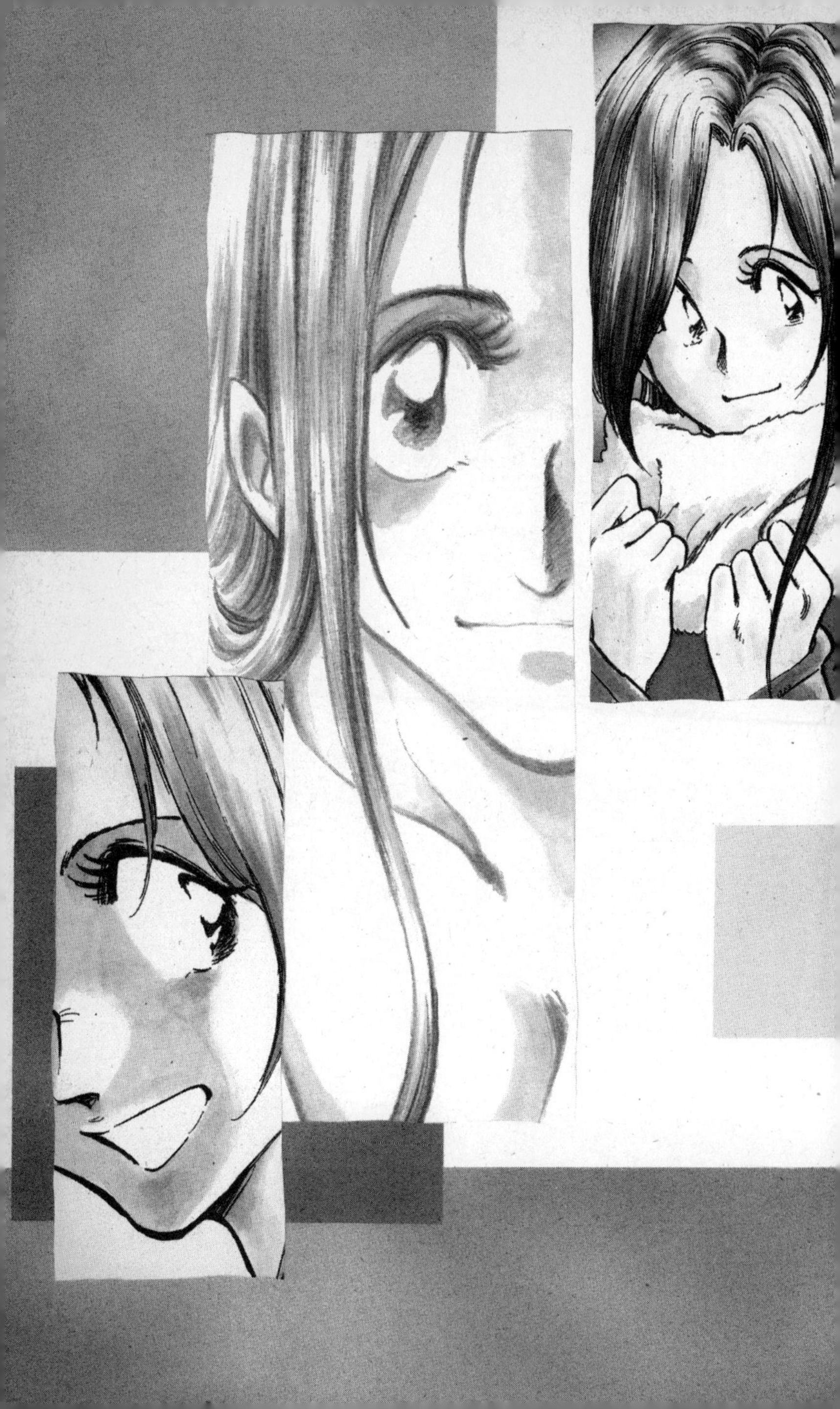

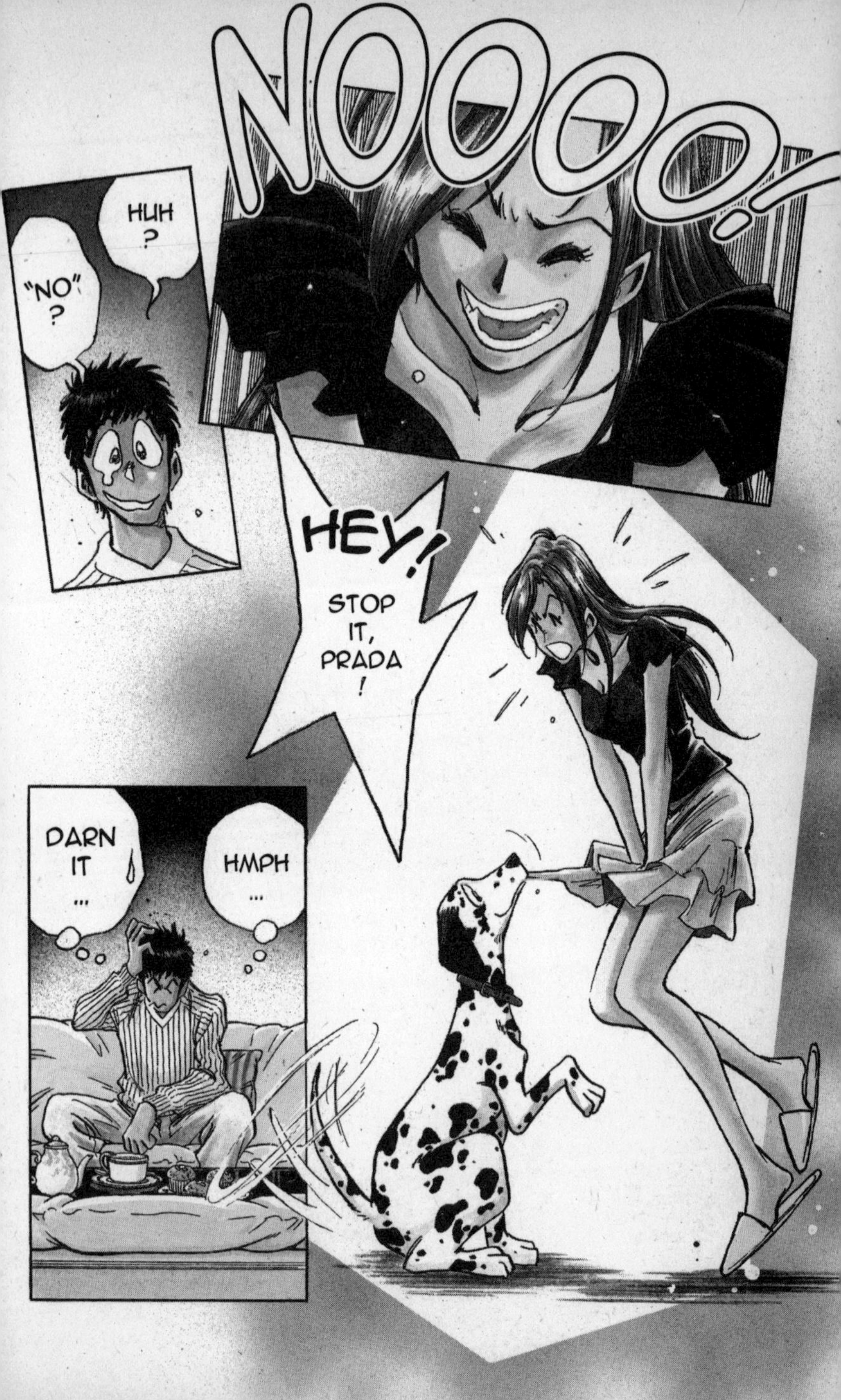
NOOOO!
HUH?
"NO"?
HEY!
STOP IT, PRADA!
HMPH...
DARN IT...

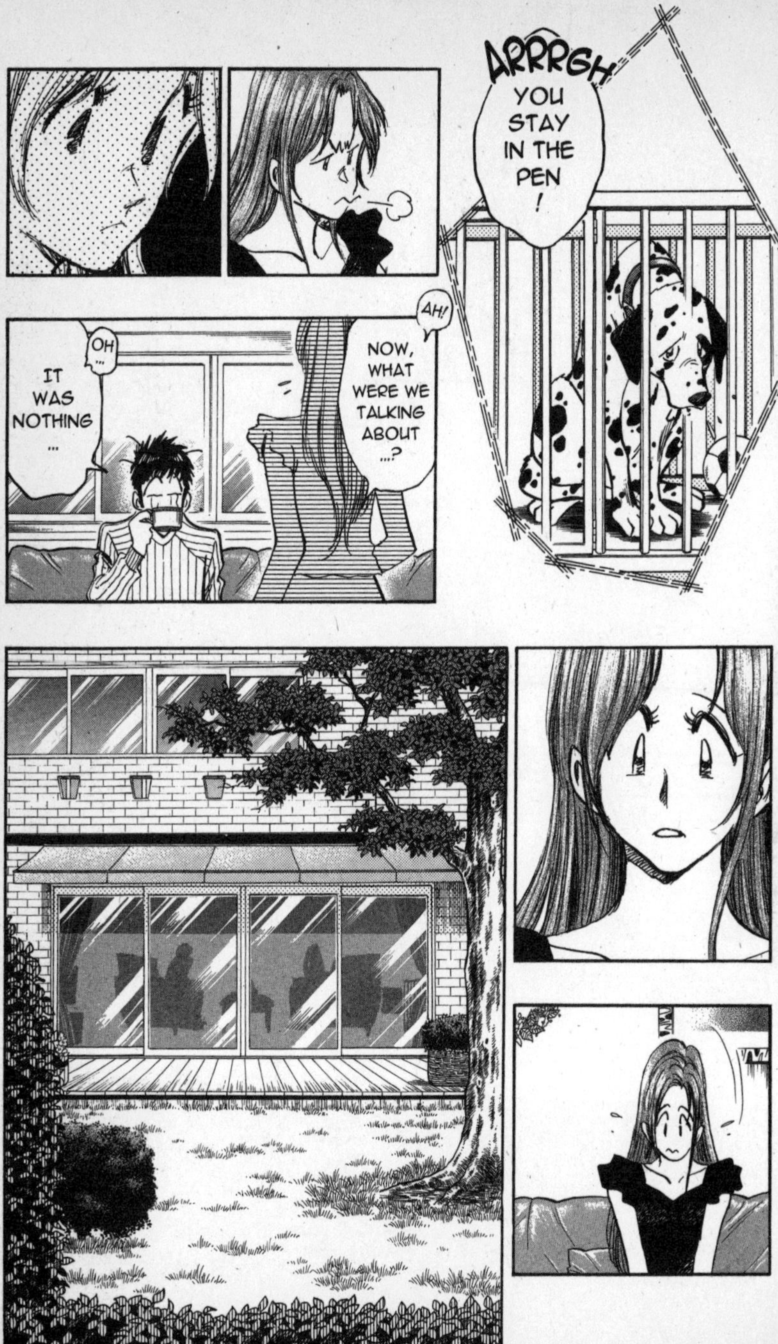
ARRRGH
YOU STAY IN THE PEN!
AH!
NOW, WHAT WERE WE TALKING ABOUT ...?
OH ...
IT WAS NOTHING ...

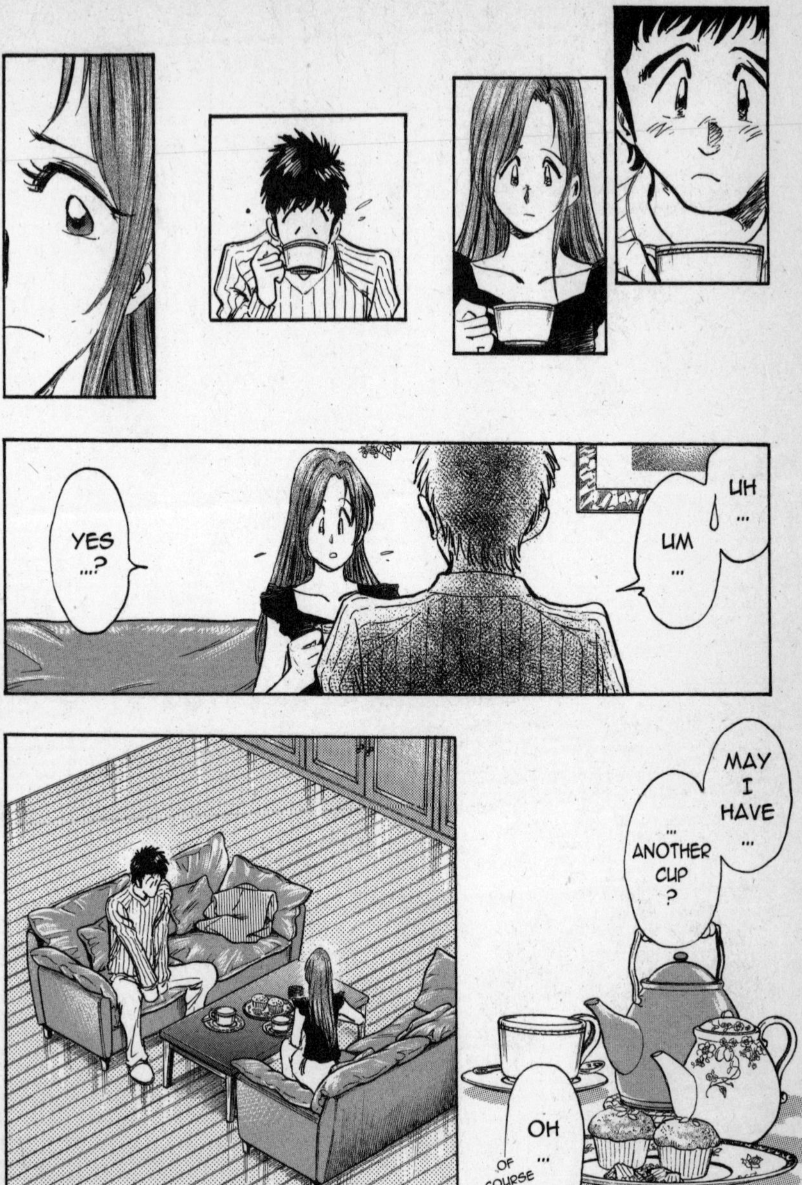
UH ... UM ...
YES ...?
MAY I HAVE ... ... ANOTHER CUP ?
OH ... OF COURSE ...

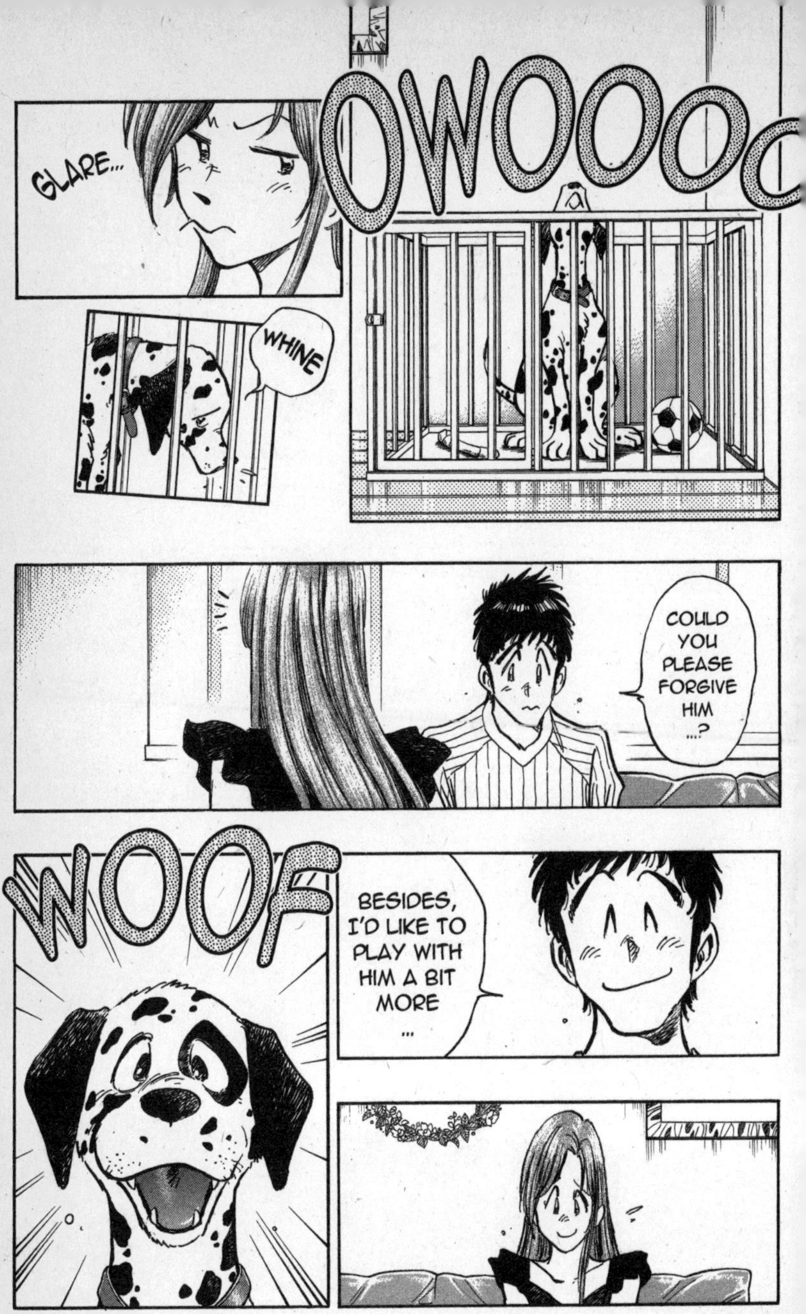

OWOOOO
GLARE...
WHINE
COULD YOU PLEASE FORGIVE HIM ...?
BESIDES, I'D LIKE TO PLAY WITH HIM A BIT MORE ...
WOOF

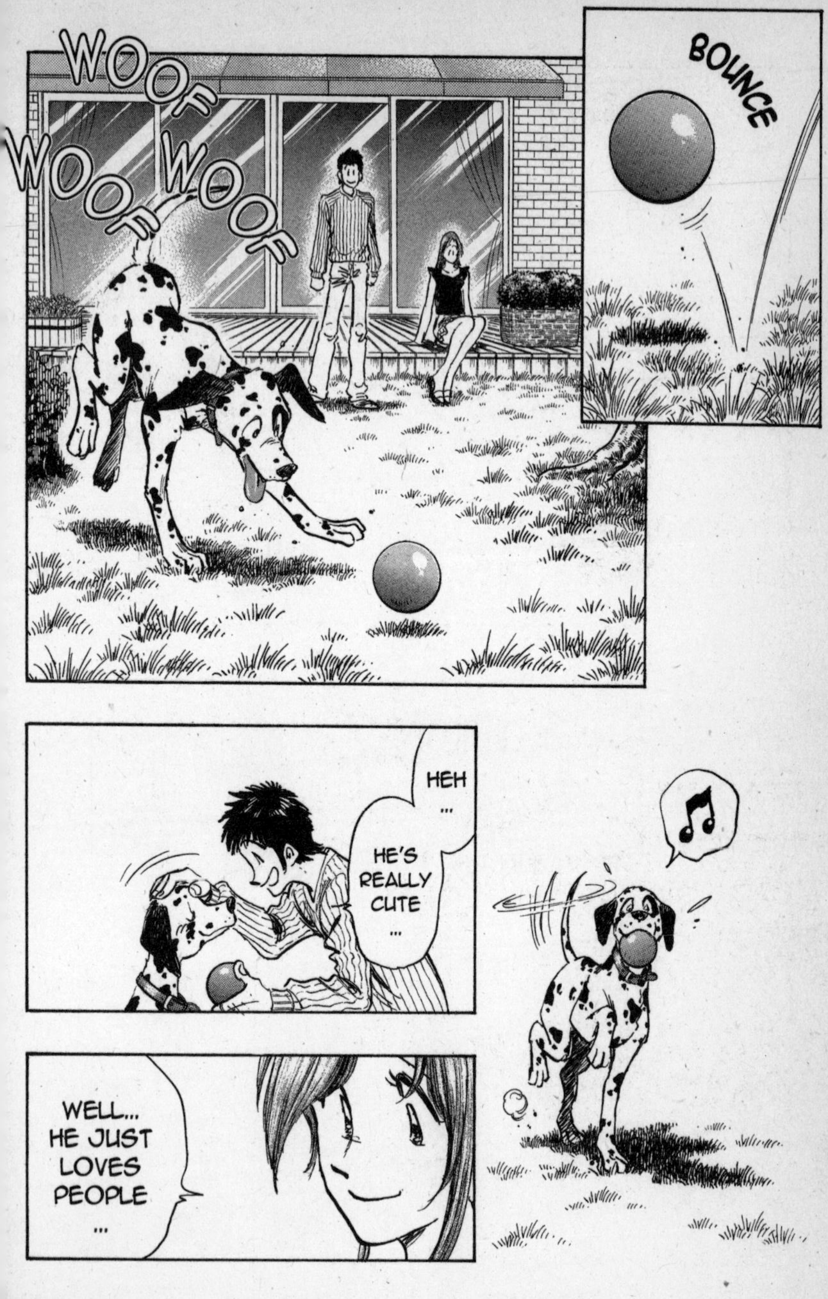
BOUNCE
WOOF WOOF
WOOF WOOF
HEH ... HE'S REALLY CUTE ...
WELL... HE JUST LOVES PEOPLE ...

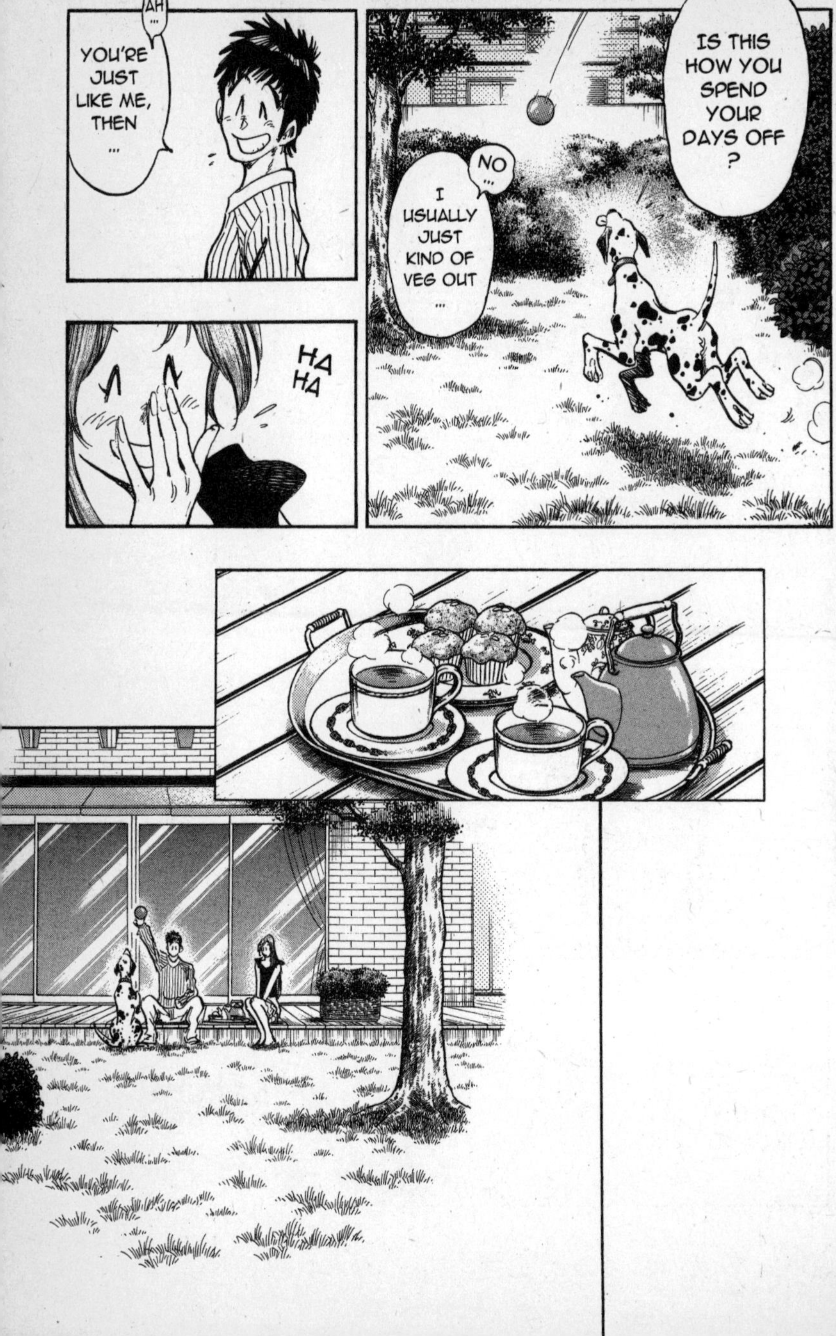
IS THIS HOW YOU SPEND YOUR DAYS OFF ?
NO ...
I USUALLY JUST KIND OF VEG OUT ...
AH ...
YOU'RE JUST LIKE ME, THEN ...
HA HA

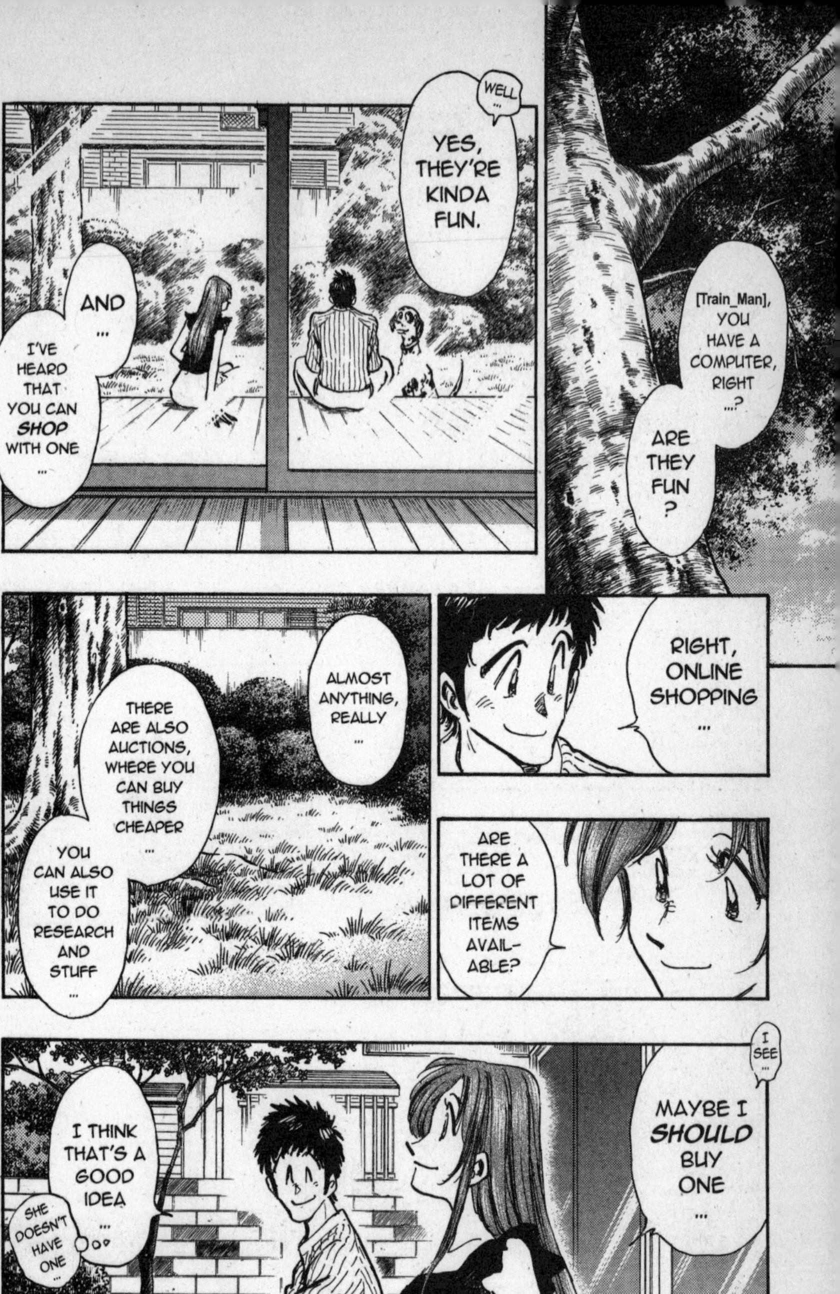
[Train_Man], YOU HAVE A COMPUTER, RIGHT ...?
ARE THEY FUN ?
WELL ...
YES, THEY'RE KINDA FUN.
AND ...
I'VE HEARD THAT YOU CAN *SHOP* WITH ONE ...
RIGHT, ONLINE SHOPPING ...
ARE THERE A LOT OF DIFFERENT ITEMS AVAIL-ABLE?
ALMOST ANYTHING, REALLY ...
THERE ARE ALSO AUCTIONS, WHERE YOU CAN BUY THINGS CHEAPER ...
YOU CAN ALSO USE IT TO DO RESEARCH AND STUFF ...
I SEE ...
MAYBE I *SHOULD* BUY ONE ...
I THINK THAT'S A GOOD IDEA ...
SHE DOESN'T HAVE ONE ...

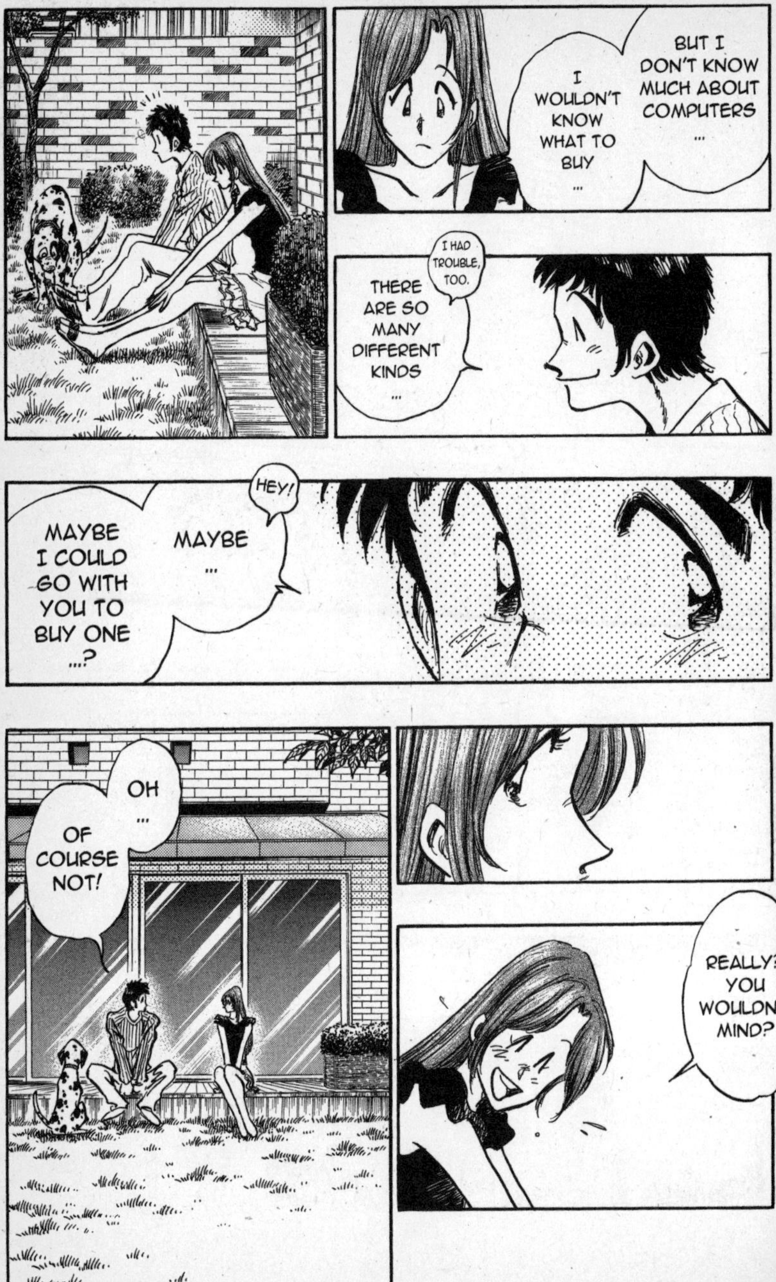
BUT I DON'T KNOW MUCH ABOUT COMPUTERS ...
I WOULDN'T KNOW WHAT TO BUY ...
I HAD TROUBLE, TOO.
THERE ARE SO MANY DIFFERENT KINDS ...
HEY!
MAYBE ...
MAYBE I COULD GO WITH YOU TO BUY ONE ...?
REALLY? YOU WOULDN MIND?
OH ...
OF COURSE NOT!

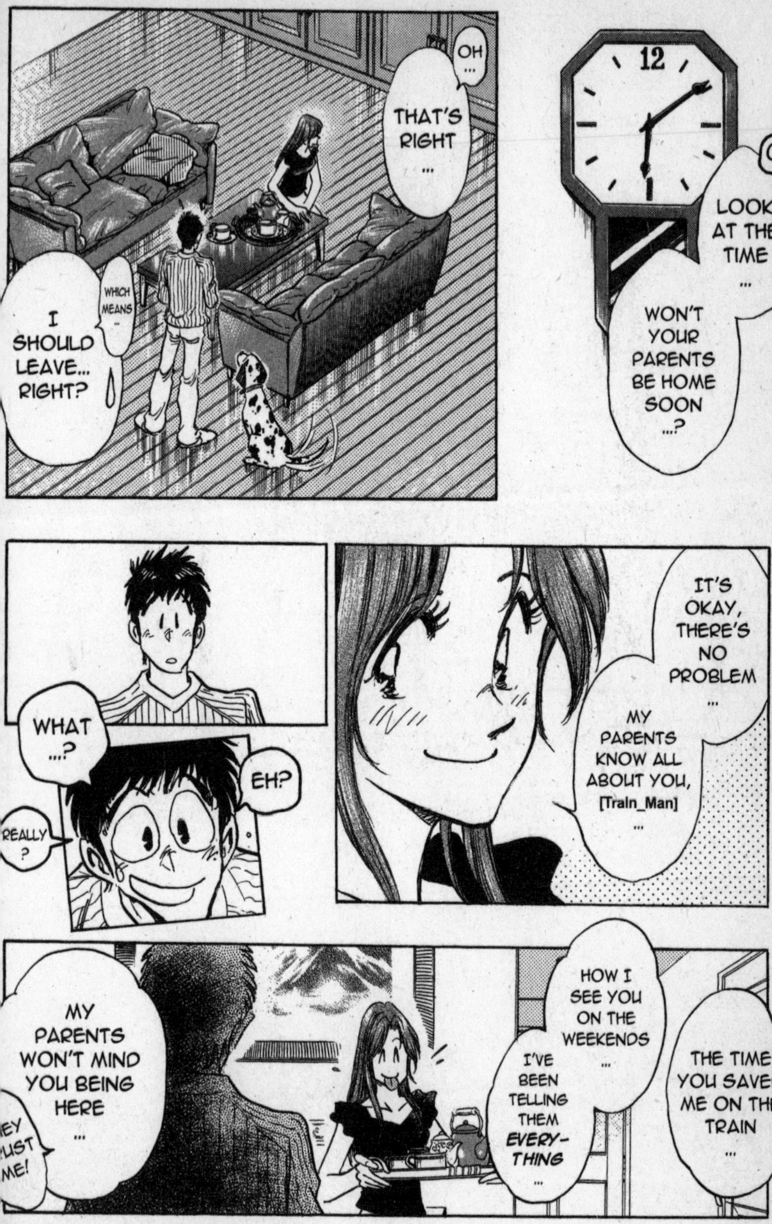
OH!
LOOK AT THE TIME ...
WON'T YOUR PARENTS BE HOME SOON ...?
OH ...
THAT'S RIGHT ...
WHICH MEANS ...
I SHOULD LEAVE... RIGHT?
IT'S OKAY, THERE'S NO PROBLEM ...
MY PARENTS KNOW ALL ABOUT YOU, [Train_Man] ...
WHAT ...?
EH?
REALLY ?
THE TIME YOU SAVED ME ON THE TRAIN ...
HOW I SEE YOU ON THE WEEKENDS ...
I'VE BEEN TELLING THEM *EVERY-THING* ...
MY PARENTS WON'T MIND YOU BEING HERE ...
EY UST ME!

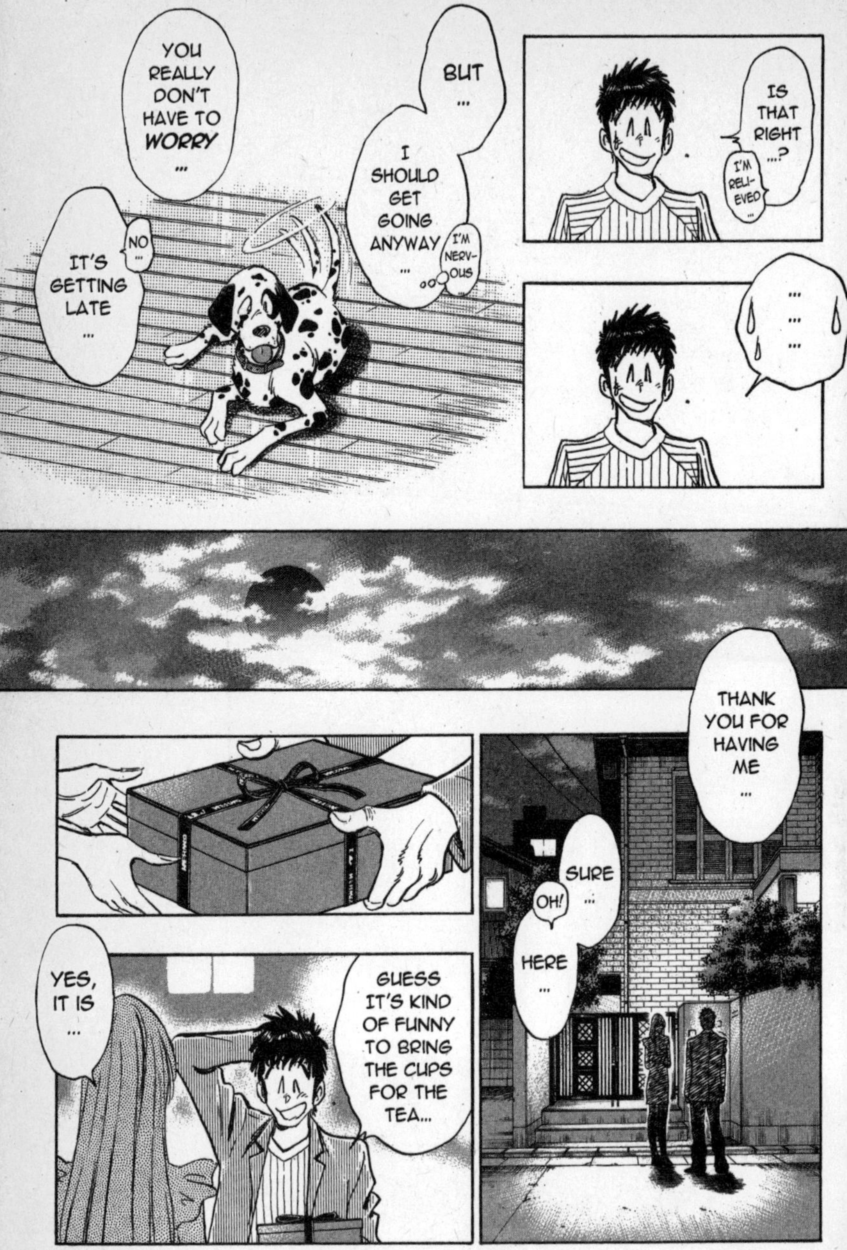
IS THAT RIGHT ...?
I'M RELIEVED ...
... ...
BUT ...
I SHOULD GET GOING ANYWAY ...
I'M NERVOUS ...
YOU REALLY DON'T HAVE TO *WORRY* ...
NO ...
IT'S GETTING LATE ...
THANK YOU FOR HAVING ME ...
SURE ...
OH!
HERE ...
GUESS IT'S KIND OF FUNNY TO BRING THE CUPS FOR THE TEA...
YES, IT IS ...

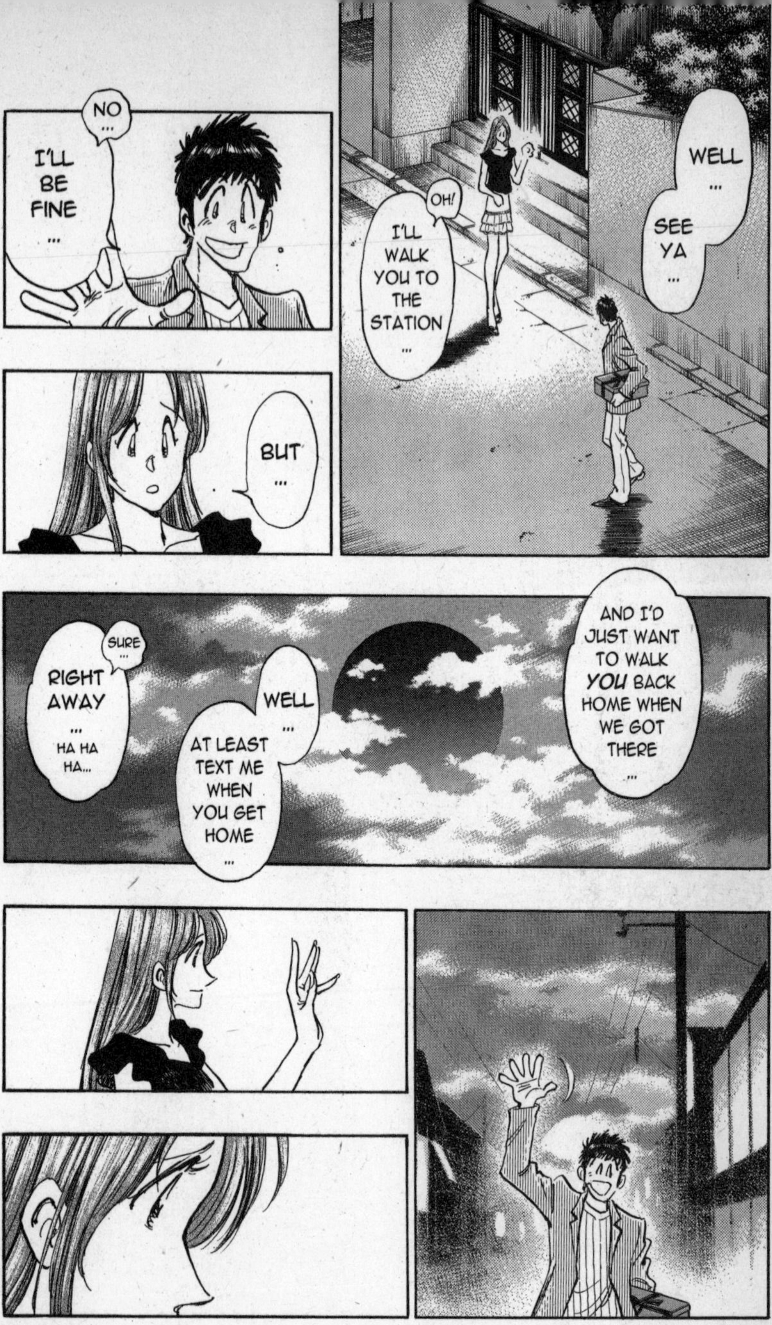
WELL ... SEE YA ...
OH! I'LL WALK YOU TO THE STATION ...
NO ... I'LL BE FINE ...
BUT ...
AND I'D JUST WANT TO WALK YOU BACK HOME WHEN WE GOT THERE ...
WELL ... AT LEAST TEXT ME WHEN YOU GET HOME ...
SURE ... RIGHT AWAY ... HA HA HA...

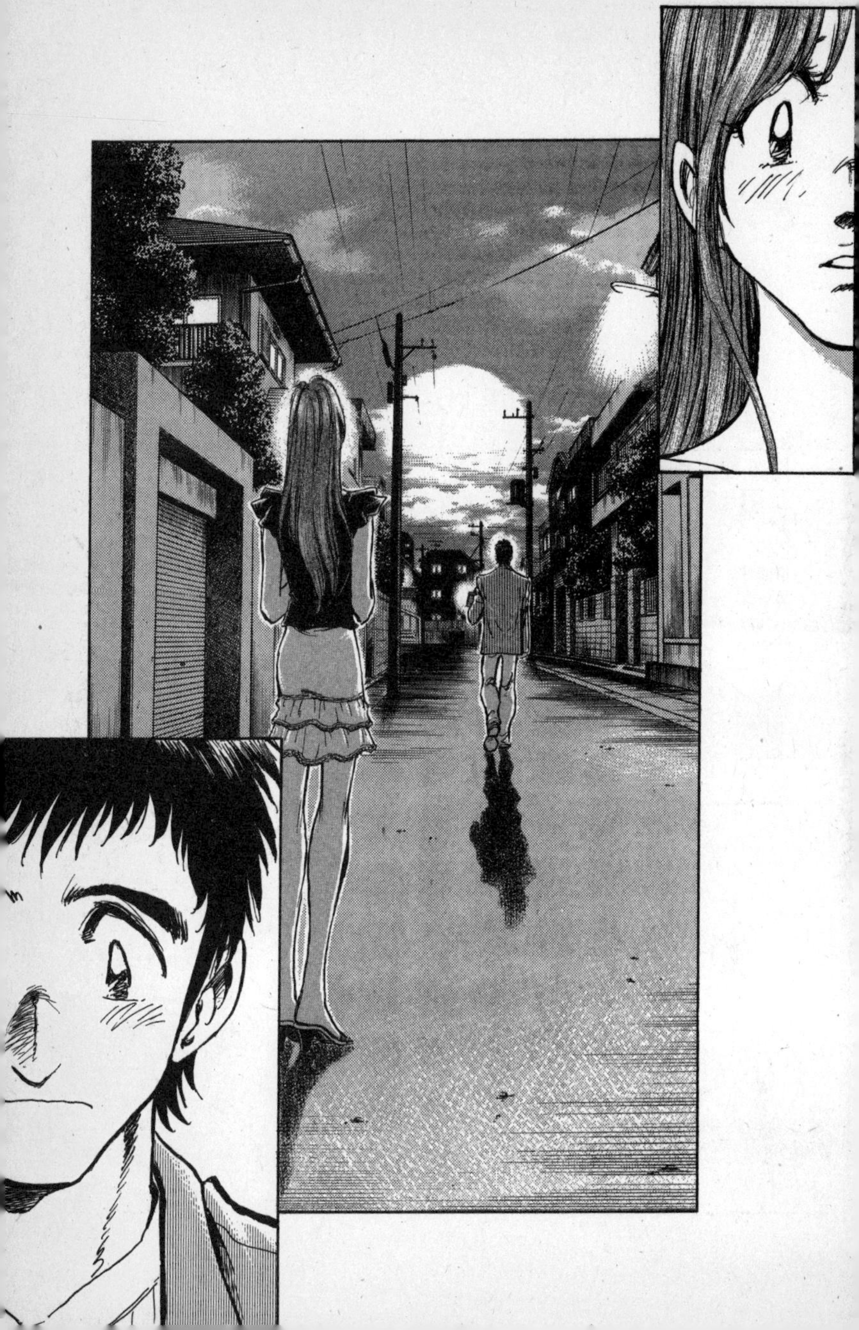

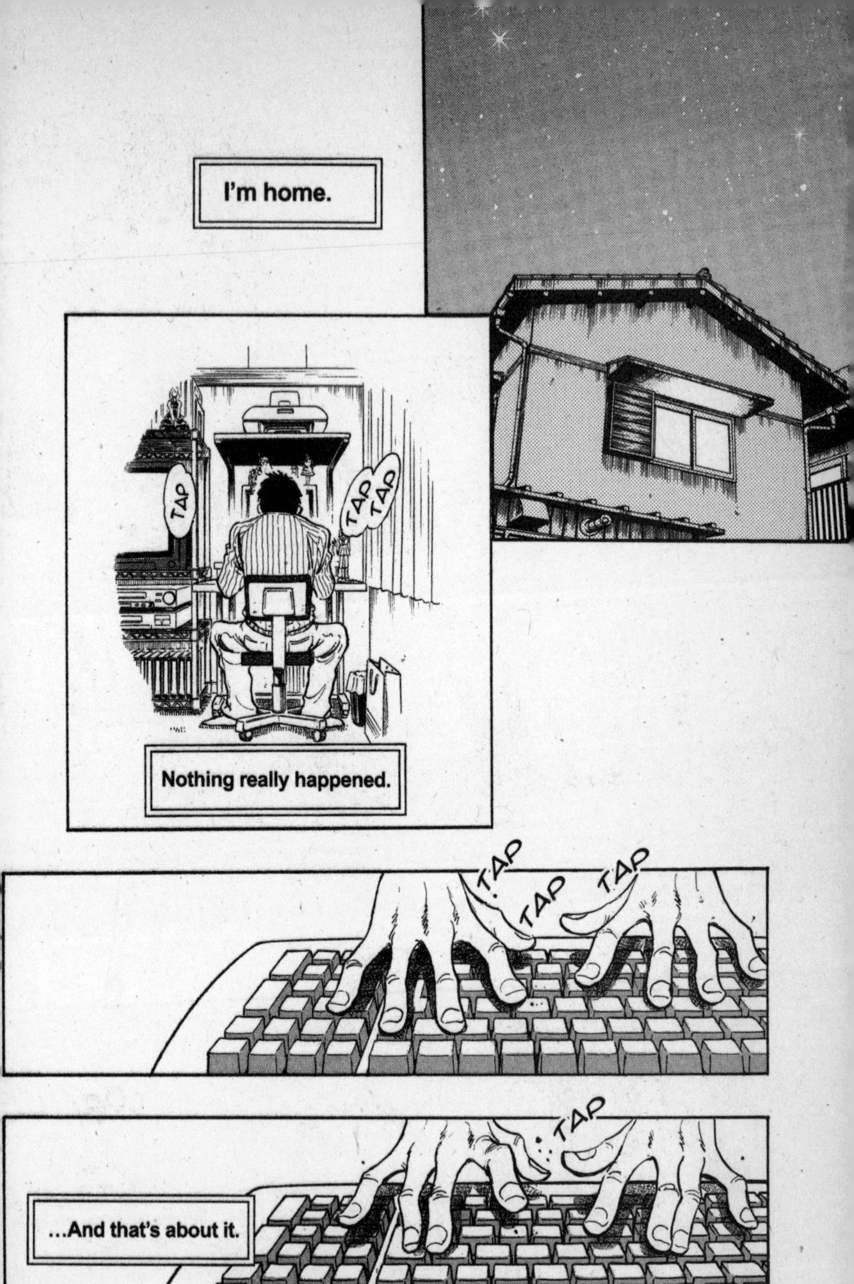
I'm home.
TAP TAP
TAP
Nothing really happened.
TAP
TAP
TAP
TAP
...And that's about it.

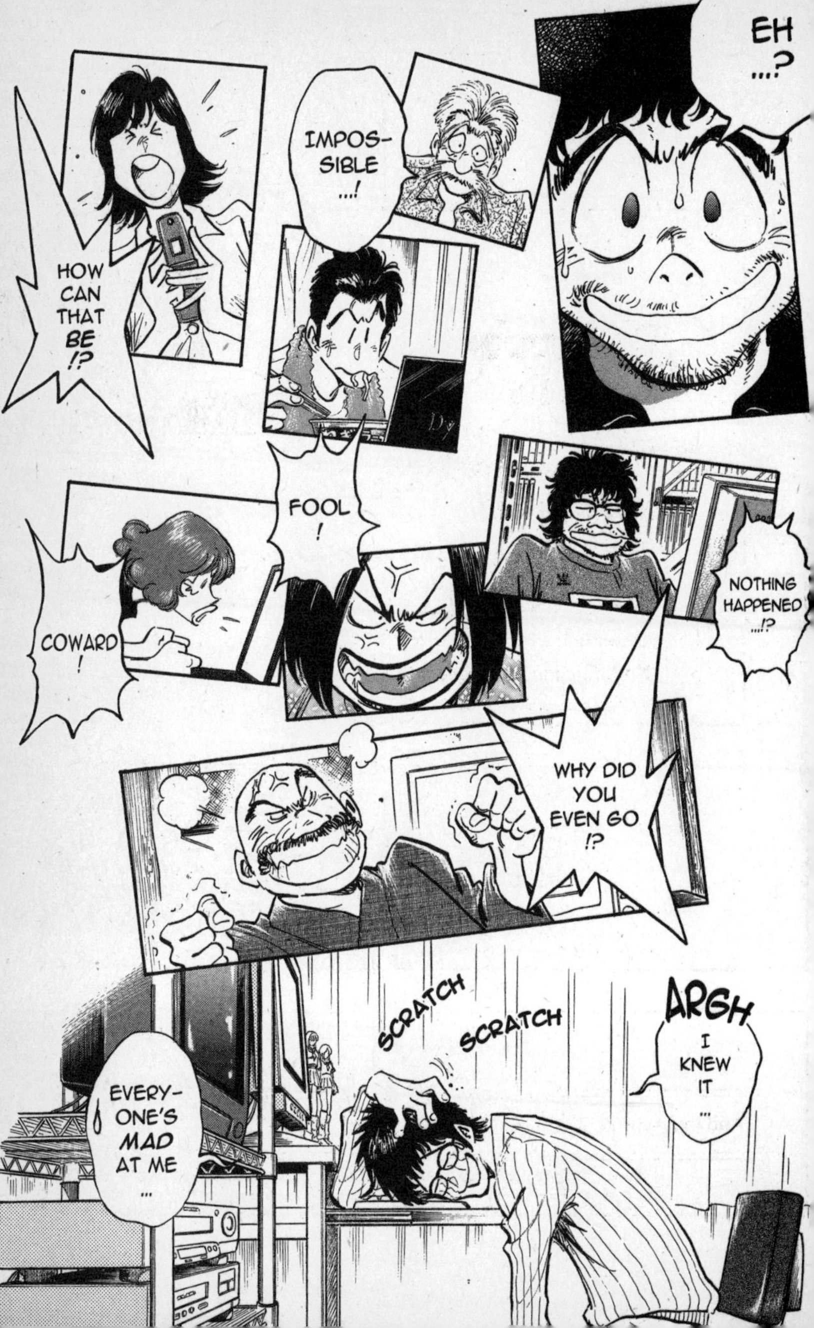
EH ...?
IMPOSSIBLE ...!
HOW CAN THAT BE !?
NOTHING HAPPENED ...!?
FOOL !
COWARD !
WHY DID YOU EVEN GO !?
ARGH
I KNEW IT ...
SCRATCH SCRATCH
EVERYONE'S MAD AT ME ...

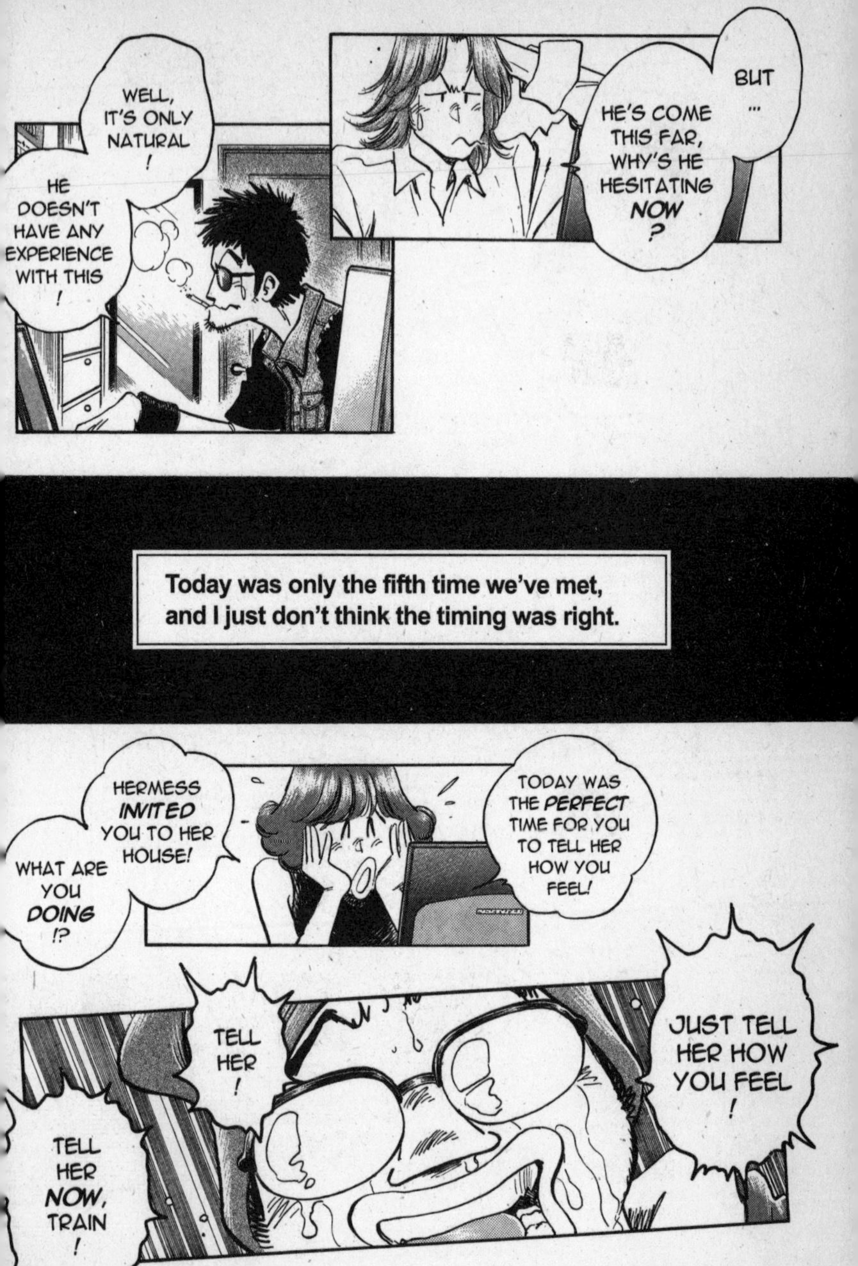
BUT ...
HE'S COME THIS FAR, WHY'S HE HESITATING *NOW*?
WELL, IT'S ONLY NATURAL!
HE DOESN'T HAVE ANY EXPERIENCE WITH THIS!
Today was only the fifth time we've met, and I just don't think the timing was right.
TODAY WAS THE *PERFECT* TIME FOR YOU TO TELL HER HOW YOU FEEL!
HERMESS *INVITED* YOU TO HER HOUSE!
WHAT ARE YOU *DOING*!?
JUST TELL HER HOW YOU FEEL!
TELL HER!
TELL HER *NOW*, TRAIN!

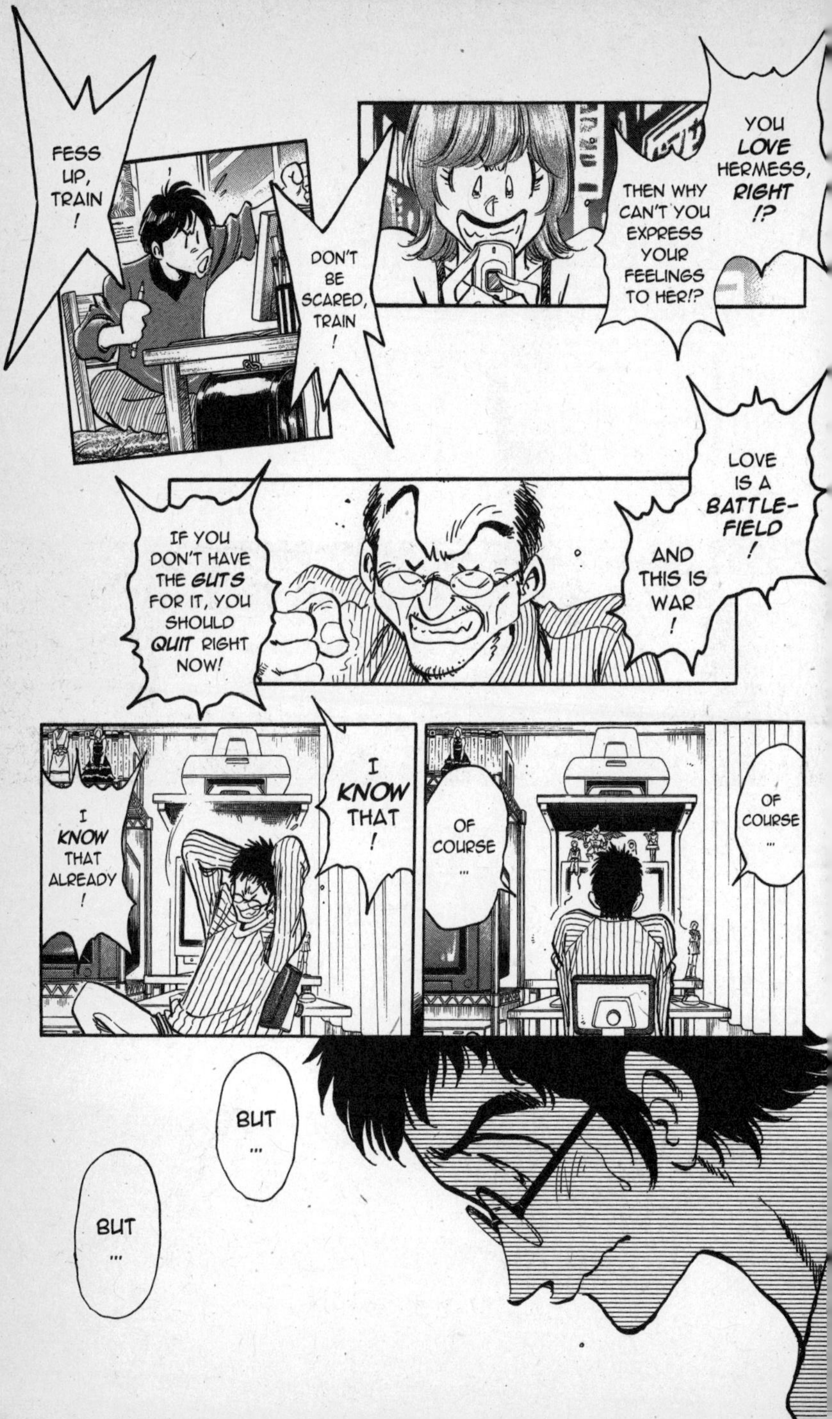

YOU LOVE HERMESS, RIGHT!?
THEN WHY CAN'T YOU EXPRESS YOUR FEELINGS TO HER!?
DON'T BE SCARED, TRAIN!
FESS UP, TRAIN!
LOVE IS A BATTLEFIELD!
AND THIS IS WAR!
IF YOU DON'T HAVE THE GUTS FOR IT, YOU SHOULD QUIT RIGHT NOW!
OF COURSE...
OF COURSE...
I KNOW THAT!
I KNOW THAT ALREADY!
BUT...
BUT...

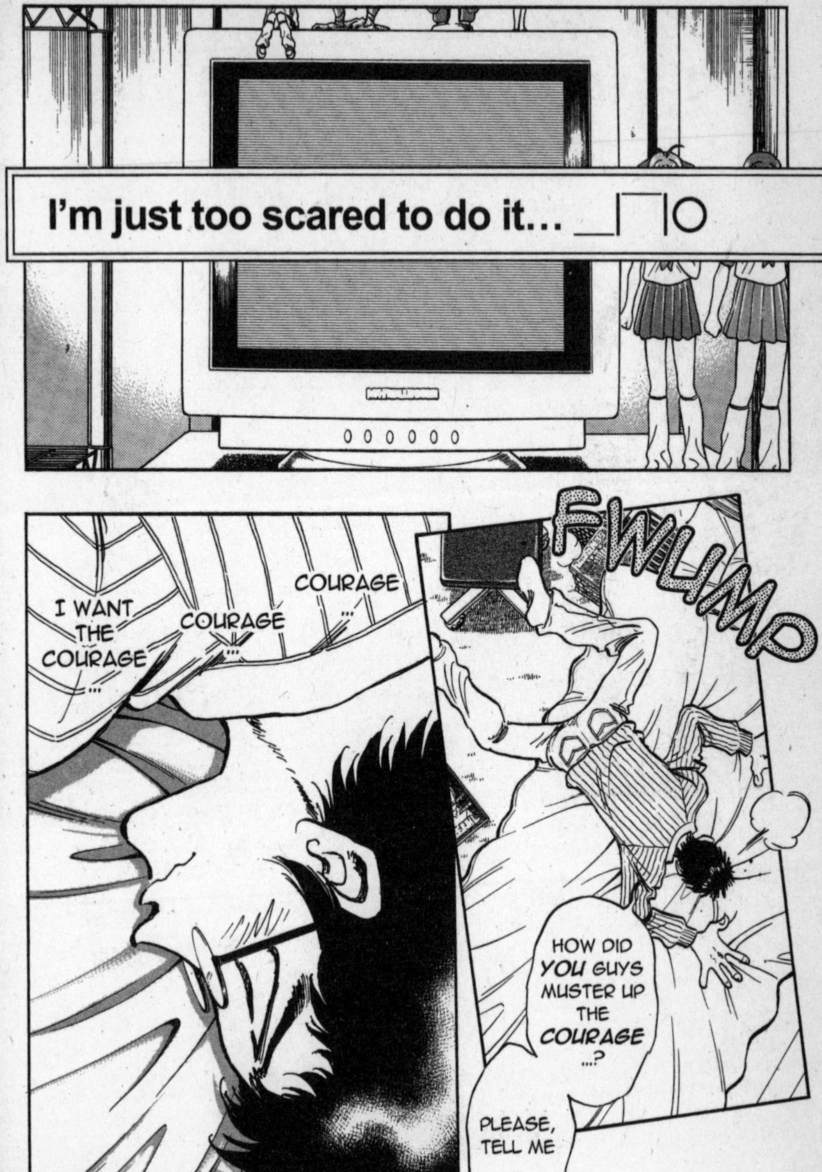
I'm just too scared to do it… _|¯|○
FWUMP
HOW DID YOU GUYS MUSTER UP THE COURAGE ...?
PLEASE, TELL ME ...
COURAGE ...
COURAGE ...
I WANT THE COURAGE ...

episode 15:
Train_Man, Carried Away

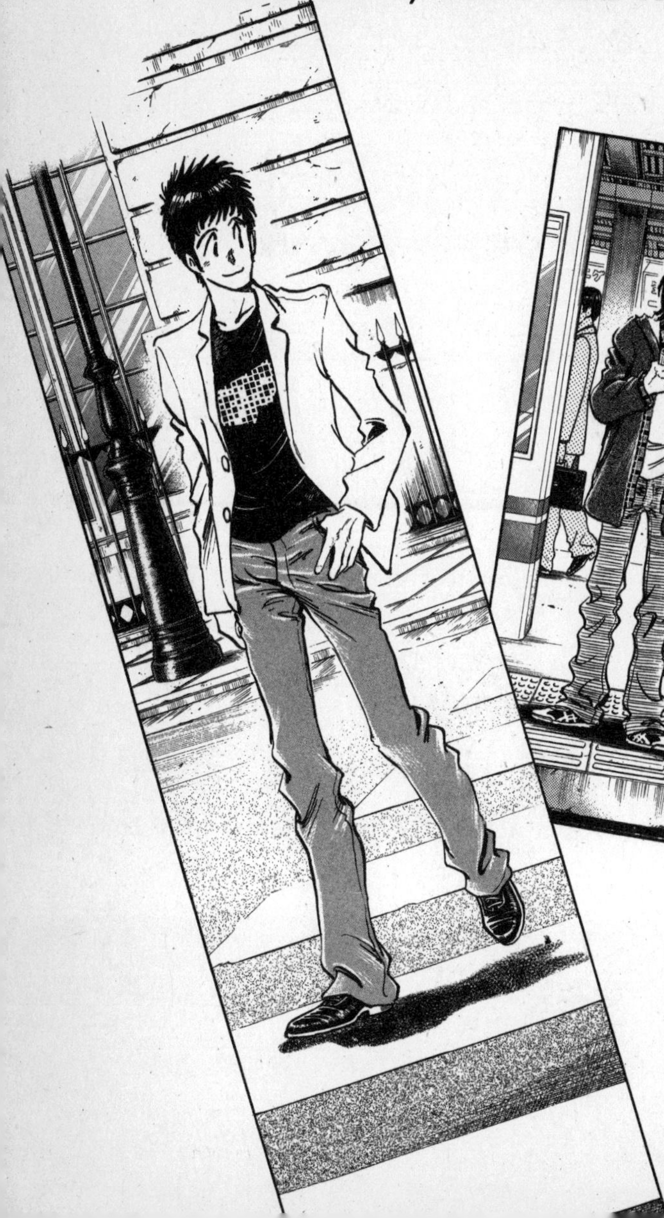

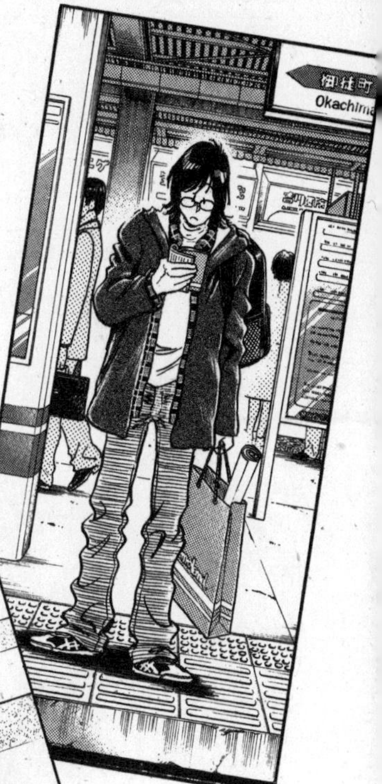
Okachima

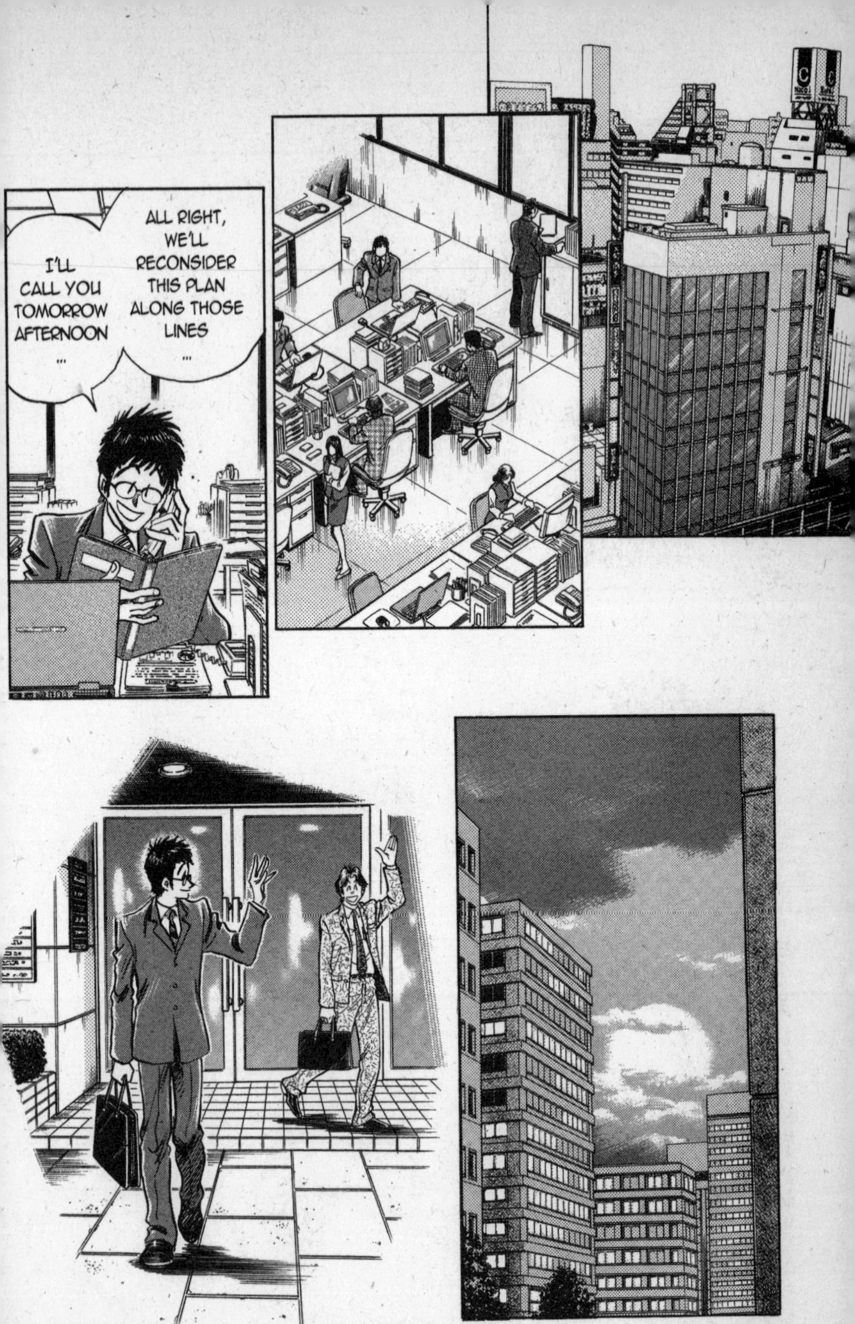
ALL RIGHT, WE'LL RECONSIDER THIS PLAN ALONG THOSE LINES ...
I'LL CALL YOU TOMORROW AFTERNOON ...

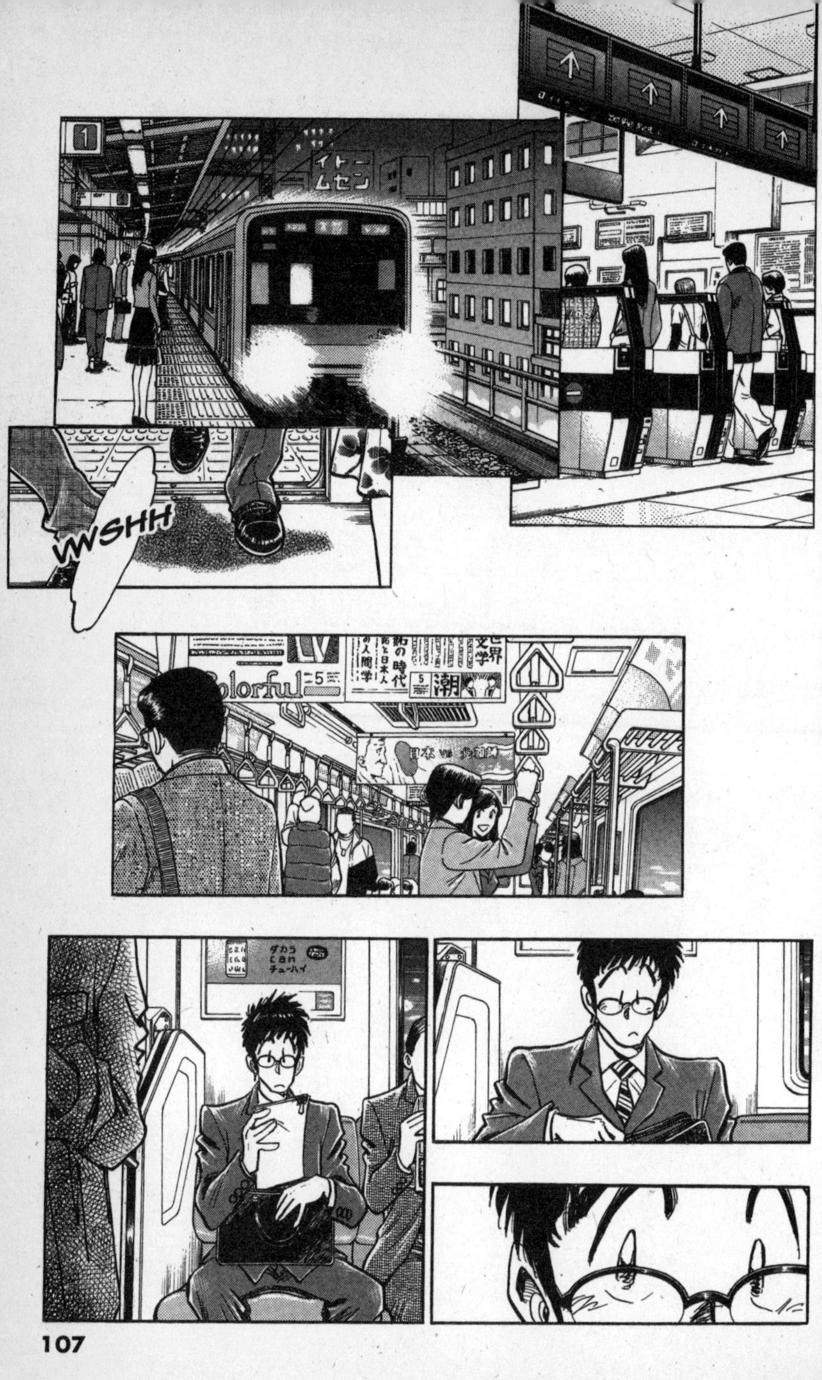
イトー
ムセン
WSHH
Colorful
潮
ダカラ
can
チューハイ

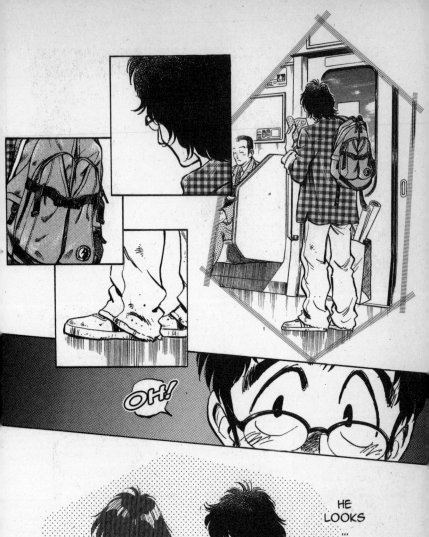

OH!

HE LOOKS ...

JUST LIKE ME ...

... WAY BACK WHEN.

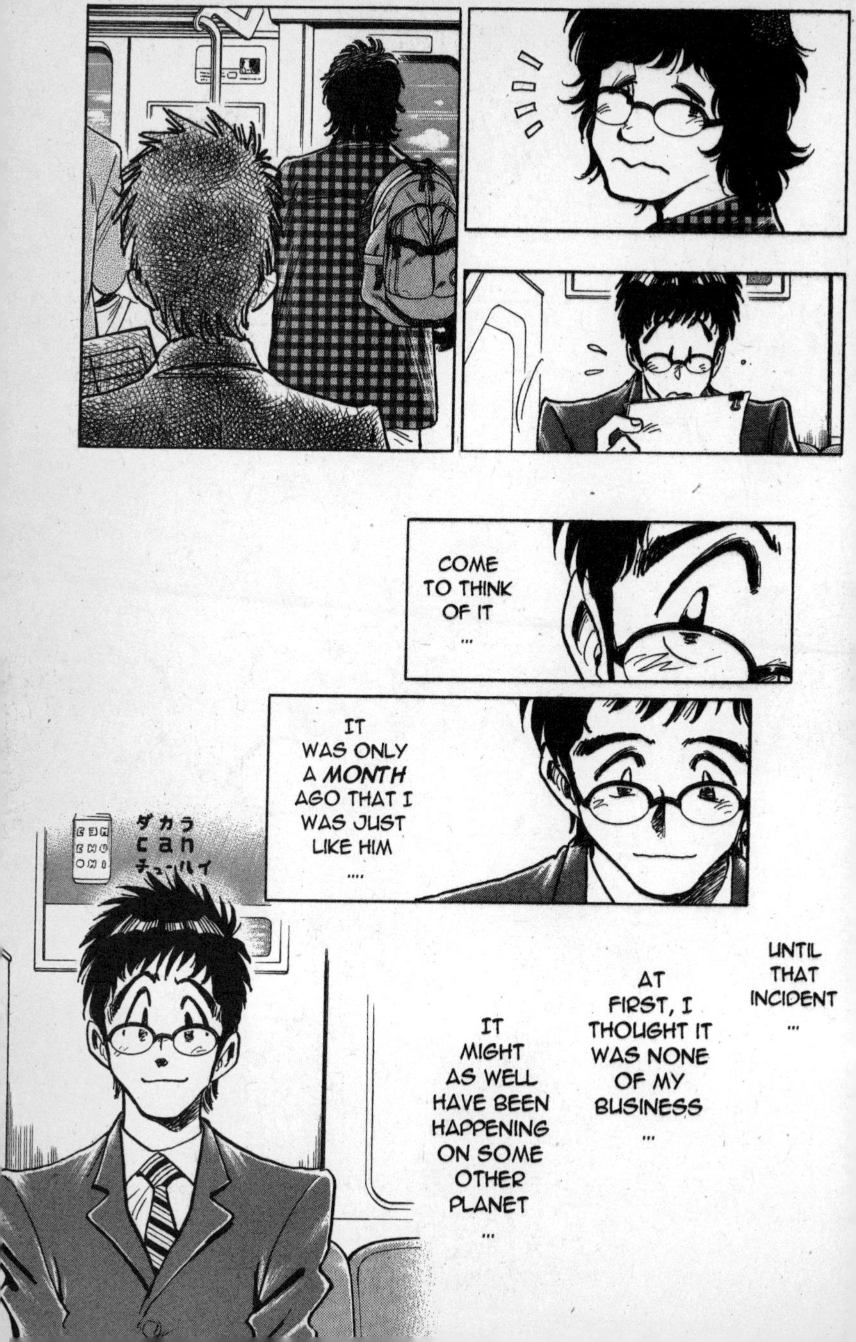
COME TO THINK OF IT ...
IT WAS ONLY A *MONTH* AGO THAT I WAS JUST LIKE HIM ....
UNTIL THAT INCIDENT ...
AT FIRST, I THOUGHT IT WAS NONE OF MY BUSINESS ...
IT MIGHT AS WELL HAVE BEEN HAPPENING ON SOME OTHER PLANET ...
ダカラ can チューハイ

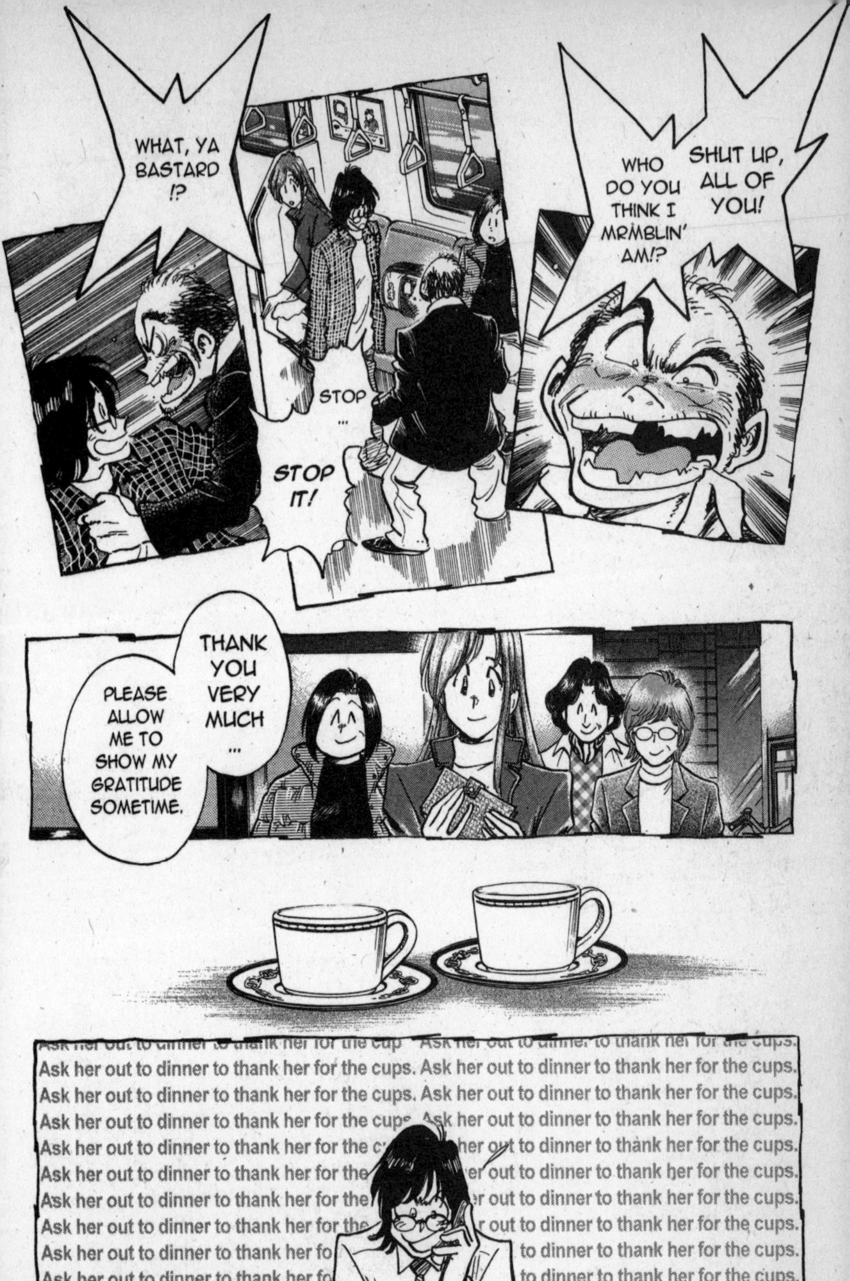
SHUT UP, ALL OF YOU!
WHO DO YOU THINK I MRMBLIN' AM!?
STOP ...
STOP IT!
WHAT, YA BASTARD !?
THANK YOU VERY MUCH ...
PLEASE ALLOW ME TO SHOW MY GRATITUDE SOMETIME.
Ask her out to dinner to thank her for the cups. Ask her out to dinner to thank her for the cups.
Ask her out to dinner to thank her for the cups. Ask her out to dinner to thank her for the cups.
Ask her out to dinner to thank her for the cups. Ask her out to dinner to thank her for the cups.
Ask her out to dinner to thank her for the c her out to dinner to thank her for the cups.
Ask her out to dinner to thank her for the out to dinner to thank her for the cups.
Ask her out to dinner to thank her for the out to dinner to thank her for the cups.
Ask her out to dinner to thank her for the out to dinner to thank her for the cups.
Ask her out to dinner to thank her fo to dinner to thank her for the cups.
Ask her out to dinner to thank her fo to dinner to thank her for the cups.

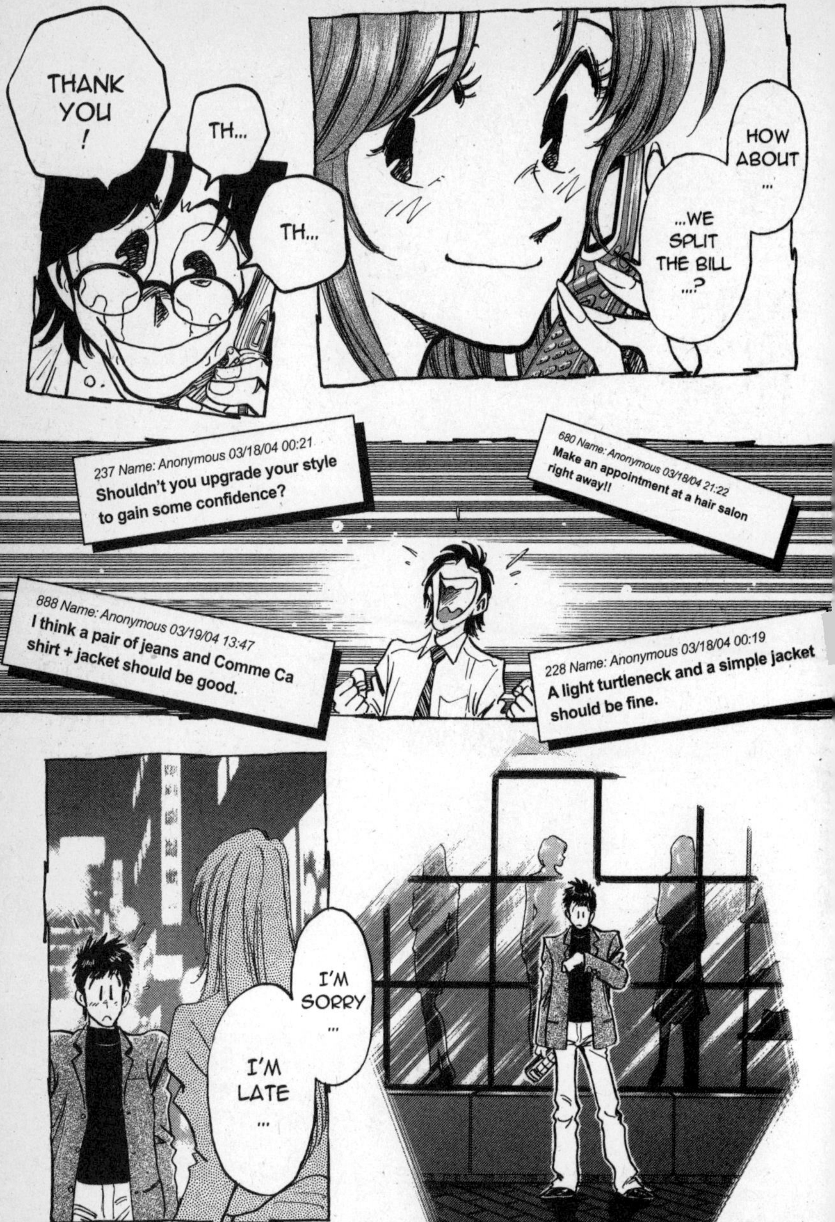
HOW ABOUT ...
...WE SPLIT THE BILL ...?
TH...
TH...
THANK YOU !
680 Name: Anonymous 03/18/04 21:22
Make an appointment at a hair salon right away!!
237 Name: Anonymous 03/18/04 00:21
Shouldn't you upgrade your style to gain some confidence?
228 Name: Anonymous 03/18/04 00:19
A light turtleneck and a simple jacket should be fine.
888 Name: Anonymous 03/19/04 13:47
I think a pair of jeans and Comme Ca shirt + jacket should be good.
I'M SORRY ...
I'M LATE ...

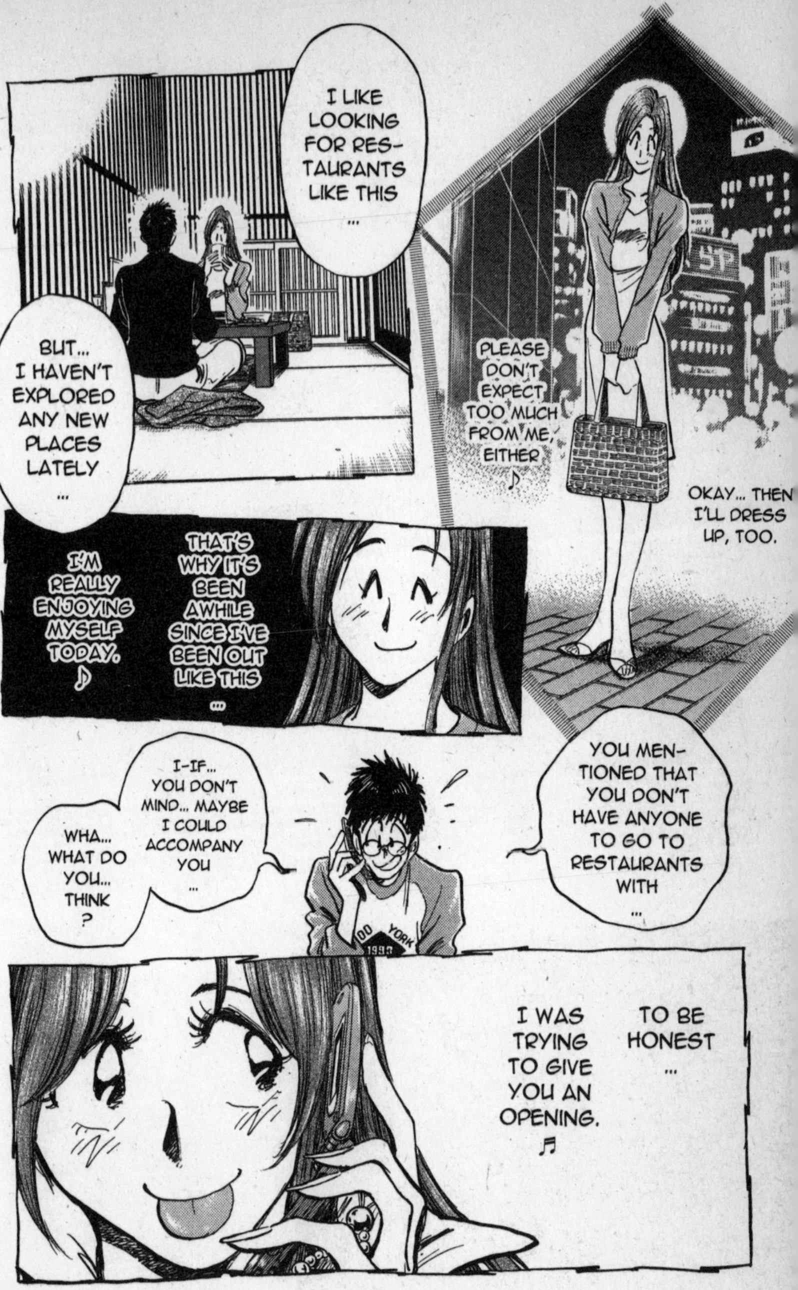
PLEASE DON'T EXPECT TOO MUCH FROM ME, EITHER ♪
OKAY... THEN I'LL DRESS UP, TOO.
I LIKE LOOKING FOR RES-TAURANTS LIKE THIS ...
BUT... I HAVEN'T EXPLORED ANY NEW PLACES LATELY ...
THAT'S WHY IT'S BEEN AWHILE SINCE I'VE BEEN OUT LIKE THIS ...
I'M REALLY ENJOYING MYSELF TODAY. ♪
YOU MEN-TIONED THAT YOU DON'T HAVE ANYONE TO GO TO RESTAURANTS WITH ...
I-IF... YOU DON'T MIND... MAYBE I COULD ACCOMPANY YOU ...
WHA... WHAT DO YOU... THINK ?
TO BE HONEST ...
I WAS TRYING TO GIVE YOU AN OPENING. ♬

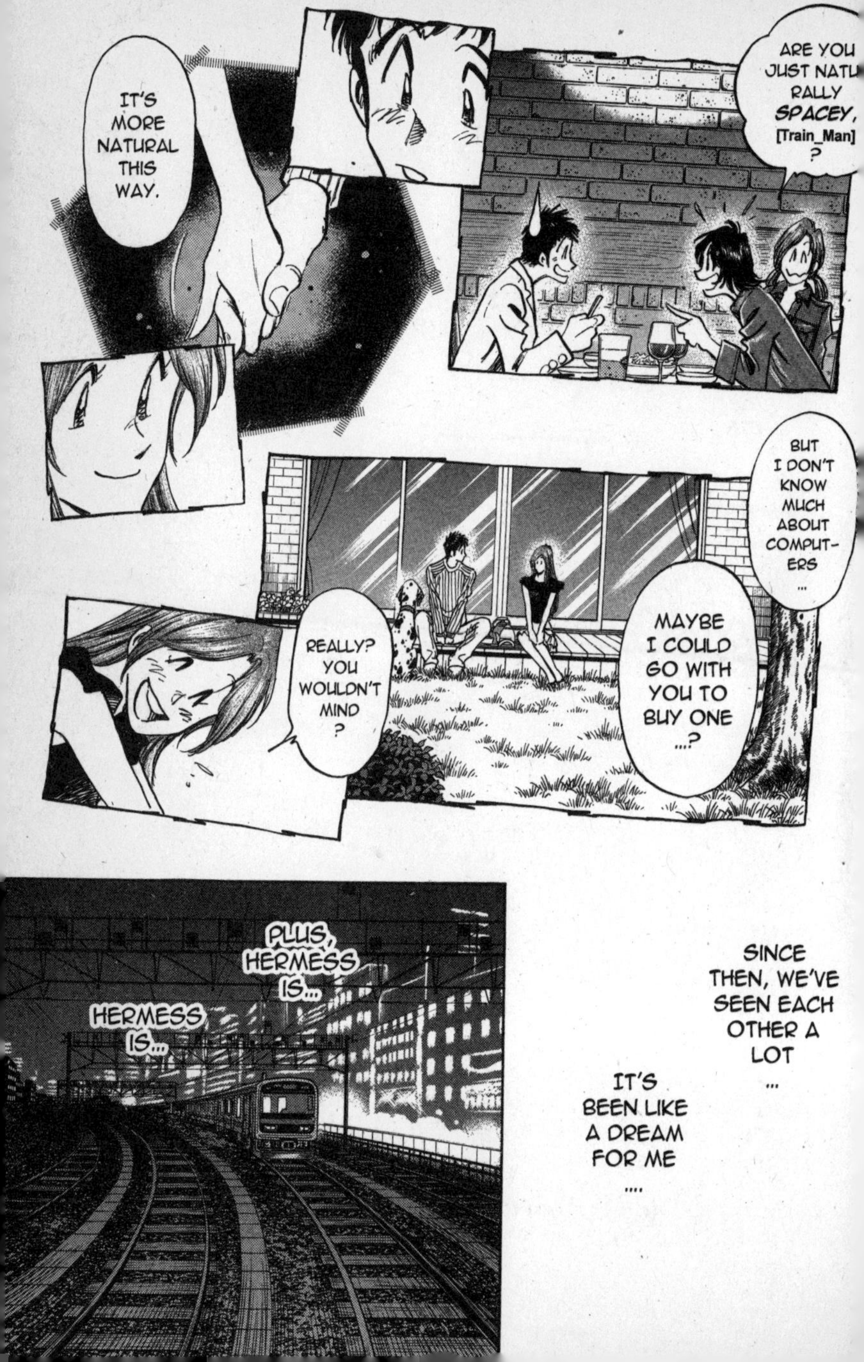
ARE YOU JUST NATURALLY SPACEY, [Train_Man]?
IT'S MORE NATURAL THIS WAY.
BUT I DON'T KNOW MUCH ABOUT COMPUTERS...
MAYBE I COULD GO WITH YOU TO BUY ONE...?
REALLY? YOU WOULDN'T MIND?
SINCE THEN, WE'VE SEEN EACH OTHER A LOT...
IT'S BEEN LIKE A DREAM FOR ME....
PLUS, HERMESS IS...
HERMESS IS...

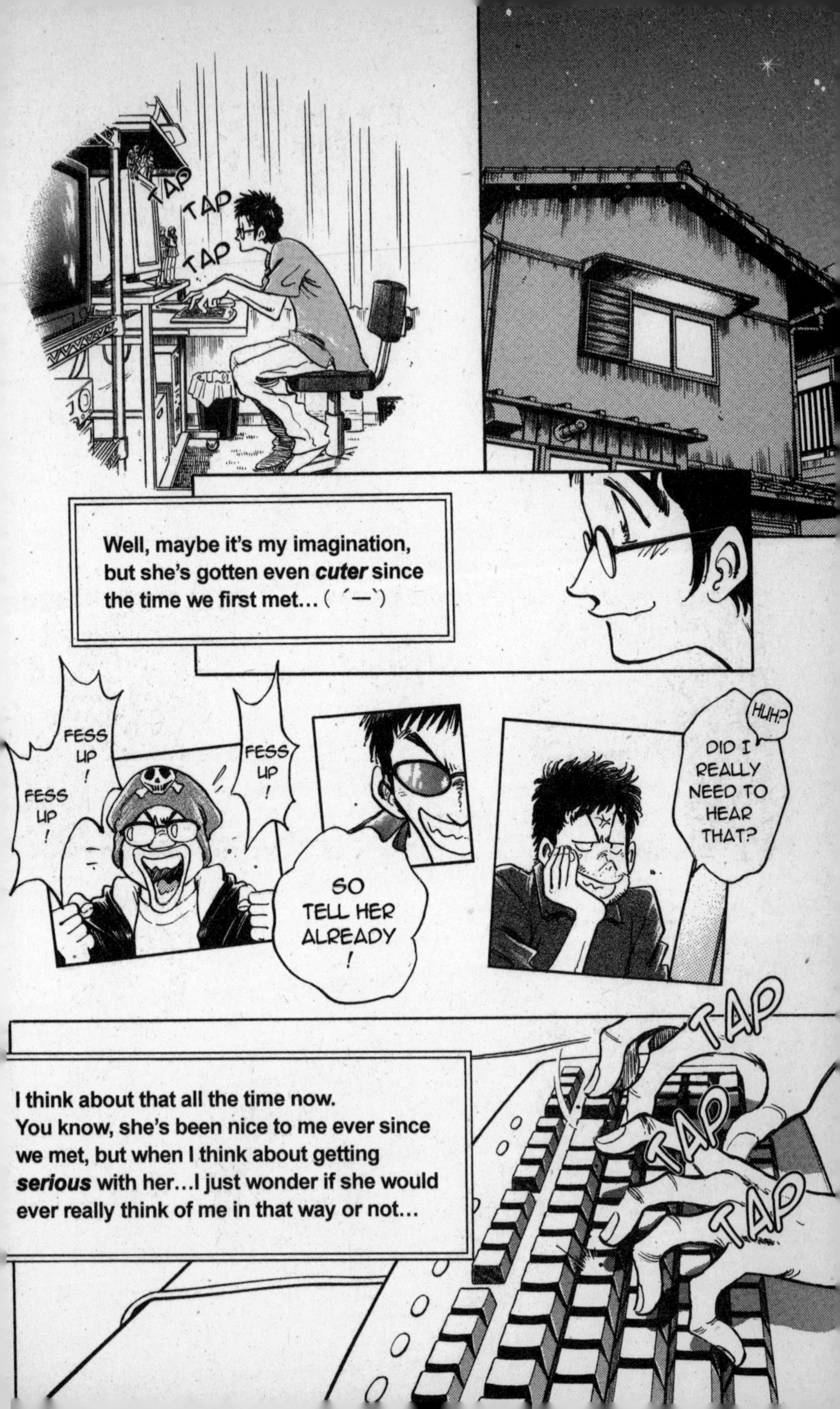
TAP
TAP
TAP
Well, maybe it's my imagination, but she's gotten even *cuter* since the time we first met… (´—`)
HUH?
DID I REALLY NEED TO HEAR THAT?
SO TELL HER ALREADY!
FESS UP!
FESS UP!
FESS UP!
I think about that all the time now.
You know, she's been nice to me ever since we met, but when I think about getting ***serious*** with her…I just wonder if she would ever really think of me in that way or not…
TAP
TAP
TAP

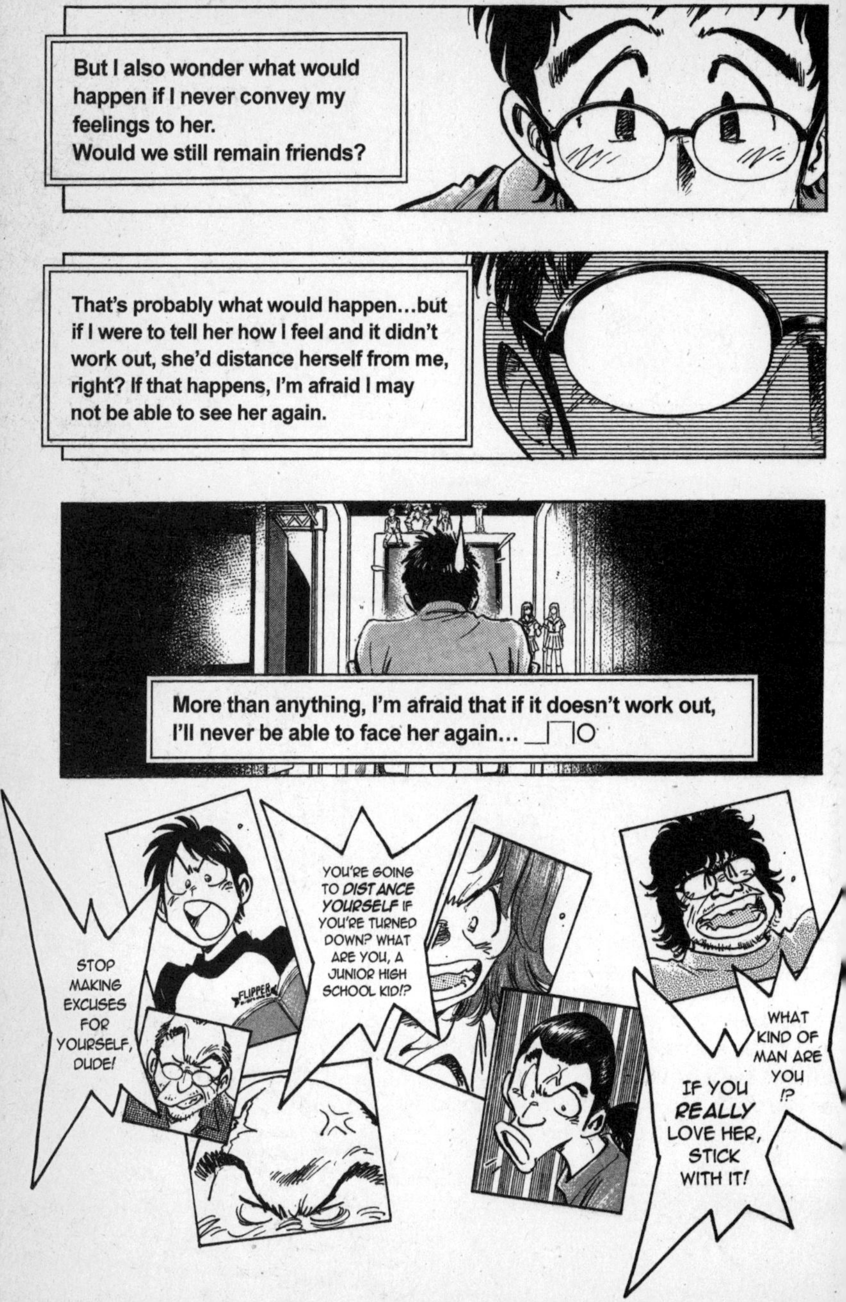
But I also wonder what would happen if I never convey my feelings to her.
Would we still remain friends?
That's probably what would happen…but if I were to tell her how I feel and it didn't work out, she'd distance herself from me, right? If that happens, I'm afraid I may not be able to see her again.
More than anything, I'm afraid that if it doesn't work out, I'll never be able to face her again… _|￣|○
WHAT KIND OF MAN ARE YOU!?
IF YOU REALLY LOVE HER, STICK WITH IT!
YOU'RE GOING TO DISTANCE YOURSELF IF YOU'RE TURNED DOWN? WHAT ARE YOU, A JUNIOR HIGH SCHOOL KID!?
STOP MAKING EXCUSES FOR YOURSELF, DUDE!
FLIPPER

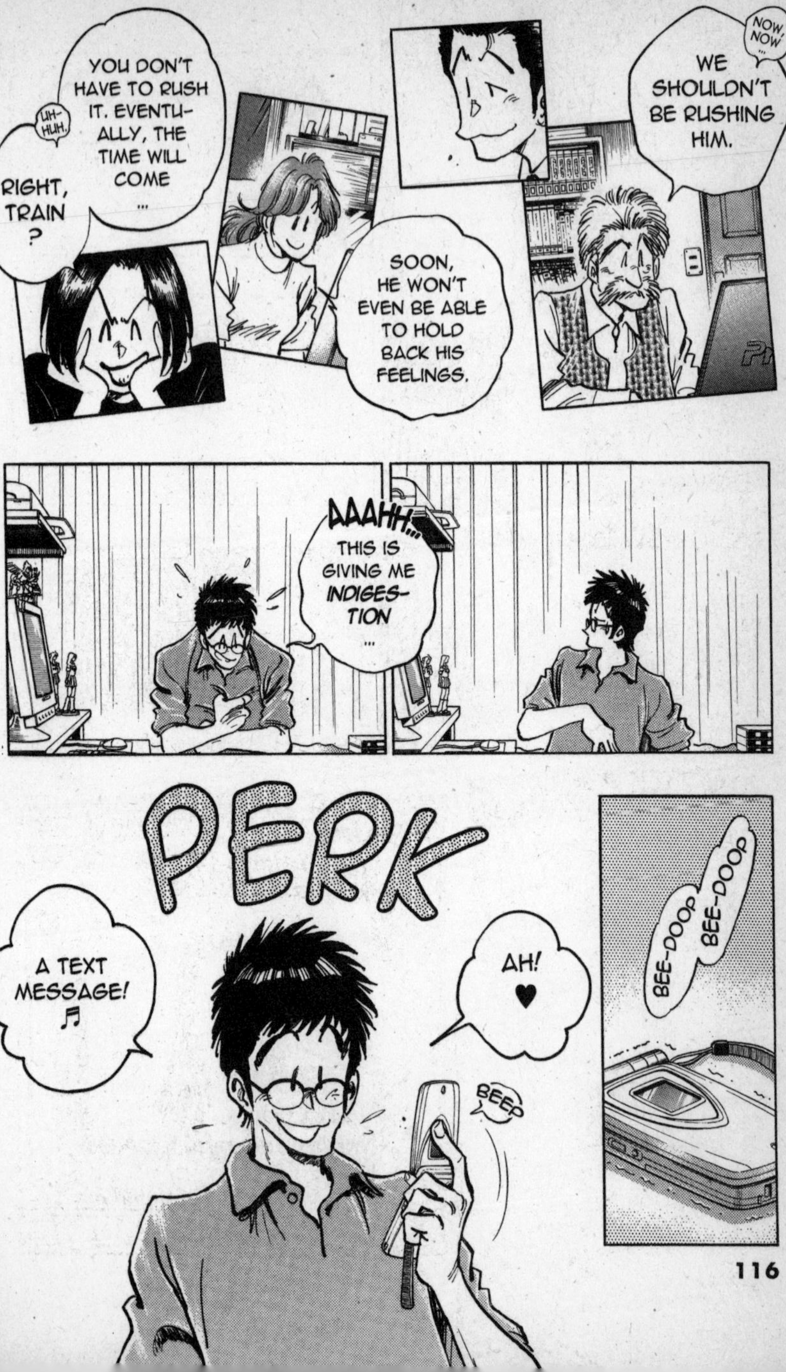
NOW, NOW...
WE SHOULDN'T BE RUSHING HIM.
SOON, HE WON'T EVEN BE ABLE TO HOLD BACK HIS FEELINGS.
YOU DON'T HAVE TO RUSH IT. EVENTU-ALLY, THE TIME WILL COME...
UH-HUH.
RIGHT, TRAIN?
AAAHH... THIS IS GIVING ME INDIGES-TION...
BEE-DOOP BEE-DOOP
PERK
AH! ♥
BEEP
A TEXT MESSAGE! ♬

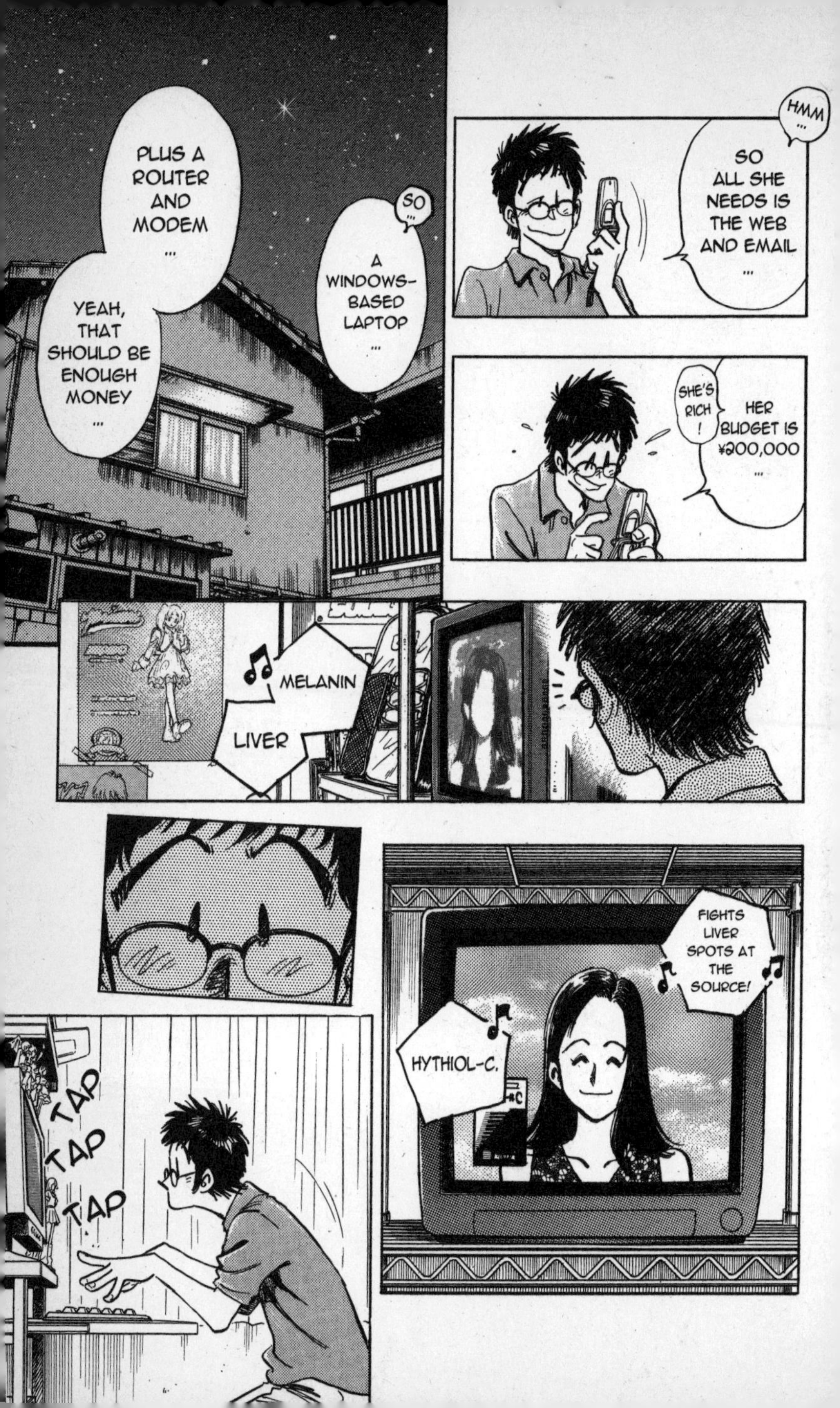
HMM ...
SO ALL SHE NEEDS IS THE WEB AND EMAIL ...
HER BUDGET IS ¥200,000 ...
SHE'S RICH !
SO ...
A WINDOWS-BASED LAPTOP ...
PLUS A ROUTER AND MODEM ...
YEAH, THAT SHOULD BE ENOUGH MONEY ...
MELANIN
LIVER
FIGHTS LIVER SPOTS AT THE SOURCE!
HYTHIOL-C.
TAP
TAP
TAP

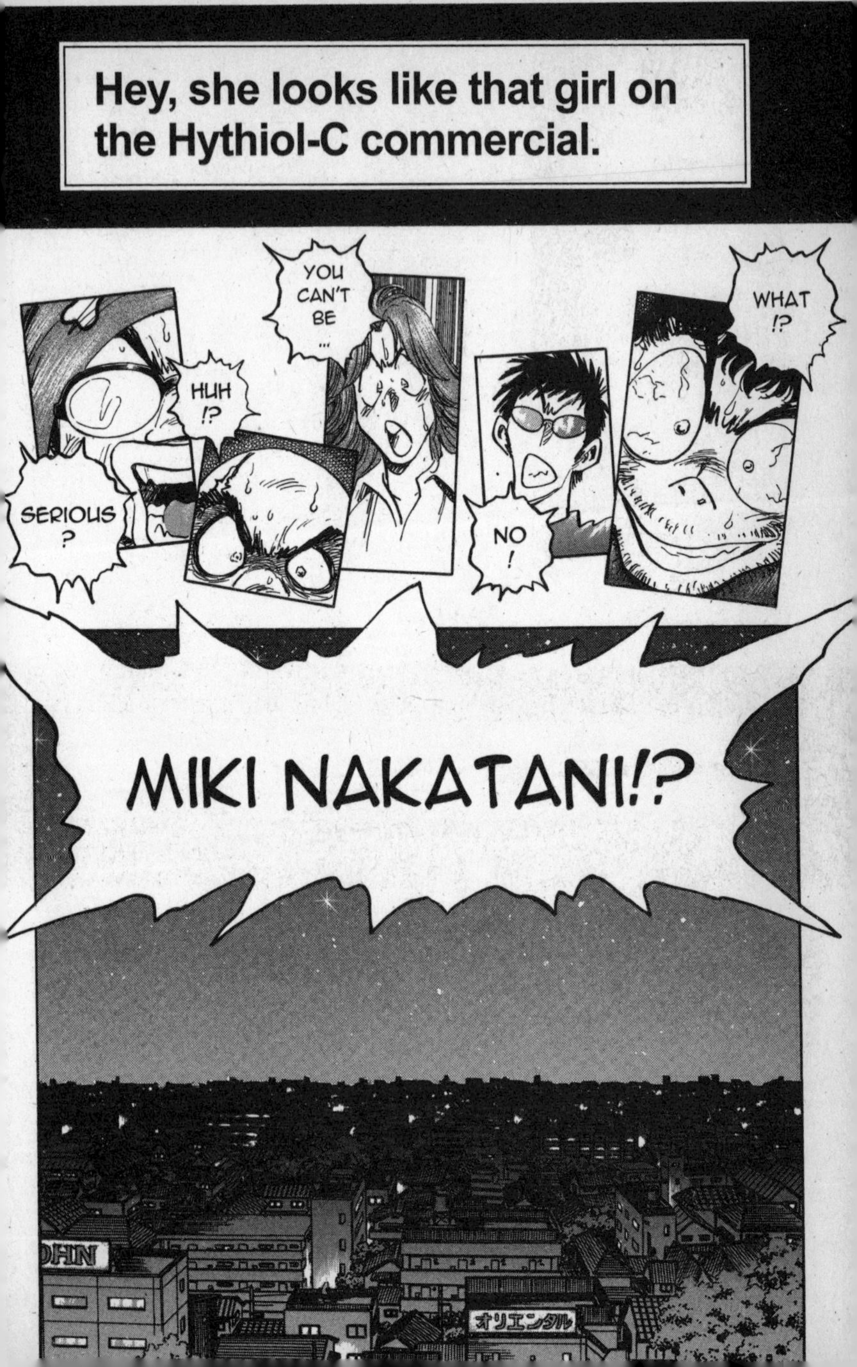
Hey, she looks like that girl on the Hythiol-C commercial.
WHAT !?
NO !
YOU CAN'T BE ...
HUH !?
SERIOUS ?
MIKI NAKATANI!?
オリエンタル

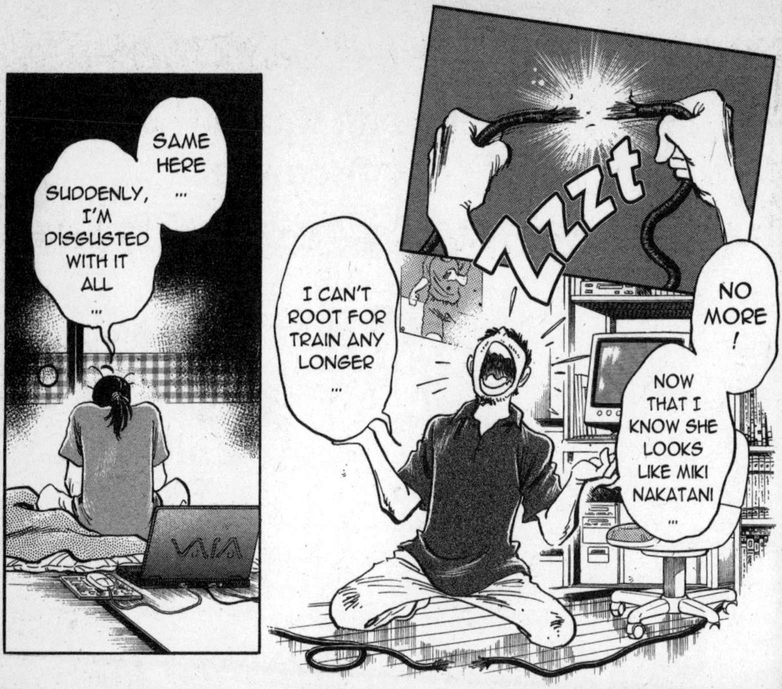
Zzzt
NO MORE!
NOW THAT I KNOW SHE LOOKS LIKE MIKI NAKATANI...
I CAN'T ROOT FOR TRAIN ANY LONGER...
SAME HERE...
SUDDENLY, I'M DISGUSTED WITH IT ALL...

But Hermess is even better looking… (´ー`)

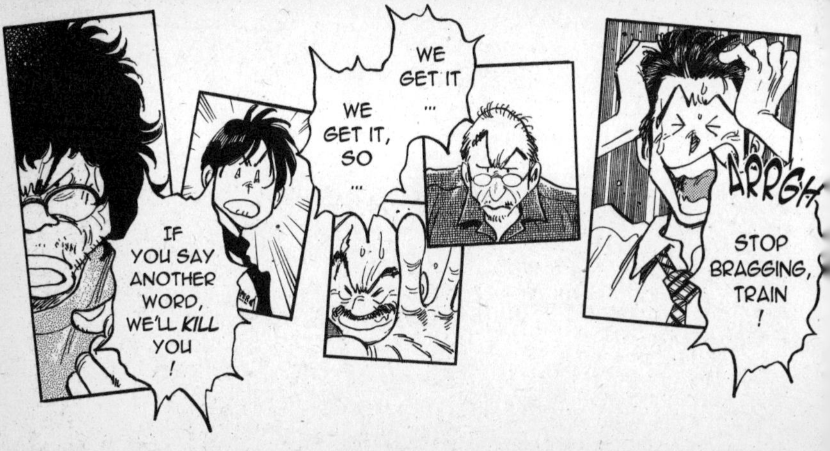
ARRGH
STOP BRAGGING, TRAIN!
WE GET IT...
WE GET IT, SO...
IF YOU SAY ANOTHER WORD, WE'LL *KILL* YOU!

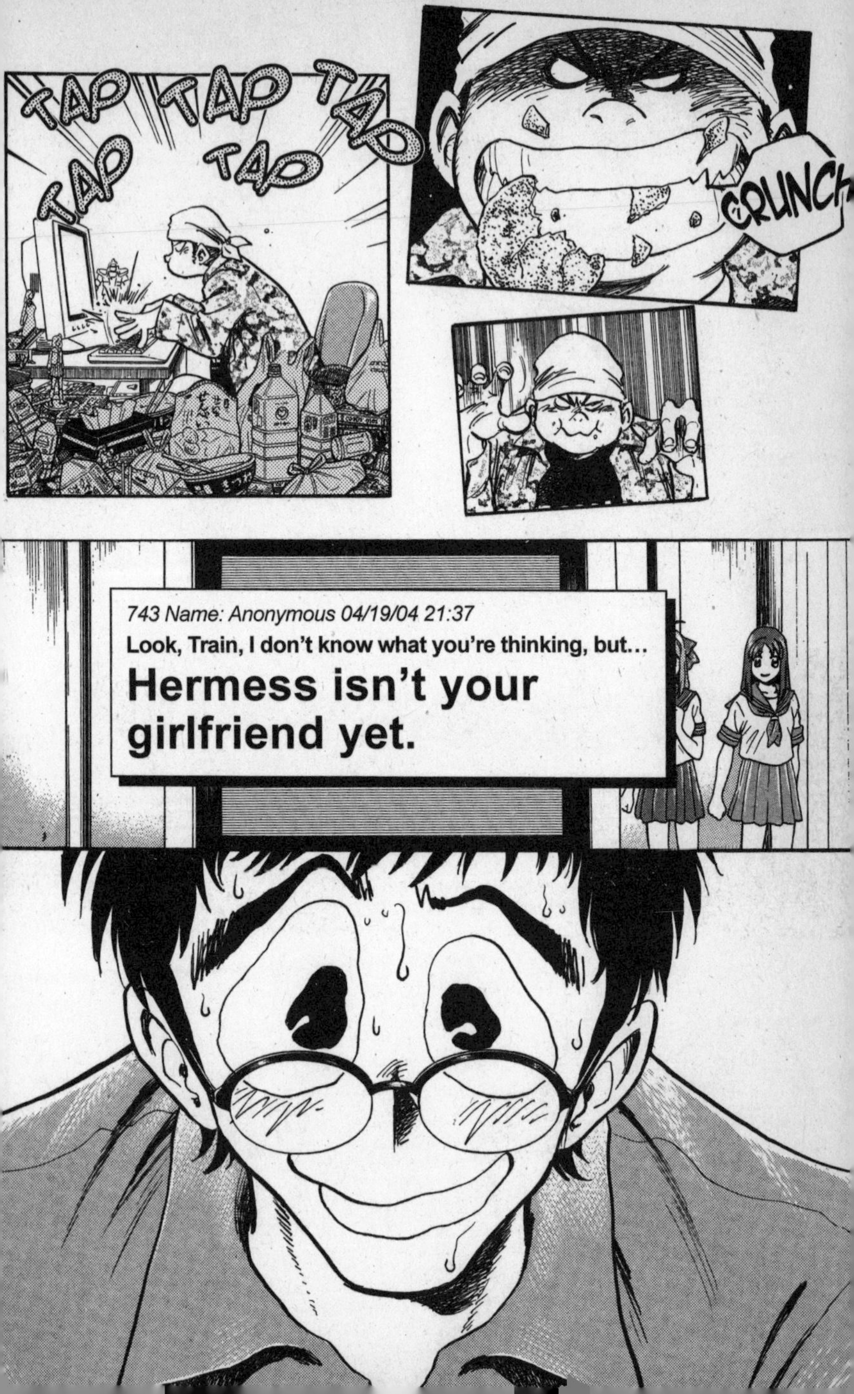
CRUNCH
TAP TAP TAP
TAP TAP
743 Name: Anonymous 04/19/04 21:37
Look, Train, I don't know what you're thinking, but…
Hermess isn't your girlfriend yet.

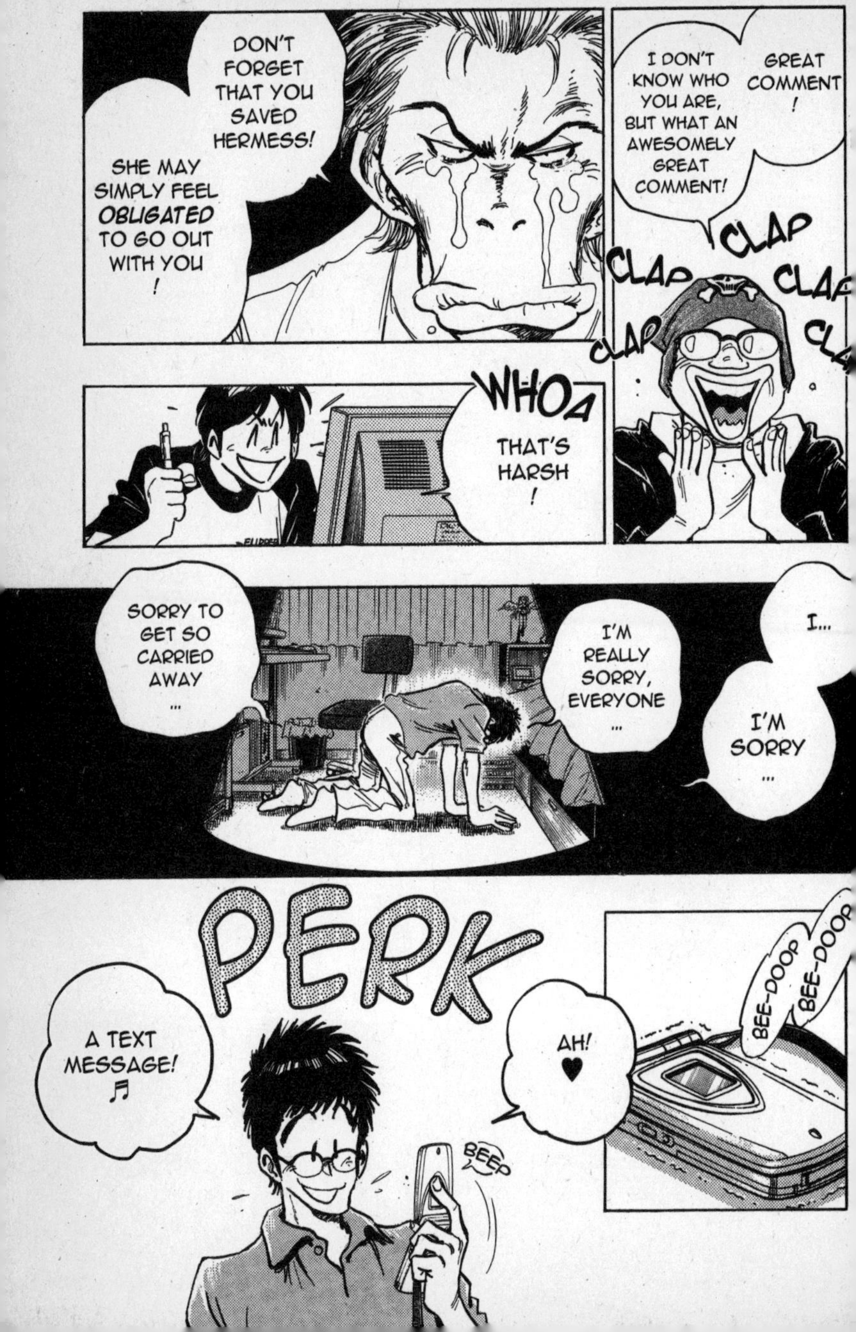
GREAT COMMENT!
I DON'T KNOW WHO YOU ARE, BUT WHAT AN AWESOMELY GREAT COMMENT!
CLAP
CLAP
CLAP
CLAP
DON'T FORGET THAT YOU SAVED HERMESS!
SHE MAY SIMPLY FEEL OBLIGATED TO GO OUT WITH YOU!
WHOA
THAT'S HARSH!
I...
I'M SORRY...
I'M REALLY SORRY, EVERYONE...
SORRY TO GET SO CARRIED AWAY...
BEE-DOOP
BEE-DOOP
PERK
AH! ♥
A TEXT MESSAGE! ♬
BEEP

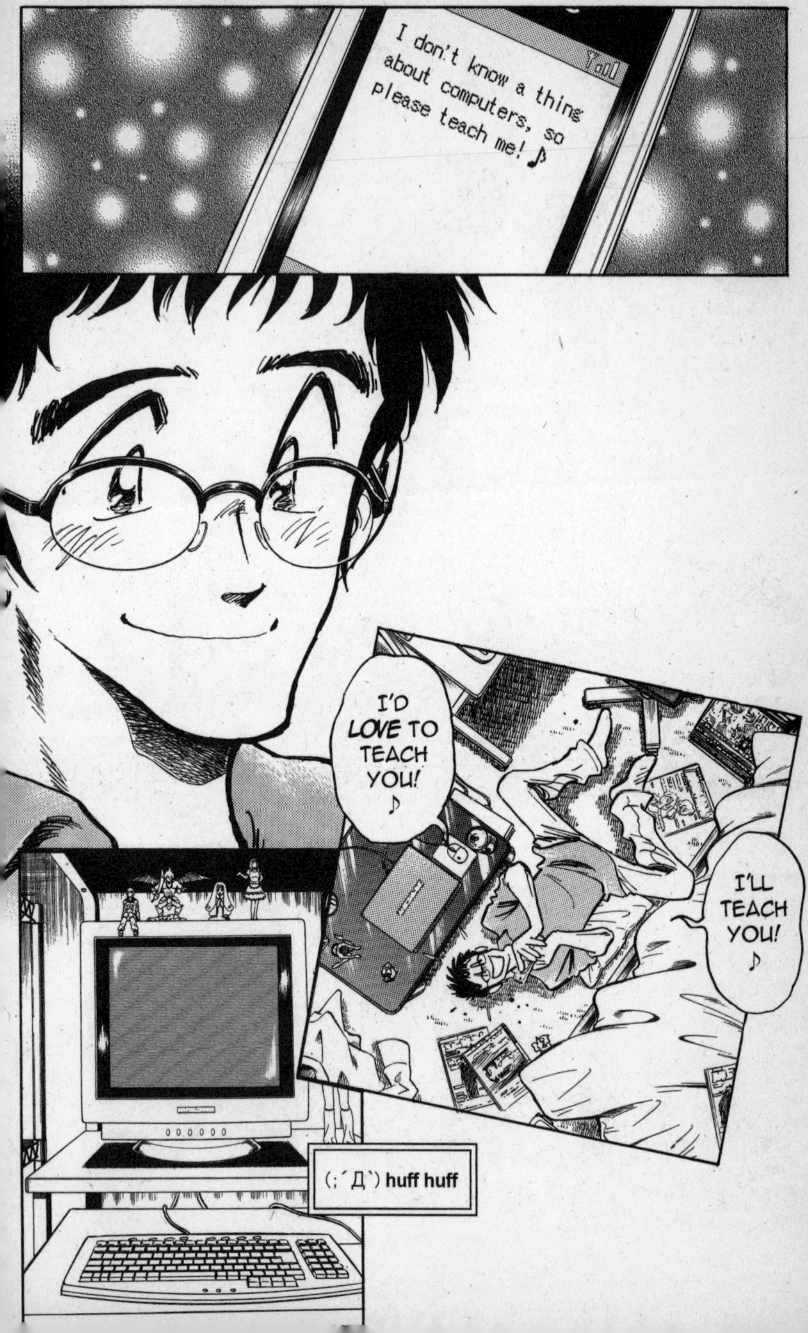
I don't know a thing about computers, so please teach me! ♪
I'D LOVE TO TEACH YOU! ♪
I'LL TEACH YOU! ♪
(;´Д`) huff huff

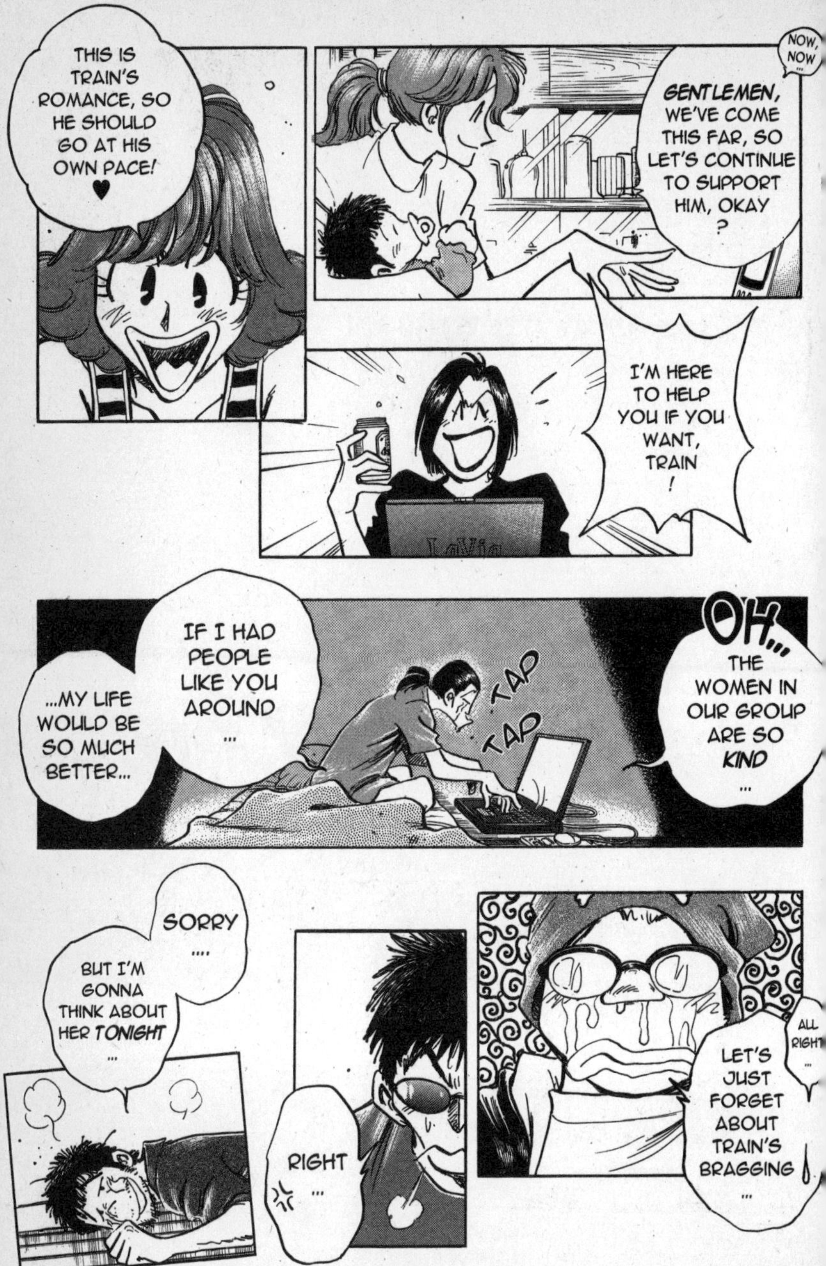
NOW, NOW ...
GENTLEMEN, WE'VE COME THIS FAR, SO LET'S CONTINUE TO SUPPORT HIM, OKAY?
I'M HERE TO HELP YOU IF YOU WANT, TRAIN!
THIS IS TRAIN'S ROMANCE, SO HE SHOULD GO AT HIS OWN PACE! ♥
OH... THE WOMEN IN OUR GROUP ARE SO KIND ...
TAP TAP
IF I HAD PEOPLE LIKE YOU AROUND ...
...MY LIFE WOULD BE SO MUCH BETTER...
ALL RIGHT ...
LET'S JUST FORGET ABOUT TRAIN'S BRAGGING ...
RIGHT ...
SORRY ....
BUT I'M GONNA THINK ABOUT HER TONIGHT ...

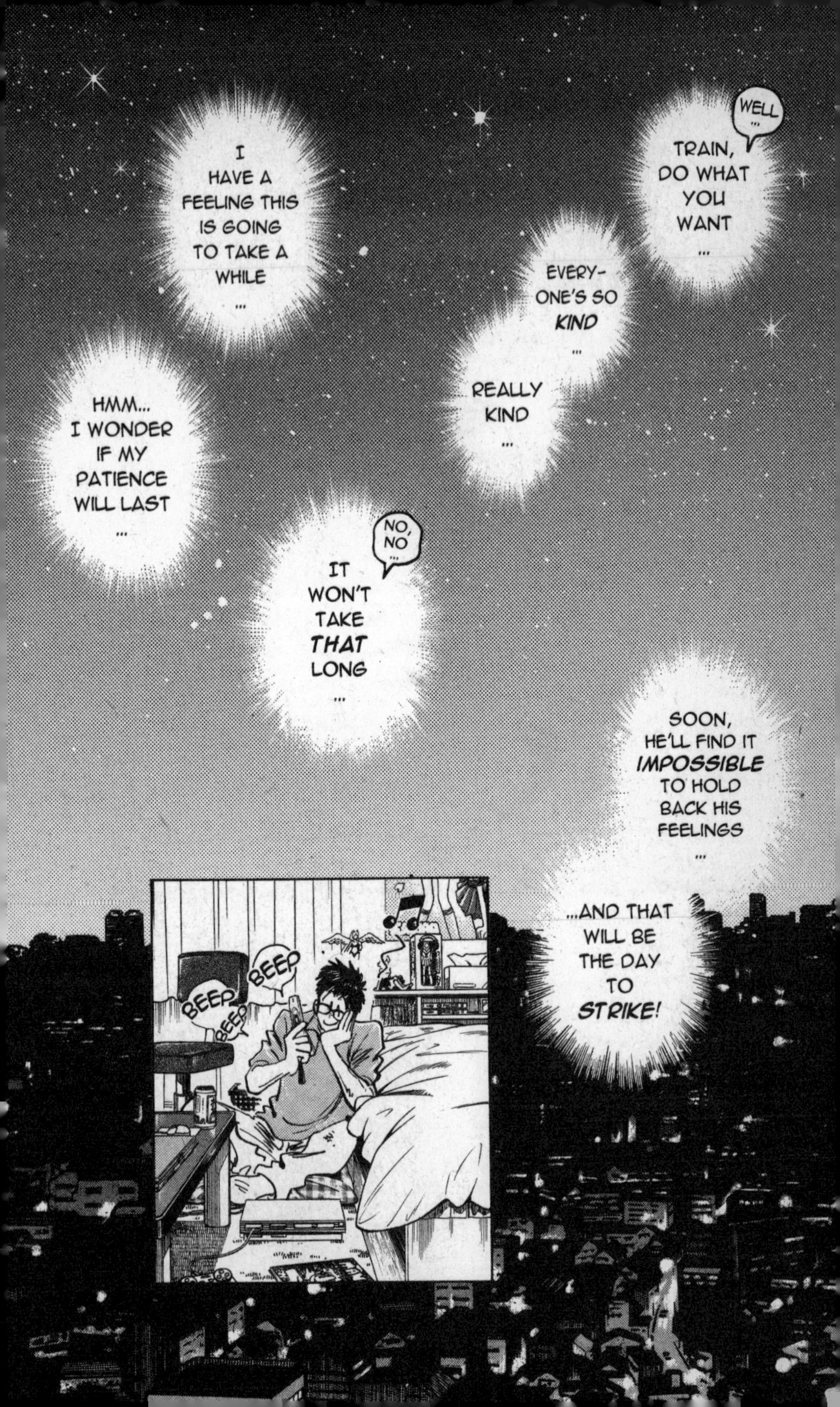
WELL ...
TRAIN, DO WHAT YOU WANT ...
EVERYONE'S SO *KIND* ...
REALLY KIND ...
I HAVE A FEELING THIS IS GOING TO TAKE A WHILE ...
HMM... I WONDER IF MY PATIENCE WILL LAST ...
NO, NO ...
IT WON'T TAKE *THAT* LONG ...
SOON, HE'LL FIND IT *IMPOSSIBLE* TO HOLD BACK HIS FEELINGS ...
...AND THAT WILL BE THE DAY TO *STRIKE!*
BEEP
BEEP
BEEP

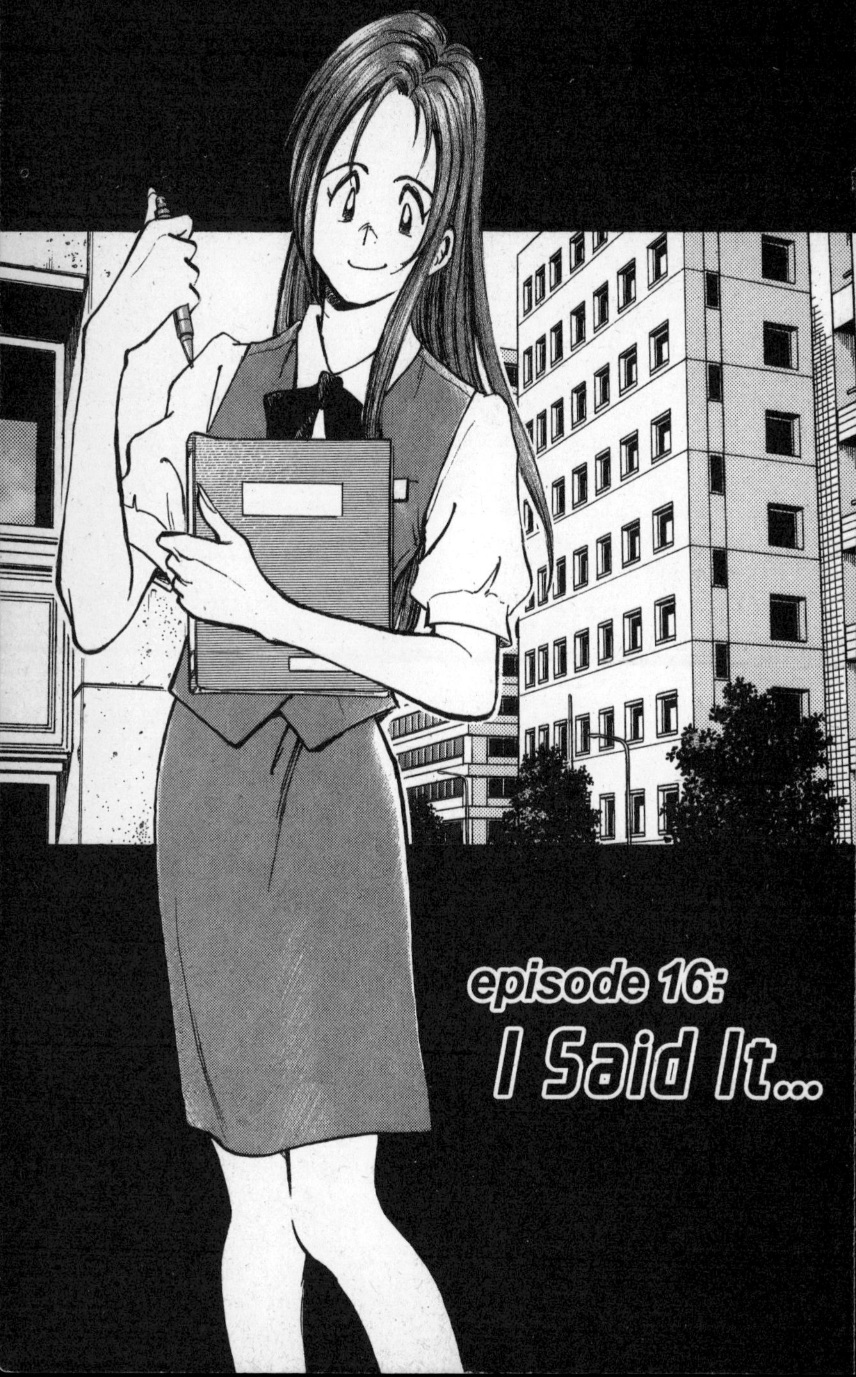
episode 16:
I Said It...

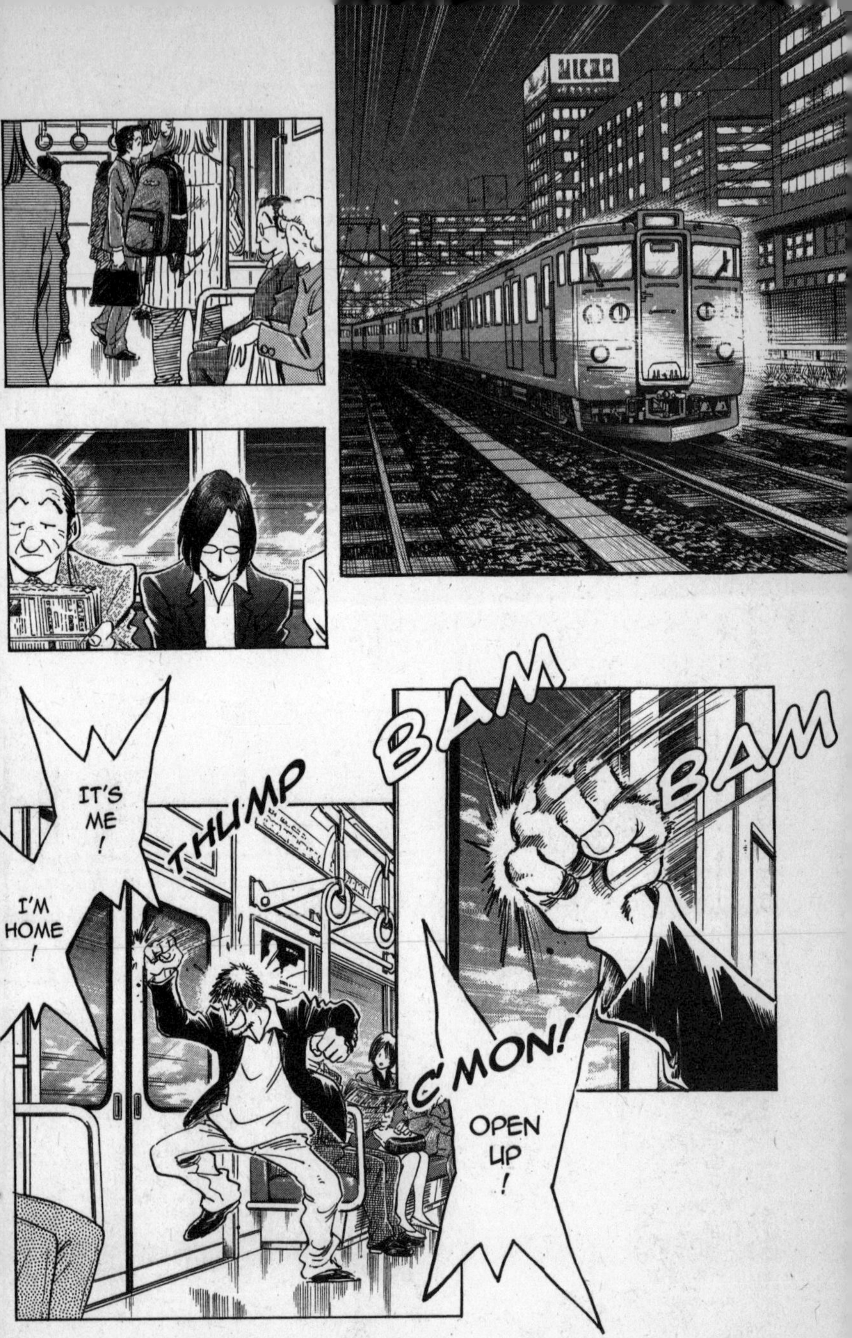
BAM
BAM
C'MON!
OPEN UP!
THUMP
IT'S ME!
I'M HOME!

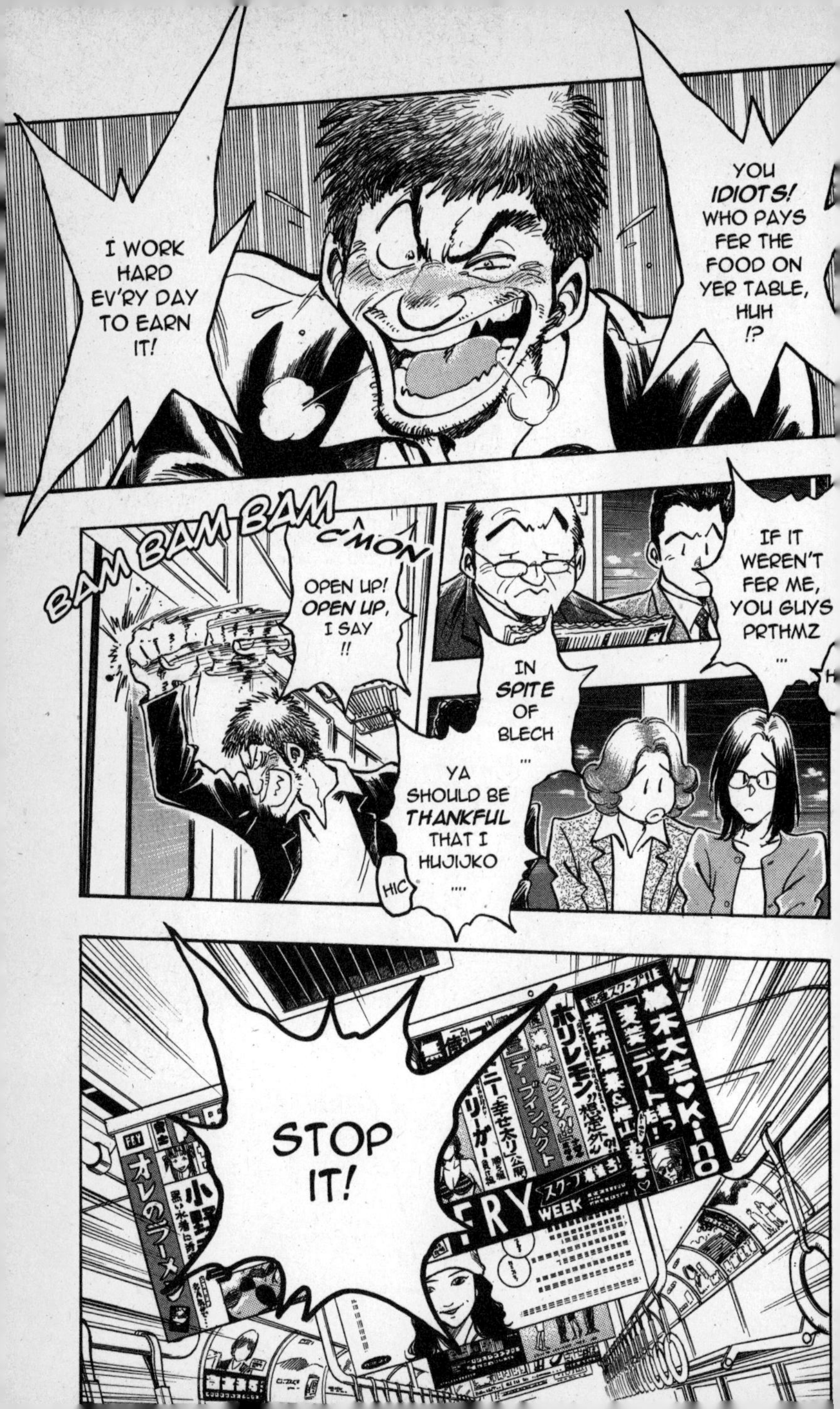

YOU IDIOTS! WHO PAYS FER THE FOOD ON YER TABLE, HUH !?
I WORK HARD EV'RY DAY TO EARN IT!
IF IT WEREN'T FER ME, YOU GUYS PRTHMZ ...
IN SPITE OF BLECH ...
YA SHOULD BE THANKFUL THAT I HUJIJKO ....
HIC
C'MON
OPEN UP! OPEN UP, I SAY !!
BAM BAM BAM
STOP IT!
FRY
WEEK

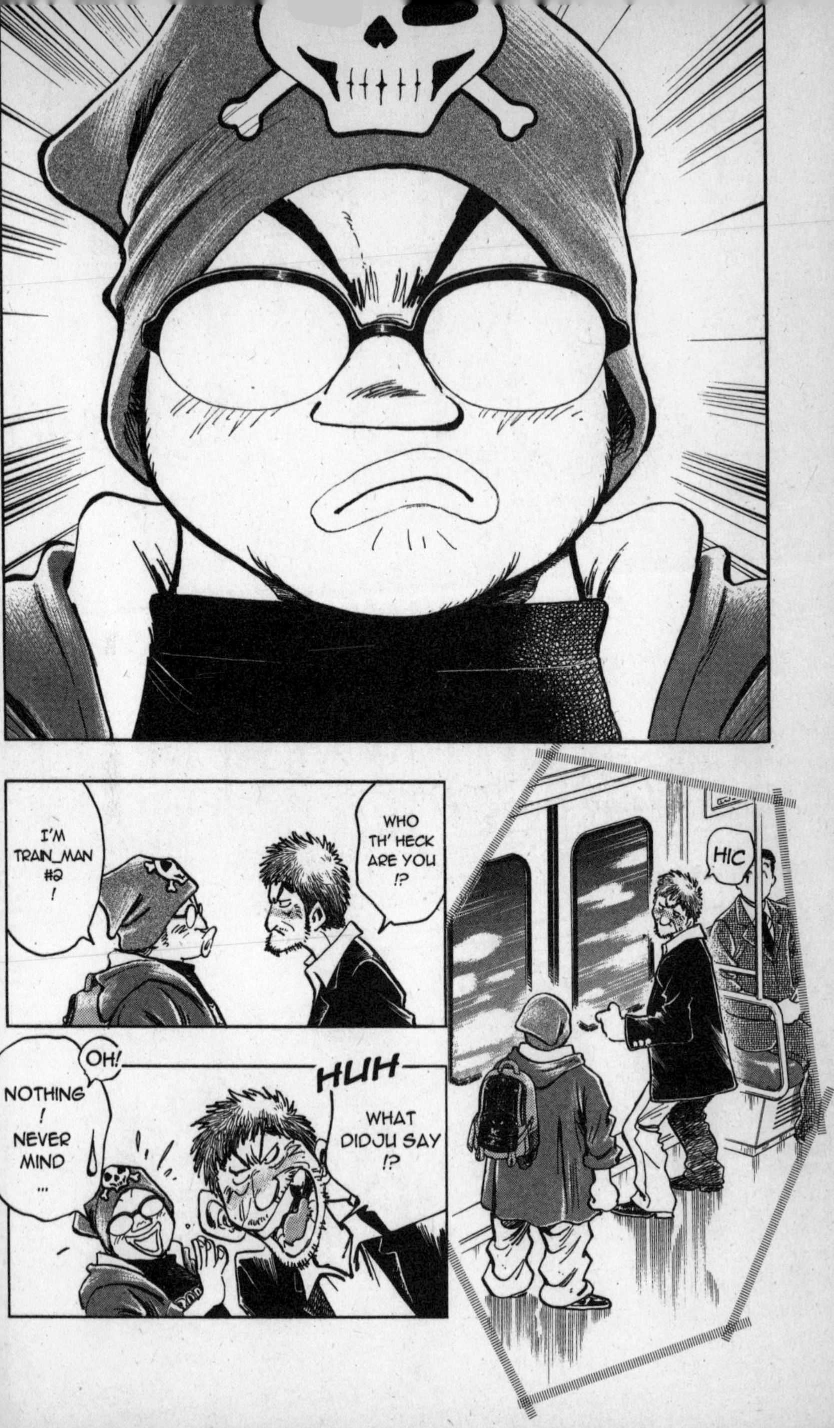
HIC
WHO TH' HECK ARE YOU !?
I'M TRAIN_MAN #2 !
HUH
WHAT DIDJU SAY !?
OH!
NOTHING ! NEVER MIND ...

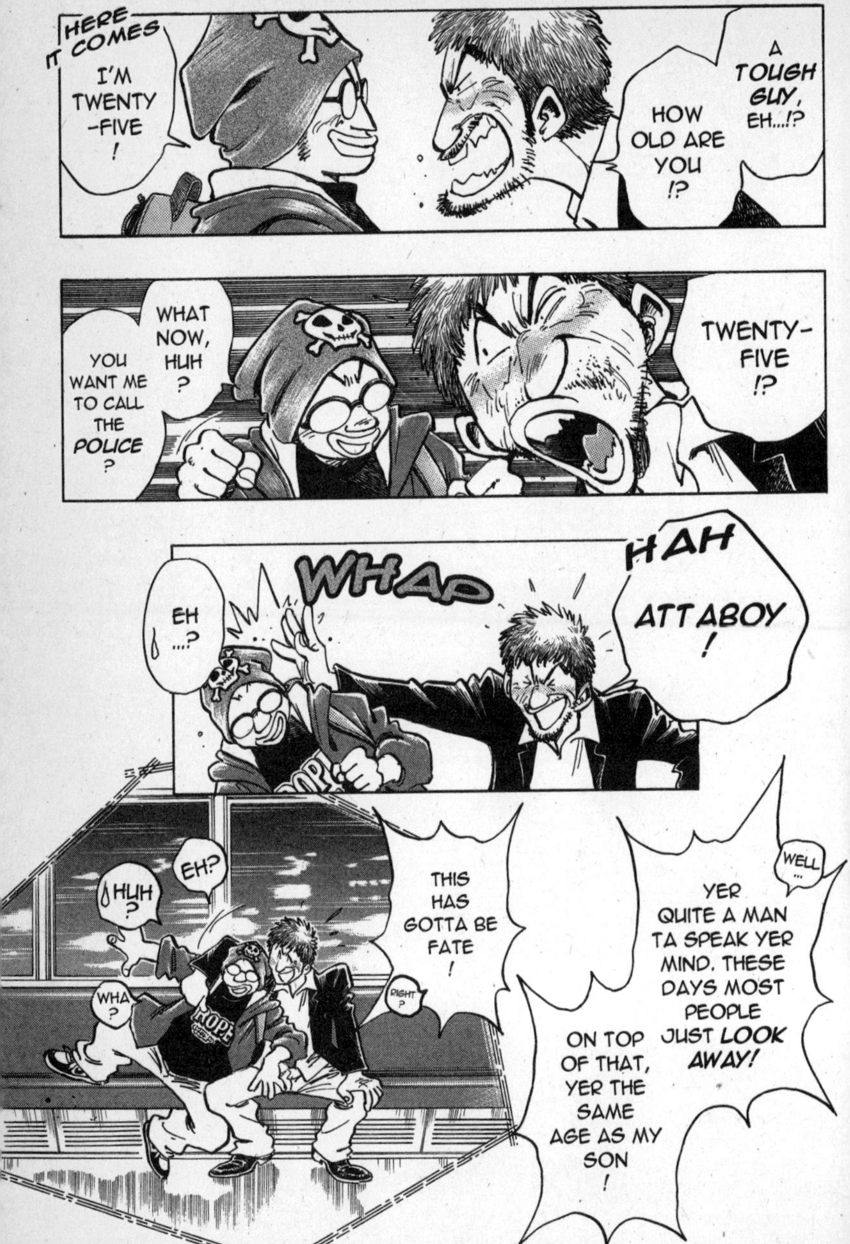
A TOUGH GUY, EH...!?
HOW OLD ARE YOU !?
HERE IT COMES
I'M TWENTY-FIVE !
TWENTY-FIVE !?
WHAT NOW, HUH ?
YOU WANT ME TO CALL THE POLICE ?
HAH
ATTABOY !
WHAP
EH ...?
WELL ...
YER QUITE A MAN TA SPEAK YER MIND. THESE DAYS MOST PEOPLE JUST LOOK AWAY!
ON TOP OF THAT, YER THE SAME AGE AS MY SON !
THIS HAS GOTTA BE FATE !
RIGHT ?
EH?
HUH ?
WHA ?

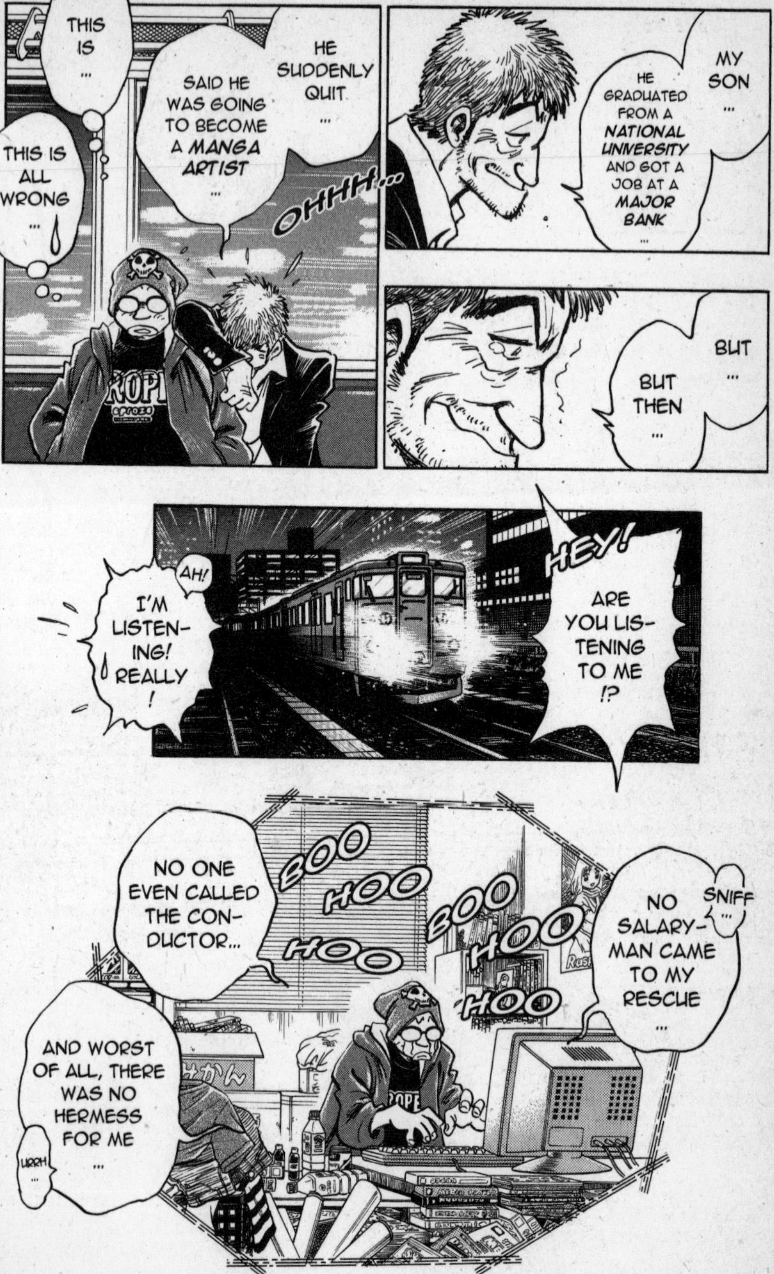
MY SON ...
HE GRADUATED FROM A NATIONAL UNIVERSITY AND GOT A JOB AT A MAJOR BANK ...
BUT ...
BUT THEN ...
HE SUDDENLY QUIT ...
SAID HE WAS GOING TO BECOME A MANGA ARTIST ...
OHHHH...
THIS IS ...
THIS IS ALL WRONG ...
HEY!
ARE YOU LIS-TENING TO ME !?
AH!
I'M LISTEN-ING! REALLY !
NO SALARY-MAN CAME TO MY RESCUE ...
SNIFF ...
BOO HOO
BOO HOO
HOO HOO
NO ONE EVEN CALLED THE CON-DUCTOR...
AND WORST OF ALL, THERE WAS NO HERMESS FOR ME ...
URRH ...

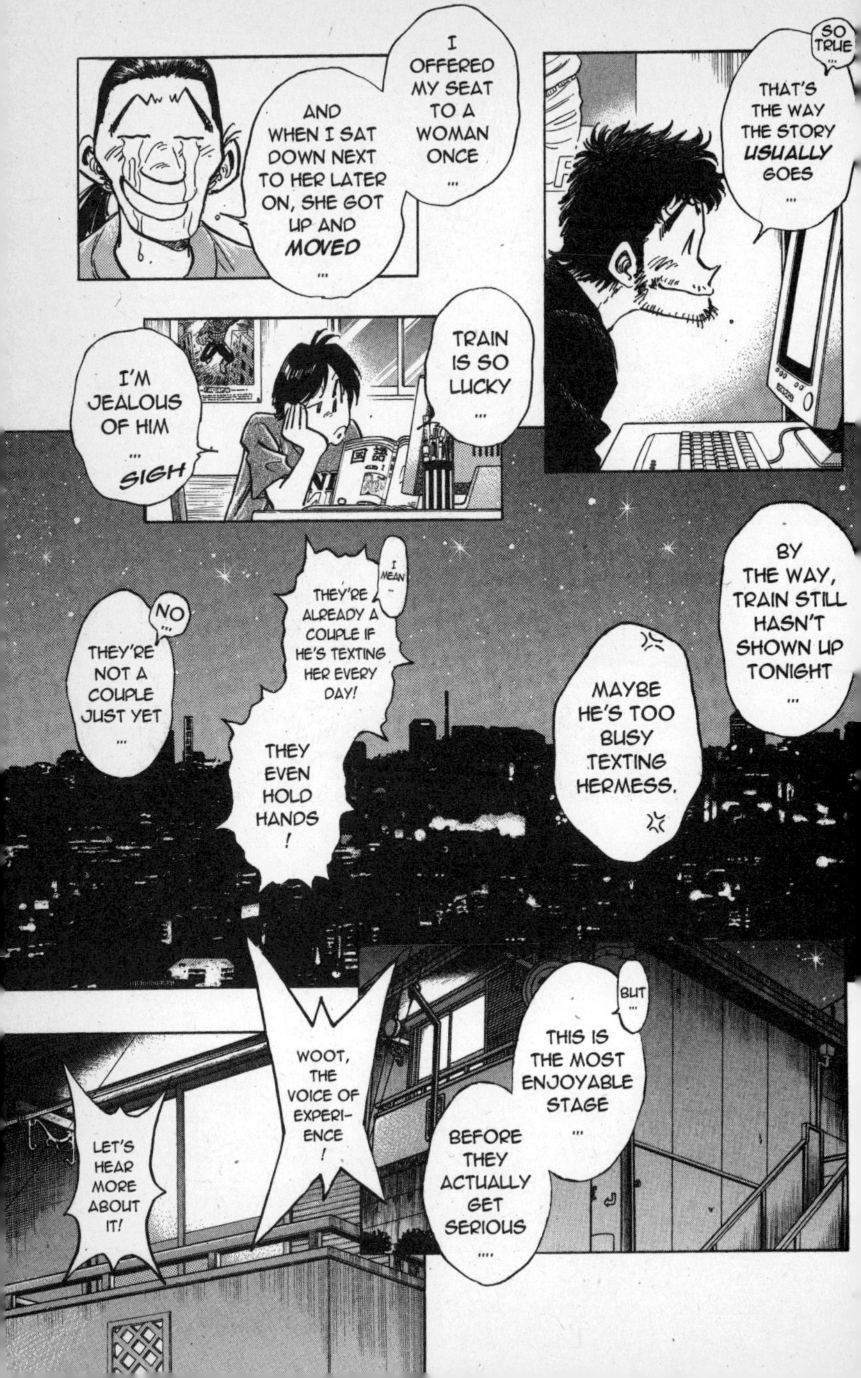
SO TRUE ...
THAT'S THE WAY THE STORY USUALLY GOES ...
I OFFERED MY SEAT TO A WOMAN ONCE ...
AND WHEN I SAT DOWN NEXT TO HER LATER ON, SHE GOT UP AND MOVED ...
TRAIN IS SO LUCKY ...
I'M JEALOUS OF HIM ... SIGH
BY THE WAY, TRAIN STILL HASN'T SHOWN UP TONIGHT ...
MAYBE HE'S TOO BUSY TEXTING HERMESS.
I MEAN ...
THEY'RE ALREADY A COUPLE IF HE'S TEXTING HER EVERY DAY!
THEY EVEN HOLD HANDS!
NO ...
THEY'RE NOT A COUPLE JUST YET ...
BUT ...
THIS IS THE MOST ENJOYABLE STAGE ...
BEFORE THEY ACTUALLY GET SERIOUS ....
WOOT, THE VOICE OF EXPERIENCE!
LET'S HEAR MORE ABOUT IT!

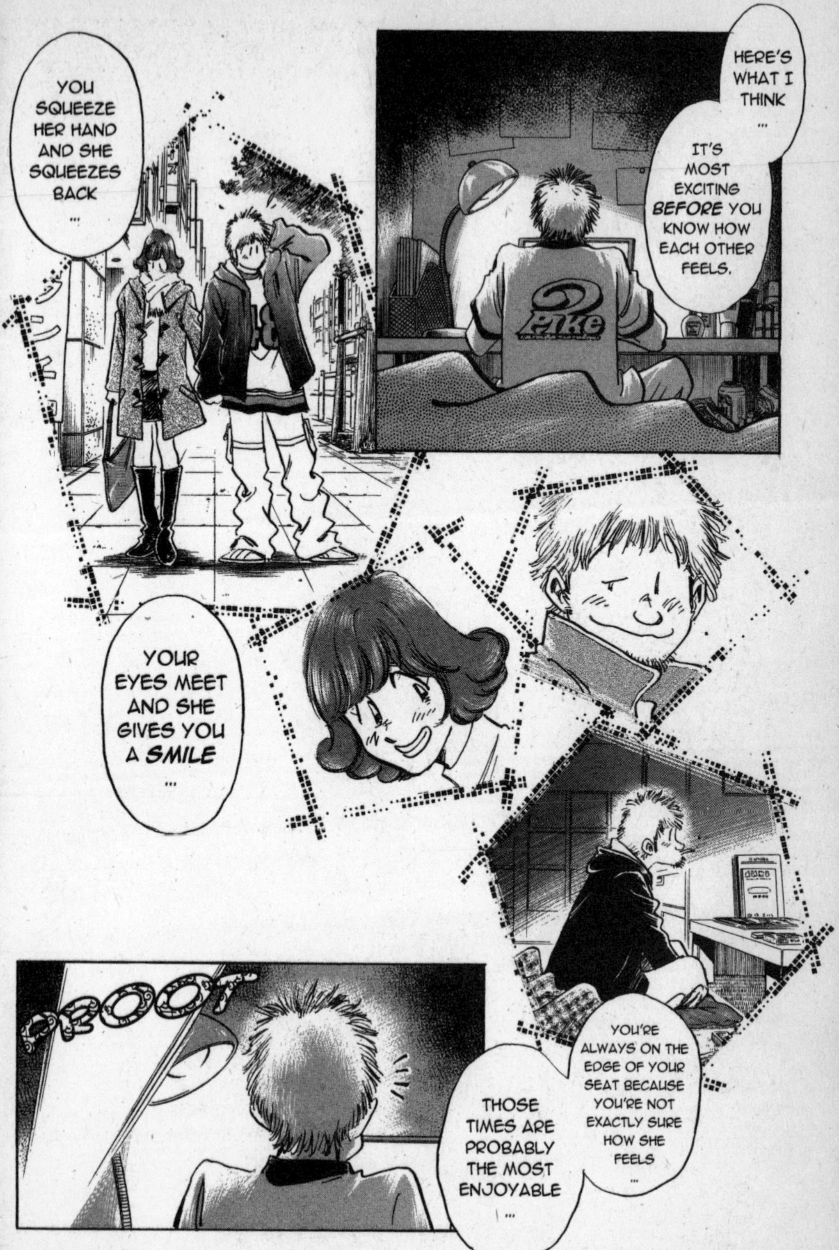
HERE'S WHAT I THINK ...
IT'S MOST EXCITING BEFORE YOU KNOW HOW EACH OTHER FEELS.
YOU SQUEEZE HER HAND AND SHE SQUEEZES BACK ...
YOUR EYES MEET AND SHE GIVES YOU A SMILE ...
YOU'RE ALWAYS ON THE EDGE OF YOUR SEAT BECAUSE YOU'RE NOT EXACTLY SURE HOW SHE FEELS ...
THOSE TIMES ARE PROBABLY THE MOST ENJOYABLE ...
PROOT

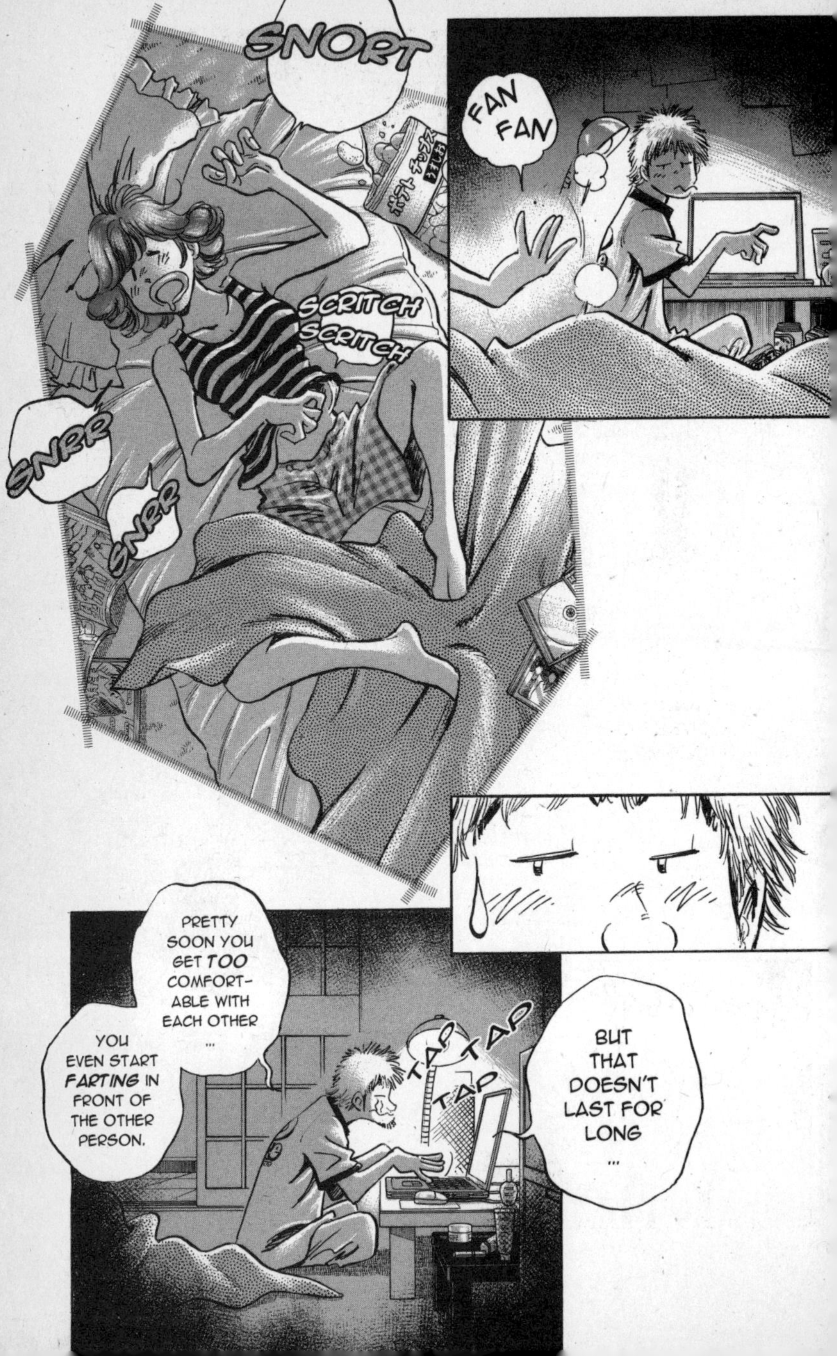
FAN FAN
SNORT
SCRITCH SCRITCH
SNRR
SNRR
BUT THAT DOESN'T LAST FOR LONG ...
PRETTY SOON YOU GET *TOO* COMFORT-ABLE WITH EACH OTHER ...
YOU EVEN START *FARTING* IN FRONT OF THE OTHER PERSON.
TAP TAP
TAP

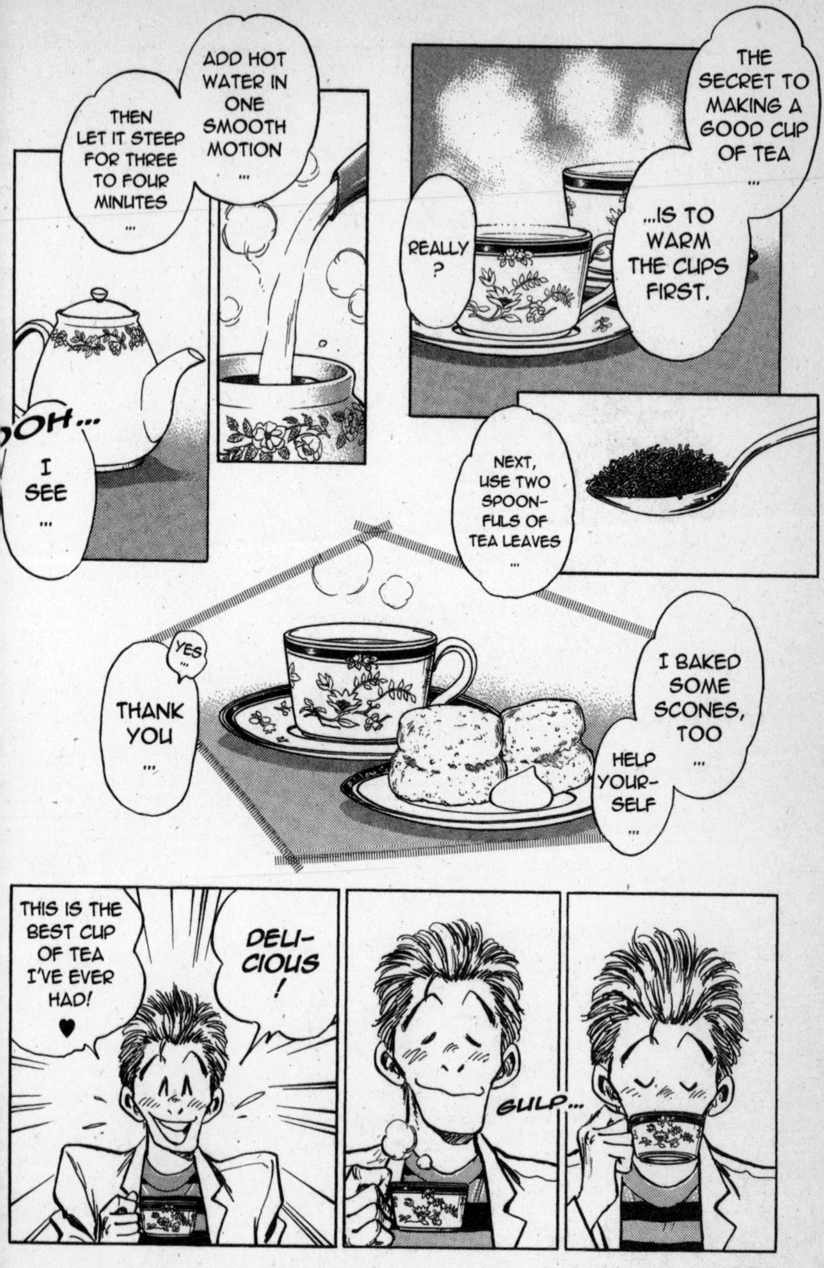
THE SECRET TO MAKING A GOOD CUP OF TEA ...
...IS TO WARM THE CUPS FIRST.
REALLY ?
NEXT, USE TWO SPOON-FULS OF TEA LEAVES ...
ADD HOT WATER IN ONE SMOOTH MOTION ...
THEN LET IT STEEP FOR THREE TO FOUR MINUTES ...
OOH...
I SEE ...
I BAKED SOME SCONES, TOO ...
HELP YOUR-SELF ...
YES ...
THANK YOU ...
GULP...
DELI-CIOUS !
THIS IS THE BEST CUP OF TEA I'VE EVER HAD! ♥

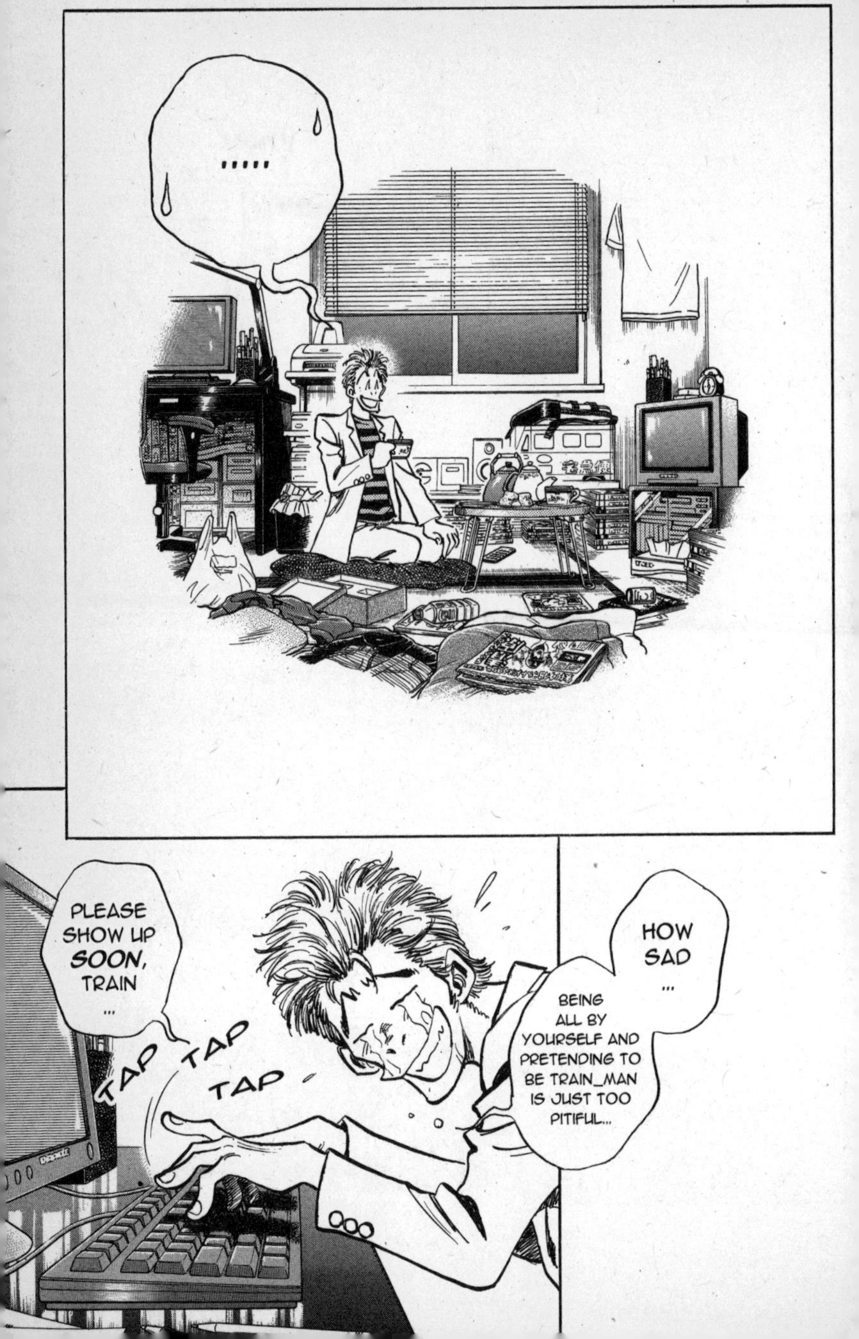
.....
HOW SAD ...
BEING ALL BY YOURSELF AND PRETENDING TO BE TRAIN_MAN IS JUST TOO PITIFUL...
PLEASE SHOW UP SOON, TRAIN ...
TAP TAP TAP

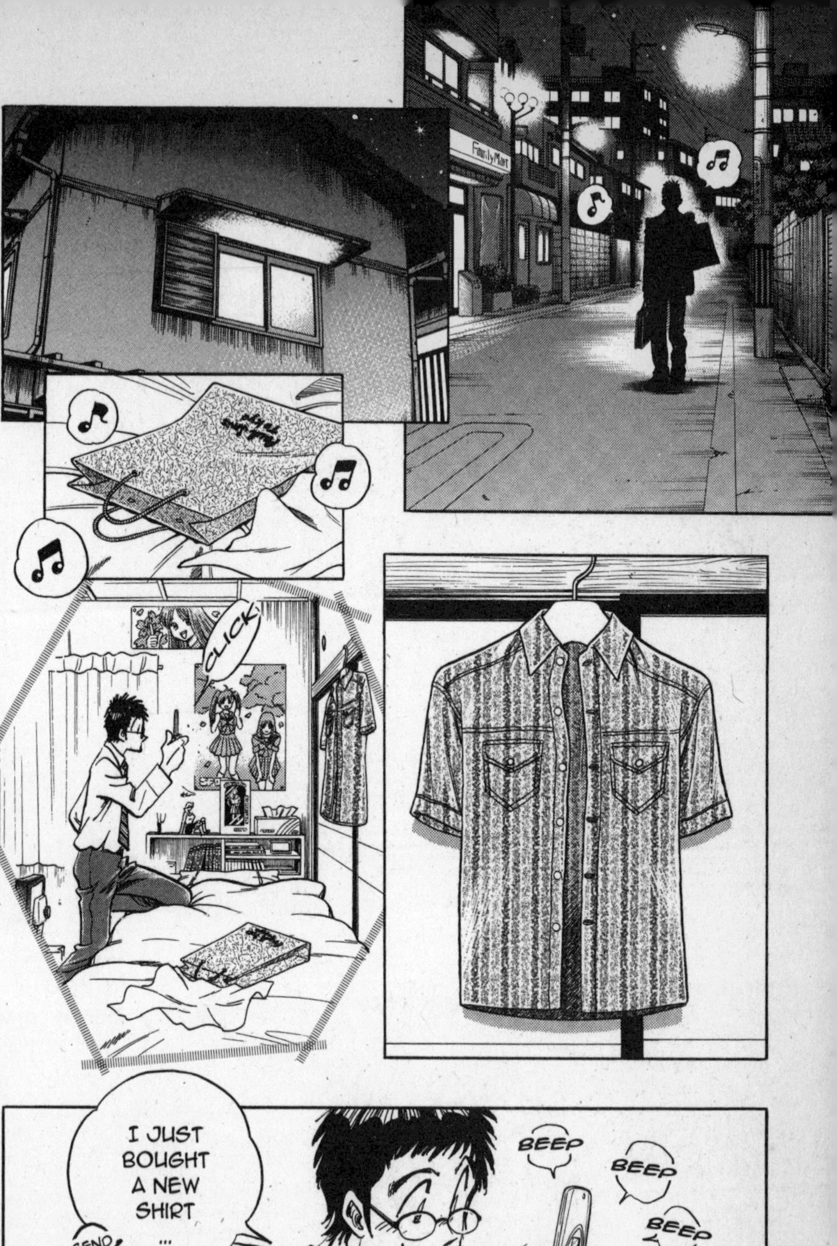
FamilyMart
CLICK
BEEP
BEEP
BEEP
I JUST BOUGHT A NEW SHIRT ...
SEND!

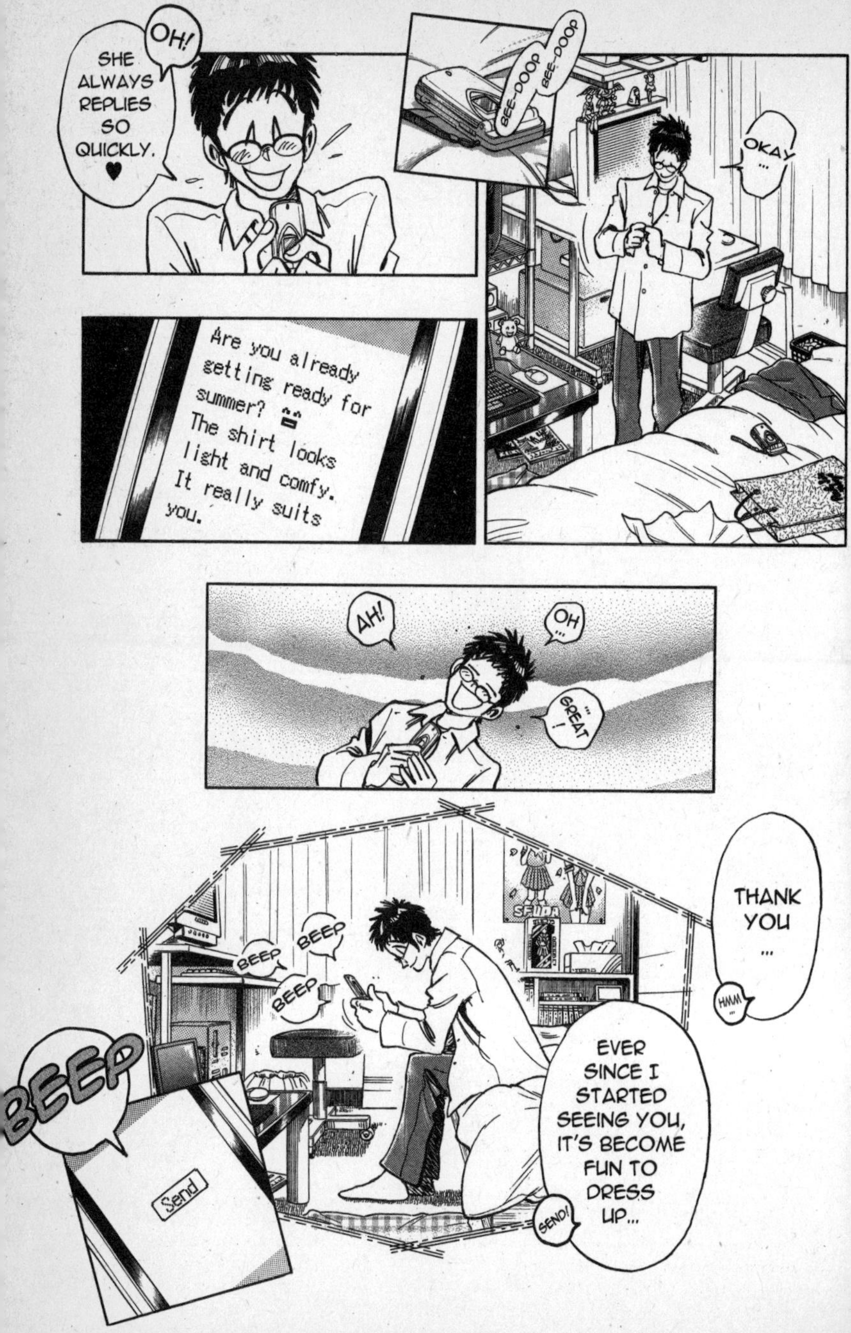
BEE-DOOP
BEE-DOOP
OKAY...
OH!
SHE ALWAYS REPLIES SO QUICKLY. ♥
Are you already getting ready for summer? The shirt looks light and comfy. It really suits you.
OH...
AH!
...GREAT!
THANK YOU...
HMM...
EVER SINCE I STARTED SEEING YOU, IT'S BECOME FUN TO DRESS UP...
SEND!
BEEP
BEEP
BEEP
BEEP
Send

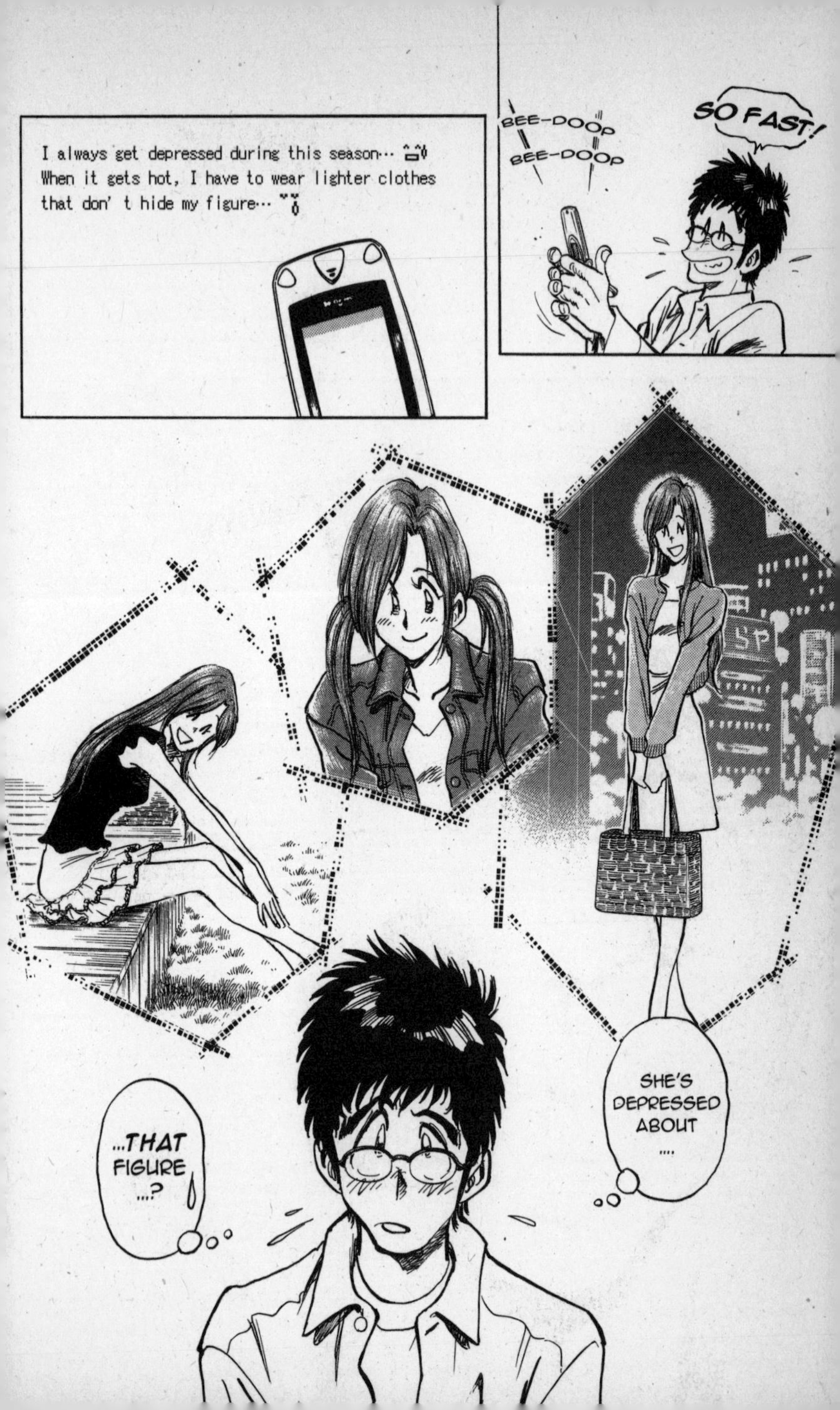
BEE-DOOP
BEE-DOOP
SO FAST!
I always get depressed during this season…
When it gets hot, I have to wear lighter clothes
that don' t hide my figure…
SHE'S DEPRESSED ABOUT ....
...THAT FIGURE ...?

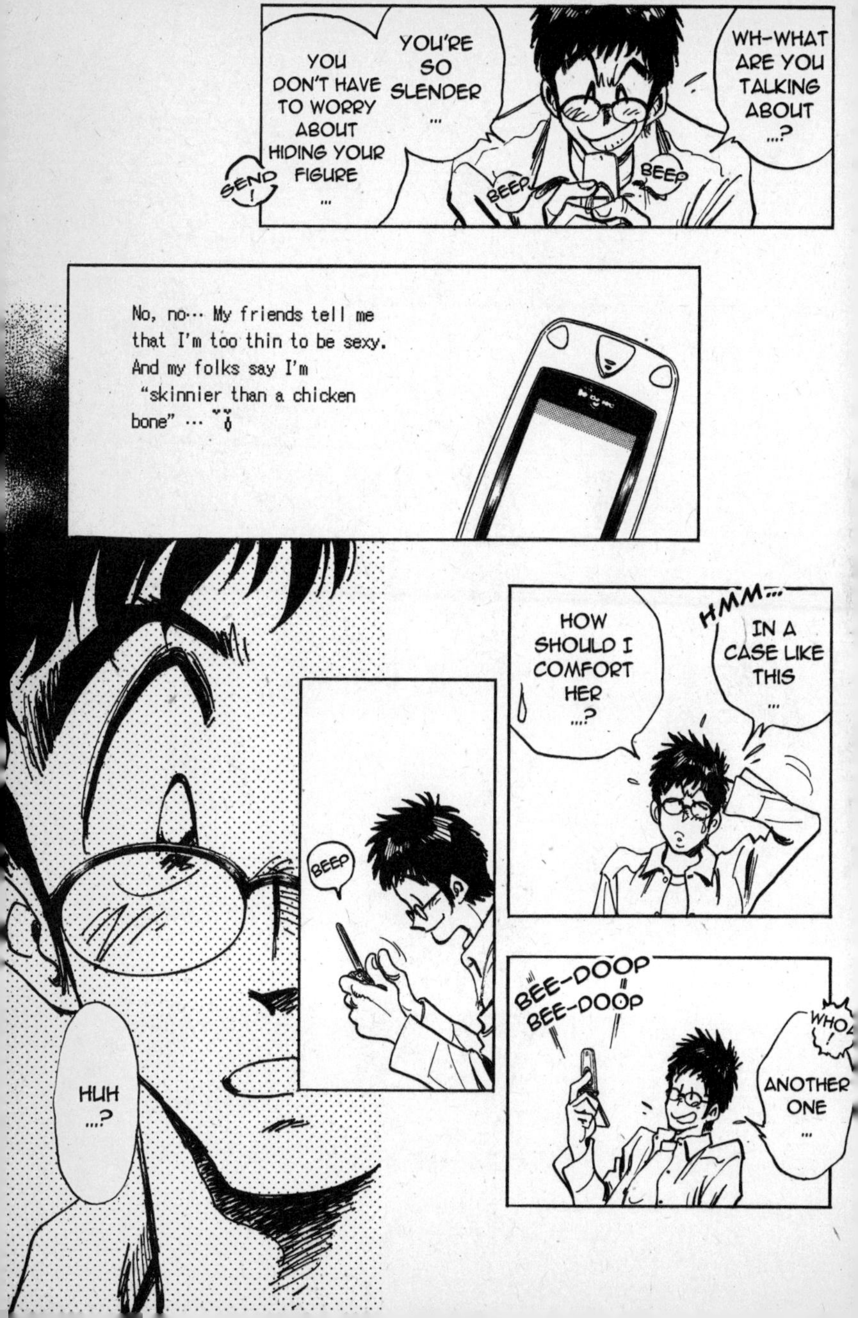
WH-WHAT ARE YOU TALKING ABOUT ...?
BEEP
BEEP
YOU'RE SO SLENDER ...
YOU DON'T HAVE TO WORRY ABOUT HIDING YOUR FIGURE ...
SEND!
No, no… My friends tell me that I'm too thin to be sexy. And my folks say I'm "skinnier than a chicken bone" …
HMM...
IN A CASE LIKE THIS ...
HOW SHOULD I COMFORT HER ...?
WHOA!
ANOTHER ONE ...
BEE-DOOP BEE-DOOP
BEEP
HUH ...?

eason that I can't

(x_x)

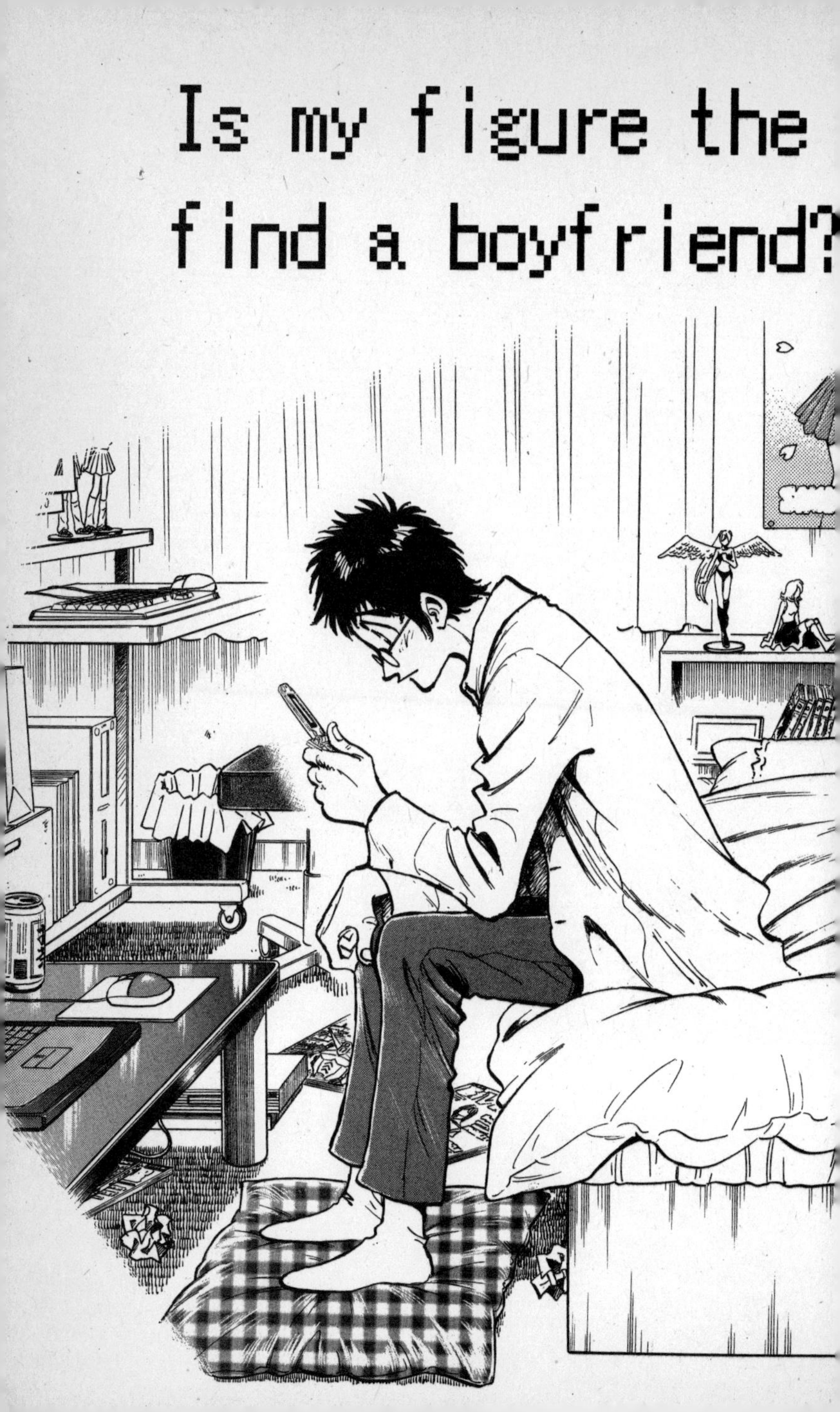
Is my figure the
find a boyfriend?

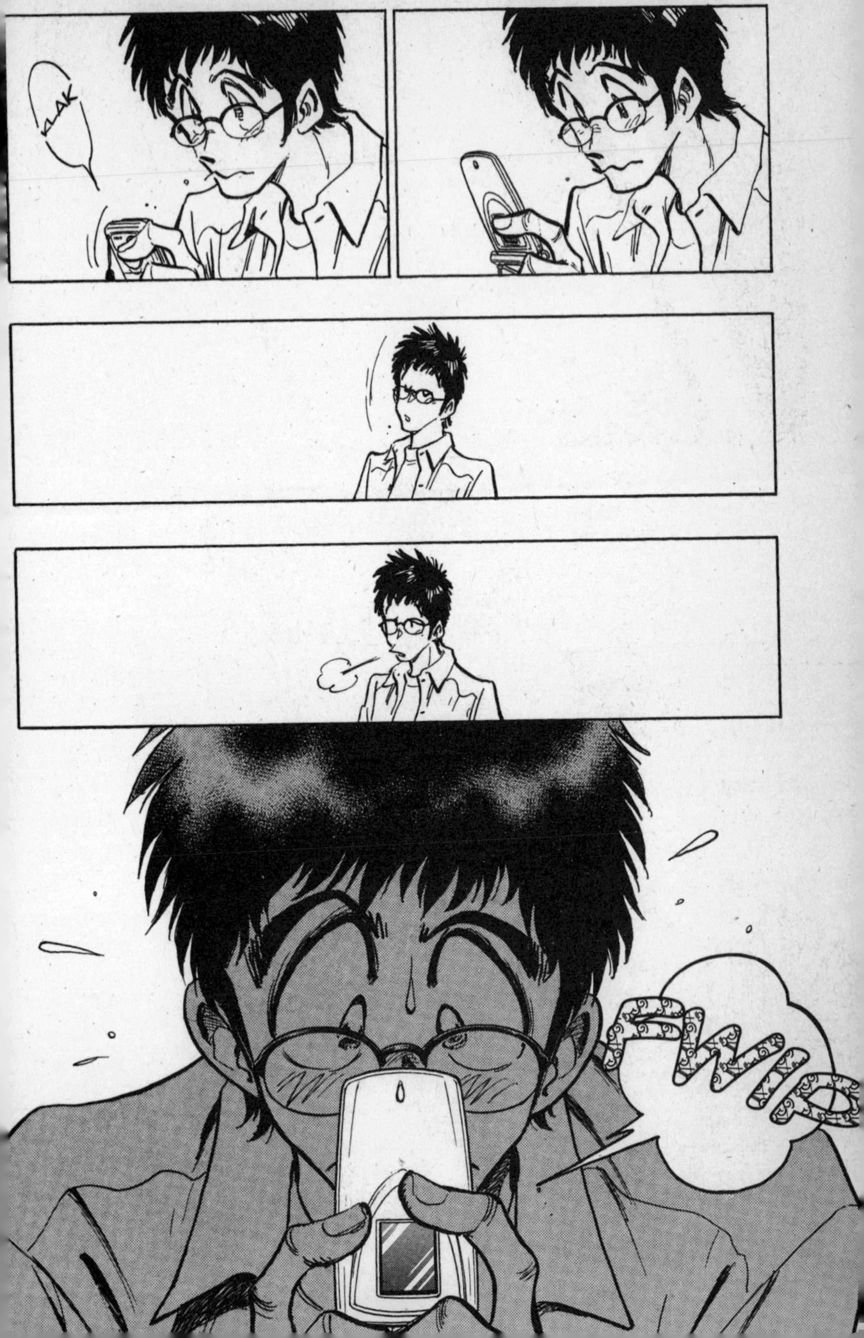
KLAK
FWIP

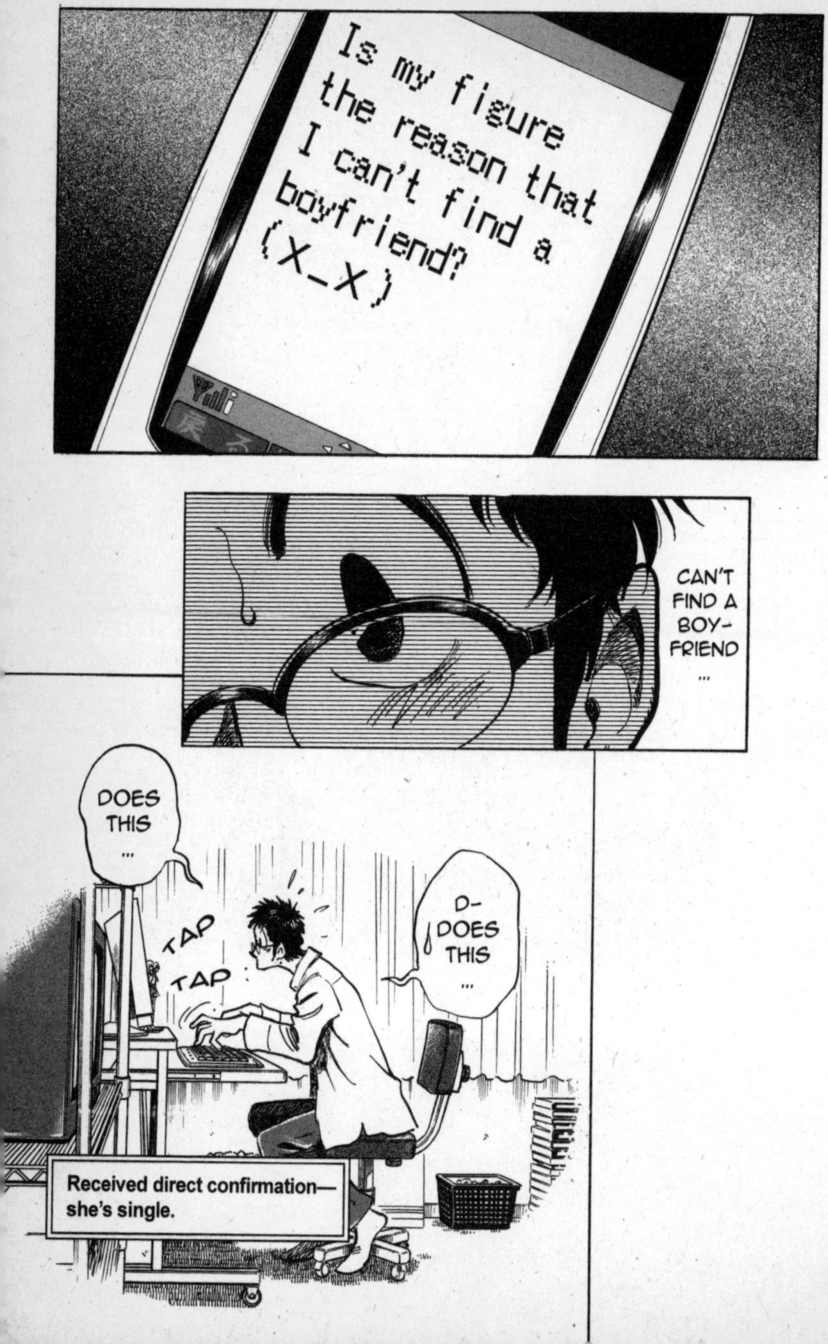
Is my figure the reason that I can't find a boyfriend? (X_X)
CAN'T FIND A BOY-FRIEND ...
DOES THIS ...
D-DOES THIS ...
TAP
TAP
Received direct confirmation—she's single.

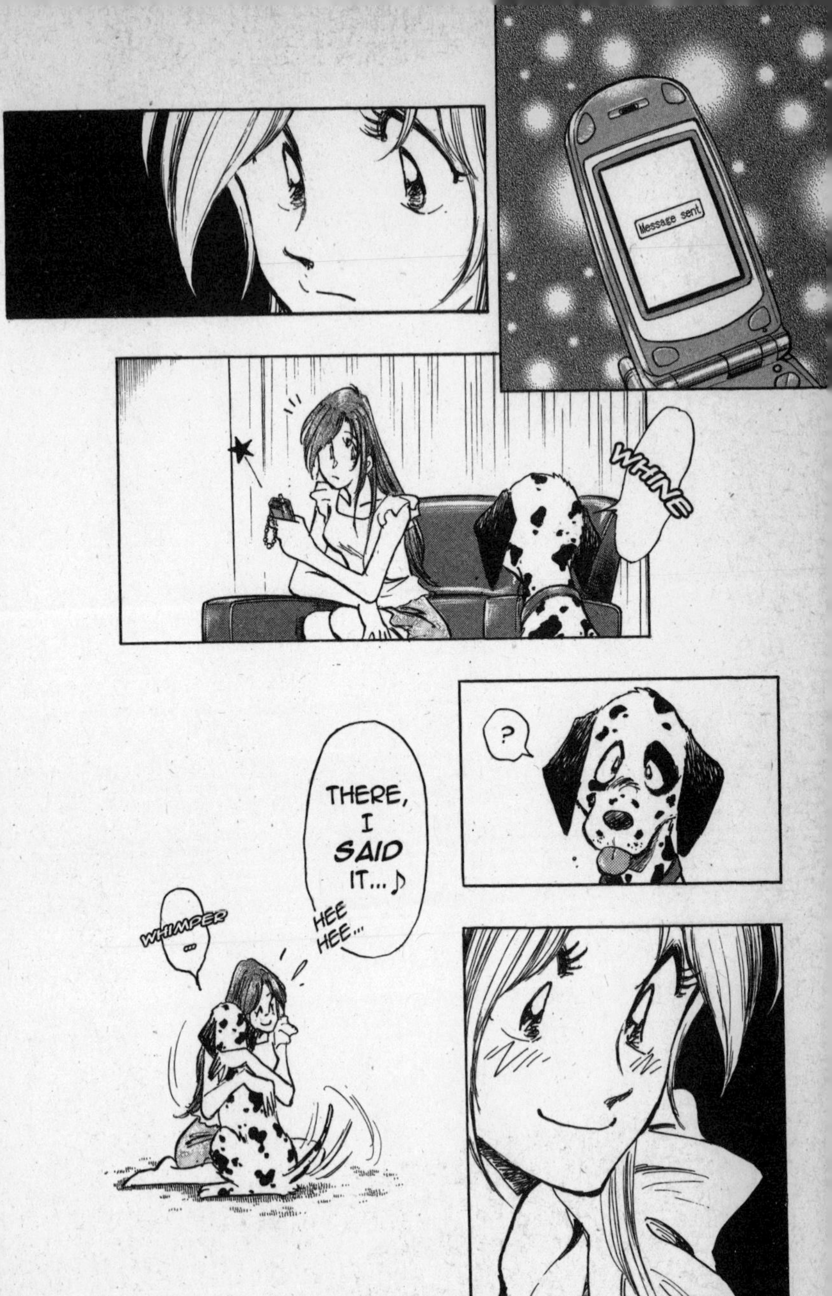
Message sent.
WHINE
?
THERE, I SAID IT...♪
HEE HEE...
WHIMPER
...

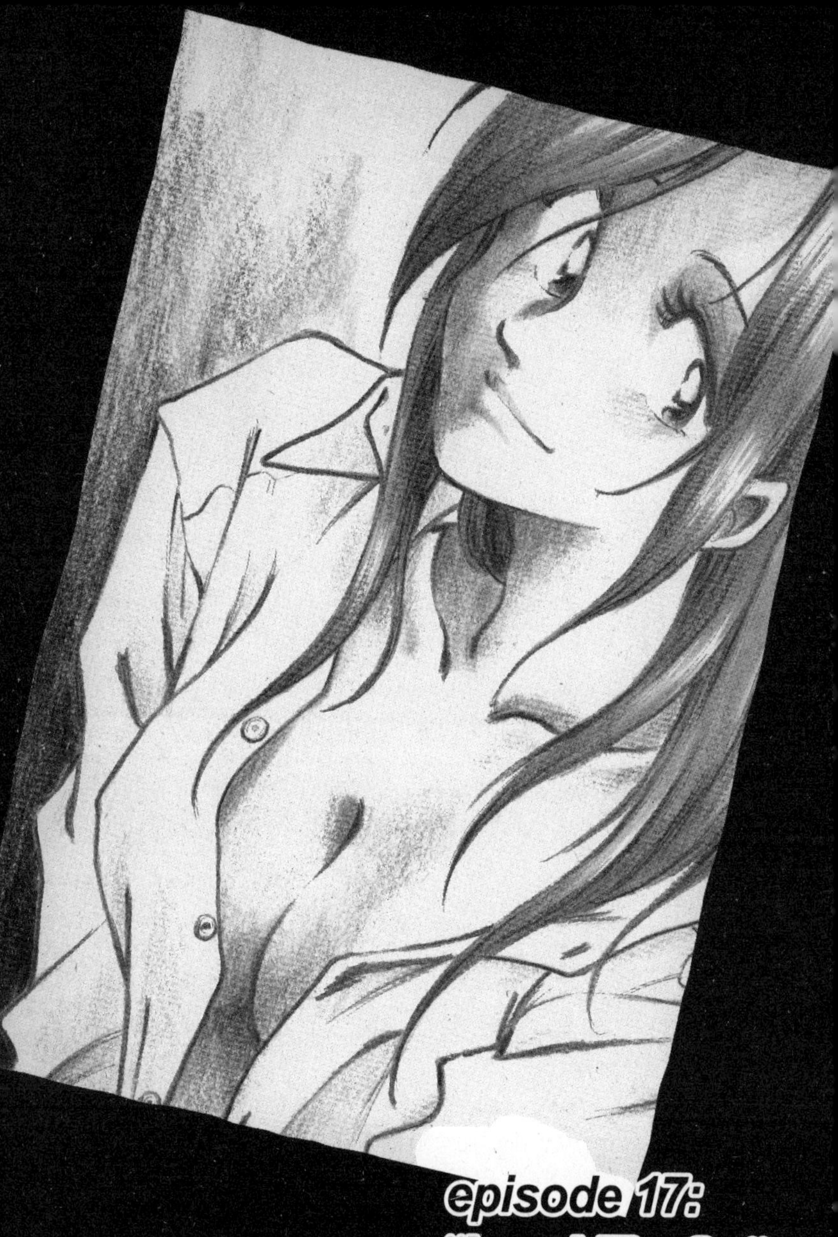

episode 17:
"Lead Me On"

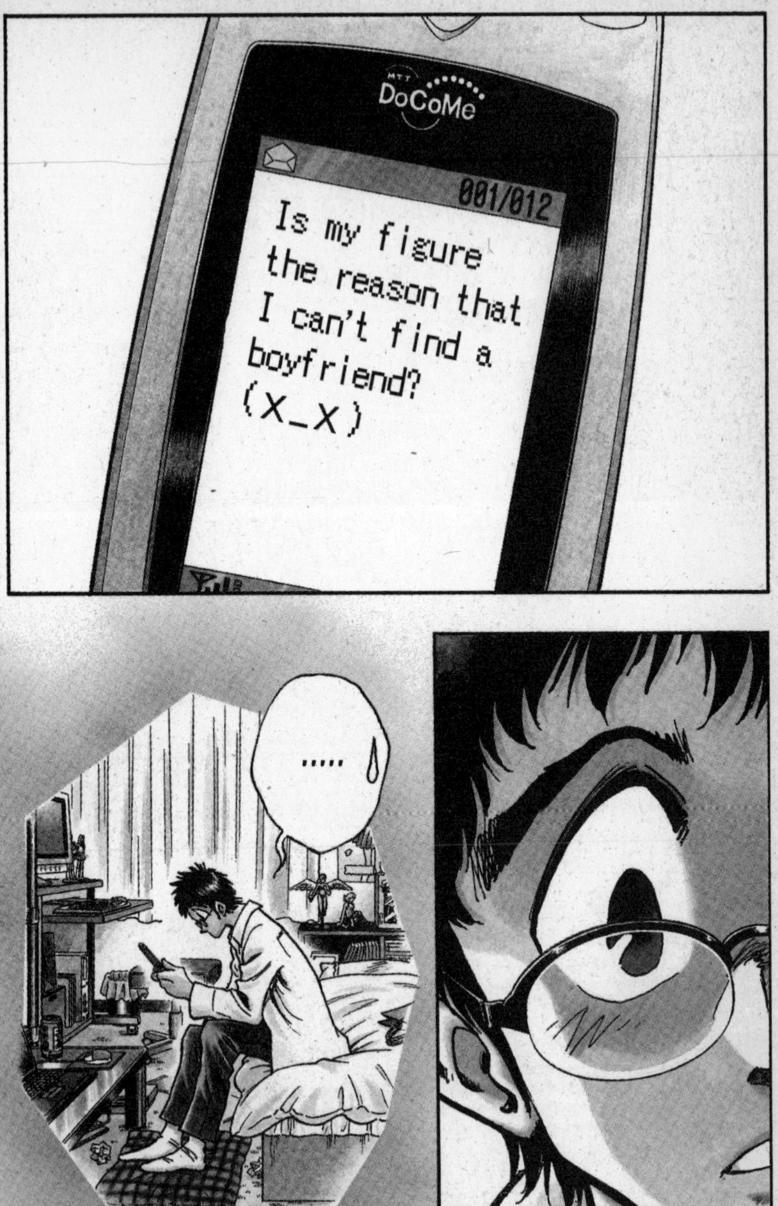
DoCoMe
001/012
Is my figure the reason that I can't find a boyfriend? (X_X)
.....

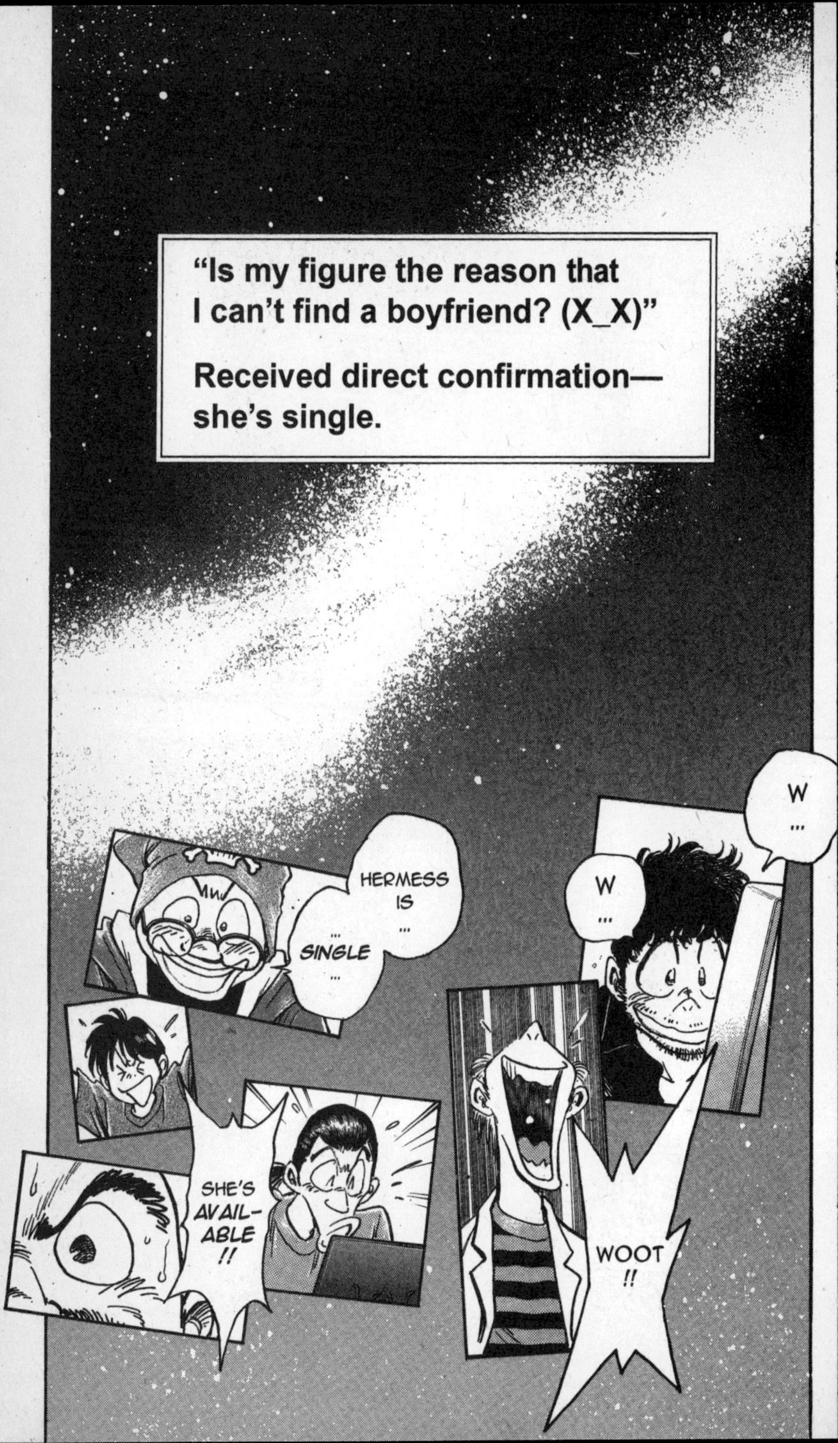
"Is my figure the reason that I can't find a boyfriend? (X_X)"
Received direct confirmation—she's single.
W ...
W ...
HERMESS IS ...
... SINGLE ...
WOOT !!
SHE'S AVAIL-ABLE !!

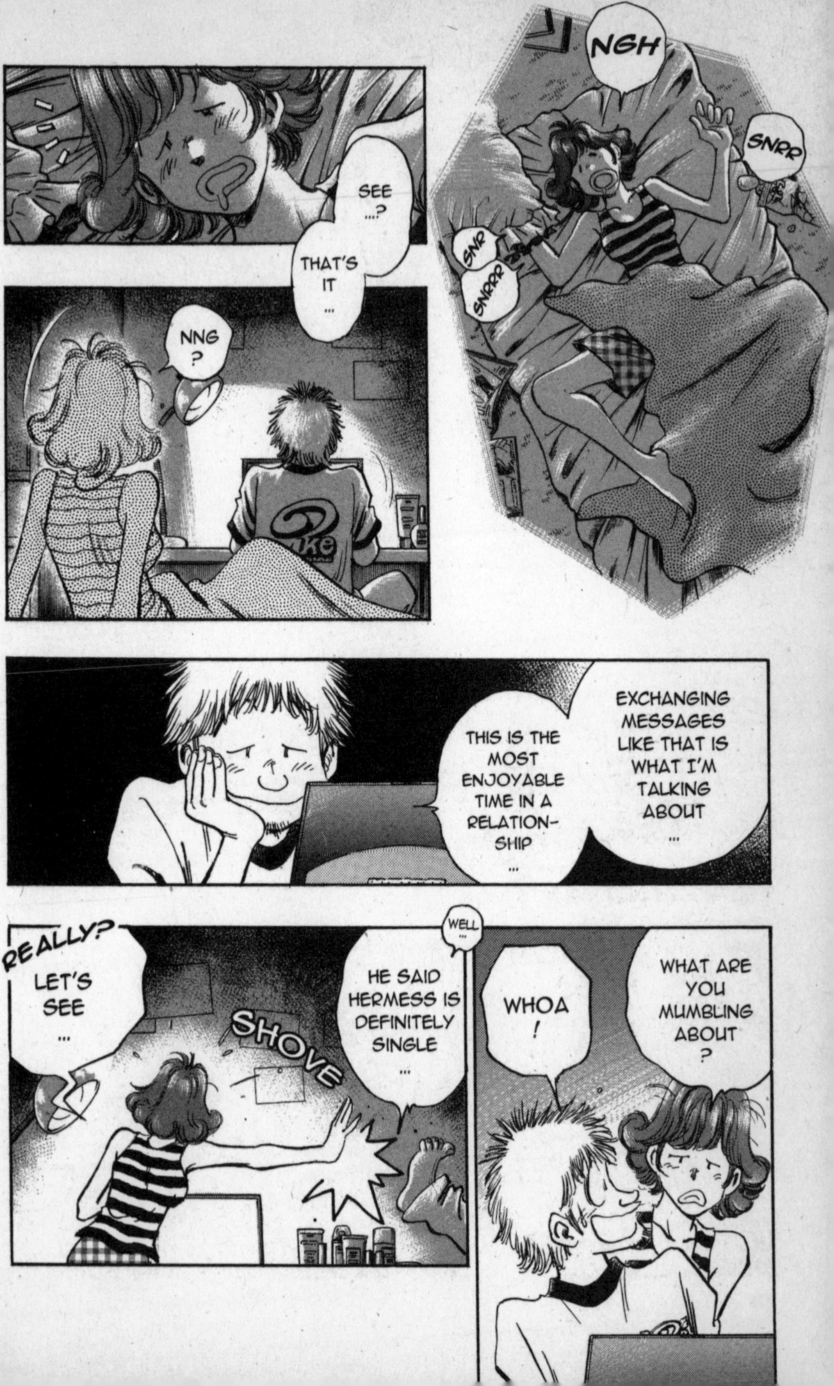
NGH
SNRR
SNR
SNRRR
SEE ...?
THAT'S IT ...
NNG ?
EXCHANGING MESSAGES LIKE THAT IS WHAT I'M TALKING ABOUT ...
THIS IS THE MOST ENJOYABLE TIME IN A RELATION-SHIP ...
WHAT ARE YOU MUMBLING ABOUT ?
WHOA !
WELL ...
HE SAID HERMESS IS DEFINITELY SINGLE ...
SHOVE
REALLY?
LET'S SEE ...

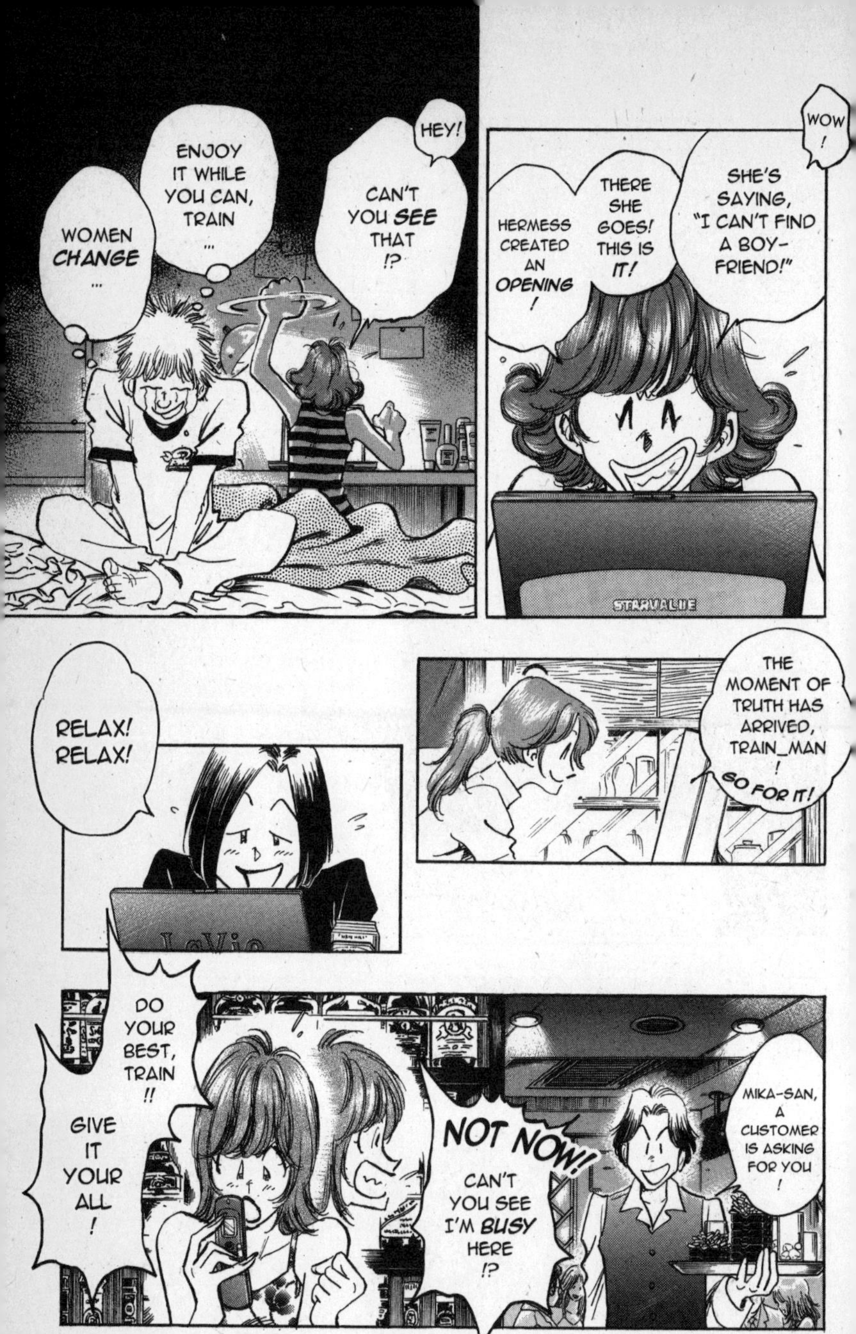
WOW!
SHE'S SAYING, "I CAN'T FIND A BOY-FRIEND!"
THERE SHE GOES! THIS IS IT!
HERMESS CREATED AN OPENING!
STARVALUE
HEY!
CAN'T YOU SEE THAT!?
ENJOY IT WHILE YOU CAN, TRAIN...
WOMEN CHANGE...
THE MOMENT OF TRUTH HAS ARRIVED, TRAIN_MAN!
GO FOR IT!
RELAX! RELAX!
MIKA-SAN, A CUSTOMER IS ASKING FOR YOU!
NOT NOW!
CAN'T YOU SEE I'M BUSY HERE!?
DO YOUR BEST, TRAIN!!
GIVE IT YOUR ALL!

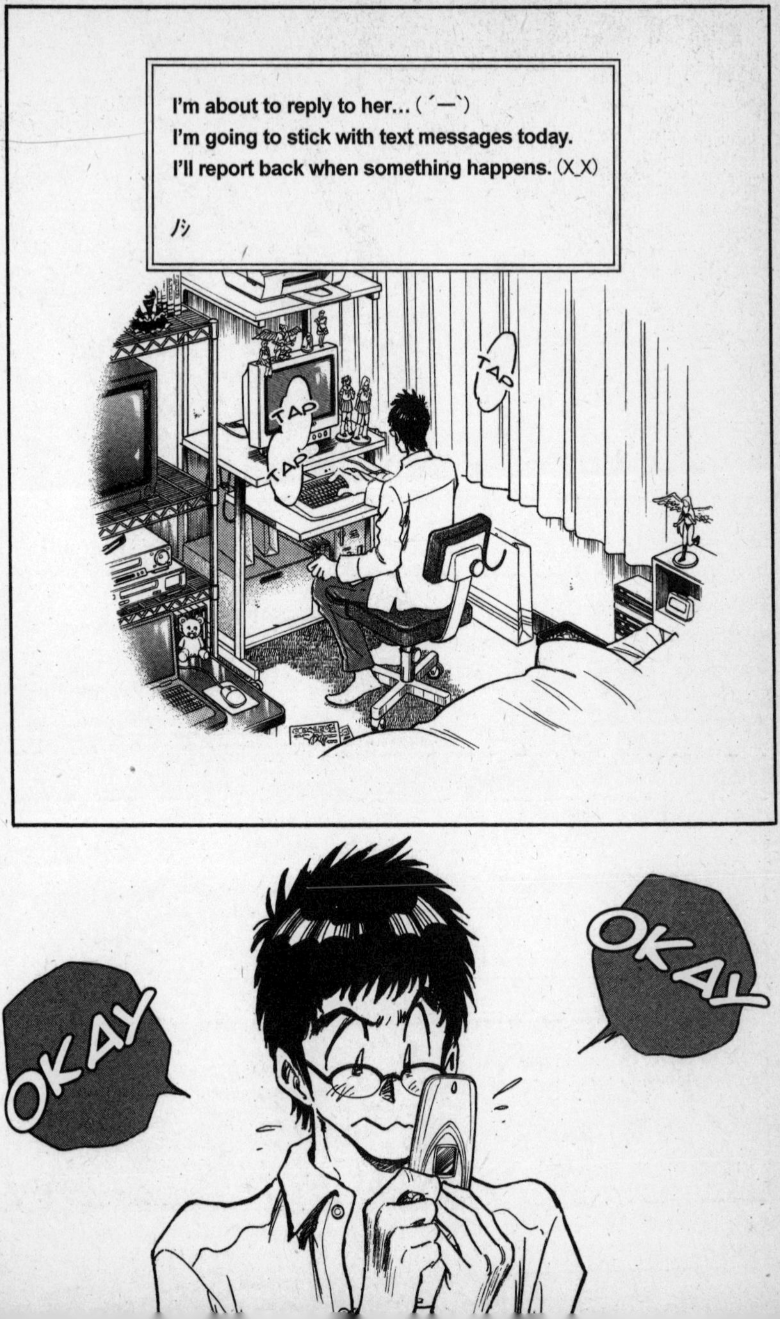

I'm about to reply to her... (´—`)
I'm going to stick with text messages today.
I'll report back when something happens. (X_X)
ノシ
TAP
TAP
TAP
OKAY
OKAY

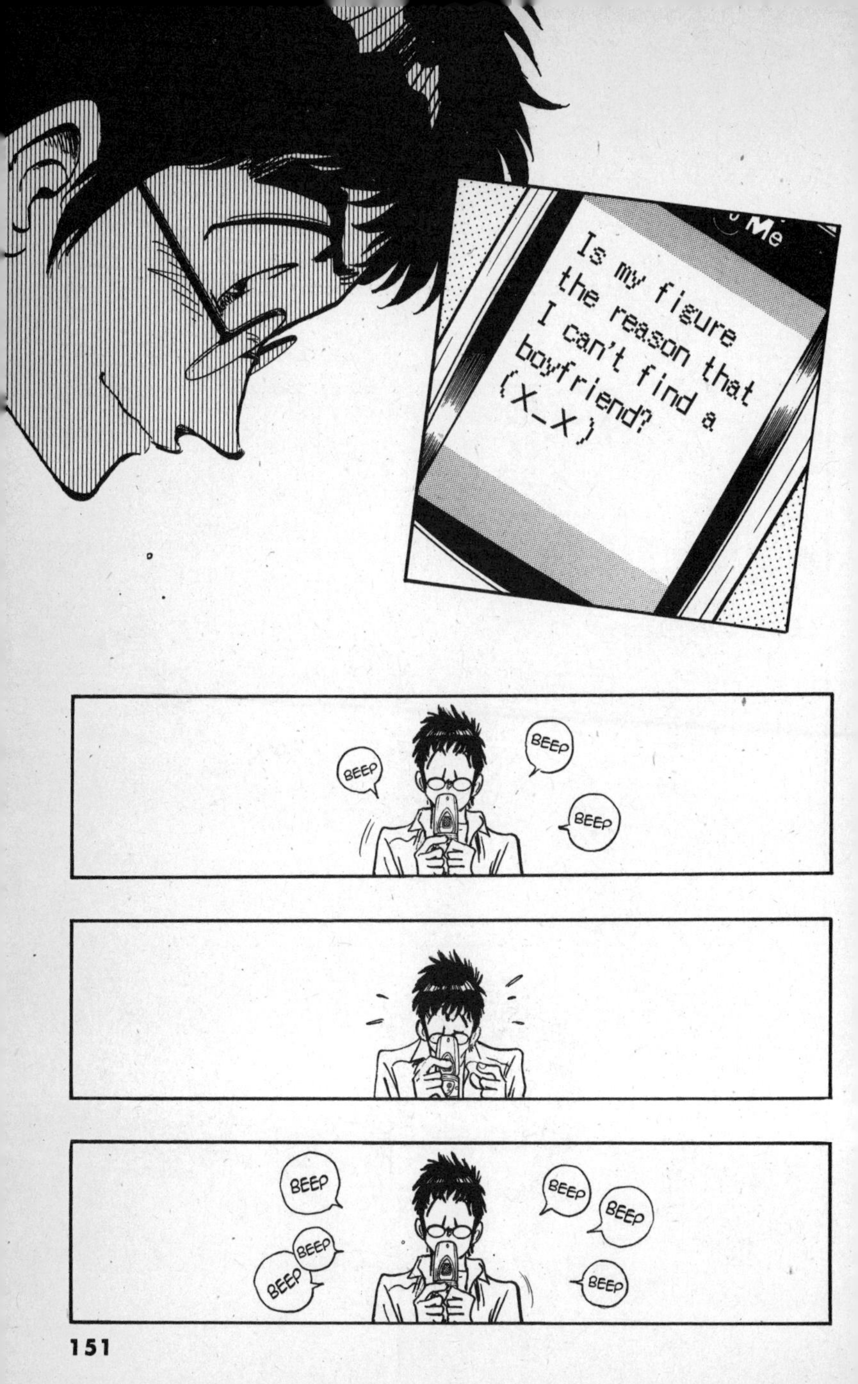
Me
Is my figure the reason that I can't find a boyfriend? (X_X)
BEEP
BEEP
BEEP
BEEP
BEEP
BEEP
BEEP
BEEP
BEEP

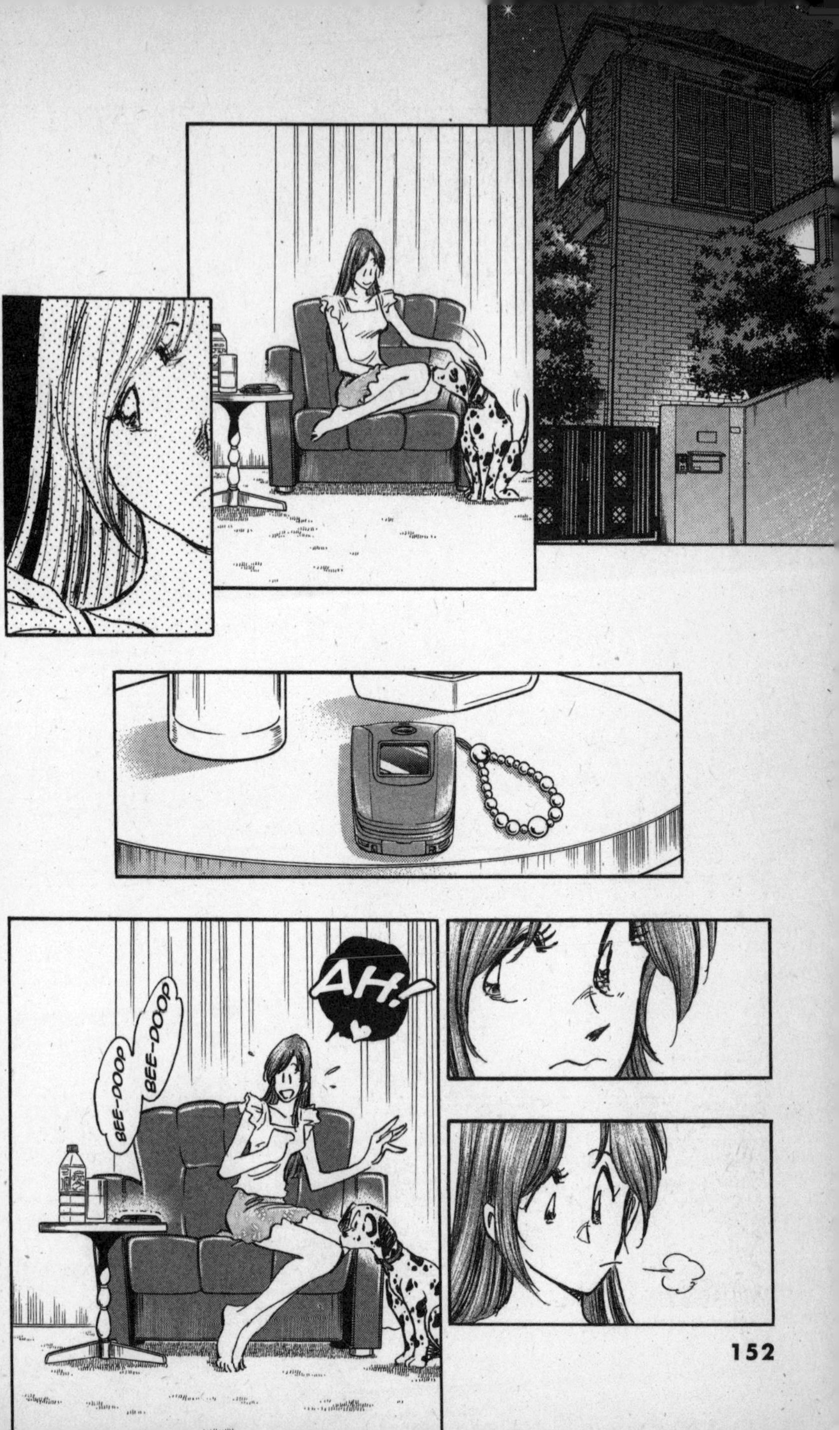
AH!
BEE-DOOP
BEE-DOOP

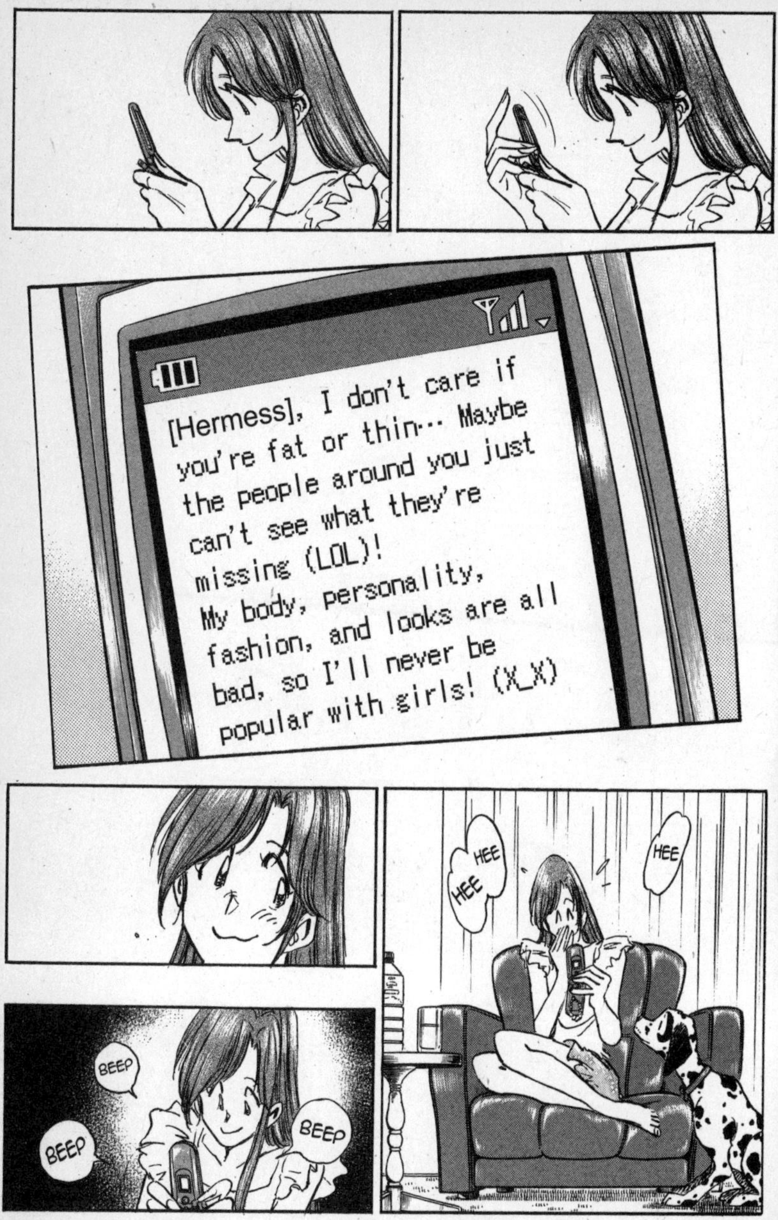
[Hermess], I don't care if
you're fat or thin… Maybe
the people around you just
can't see what they're
missing (LOL)!
My body, personality,
fashion, and looks are all
bad, so I'll never be
popular with girls! (X_X)
HEE
HEE HEE
BEEP
BEEP
BEEP

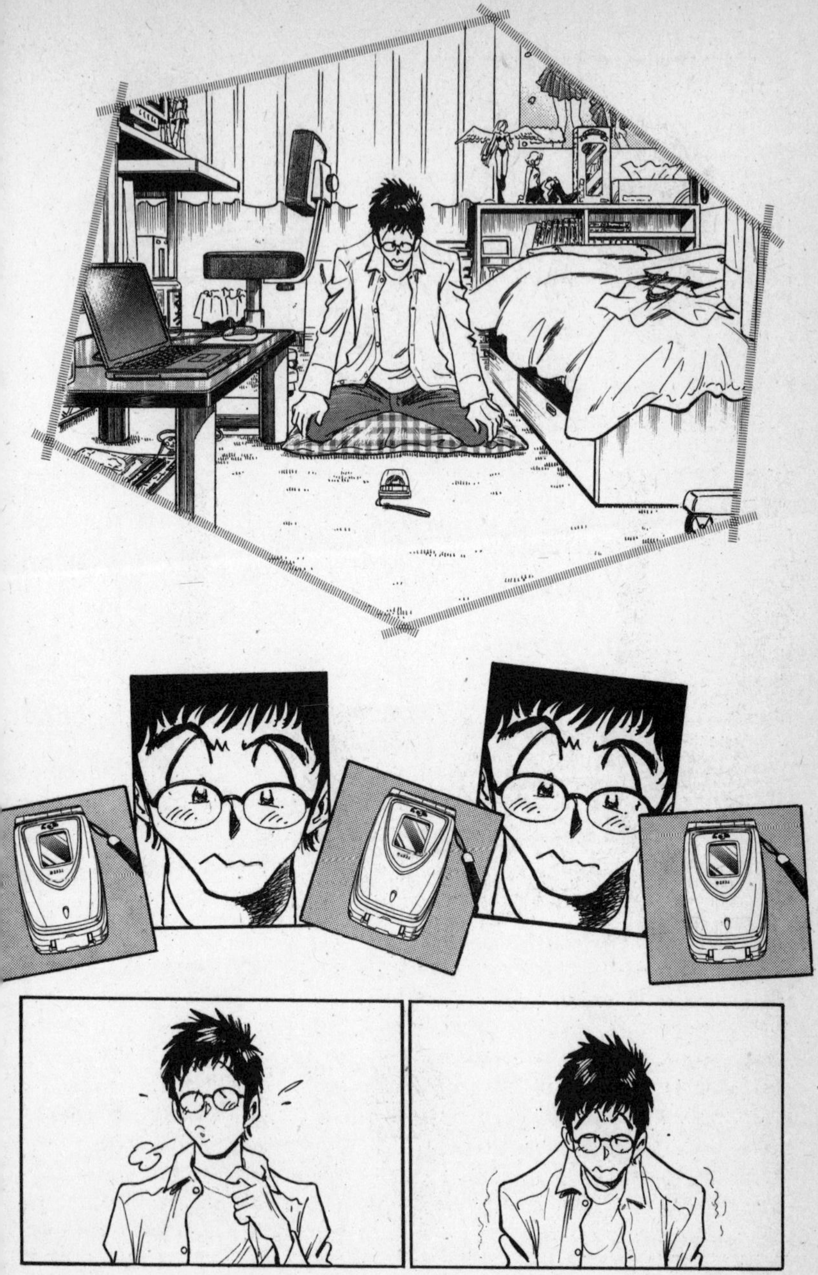

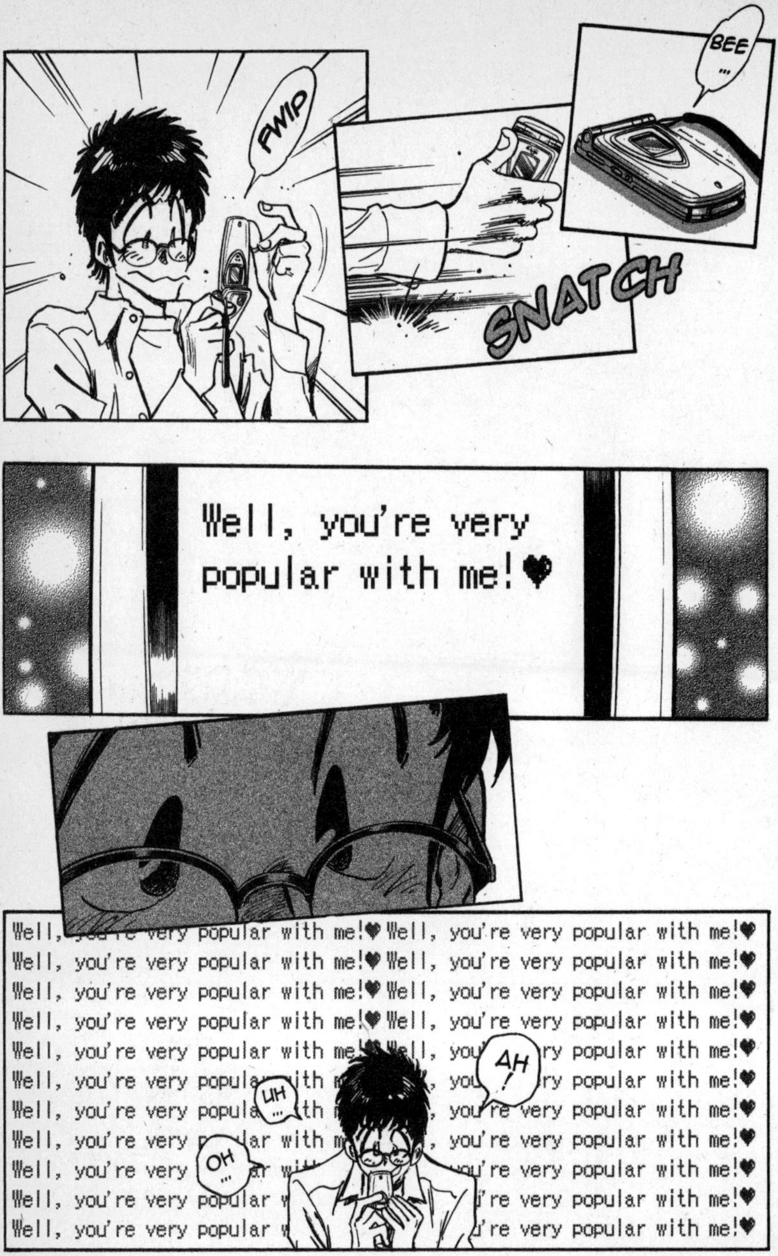
BEE...
SNATCH
FWIP
Well, you're very popular with me!♥
Well, you're very popular with me!♥ Well, you're very popular with me!♥
Well, you're very popular with me!♥ Well, you're very popular with me!♥
Well, you're very popular with me!♥ Well, you're very popular with me!♥
AH!
UH...
OH...

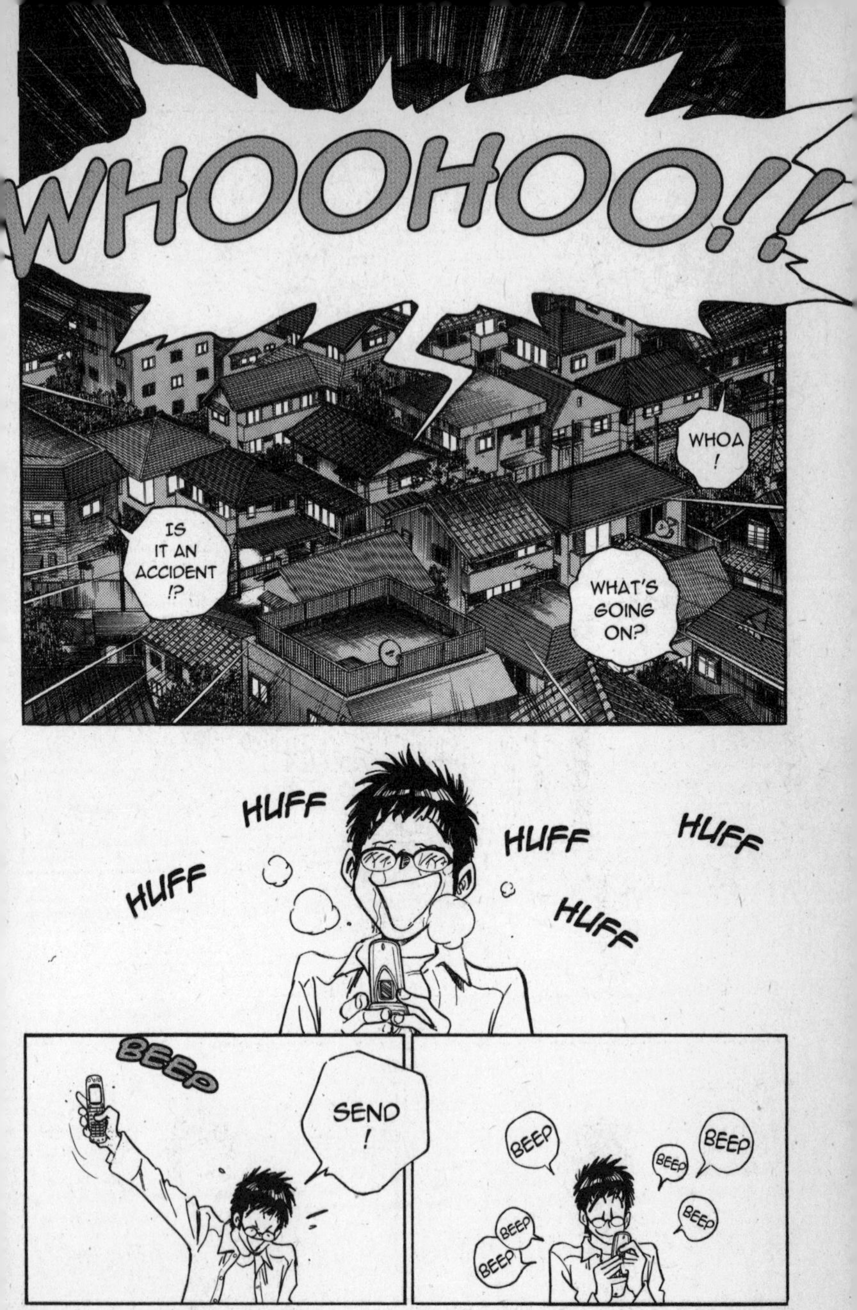
WHOOHOO!!
WHOA!
WHAT'S GOING ON?
IS IT AN ACCIDENT!?
HUFF
HUFF
HUFF
HUFF
HUFF
BEEP
BEEP
BEEP
BEEP
BEEP
BEEP
BEEP
SEND!

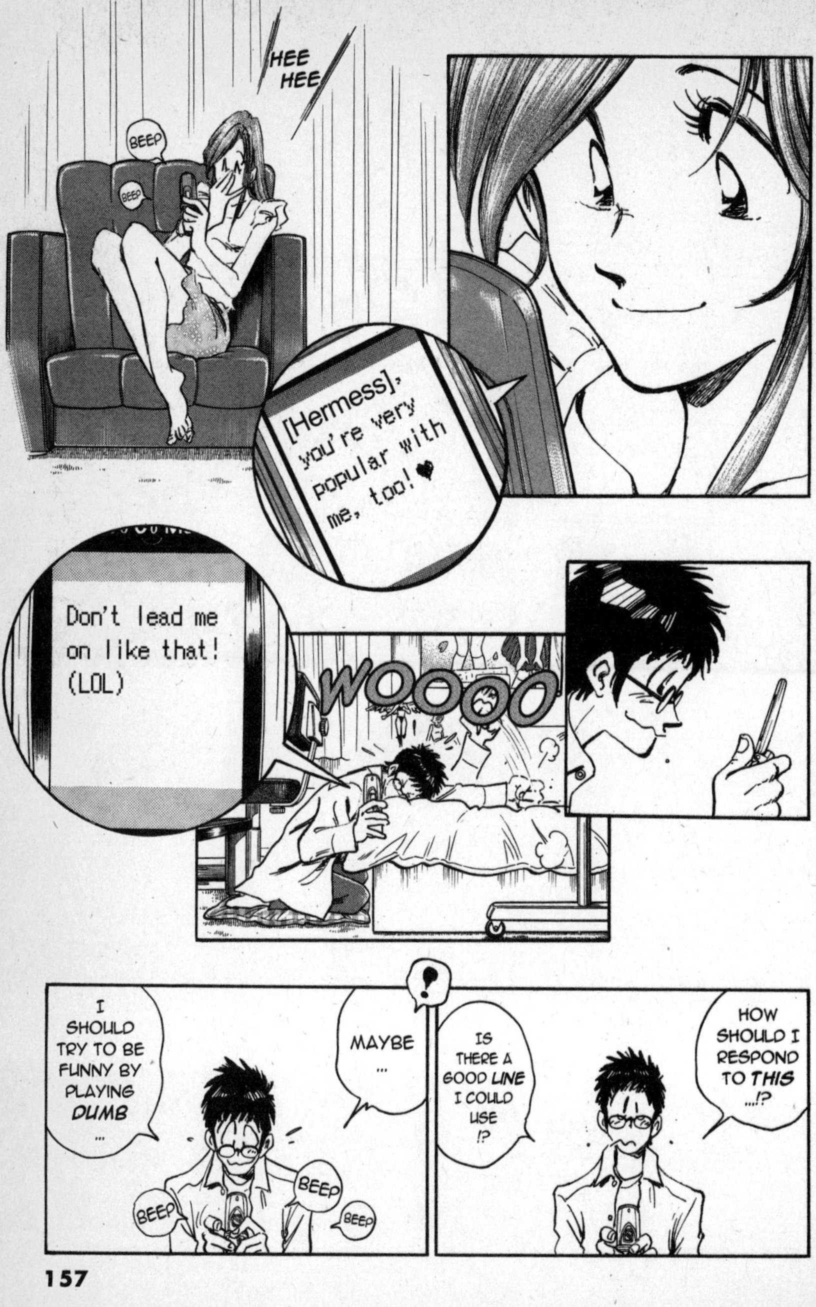

[Hermess], you're very popular with me, too! ❤
HEE HEE
BEEP
BEEP
Don't lead me on like that! (LOL)
WOOOO
HOW SHOULD I RESPOND TO THIS ...!?
IS THERE A GOOD LINE I COULD USE !?
!?
MAYBE ...
I SHOULD TRY TO BE FUNNY BY PLAYING DUMB ...
BEEP
BEEP
BEEP

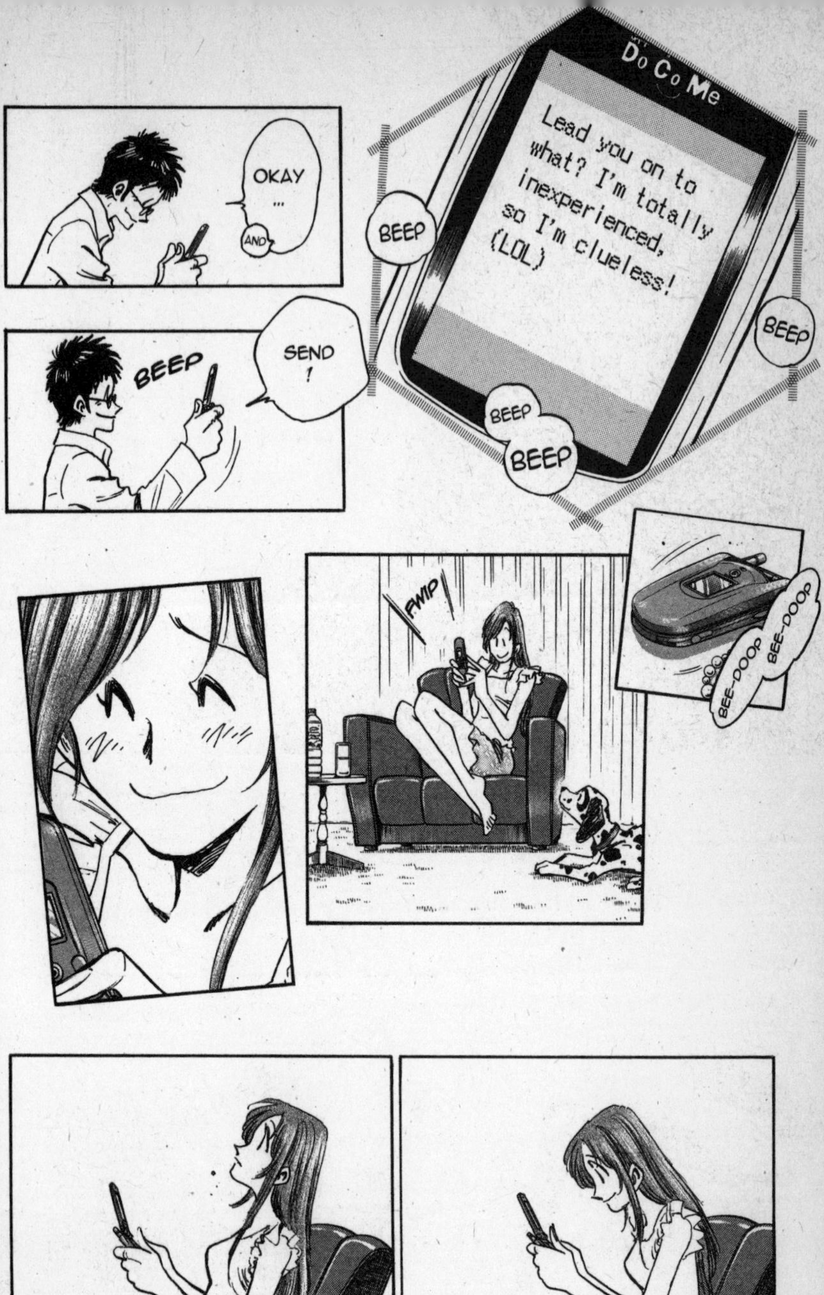

DoCoMe
Lead you on to what? I'm totally inexperienced, so I'm clueless! (LOL)
BEEP
BEEP
BEEP
BEEP
OKAY ...
AND
BEEP
SEND!
BEE-DOOP
BEE-DOOP
FWIP

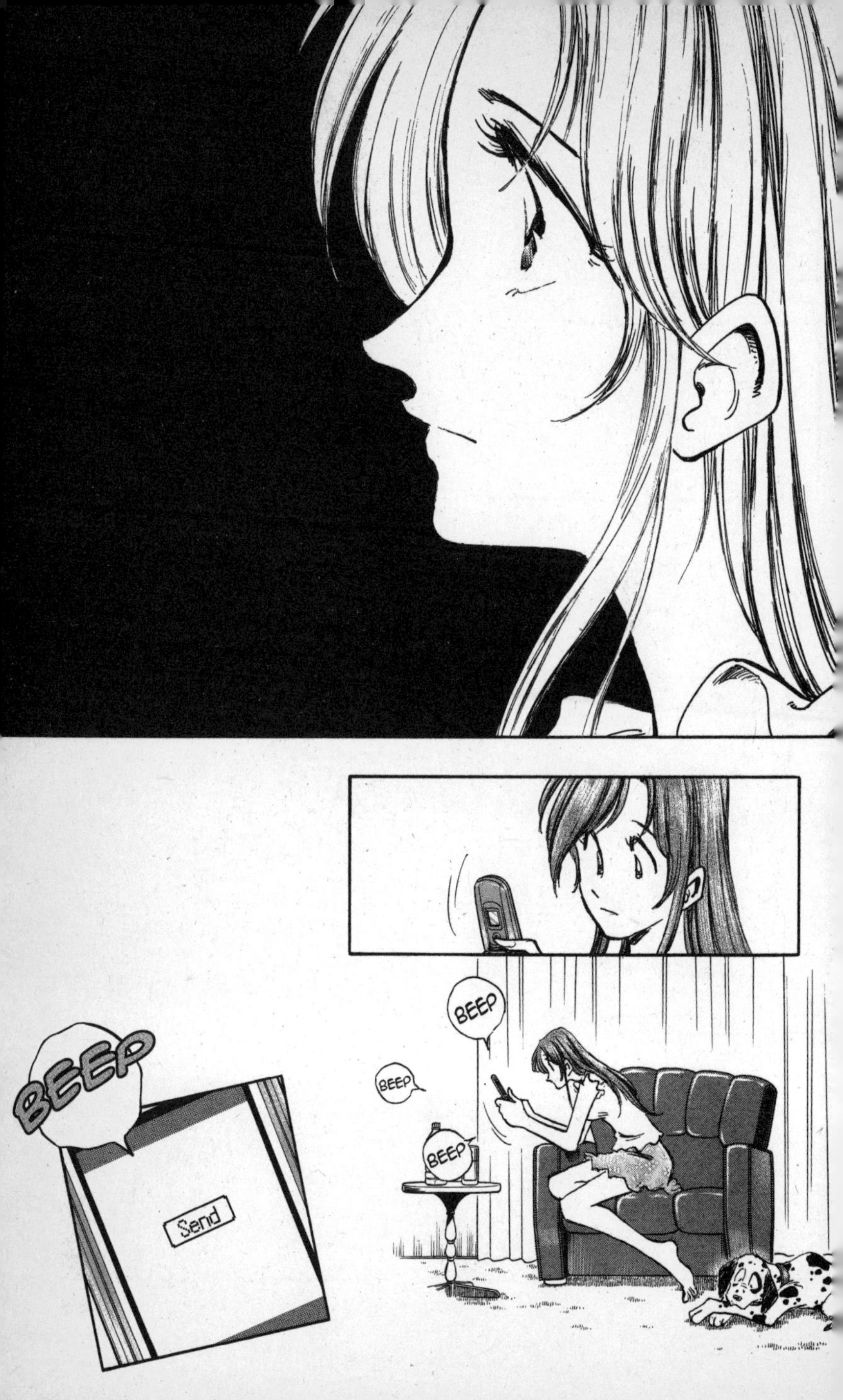
BEEP
BEEP
BEEP
BEEP
Send

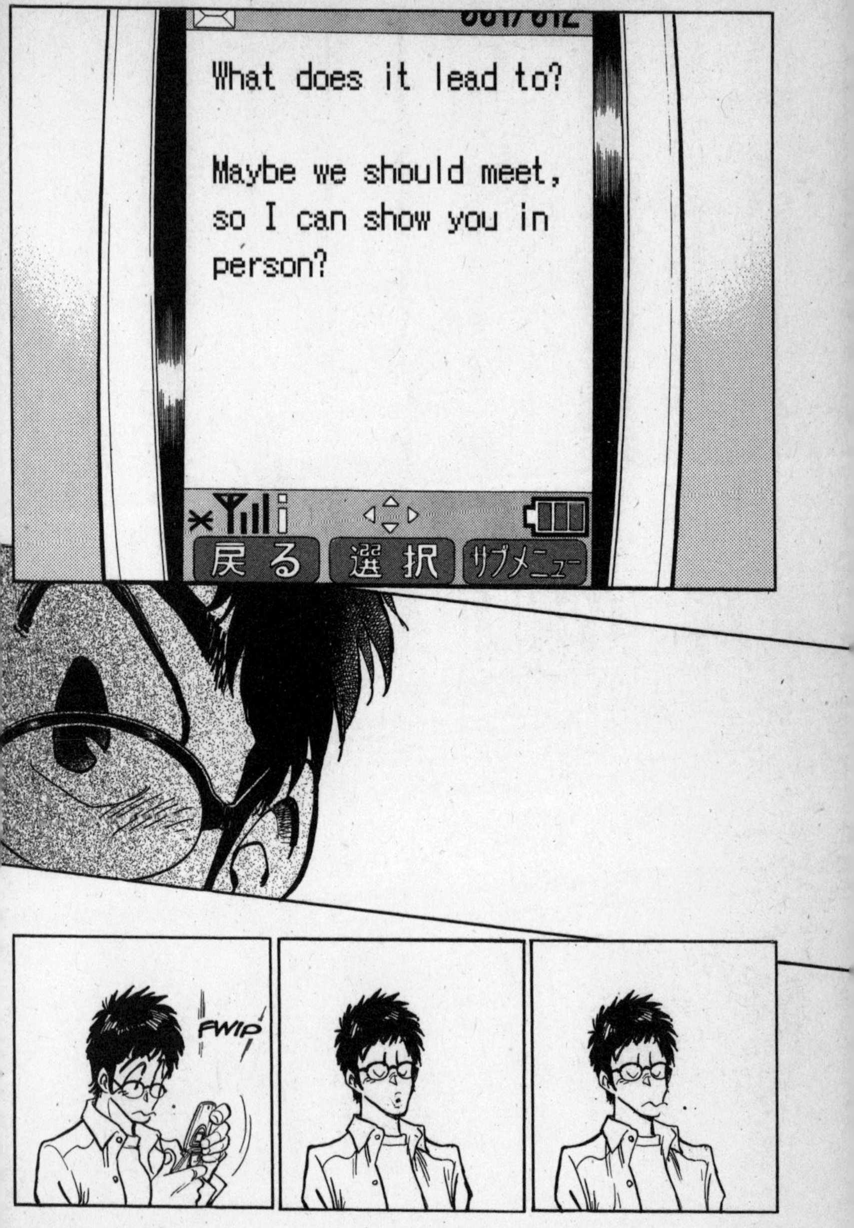
What does it lead to?
Maybe we should meet, so I can show you in person?
戻る
選択
サブメニュー
FWIP

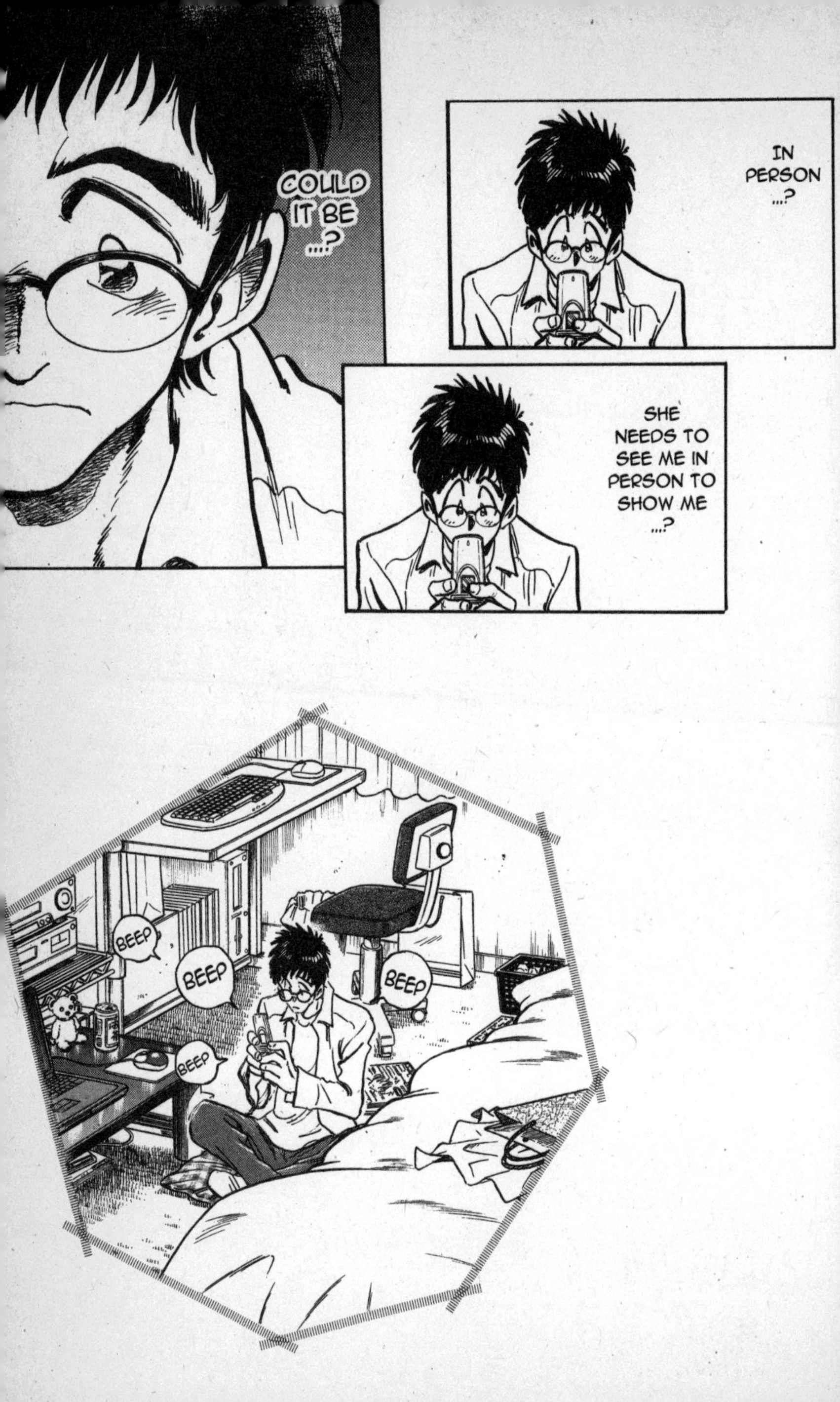
IN PERSON ...?
SHE NEEDS TO SEE ME IN PERSON TO SHOW ME ...?
COULD IT BE ...?
BEEP
BEEP
BEEP
BEEP

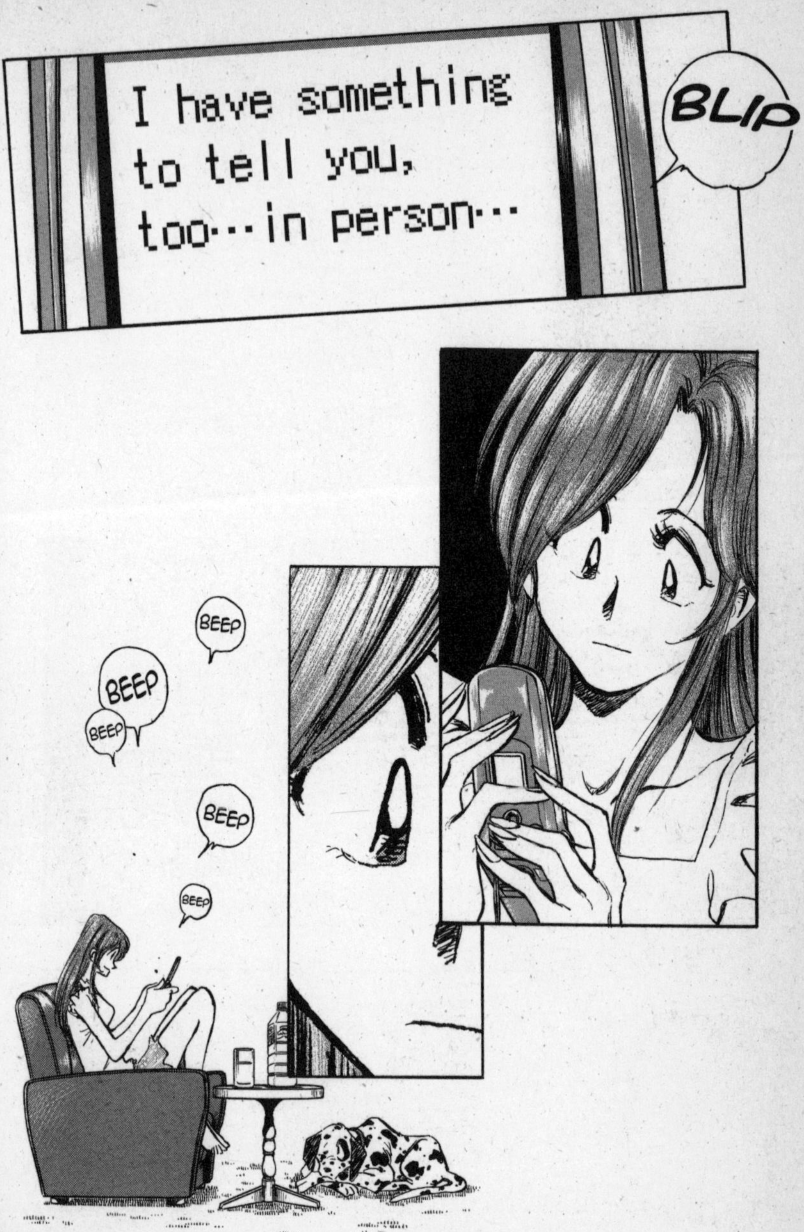
I have something to tell you, too···in person···
BLIP
BEEP
BEEP
BEEP
BEEP
BEEP

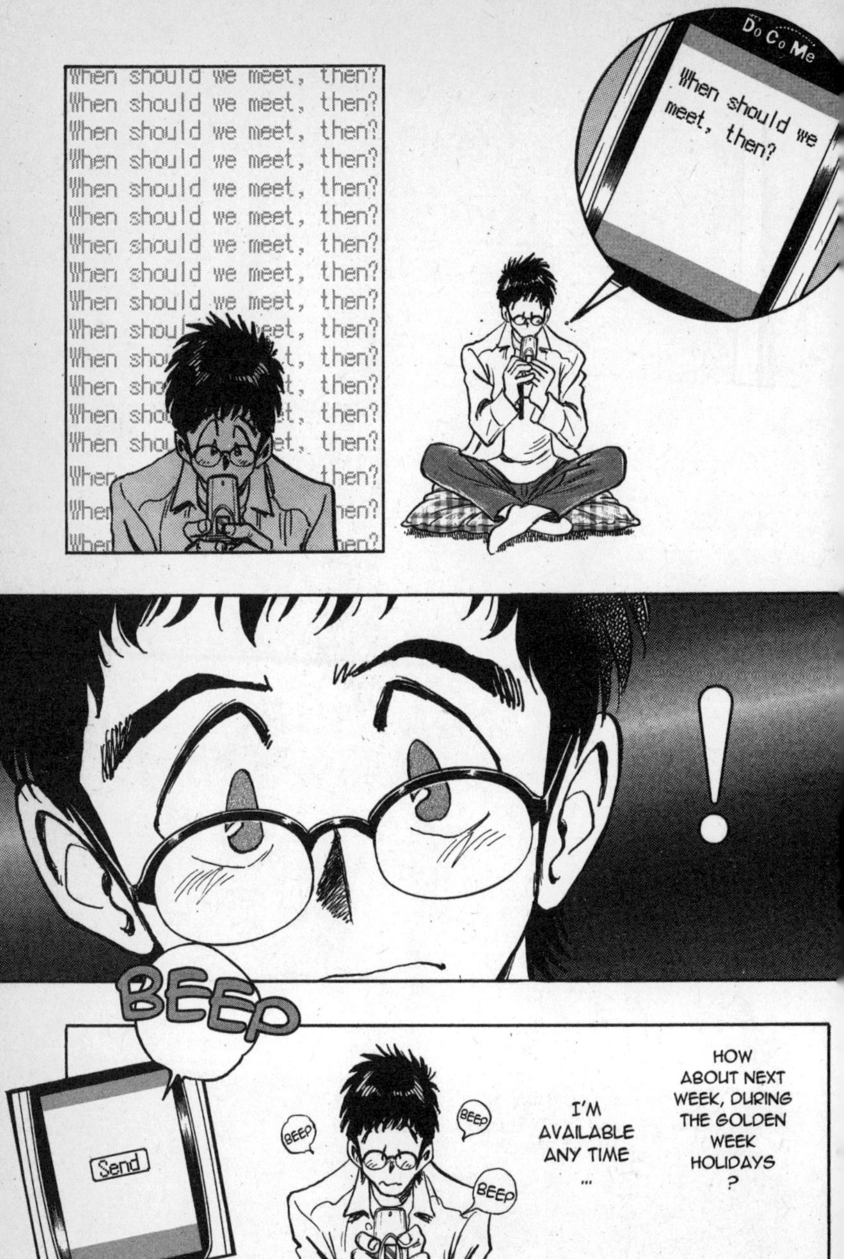

DoCoMe
When should we meet, then?
When should we meet, then?
When should we meet, then?
When should we meet, then?
When should we meet, then?
When should we meet, then?
When should we meet, then?
When should we meet, then?
When should we meet, then?
When should we meet, then?
!
HOW ABOUT NEXT WEEK, DURING THE GOLDEN WEEK HOLIDAYS ?
I'M AVAILABLE ANY TIME ...
BEEP
BEEP
BEEP
BEEP
Send

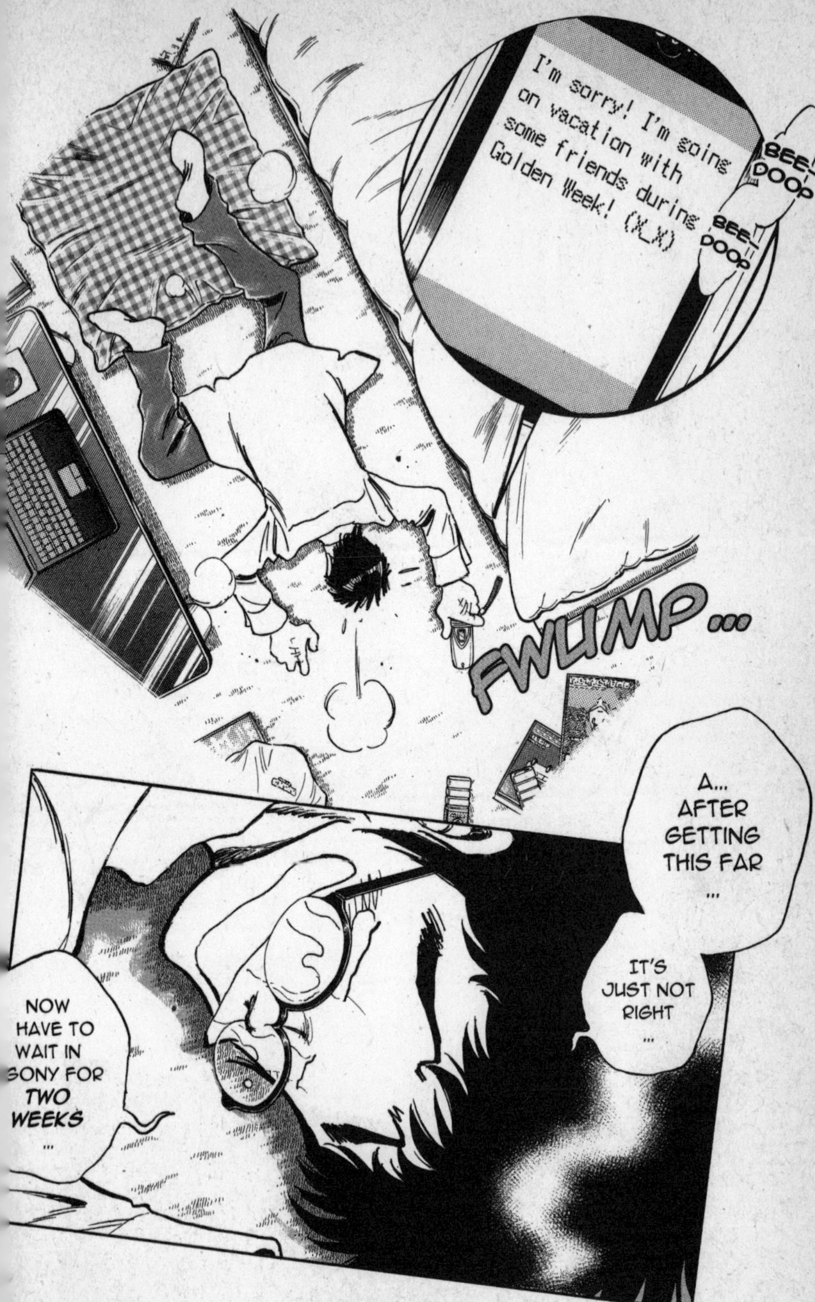

I'm sorry! I'm going on vacation with some friends during Golden Week! (X_X)
BEE-DOOP
BEE-DOOP
FWUMP...
A... AFTER GETTING THIS FAR ...
IT'S JUST NOT RIGHT ...
NOW HAVE TO WAIT IN SONY FOR TWO WEEKS ...

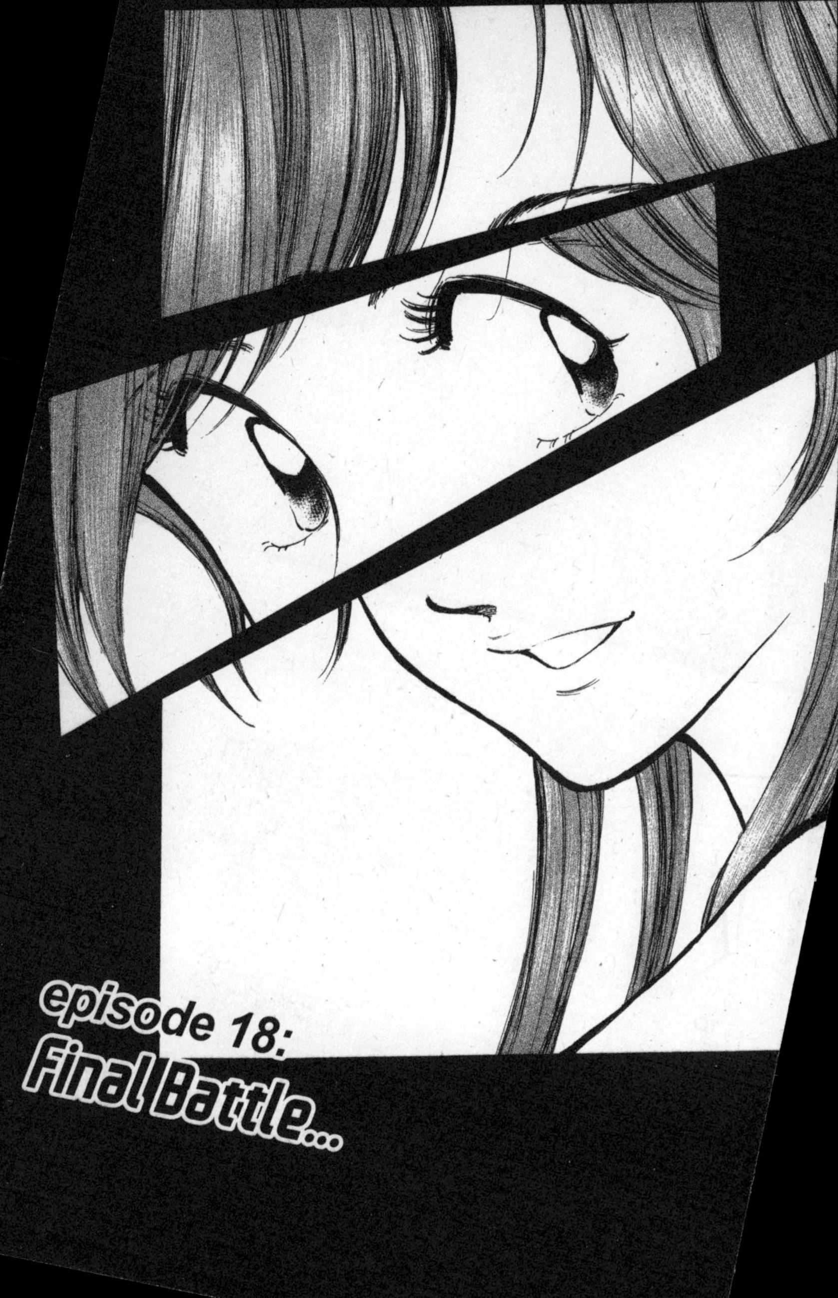
episode 18:
Final Battle...

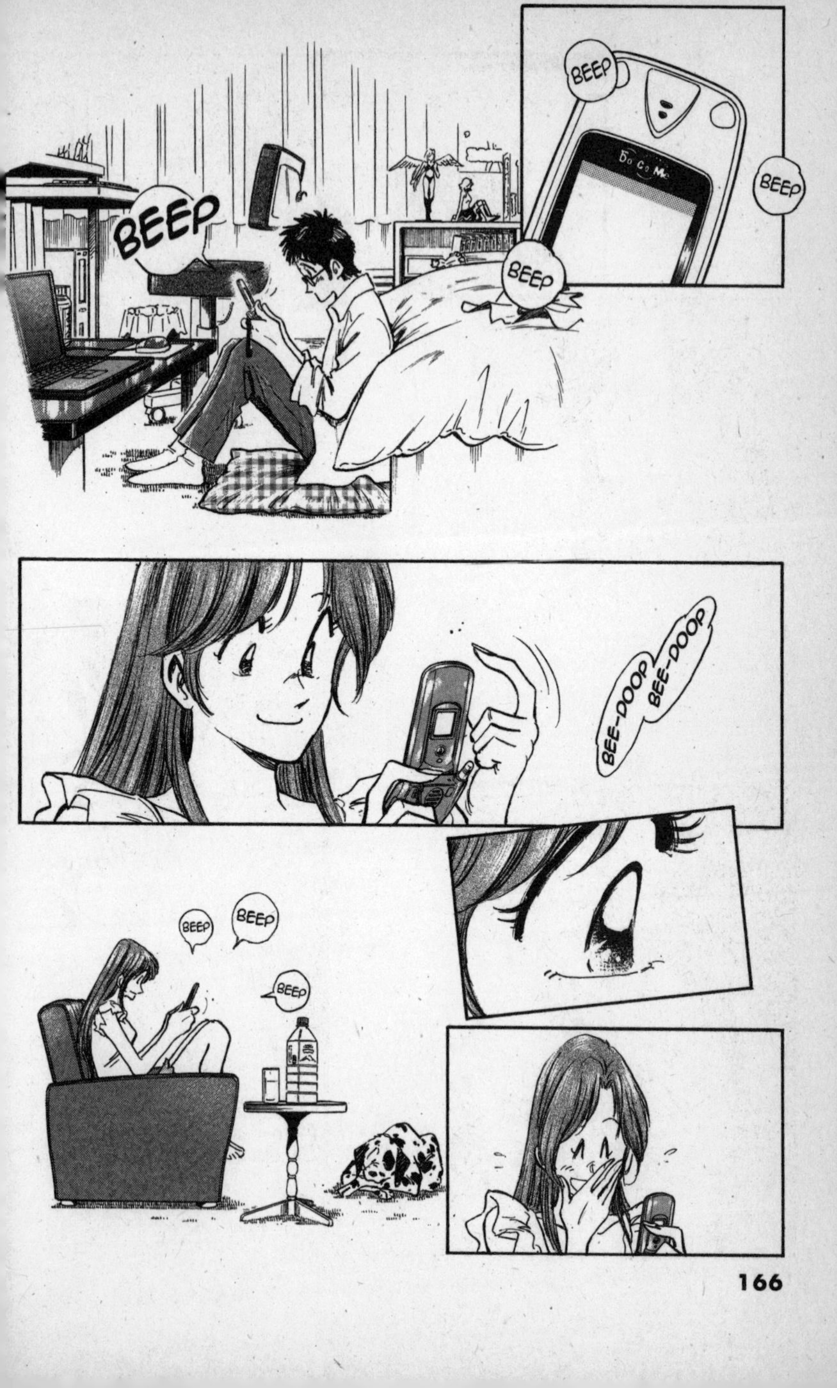
BEEP
BEEP
BEEP
BEEP
BEE-DOOP
BEE-DOOP
BEEP
BEEP
BEEP

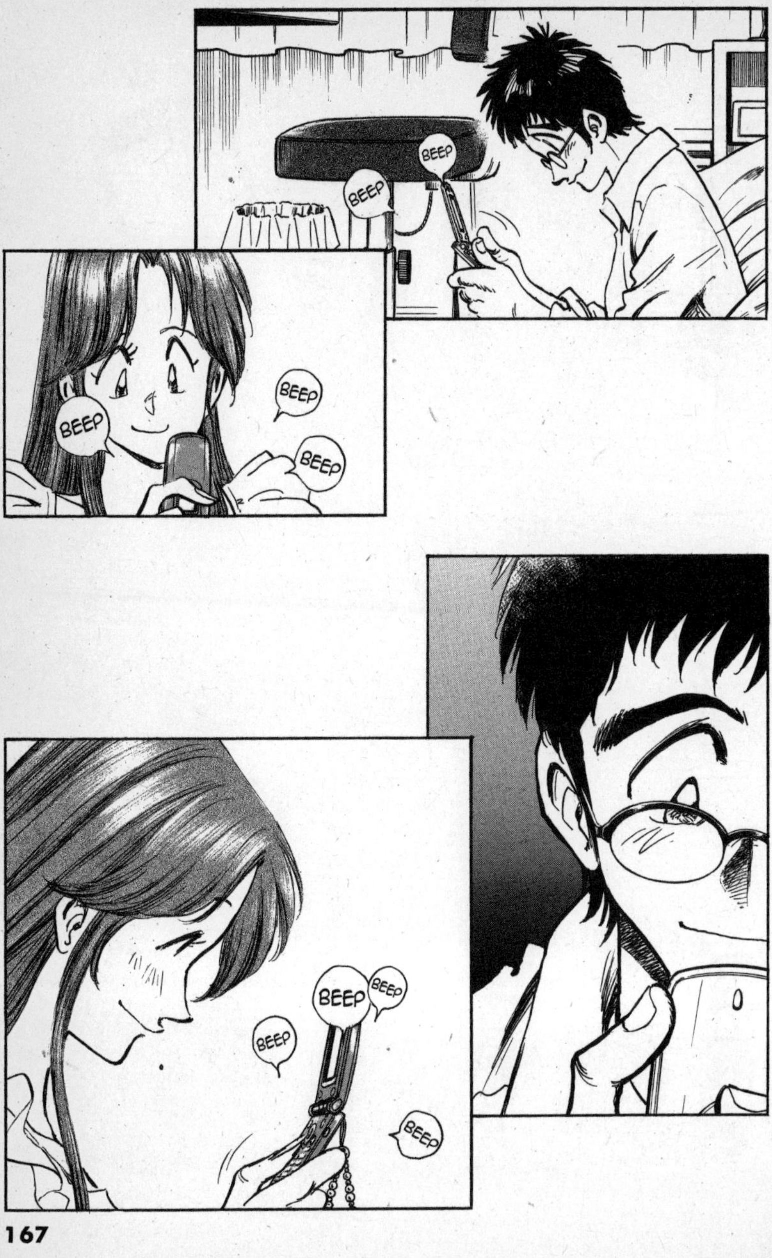
BEEP
BEEP
BEEP
BEEP
BEEP
BEEP
BEEP
BEEP
BEEP

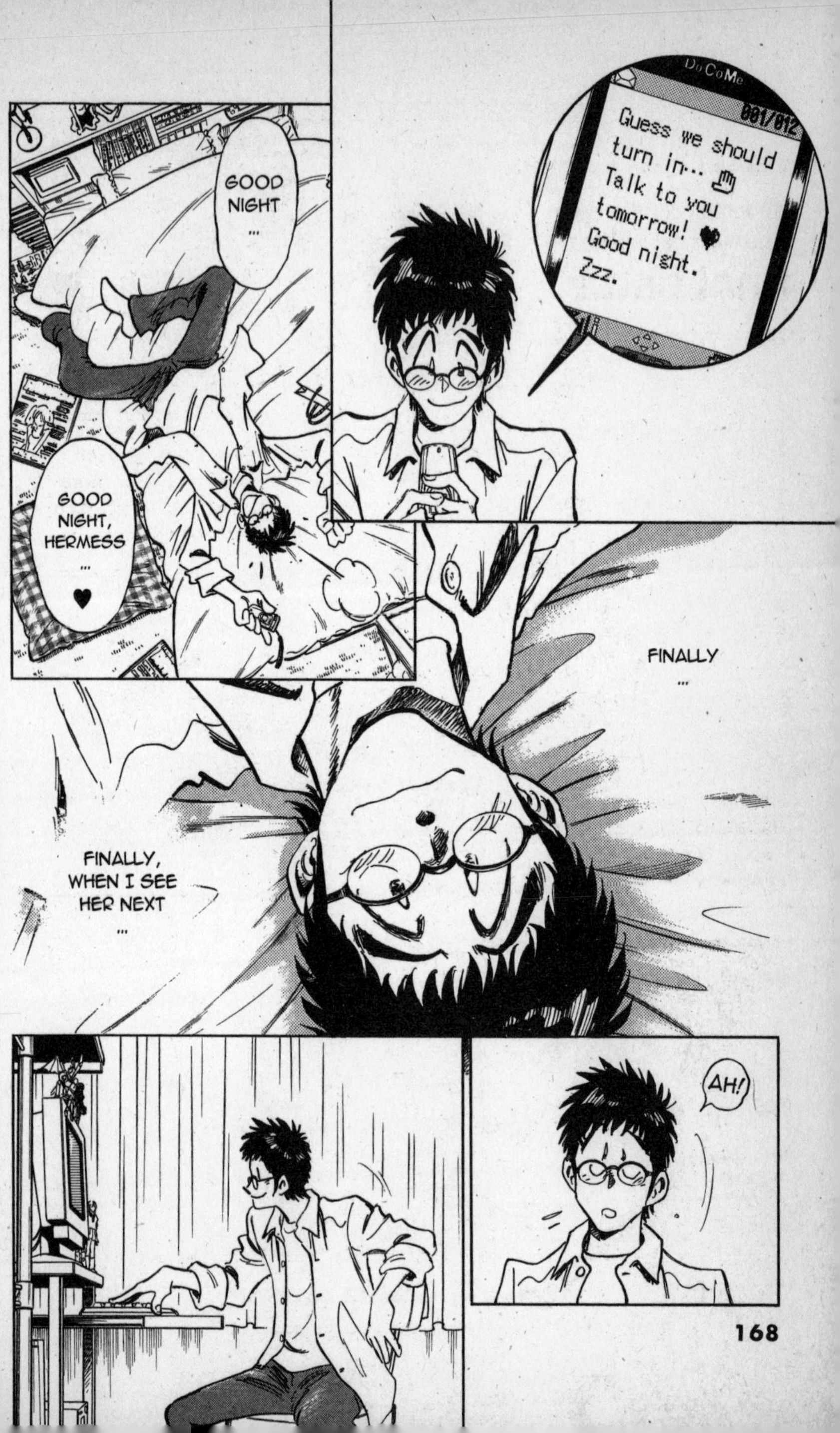
DoCoMe
001/012
Guess we should turn in... Talk to you tomorrow! ♥ Good night. Zzz.
GOOD NIGHT ...
GOOD NIGHT, HERMESS ... ♥
FINALLY ...
FINALLY, WHEN I SEE HER NEXT ...
AH!

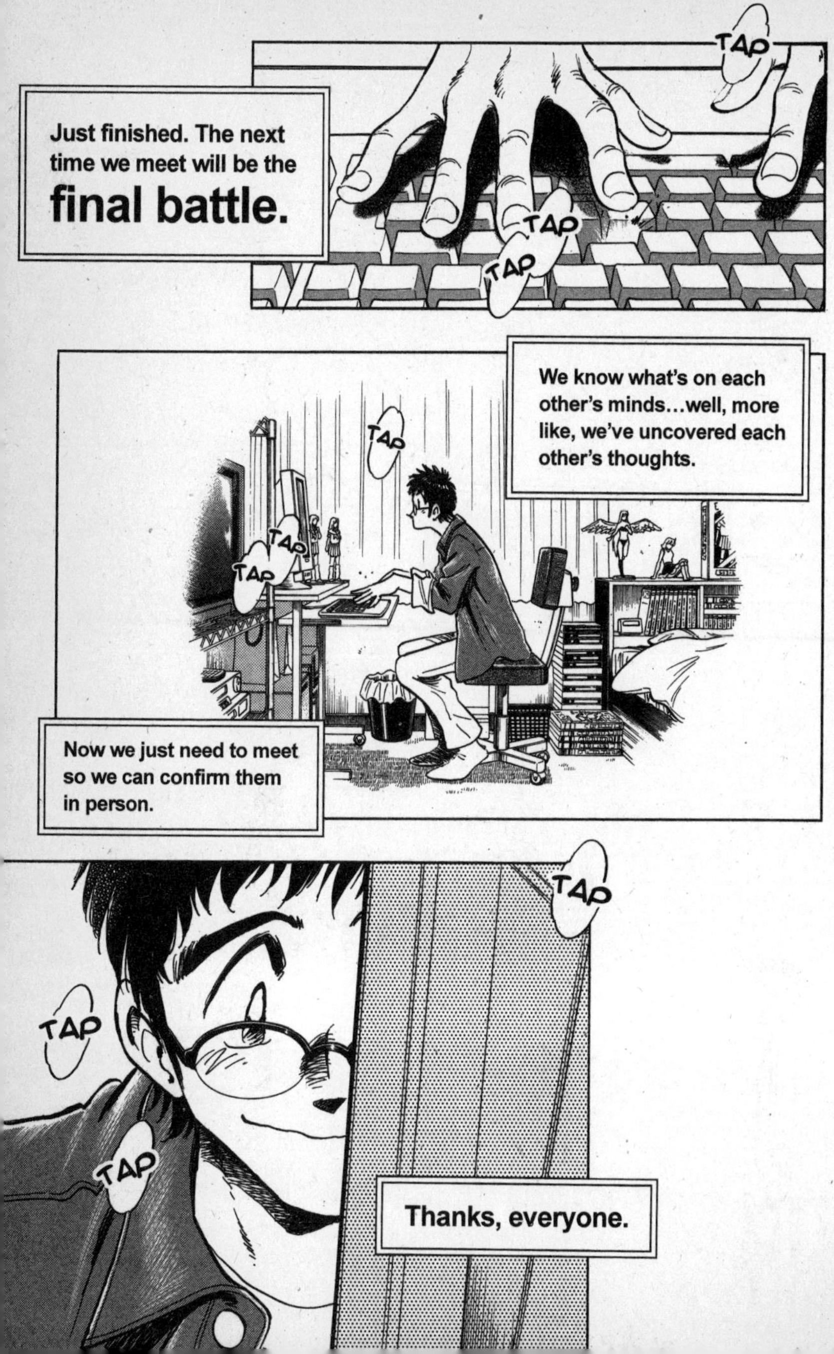
TAP
TAP
TAP
Just finished. The next time we meet will be the **final battle.**
We know what's on each other's minds…well, more like, we've uncovered each other's thoughts.
TAP
TAP
TAP
Now we just need to meet so we can confirm them in person.
TAP
TAP
TAP
Thanks, everyone.

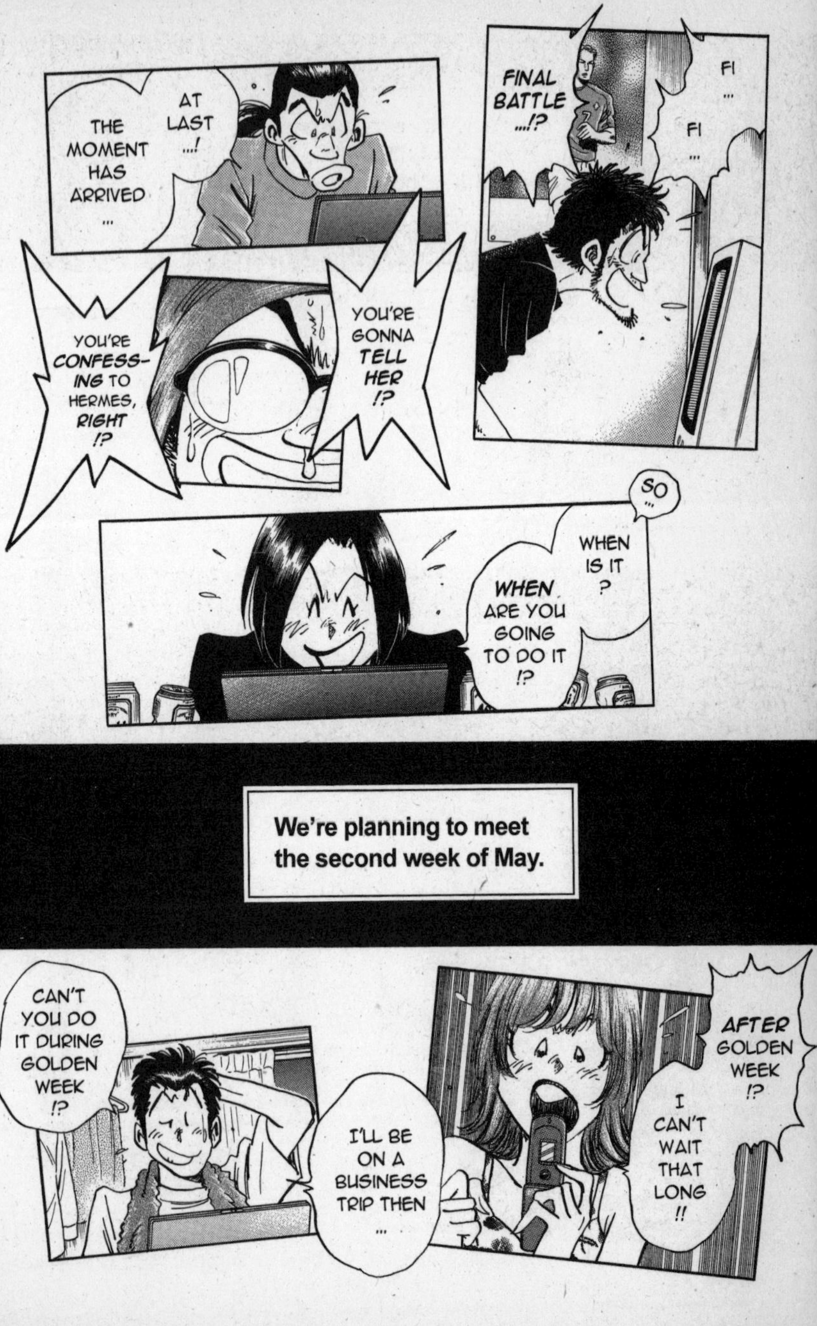
FI ... FI ...
FINAL BATTLE ...!?
AT LAST ...!
THE MOMENT HAS ARRIVED ...
YOU'RE GONNA TELL HER !?
YOU'RE CONFESSING TO HERMES, RIGHT !?
SO ...
WHEN IS IT ?
WHEN ARE YOU GOING TO DO IT !?
We're planning to meet the second week of May.
AFTER GOLDEN WEEK !?
I CAN'T WAIT THAT LONG !!
CAN'T YOU DO IT DURING GOLDEN WEEK !?
I'LL BE ON A BUSINESS TRIP THEN ...

She's going on a trip from the 29th to the 4th. I can see her on the fifth, though.

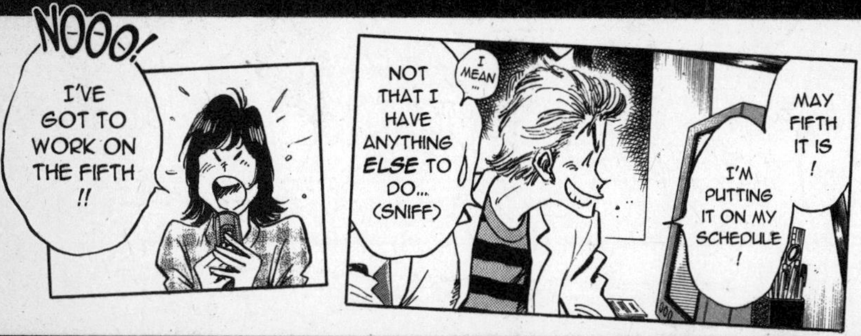
MAY FIFTH IT IS!
I'M PUTTING IT ON MY SCHEDULE!
I MEAN...
NOT THAT I HAVE ANYTHING ELSE TO DO... (SNIFF)
NOOO!
I'VE GOT TO WORK ON THE FIFTH!!

I think she'll be tired after the trip, so I don't want to push it too much.

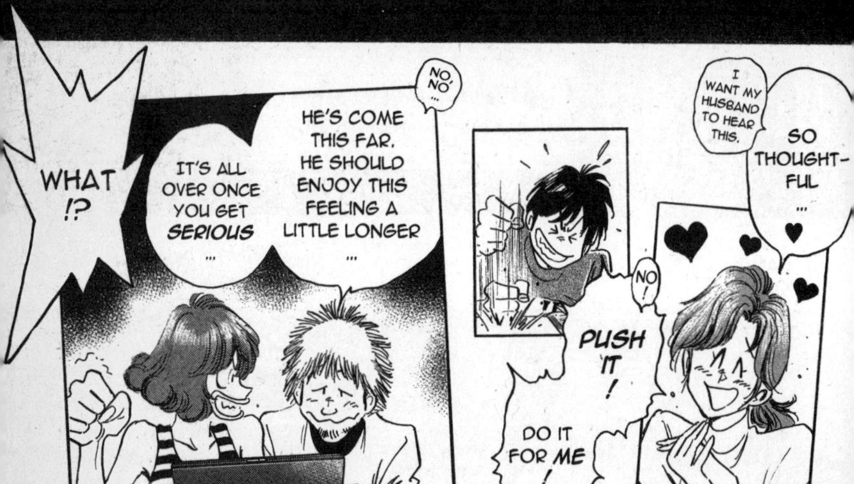
SO THOUGHTFUL...
I WANT MY HUSBAND TO HEAR THIS.
NO!
PUSH IT!
DO IT FOR ME!
NO, NO...
HE'S COME THIS FAR. HE SHOULD ENJOY THIS FEELING A LITTLE LONGER...
IT'S ALL OVER ONCE YOU GET SERIOUS...
WHAT!?

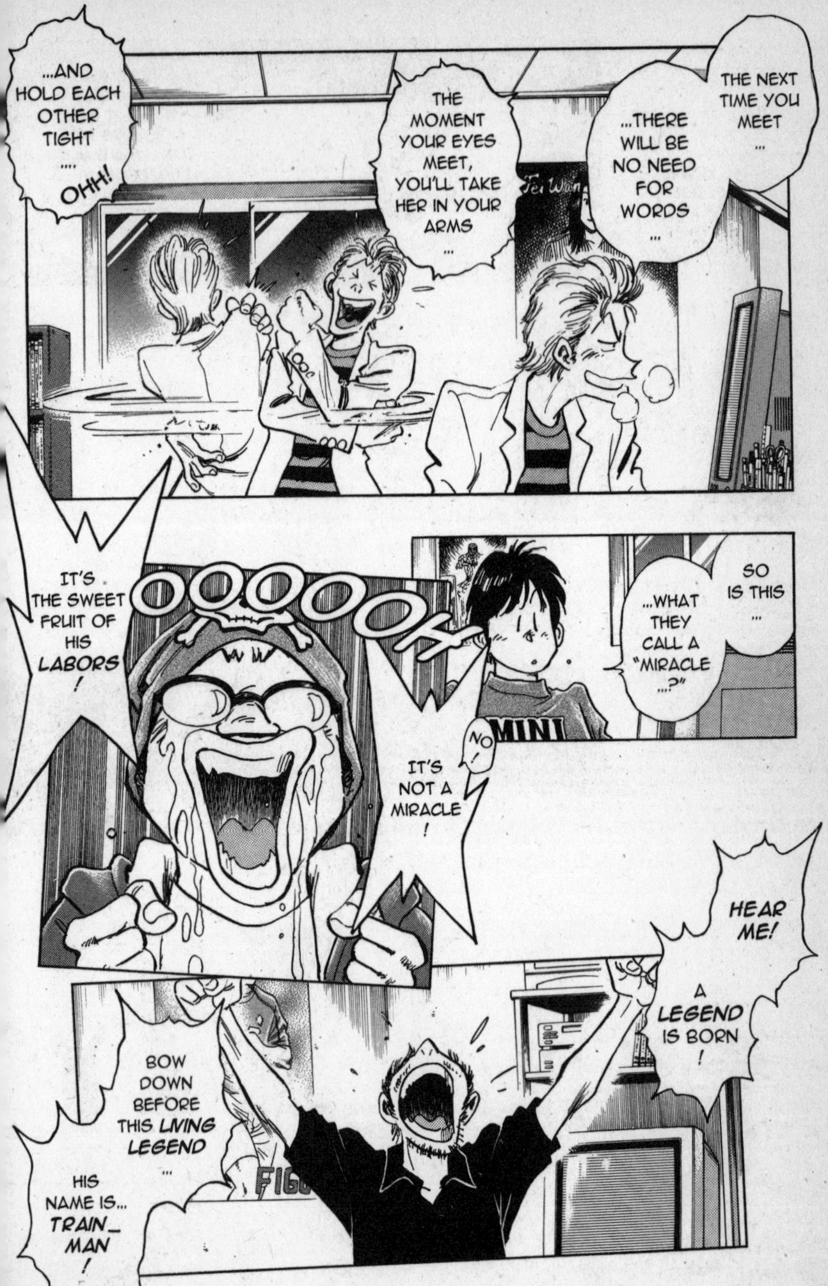
THE NEXT TIME YOU MEET ...
...THERE WILL BE NO NEED FOR WORDS ...
THE MOMENT YOUR EYES MEET, YOU'LL TAKE HER IN YOUR ARMS ...
...AND HOLD EACH OTHER TIGHT .... OHH!
SO IS THIS ...
...WHAT THEY CALL A "MIRACLE ...?"
NO!
IT'S NOT A MIRACLE!
IT'S THE SWEET FRUIT OF HIS LABORS!
OOOOOOH
HEAR ME!
A LEGEND IS BORN!
BOW DOWN BEFORE THIS LIVING LEGEND ...
HIS NAME IS... TRAIN_MAN!

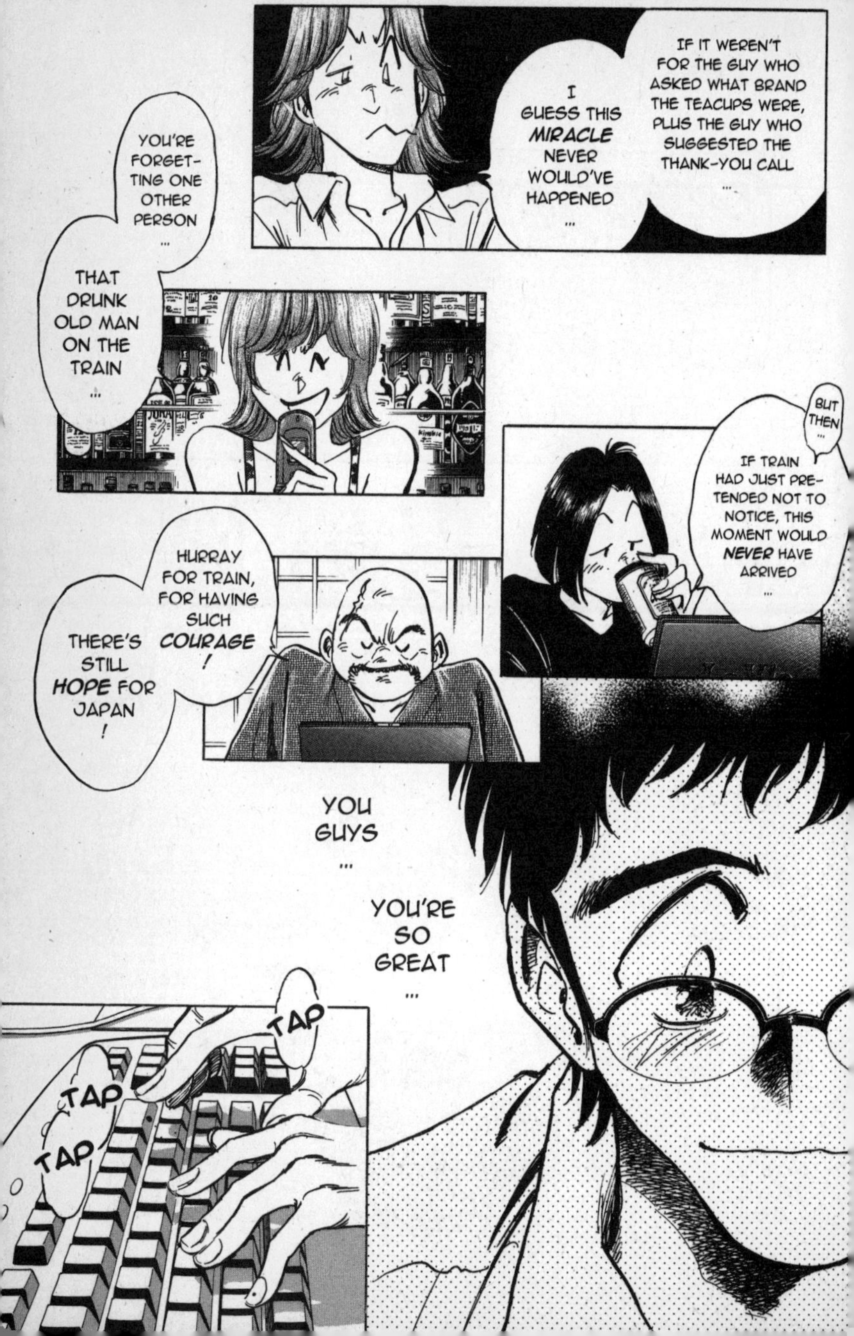
IF IT WEREN'T FOR THE GUY WHO ASKED WHAT BRAND THE TEACUPS WERE, PLUS THE GUY WHO SUGGESTED THE THANK-YOU CALL ...
I GUESS THIS MIRACLE NEVER WOULD'VE HAPPENED ...
YOU'RE FORGET-TING ONE OTHER PERSON ...
THAT DRUNK OLD MAN ON THE TRAIN ...
BUT THEN ...
IF TRAIN HAD JUST PRE-TENDED NOT TO NOTICE, THIS MOMENT WOULD NEVER HAVE ARRIVED ...
HURRAY FOR TRAIN, FOR HAVING SUCH COURAGE !
THERE'S STILL HOPE FOR JAPAN !
YOU GUYS ...
YOU'RE SO GREAT ...
TAP
TAP
TAP

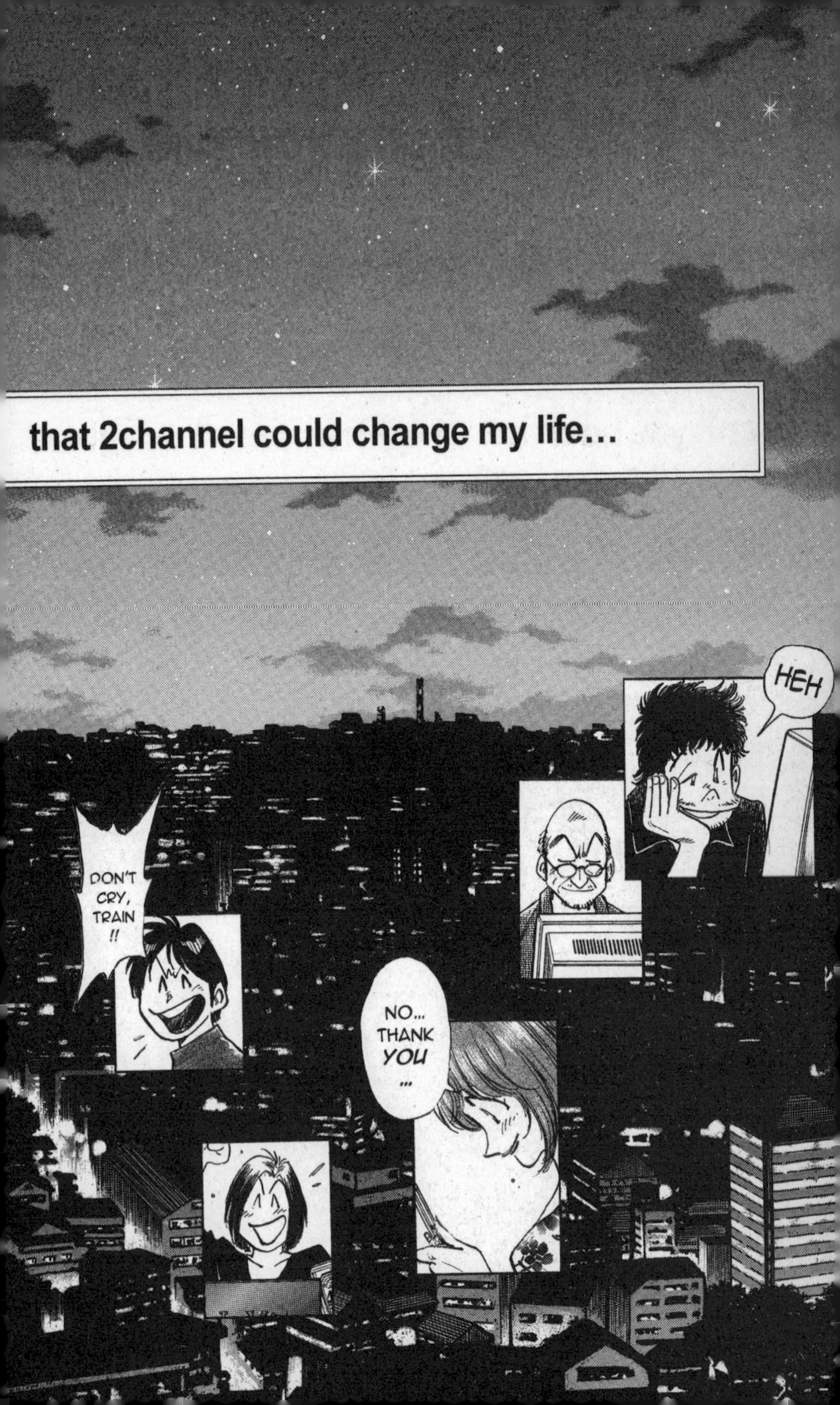
that 2channel could change my life…
HEH
DON'T CRY, TRAIN !!
NO... THANK YOU ...

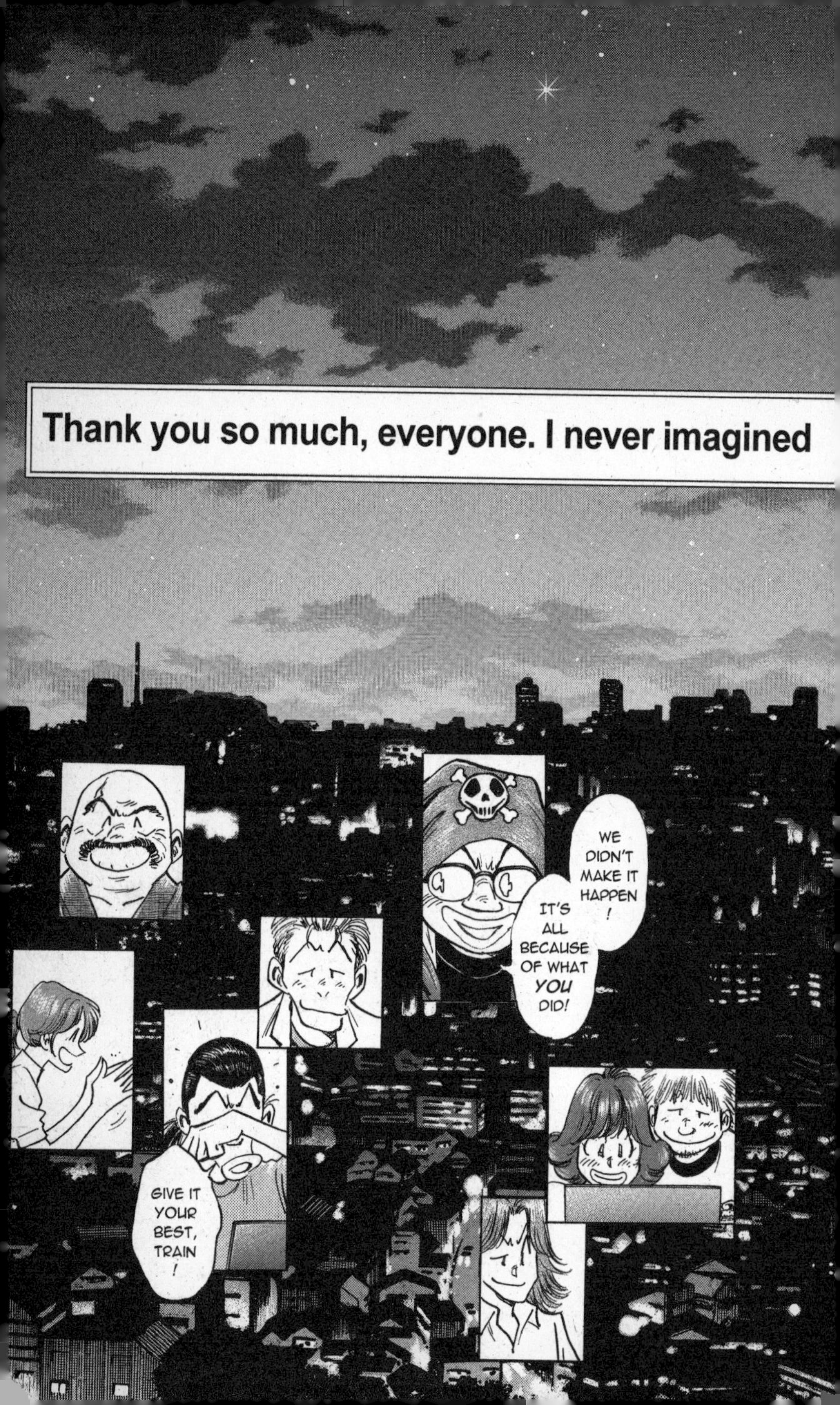
Thank you so much, everyone. I never imagined
WE DIDN'T MAKE IT HAPPEN!
IT'S ALL BECAUSE OF WHAT YOU DID!
GIVE IT YOUR BEST, TRAIN!

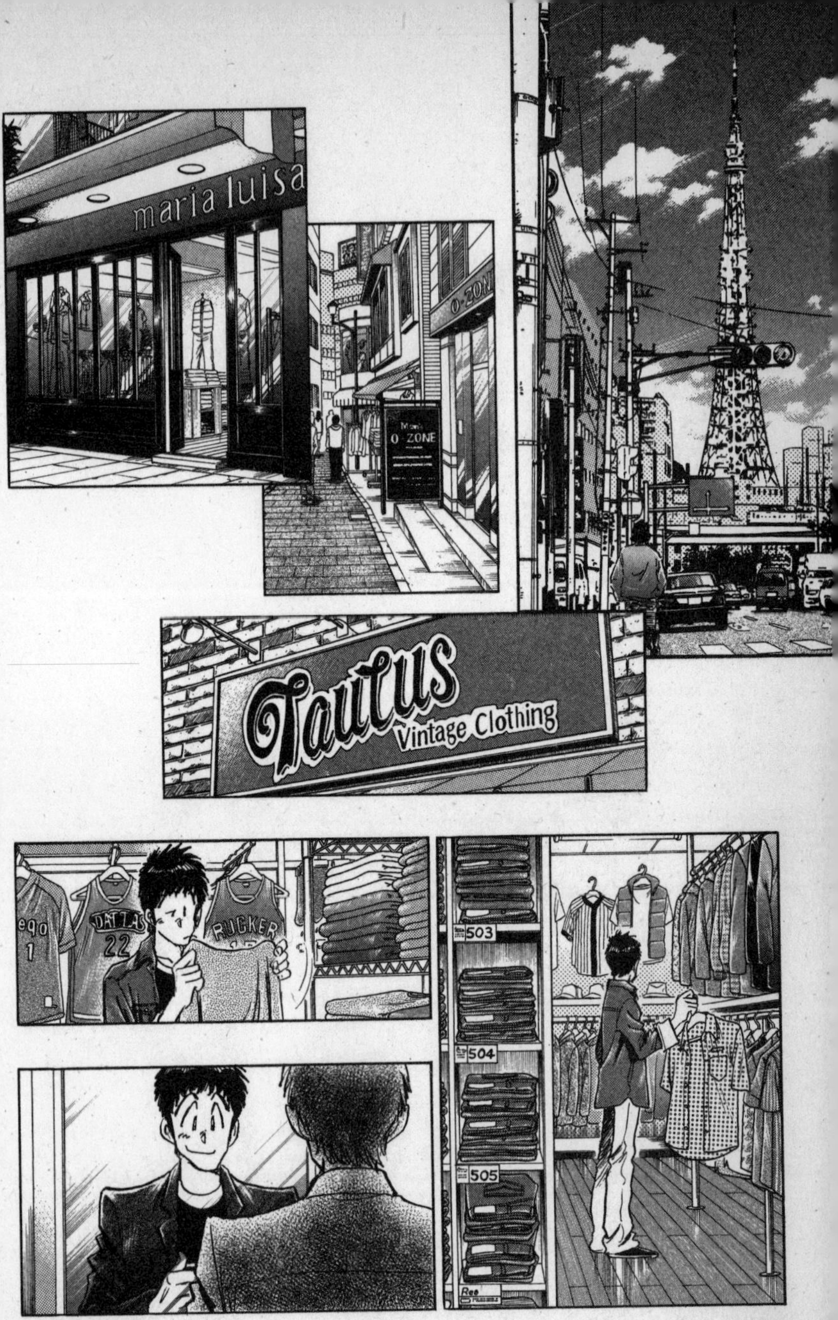
O-ZONE
Men's
O-ZONE
maria luisa
Taurus
Vintage Clothing
503
504
505
DALLAS
22
RUCKER

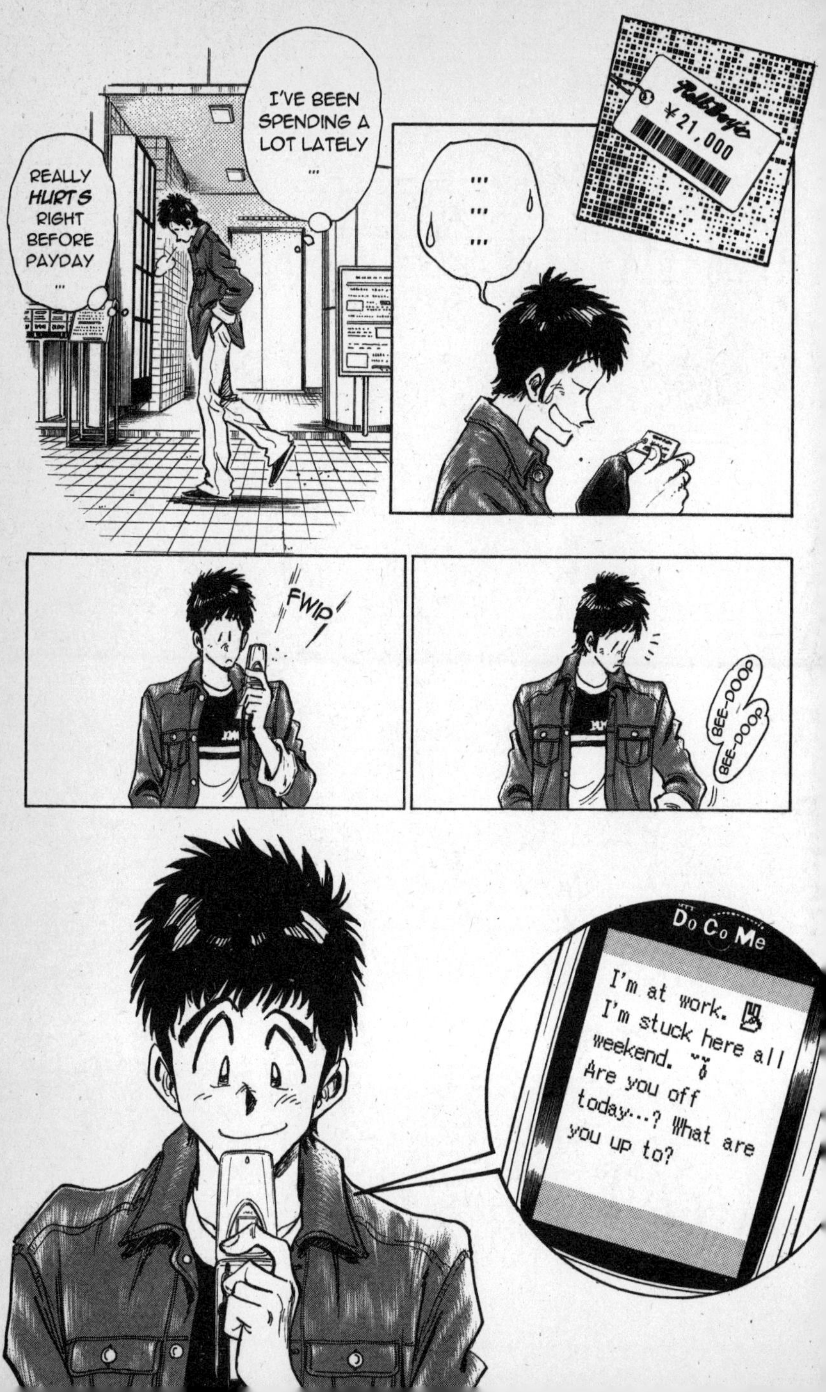
¥21,000
...
...
...
I'VE BEEN SPENDING A LOT LATELY ...
REALLY HURTS RIGHT BEFORE PAYDAY ...
BEE-DOOP
BEE-DOOP
FWIP
DoCoMe
I'm at work. I'm stuck here all weekend. Are you off today...? What are you up to?

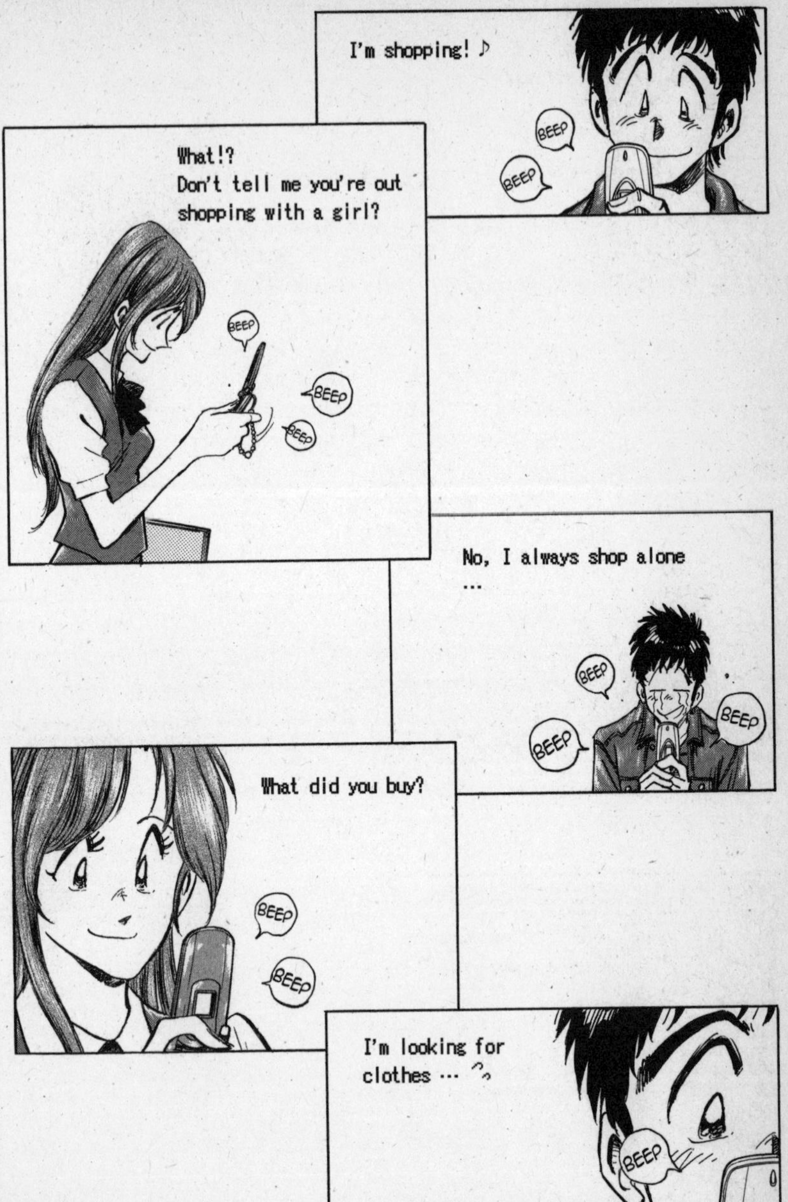
I'm shopping! ♪
BEEP
BEEP
What!?
Don't tell me you're out shopping with a girl?
BEEP
BEEP
BEEP
No, I always shop alone
···
BEEP
BEEP
BEEP
What did you buy?
BEEP
BEEP
I'm looking for
clothes ···
BEEP

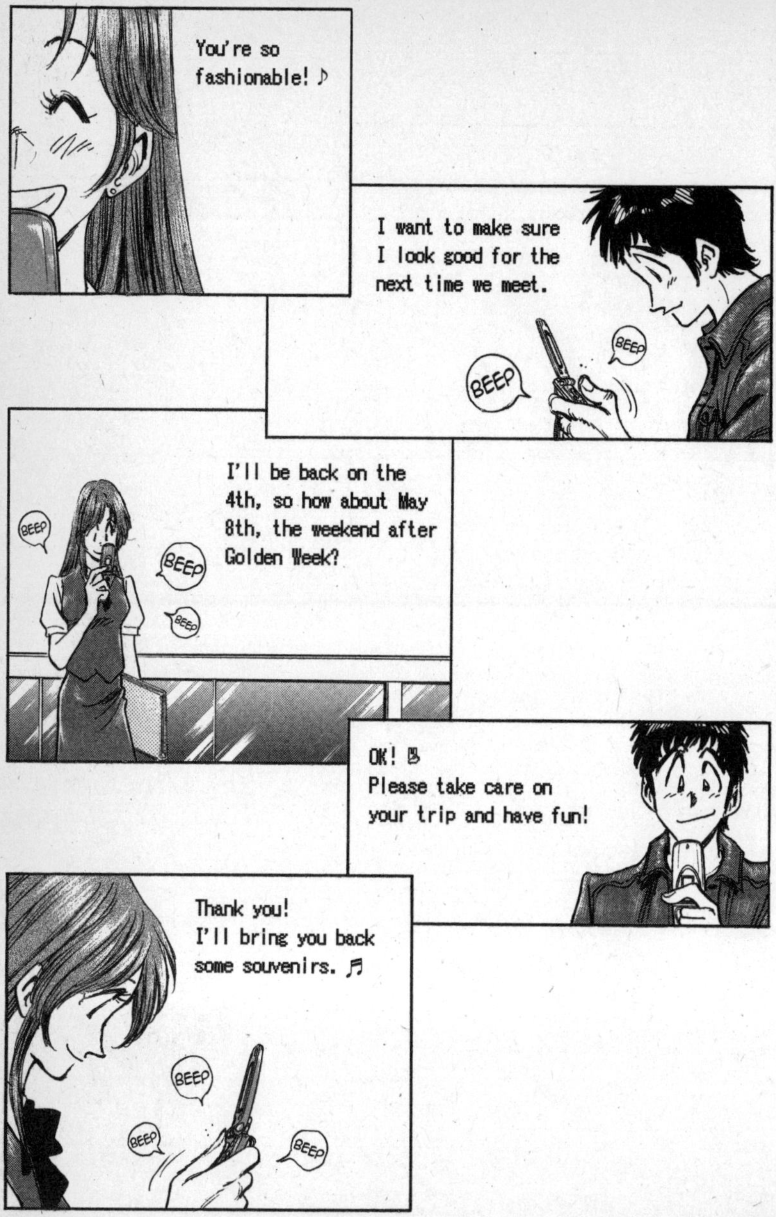
You're so fashionable! ♪
I want to make sure I look good for the next time we meet.
BEEP
BEEP
I'll be back on the 4th, so how about May 8th, the weekend after Golden Week?
BEEP
BEEP
BEEP
OK!
Please take care on your trip and have fun!
Thank you!
I'll bring you back some souvenirs. ♬
BEEP
BEEP
BEEP

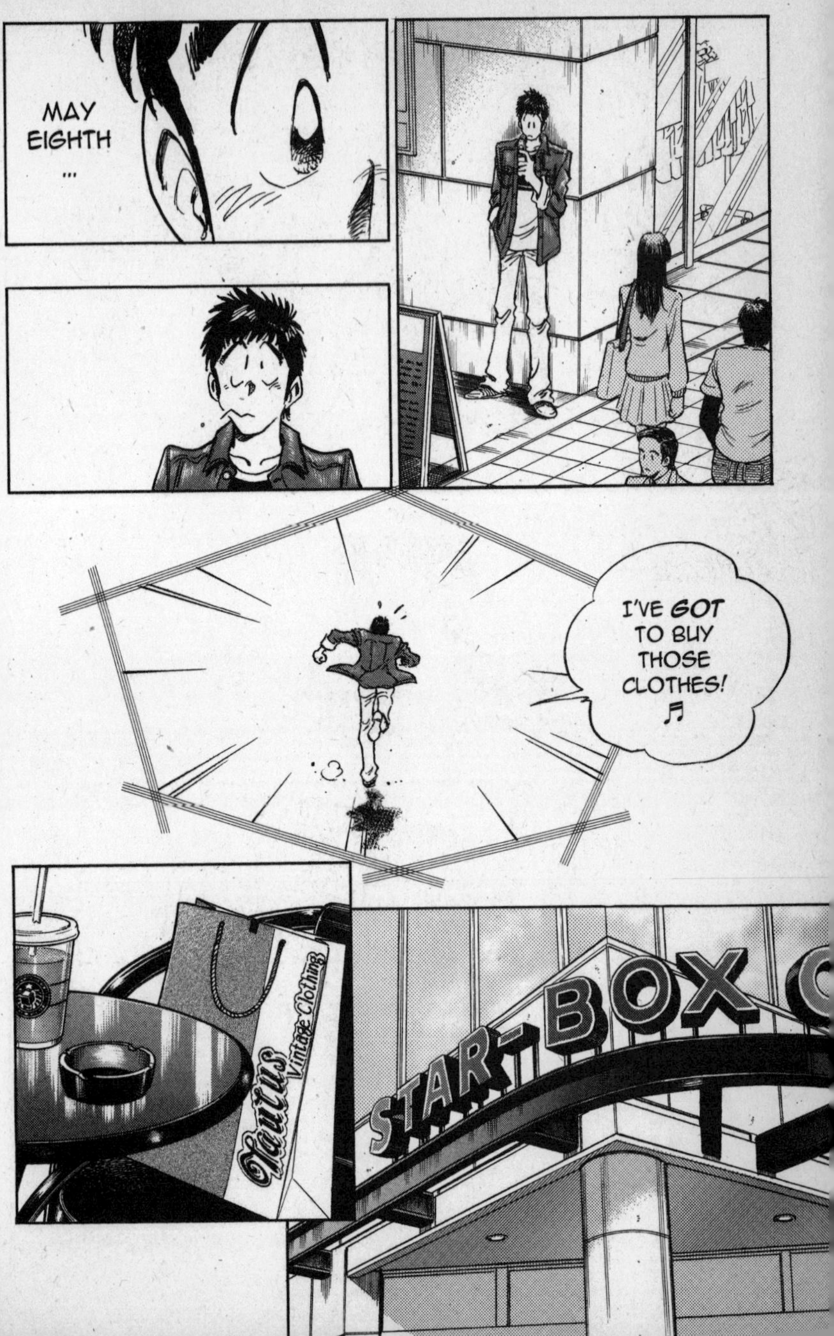
MAY EIGHTH ...
I'VE **GOT** TO BUY THOSE CLOTHES! ♬
STAR-BOX
Nautus Vintage Clothing

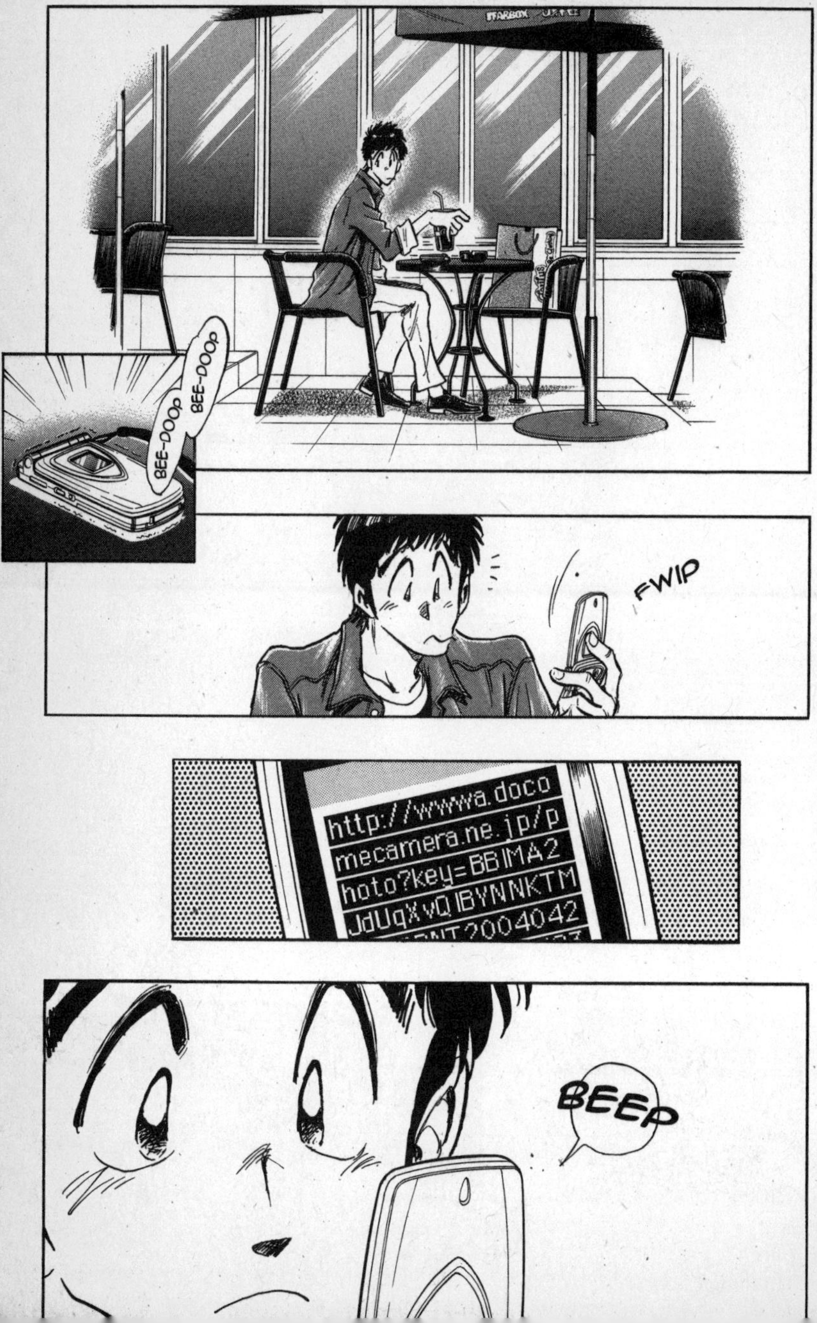
BEE-DOOP BEE-DOOP
FWIP
http://wwwa.doco
mecamera.ne.jp/p
hoto?key=BBIMA2
JdUqXvQIBYNNKTM
NT2004042
BEEP

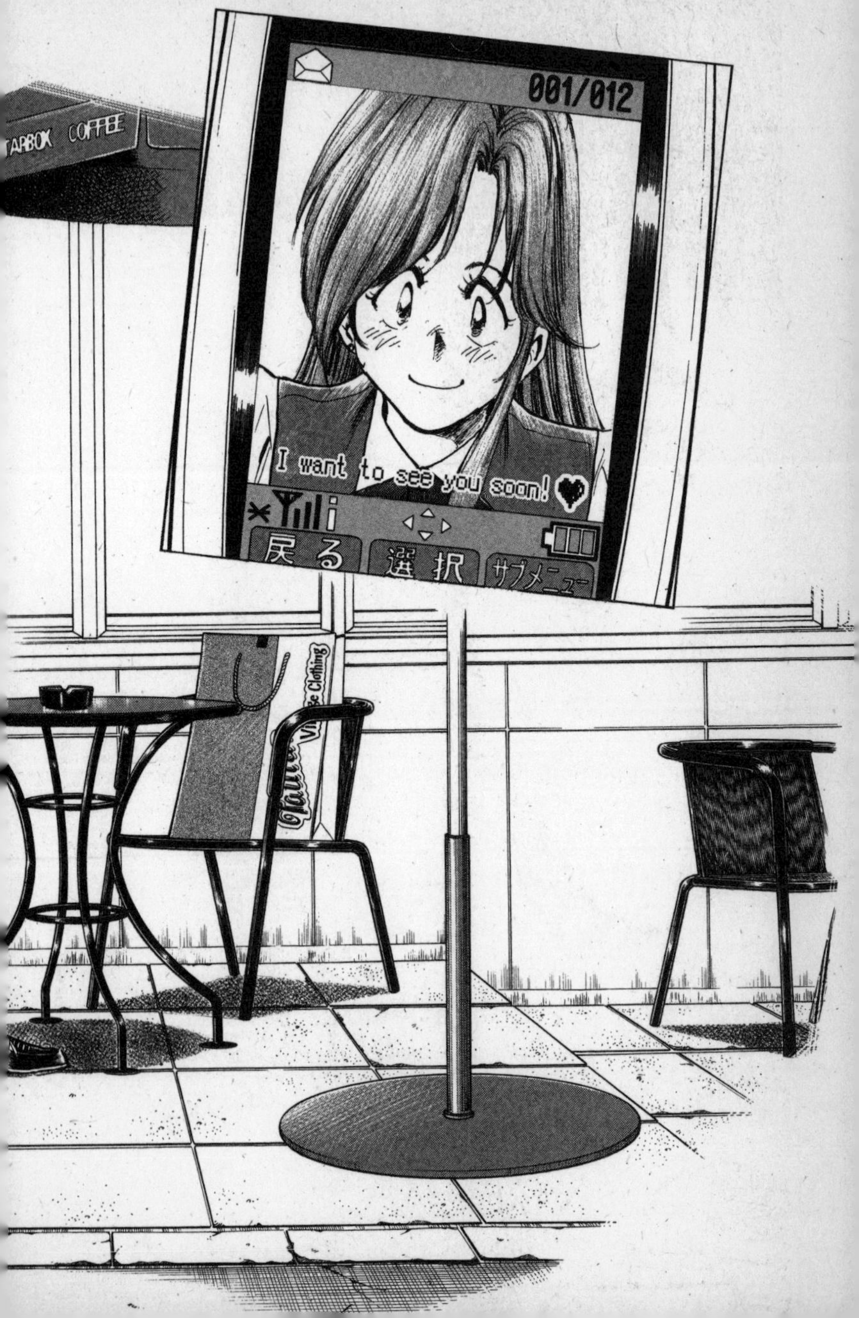

001/012
I want to see you soon!
戻る
選択
サブメニュー
TARBOX COFFEE
Vintage Clothing

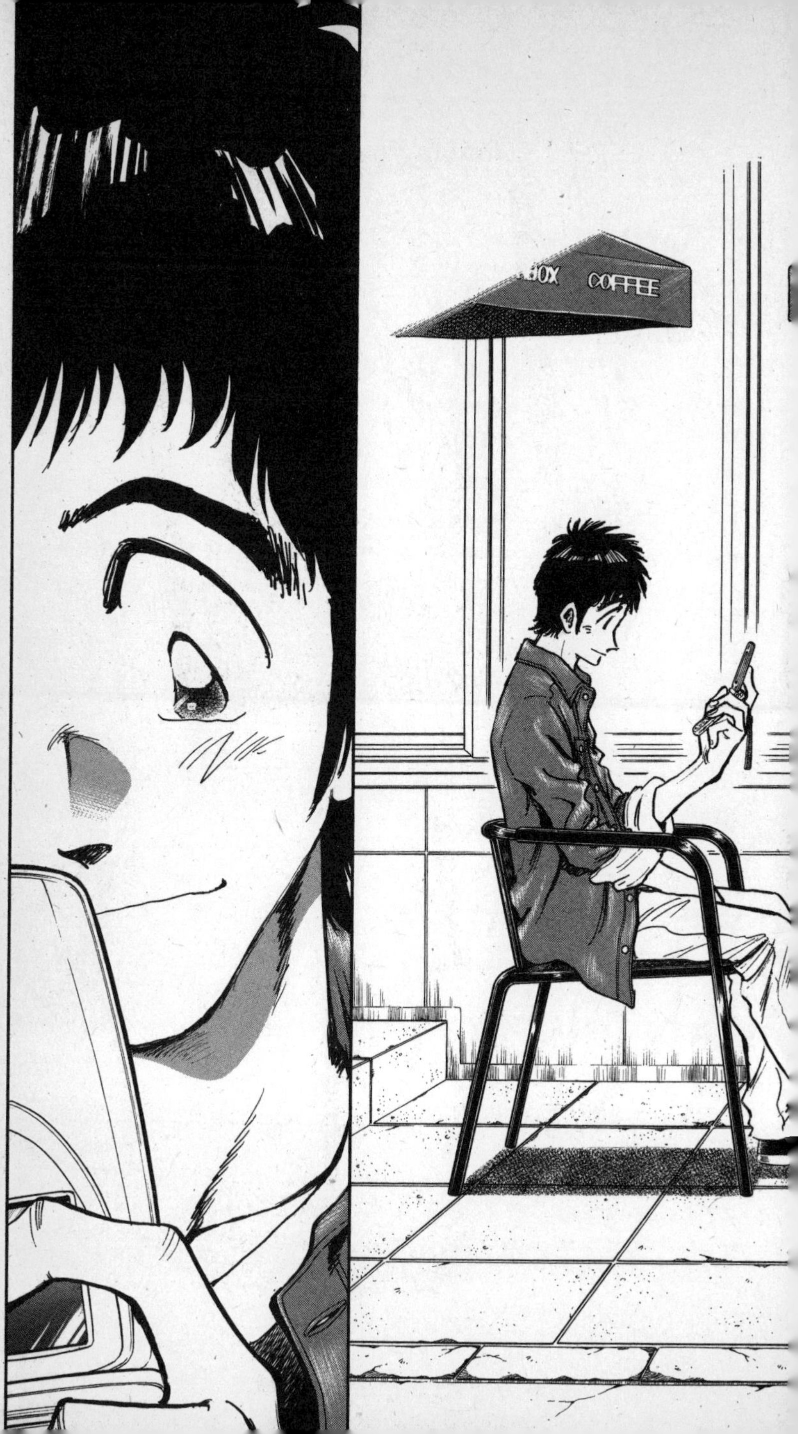
COFFEE

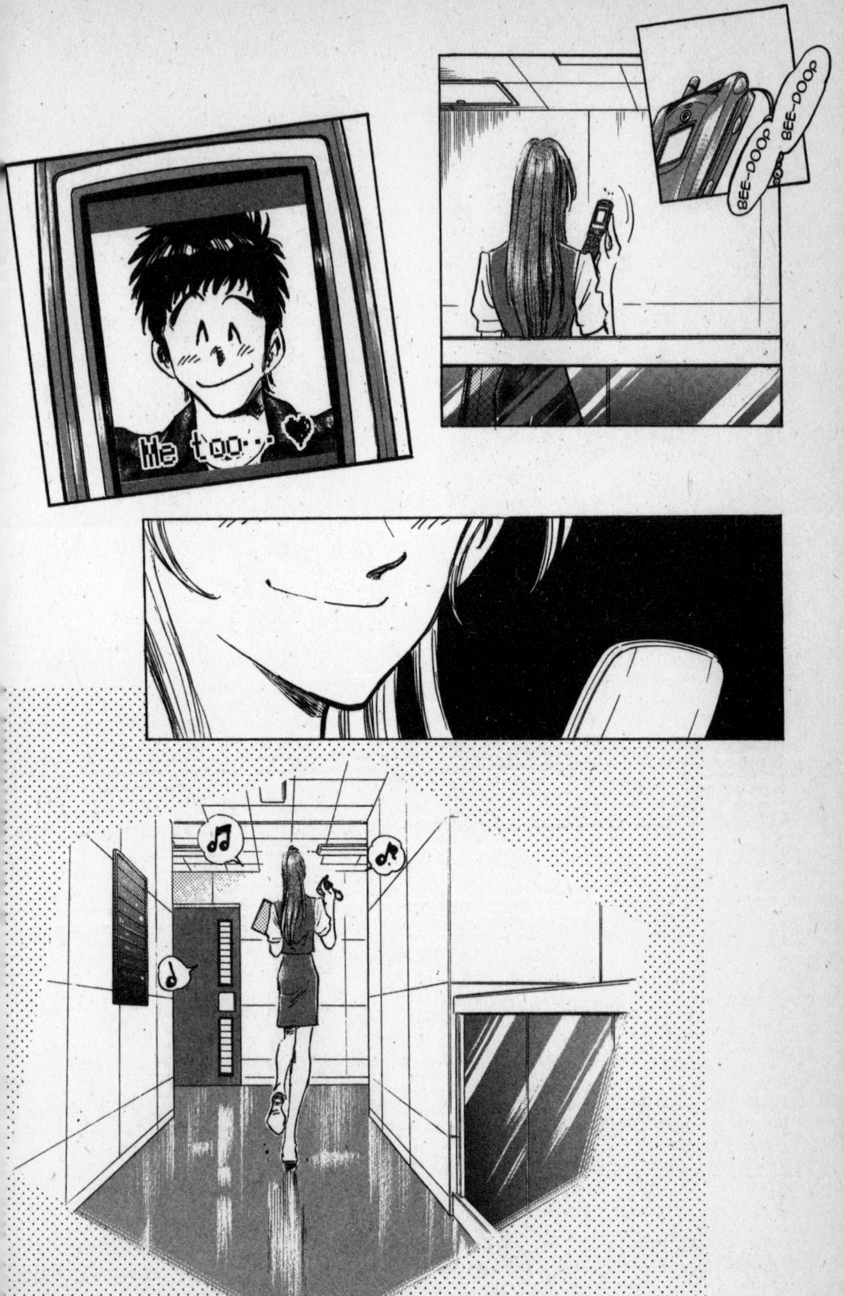
BEE-DOOP BEE-DOOP
BEE-DOOP
Me too... ♥

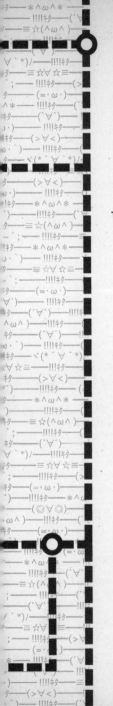

Train_Man
Densha Otoko
Volume 2
VIZ Media Edition

Story and Art by
HIDENORI HARA
Based on *Densha Otoko* by
HITORI NAKANO

Translation/Cindy Yamauchi (REGION FREE Japan Artist Network)
English Adaptation/Mark Giambruno
Touch-Up Art & Lettering/James Tonjes, Jack Blazkiewicz (RJP-PRO, Inc.)
Design/Izumi Hirayama
Editor/Andy Nakatani

Managing Editor/Annette Roman
Editorial Director/Elizabeth Kawasaki
Editor in Chief/Alvin Lu
Sr. Director of Acquisitions/Rika Inouye
Sr. VP of Marketing/Liza Coppola
Exec. VP of Sales & Marketing/John Easum
Publisher/Hyoe Narita

Printed in the U.S.A.

Published by VIZ Media, LLC
P.O. Box 77010
San Francisco, CA 94107

10 9 8 7 6 5 4 3 2 1
First printing, December 2006

www.viz.com
store.viz.com

VIZ MEDIA™

RATED T FOR TEEN

PARENTAL ADVISORY
DENSHA OTOKO: TRAIN_MAN is rated T for Teen and is recommended for ages 13 and up.

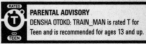

Who Is Hidenori Hara?

Hidenori Hara is a 20-year veteran manga artist who specializes in the coming-of-age romance genre. Previous works include *Fuyu Monogatari* (Winter Tale), *Someday*, and *Regatta*. Hara's work has been serialized in *Shonen Sunday*, *Big Comics Spirits*, and *Young Sunday*. His most recent project is *Hoshi no Furu Machi: When You Wish Upon a Star.*

Who Is Hitori Nakano?

Densha Otoko was based on an online thread on 2Channel, Japan's largest Internet bulletin board site. The fictitious name, Hitori Nakano, was selected as the author's name when this story was published in book format. When read in the Japanese order, with surname followed by given name, Nakano Hitori is a homonym for a phrase which means "one among many"–representing all the single men who gathered on the online discussion forum which hosted this thread.

What is Akihabara?

Akihabara is Tokyo's shopping mecca for electronics and software. Akihabara, or Akiba for short, has also become famous for being a center of otaku culture with throngs of stores selling anime, video games and other ancillary merchandise.

What is on the background of the cover?

"‡夕―――(ﾟ∀ﾟ)―――!!!!" is used in the background of the front and back covers and would be transliterated as "Kita―――(ﾟ∀ﾟ)―――!!!!"
"Kita" literally means "(it) came." Sometimes it's used literally, such as when finally receiving a long-awaited e-mail or phone call, but it is also used in the sense of being emotionally moved, or even as a reaction to something like strong wasabi. It has been localized in this series as "w00t." The other symbols on the cover are all examples of Japanese emoticons. For example (ﾟ∀ﾟ) represents an excited face. Japanese emoticons have been retained throughout this manga. A few other examples of note include the following:

(;ﾟ∀ﾟ)=3	An excited face with sweat or tears running down the side of its face. The "=3" represents a puff of air to accompany the panting.
_| ̄|○	A man down on his hands and knees in shame.
\(ﾟДﾟ)/	Excited face with open mouth and hands waving in the air.

What is "drftgyhujikolp;["?

"drftgyhujikolp;["can represent extreme exasperation, surprise, or anything else that cannot be expressed in words. It's formed by taking a couple fingers and dragging them across a standard QWERTY keyboard.

Fullmetal Alchemist Profiles

Get the background story and world history of the manga, plus:

- Character bios
- New, original artwork
- Interview with creator Hiromu Arakawa
- Bonus manga episode only available in this book

Fullmetal Alchemist Anime Profiles

Stay on top of your favorite episodes and characters with:

- Actual cel artwork from the TV series
- Summaries of all 51 TV episodes
- Definitive cast biographies
- Exclusive poster for your wall

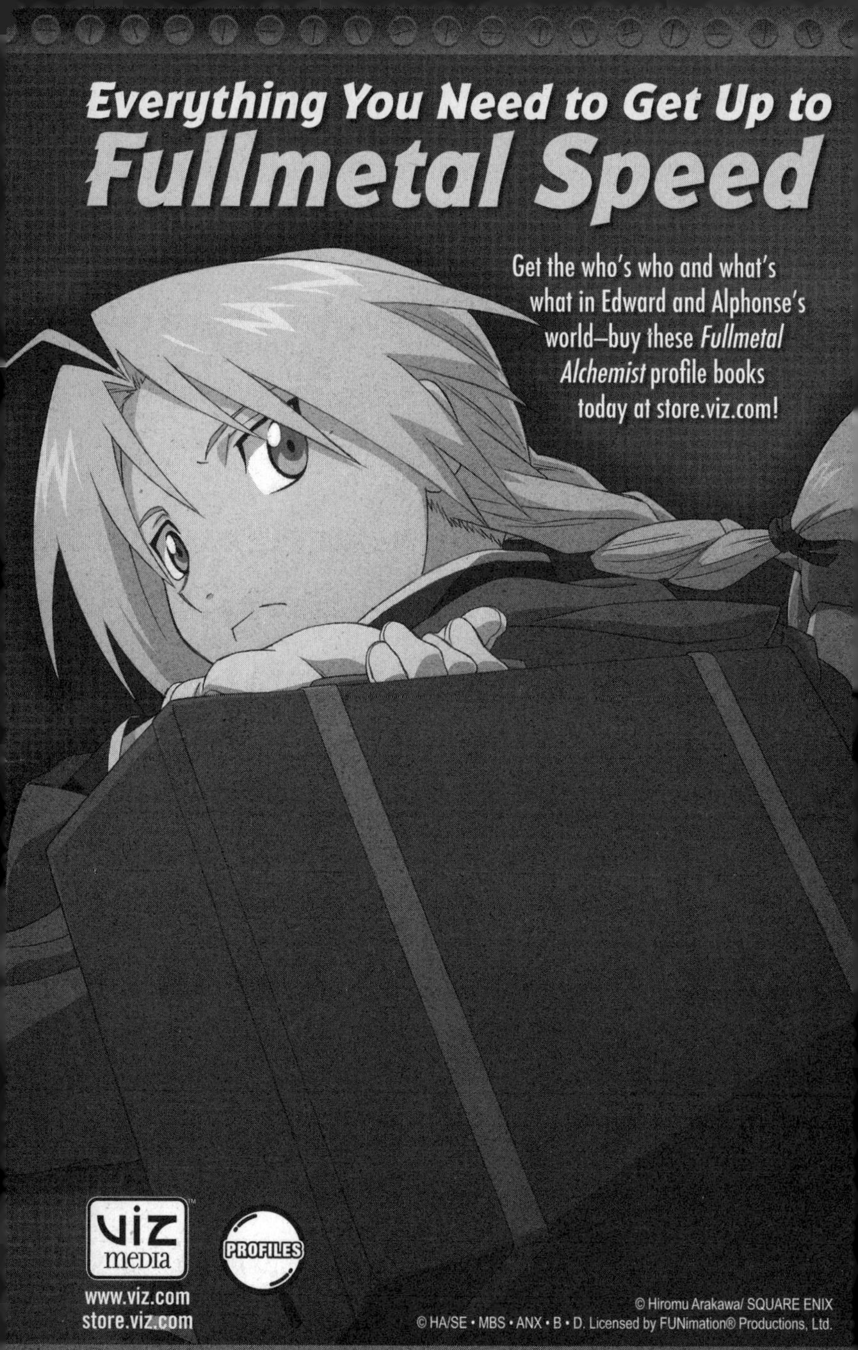

Everything You Need to Get Up to
Fullmetal Speed
Get the who's who and what's what in Edward and Alphonse's world—buy these *Fullmetal Alchemist* profile books today at store.viz.com!
VIZ media
PROFILES
www.viz.com
store.viz.com
© Hiromu Arakawa/ SQUARE ENIX
© HA/SE • MBS • ANX • B • D. Licensed by FUNimation® Productions, Ltd.

LOVE MANGA?
LET US KNOW WHAT YOU THINK!